Money, Valuation and Growth

We have experienced an era of extreme anti-inflationary policy combined with debts and deficits, the result of which has been a decrease in social stability. This book examines how using mainstream theory as the basis for economic decisions leads to misunderstandings of central concepts of our economic reality. It aims to establish a better understanding of the discrepancies between the current mainstream economic theory and the economy experienced in business and politics.

This ambitious and wide-ranging volume begins the project of rethinking the approach of economics to money. In this new light, concepts such as valuation, price, uncertainty, growth and aggregation are interpreted differently, even as analytical inconsistencies and even intrinsic contradictions between these concepts arise. A central theme of the book is the use of money as a measure and whether the disconnect between money as a form of measurement and money as it is used in the real world can be maintained.

This book calls for a radical rethinking of the basis of much of the modern study of economics. It will be of interest to researchers concerned with monetary economics, finance, political economy and economic philosophy.

Hasse Ekstedt is a Senior Researcher in the School of Public Administration at the University of Gothenburg, Sweden.

Routledge International Studies in Money and Banking

For a complete list of titles in this series, please visit www.routledge.com

Money, Valuation and Growth

Conceptualizations and contradictions
of the money economy

Hasse Ekstedt

LONDON AND NEW YORK

First published 2016 by Routledge

2 Park Square, Milton Park, Abingdon, Oxon OX14 4RN
711 Third Avenue, New York, NY 10017, USA

Routledge is an imprint of the Taylor & Francis Group, an informa business

First issued in paperback 2017

British Library Cataloguing in Publication Data
A catalogue record for this book is available from the British Library

Library of Congress Cataloging in Publication Data
A catalog record for this book has been requested

ISBN: 978-1-138-78215-0 (hbk)
ISBN: 978-1-138-29996-2 (pbk)

Typeset in Times New Roman
by Cenveo Publisher Services

Contents

List of Figures

Figures

List of Tables

Preface

'Cash is King' – so it is for people in business, so it is for households and so it is for states. When we listen to state budget discussions in media we get the impression that $1 billion invested in housing is the same as if it is invested in education systems, it is only a matter of priorities. An influential Swedish politician said once that one SEK is one SEK irrespective of under which heading in the state budget we put it, it is a matter of accounting.

Currently state debts are discussed internationally and in most countries, and it is quite natural to expect the same responsibilities from the states as from individuals.

May be we can accept the two first statements but when we come to the third there is something funny about it. What do we really mean by the word *responsibility*? In the first two statements we were discussing an aggregate level, the state, and how decision makers on this level should decide. But in the third statement we are comparing two radically different levels of aggregation. With respect to this statement wouldn't it be wise to let those who have taken the financial decisions, for the rise of the debt, pay? We could follow what they did in old Athens as we are told by Thucydides. After a couple of years they let the people cast their votes about whether the elected rulers were to be seen as seducers of the people or not. If yes, they could be sentenced to be either thrown down from Acropolis, the mild sentence, or be ostracized for life, the severe sentence. Both those alternatives have their drawbacks: either chaos or rigorous dictatorship comes to mind. So we probably have to let the taxpayers pay, but if so how do we distribute it among taxpayers?

A rather comfortable solution is of course to pay with newly fresh printed money bills, what's wrong with that?

Well we can go on like this but the thing is that aggregation and aggregates are probably the most problematic issue when it comes to money. Not even the two first statements are that simple when we scrutinize them in depth. David Hume tells us that money is the lubricant of the society in its development, but greasing the lock is different from greasing the hinges on a door and so it is for the state: different ways of using money on the aggregate level give different effects.

The underlying problem in this book is consequently money in its different shapes. Early in my studies I had some problems with quantity theory. Price level and GDP I could then understand but what was money and velocity of money? Nowadays my difficulties have been to enlarge all four variables.

That is why in this book we start the discussion of quantity theory with the *quantity identity* which is completely undetermined but always true. We have something which we call money but the concept seems to fade away every time when we decide to scrutinize it. We will regard the concept of money as a complex structure where the intrinsic features are not always commensurable and sometimes even contradictory.

In fact much of our analysis is to be traced back to the problem of atomistic and complex variables. This is also another path into Keynes' analysis. He actually started his philosophy studies in Cambridge with this very problem.

Consequently this book can be seen as a kind of interface between economics and philosophy since we also have to distance economics as a social science from natural sciences. Not that associations to methods in natural sciences are necessarily wrong but the main difference is that physics deals with objects and economics deals with subjects and that is fundamental.

Mathematics is an integral part of economics. Some claim that this has destroyed the whole subject of economics and we should go back to non-mathematical analysis. Our attitude is that mathematics/logics is an essential part of scientific analysis but that does not mean that we must press reality into a certain type of mathematic reasoning. We will show how the juxtaposition of atomic and complex variables confuses both logics and mind. Furthermore we will take Keynes' attitude to econometrics that using mathematics and statistics for deriving exact parameter structures is doubtful not to say a direct obstacle for analysis of economic and social structures.

The basic problem, in my opinion, underlying the peculiarities of economic theory is that as the welfare of human beings is the ultimate purpose of all economic activities, but the human being is also the most important production factor. Human beings are subjects and thus final causes, but as production factors she is nothing but an object.

Acknowledgements

I have had an intensive intellectual exchange with my friend and earlier co-writer Dr. Angelo Fusari, former Director of Research at the Institute of Studies and Economic Analysis, ISAE, Rome. He works more with the general research methodology in social science and his book *Methodological Misconceptions in the Social Sciences* (Springer 2014) has been of utmost importance for me.

The philosophical side of Keynes has been of utmost interest for me in this book and I am grateful to Lord Robert Skidelsky, Emeritus Professor at the University of Warwick, for interesting discussions on Keynes' philosophical contributions and his kind help in sending me a draft from an early paper by Keynes (1903) where Keynes rejects additive aggregation.

I have had many and fruitful discussions on welfare and health economics with my friend Senior Lecturer José Ferraz-Nunes, University of Gothenburg. This has been of importance for me.

My thoughts at this moment go also to my teacher, co-researcher and great friend, the late Professor Lars Westberg with whom I discussed most of the problems which are outlined in this book. He died as a young man of 88 years but that was just a figure for administrative purposes.

I also want to thank Mr Fredrik Ekstedt, MSc. Maths and BA Economics, analyst at the Swedish Export Credit Cooperation for his help with more intricate mathematical and financial problems. I also want to thank Dr Med Anna Ekstedt for interesting discussions on medicine, particularly psychiatry, with respect to picturing and interpreting the reality, she brought to my attention to Karin Johannisson's book *Signs*, a history of medical diagnosis and treatments, which was of great use for the Epilogue.

The help of my wife Barbro Ekstedt, former linguist at the Council of the European Union in Brussels, has been indispensable in correcting my language and most of all put her finger on weak logics and blurred reasoning. I am in deep debt to her and give her my respect and love.

Finally, the two most important people for me who keep me physically and intellectually alert and also fill me with hope and dreams are my grandchildren Olivia and Elias, who see the things discussed in this book as rather trivial compared to the excitements of following a butterfly or the miracle of the knotty tree and I have to agree with them deep in my heart. I give them my love.

Introduction

When I started my university studies in economics in the middle of the 1960s, I was told that the problem of governing the stability of the economy was theoretically solved and, if we disregarded some political discrepancies of minor importance, it was also practically solved. With respect to the increasing scientific knowledge of the conditions of economic growth, we were also more or less able to administer the long run growth. During the years around 1969 there were regular international conferences on saving the Bretton Woods system. After the conferences, bulletins were published which stated that the problems were 'solved once and for all'. These conferences where held at shorter and shorter intervals and in the final instance, the interval was only three months. Thus I learnt that 'once and for all' meant about three months.

The Nobel laureate, Robert Lucas, declared in his presidential address of 2003 to the American Economic Association, that the 'central problem of depression-prevention has been solved, for all practical purposes, and has in fact been solved for many decades'. Currently, however, we know that Lucas perhaps was a bit optimistic in his declaration.

The heritage from Newton of mechanical equilibrium based on mathematical postulate and axioms often leads to intellectual obscureness in empirical sciences. Economic policy is, as other forms of policy, subject to Machiavelli's and Bismarck's general attitude 'Politik ist die Kunst des Möglichen' and reading Machiavelli's *Prince*, even the Monarch/Tyrant had to submit to the fact that humans are subjects and thus final causes.[1]

In some sense history repeats itself, particularly when it comes to overestimating the current knowledge. It is said that there are two sorts of provincialism: the spatial and the temporal, of which the latter is the far worse. Current fashion grown from methodological, often technical, advancements in conjunction with ideological idiosyncrasies influences methodologies, conceptualizations and definitions of perceived economic and social problems. Sometimes historical analysis and studies of analytical forms from other sciences may render insight into the relative non-uniqueness of the current problems as well as current analytical patterns, but unfortunately excessive specialization excludes such excursions.

One way to look at the economy is in terms of the social/cultural, where market reactions and expectations formation are based on these socio-cultural patterns. The other way is to look at the economy as a complete equilibrium system governed by objective economic forces. The latter leads to the result that we might study parts independently of each other, given the fundamental axiomatic structure, and then add our result to the total knowledge of the system. This follows from the assumed additive structure of the system. The first approach's drawback is that general models and results seldom can be derived. On the other hand, since such an approach has to be integrated with other social sciences, results, although less general and inter-temporal, tend to be more founded in the empirical world. Realizing that humans are to be seen as subjects and thus, with respect to causal structures as local and temporal final causes forces us to look, not for general results, but for locally and temporally inert structures. The scientific awareness of inertia and irreversible processes will by necessity affect theoretical advancements as well as empirical modelling and give rise to an analysis where the existence of local and temporal equilibria is inter-foliated with structural breakdowns, sometimes addressed as chaotic behaviour.

The second approach is from a technical point of view satisfactory with respect to the preciseness of the logical structure as well as of the derived analytical results which are relatively easy to transform into a statistical hypothesis. The problem is that the logical structure is postulated a priori and not derived from empirical studies. With respect to the neoclassical general equilibrium theory the axioms are identical to those which are necessary for creating n-dimensional Euclidian (measurable) space. So when Jean Baptiste Say (1803: 246) claims that:

> Value may be estimated in the way of price; but it cannot be measured, that is to say, compared with a known and invariable measure of intensity, for no such measure has yet been discovered[;]

it was also a declaration of a non-equilibrium economic theory. Economic theory has to comply with the current socio-political environment. Still however economics is the science of allocation and distribution of scarce resources but there are no general solutions to that even in our globalized world.

In Chapter 1 we will show how economists such as Mill and Jevons struggled with the concept and logics of utility as possible to attach to the economic sphere, but the ultimate link between the inner space of utility and the outer space of commodities cannot be postulated other than by assumptions. In the ultimate Arrow and Debreu approach, the pure mathematical essentials are supposed to hold in order to show an existence of something called general equilibrium but this does not comply with Say's condition of 'a known and invariable measure of intensity' since the measure only holds for a particular equilibrium and if this is perturbed we do not possess a measure fulfilling Say's condition. This has led to a great confusion. Shall we assume that we live in an eternal general equilibrium or shall we assume that we live in a temporary general equilibrium which changes according to some trajectory or do we live in a state of eternal disequilibrium?

We will show that if the second and the third alternatives are the case, then many conclusions concerning the relation between microscopic and macroscopic levels built on the general equilibrium theory are false.

Economic Theory and Economic Modelling

In practice, models are used which allude to neoclassical and/or Keynesian approaches in form of more or less advanced equation systems. These are generally rather à-theoretic in the sense that they neither discuss the character of concepts nor their spatial and temporal existence. At best we can say that it is a momentary picture, where certain inertia is assumed, of some relations between variables. The problems will normally rise in relation to aggregation and dynamics.

Our attitude in this book is that economics is based on an obsolete theoretical foundation, the neoclassical theory, with respect to a modern economy. Furthermore eventual theoretical progress like Keynes' works based on both philosophy and economics are poorly digested and even more poorly integrated in the neoclassical foundation.

Economic modelling which is the almost necessary outcome of economic theory has a microscopic and a macroscopic branch. In a sense an economic model could be seen as a kind of laboratory where we are able to conduct experiments. We may of course say that the ongoing economic policy implementations in different countries are a gigantesque experiment but on the matter of controlling the experiment we might be a bit doubtful with respect to its scientific design. Thus when we look at economic theory from abstract philosophical or mathematical views we must never forget that economic modelling for practical purposes might be an ultimate end of these exercises. The models are then used for political purposes and economic theorists sometimes regard themselves as innocent in that business although Keynes was obviously of the contrary opinion (Keynes 1936 [1973]: 383).

However economic modelling has a different role compared with natural sciences. In natural sciences models are basically designs of experimental activities which have the purpose of refining the theory/parameter structure of the model. A change in experimental design will have consequences for the outcome of the experiment in question. In fact, given a mathematical model in natural sciences, the ultimate purpose of the experiments is to actually *find* the relevant parametric structure with respect to *numbers*. This implies of course that the experiments are performed under the assumption of sufficient inertia, which implies utmost care of the environmental conditions.

Economic modelling does not have these possibilities, particularly so in the case of macroscopic models. Using statistical methods gives us at best a view of historical states but there are no certain proofs that the parameter structures so achieved have any bearing on current or future conditions. Keynes actually stresses this point in a letter to Roy Harrod, 10 July 1938 (Keynes *Collected Works*, 1938)

> My point against Tinbergen is a different one. In chemistry and physics and other natural sciences the object of experiment is to fill in the actual values of the various quantities and factors appearing in an equation or a formula; and the work when done is once and for all. In economics that is not the case, and to convert a model into a quantitative formula is to destroy its usefulness as an instrument of thought. Tinbergen endeavours to work out the variable quantities in a particular case, or perhaps in the average of several particular cases, and he then suggests that the quantitative formula so obtained has general validity. Yet in fact, by filling in figures, which one can be quite sure will not apply next time, so far from increasing the value of his instrument, he has destroyed it. All the statisticians tend that way. Colin, for example, has recently persuaded himself that the propensity to consume in terms of money is constant at all phases of the credit cycle. He works out a figure for it and proposes to predict by using the result, regardless of the fact that his own investigations clearly show that it is not constant, in addition to the strong a priori reasons for regarding it as most unlikely that it can be so.
>
> (We will often refer to this letter in the book and name it *Keynes' letter to Harrod*. These two had a quite intensive correspondence but for our purposes we generally mean this very letter.)

The quote has nothing to do with how to model the world, interpretation of data or effect on technical skills in statistics and computing. It is based on a philosophical attitude to social sciences in relation to natural sciences and it has to do with the conceptualization of fundamental variables. It mainly directs attention to the difference between atomistic variables and complex variables which is a fundamental difference in mathematics and analytical philosophy. Alluding to economic modelling, we might say that these distinctions equate to looking at mathematics as a logical language in comparison with the approach that mathematics is some sort of abstract computer. By the means that using mathematics in the first sense often implies an abstract study of forms, in economics of dynamic forms. We will follow Keynes and claim that the focus on deriving productive analytical theorems in Popper's sense is, if not devastating for economics when analysing the macroscopic level, it is an obstacle for deeper knowledge.[2] This has nothing *per se* to do with the use of mathematical and logical techniques but with the very complex character of economic concepts. The most important conceptual confusion regarding whether humans are subjects or not follows from the most fundamental paradox in economics: Arrow's paradox.[3]

The dominating neoclassical way of concentrating upon a very simply defined general equilibrium leaves economic science with no answer to the concept of complexity; money as one of the most important concepts in the daily workings of an economy cannot even be properly defined. It does not matter if we say that we focus on the market exchange if the medium of exchange has features which are an anomaly to money as a medium of exchange, and which even leads to contradictions intrinsic to the very concept of money.

In Chapter 2 we will discuss Keynes' attitude in relation to Russell and the two philosophers/physicists Brody and Torretti with respect to atomistic and complex variables and we will also touch slightly on Russell's classical question on the existence of negative facts. Suffice to say here that this is another watershed between social and natural sciences in methodological respects.

This methodological difference follows, as mentioned, however from an onto-logical watershed with respect to the research objects. The opinion in this book is that economics is a science analysing subjects and the economists themselves are acting subjects so the political use is an *immanent* part of the research process.

This brings us to the question of objective and normative research. Since economics is a social science and has individuals and social organisms as the prime research objects who, we claim, ought to be regarded as subjects and subsequently to be seen as local and temporal final causes. Since the researcher is an individual as is his subject, objective research in its deepest sense is thus impossible according to Gödel's paradox.[4] Nevertheless even if we explicitly want to pursue normative research we must scrutinize our concepts and methods in order to achieve a maximal result of our research. Such a scrutiny must as far as possible be independent of our normative frame.

Thus our aim is to scrutinize conceptualizations and consistencies of concepts and methods concerning the money economy. As a consequence of our approach that humans are subjects and thereby to be seen as final causes, we disregard constructions like 'invisible hand' or similar which are to be regarded as meta-physics: this also includes universal forces as evolutionary processes like Darwinism. These are not necessarily false but until we get a rather precise analysis of the temporal structure we prefer to regard experiences, education of individuals and their memory, which might be assumed to be possible to commu-nicate, as a highly potent cause of development for better or worse, what are the differences in the definition of *development* in an objective and a normative sense? This seems to imply a highly individualistic approach but given that humans are social creatures the very form of social structure is important for the communication and interaction between the individuals and thus also for the communication and the ability of implementation of ideas.[5]

When it comes to *microscopic studies* rich data sources and sophisticated statistical techniques make it sometimes possible to make parallel studies linked to sociological and political studies as complements, which makes these kinds of studies rather different from macroscopic studies. Often the limitations of the studies are appropriately limited in space and time, and theoretical and statistical problems are shared with other sciences. The models used are generally rather well defined both structurally and conceptually and resemble to a certain degree medical statistical studies and I suppose the virtues and the vices are much the same although the economists generally lack the clinical level of those studies, which is a substantial drawback. Generally we might say that economic micro-scopic studies/modelling are somewhat similar to, if inertia is high, microscopic studies/modelling in natural sciences. The rich abundance of statistical material makes it almost possible to create a sort of laboratory given inertia and repetitiveness. Furthermore these microscopic studies concern individual behaviour irrespective of any links to some general equilibrium concept. We will in this book connect ourselves to microscopic studies from different times and areas since they, within limits, help us to see different views of basic concepts. The problem with these kinds of studies is to explain the causes of the observed inertia and of course the problem of aggregation. Here is a field for important co-operation between most of the social sciences including social-medicine and history. We will, however, in this book disregard these important research fields since it is outside our scope, although it is probably one of the most fruitful research directions to increase our knowledge of the economic system.

Unfortunately the praise of the relative quality of economic microscopic studies generally does not hold for *macroscopic studies*. Variables are diffuse, the links between static and dynamic models are poor and interrelations between the real and financial economy unclear. Besides this statistical material is rather poor due to the aggregation of data which drag parts of the theory into data which should be explained by the theory. To this we add the whole bulk of complex problems of aggregation per se.

Let us however immediately say that economic macroscopic modelling has no equivalent modelling in natural sciences except for astronomy, but in astronomy the breach in relation to the microscopic physical theories is almost complete both with respect to concepts and methods. Sometimes one gets the feeling that the rift between macro and micro states almost enters the metaphysical spheres. Macroscopic research in economics concerns the entire social body and somehow tries to link this to individual and/or group behaviour. If we look at medicine for example, the different specialities work side by side with traditionally little connection with each other although it is nowadays clearly changing, but specialities such as cardiology, psychiatry and social medicine are hard to merge.

To perhaps overstate it a bit: economics seems to be the only science today where the conflicts, theoretical as well as empirical, between the microscopic and the macroscopic worlds are profoundly recognized and a vital part of the scientific development and disputes.

The axes around which the disputes move in the deepest sense, are the axiomatic structure of the neoclassical theory, Arrow's paradox, uncertainty and the role of money.

By uncertainty we do not only refer to the individual agents but also to the science itself, the very problem of empirical induction.

Some Comments on the Philosophical Foundations of Economics

A central issue in this book is to scrutinize the conceptualization of the theory of economics. It is said that the neoclassical theory is based upon a Newtonian approach to the world. In some sense this is true with respect to economic dynamics and practical handling of economic models. We often think of an equilibrium as some kind of sink whereto the economy returns if perturbed. Keynes also discussed in a similar way in General Theory of Employment Interest and Money, (further on shortened to GT) in Chapter 17 why the economy oscillates but the oscillations seldom exceed some limits. Thus it is a similarity between the neoclassical approach and Keynes' discussion which might induce the thinking of Keynes' thoughts as a kind of dynamic specification of the neoclassical theory. This is however wrong.

The neoclassical theory is an a priori defined axiomatic structure which shows the existence of an equilibrium of certain characteristics but this equilibrium is nowhere dense, thus it has no environment, thus no mathematical structure outside that very equilibrium. That means that we can hardly define any kind of convergence rule since we have to start in disequilibrium and show how that develops into an equilibrium although the disequilibrium cannot be defined by the axioms.

Keynes however discusses economic oscillations and their limitations with respect to social and socioeconomic structures. Thus Keynes' discussion and the neoclassical equilibrium are in fact contradictions in terms.

From a philosophical point of view the neoclassical theory is rich with respect to the problem of conceptualization. The theory basically concerns a barter economy and has been developed into a mathematical perfection with respect to clarity and intrinsic consistency but it fails to define central concepts such as money as we conceive it in the everyday use. We concentrate in this book on the money economy but actually the systematic conceptualization of the neoclassical theory has made it difficult to find alternative concepts expressing the different roles of money as it appears in the *money economy*. When discussing Keynesianism, as it appears in modelling, it is sometimes rather difficult to see the difference between a Keynesian equilibrium and a neoclassical one since the money which appears often is expressed as a market of the same characteristics as other markets, which in fact is true in some sense, but the money markets not only deal with money as a medium of exchange but also as liquidity and money as the denomination factor for assets and liabilities. With respect to liquidity such a concept only becomes interesting if a market system is open to uncertainty, which is not the same as risk. It is exactly here where we have to consider the quote from Keynes' letter to Harrod, and shove ourselves into a different theoretical universe.

Thus, although our interest is the *money economy* we need to scrutinize the barter economy as it appears in the neoclassical theory, which we based on results in Ekstedt and Fusari (2010) and Ekstedt (2012).

The neoclassical equilibrium is not something which falls out of an ordinary system of equations with some variable and parameter structure, its variables and structure must be defined within an axiomatic structure. However, as we will see, this axiomatic structure happens to be a measurable Euclidian space, with the addition of an axiom of local non-satiation, which grants that the convex hull of the feasible set is reached. Thus in fact since virtually all economic models are defined for real analytic functions the neoclassical equilibrium should fall out as a solution, given the axiom of local non-satiation. The neoclassical theory does not put any restrictions on the mathematical manipulations but on the agents and the commodities. That means that all restrictions are used to squeeze agents and commodities into atomistic definitions suitable for mathematical analysis.

Consequently we could say that from a technical point of view there is no difference between a neoclassical and a Keynesian equilibrium. That is probably why some scholars just see Keynesianism as an extension of the neoclassical model and furthermore if we take the axiomatic structure lightly and treat it as 'some stylized facts of the market economy', we can just dismiss the whole show of discussing Keynesianism and the neoclassical model.

We mentioned above some technical particulars of the neoclassical axiomatic structure which prevent the utilization of standard stability analysis. But there is a deeper problem with respect to this, namely that the general equilibrium has an intrinsic normative value, with respect to efficiency, which normal equilibria in dynamic modelling lacks and has to be imposed exogenously if the analysis so demands.

Thus alluding to Newton's world the equilibrium grants an ordered and efficient existence.

However the 'Newtonian world' was hardly established before a fundamental breach in the appearance of the physical world: *the entropy principle*, discovered by Lazare Carnot (1803) and Rudolph Clausius (1855), where the latter formulated Clausius theorem which imply that the total amount of heat absorption of a closed system with cyclical changes is zero in case of reversibility and below zero in case of non-reversibility. The basic empirical observation for the 2nd thermodynamic law is the spread of heat between a system and its environment which in the entropy concept is generalized to the universal distribution of energy. We will deal with this principle later on from several angles.

Newtonian physics gave us an ordered universe where equilibrium was the key concept, not only as an analytical tool but as a normative state of art. The detection of the entropy principle threw physics into chaos in the sense that there was no intrinsic equilibrium but a dynamic development which was apart from any type of equilibrium trajectory.

Physics, since the times of Carnot and Clausius, beginning/mid nineteenth century, has been obedient to the second law of thermodynamics which introduced a universal increase of entropy. Certainly we can imagine subsystems with decreasing entropy but only at the expense of a proportionally higher increase of entropy in the environment of the subsystems in question and, as in a thunderstorm, it is not unreasonable to expect a violent equilibration when the differences between the subsystem and its environment with respect to entropy has grown too big. Physical equilibrium in a general sense is therefore not linked to a normative state but to a state where the distribution of energy is uniform and equal to the non-existence of any system: we might call it the death of any form of system.

This state is indeed stable although we say it is a non-deterministic chaos, it is a physical state of absolute stability. This state of highest possible entropy seems also rather unpleasant, according to physicists with a temperature of 0 K° approximately −273 C°.

Certainly this equilibrium is a sort of normative value in the sense that it shows us an end of the universal process of increasing entropy but on this road we may live in subsystems where the entropy seems to be decreasing: light and the photosynthesis may create decent life conditions.

The funny thing is that the general equilibrium theory in economics may be interpreted in two different ways on the universal level: one way is an analogy to the equilibrium of physics when we have an even distribution of entropy, the death of the system. The other way of interpretation is more intriguing and is linked to the Nash equilibrium of a number of agents approaching infinity. In the first interpretation we may see the individual space of action as maximization of utility restricted by the other agents' utility maximization. This means that allowed actions are allowed for all agents and non-allowed actions are not allowed for any agent. We might interpret this state in terms of Kant's ethical imperative and implies a totally static society.[6]

Consequently, in the second interpretation we disregard an autonomous process like the universal entropy increase but say that given any distribution there exists a Kantian solution which we then might define as the Pareto optimum.

Both interpretations however imply a static equilibrium and this is why we may reject the existence of stability analysis in the sense that we have a dynamic system which may *move* towards an equilibrium. The general equilibrium is nowhere dense.

Dynamics and Stability

The static feature of a general equilibrium makes the economic analysis of dynamics rather poor. We mentioned in a footnote above analysis of waves and weather systems, which shows a rich variety of dynamical forms. Certainly the concept of equilibrium is there but just in a local and temporal way when the parameter structures happen to be structurally stable.

To claim the existence of a general equilibrium and analysing different equilibria when the state of non-equilibrium is not even defined seems to be a bit adventurous from a philosophical point of view. The fundamental reason for this is the fact that the economic theory is based on a priori axioms which create a state of equilibrium which in a topological sense is nowhere dense, as mentioned above. We will discuss this more comprehensively later on in the book. This means that from a logical point of view when we are accepting the neoclassical general equilibrium concept we also reject the existence of a stability analysis *based on the same topological characteristics as the very general equilibrium*. From this point of view the theory of rational expectations in Lucas' version is correct: you are actually expecting the very same equilibrium which you are a part of, since there are no logical grounds for expecting any other type of equilibrium. True that distribution may change but then the new equilibrium is, and must be, a fait accompli. Thus when it comes to, so to say, short run dynamics that is counteracting movements to perturbations, the neoclassical theory is indeed problematic.

However looking at long run matters there is of course a possibility that we are in a prevailing equilibrium which is symmetrically expanding leaving the price vector unchanged. The drawback with this hypothesis is of course that we then also must assume that the preference structure is left unaffected by the growth process, which might be difficult for other social sciences to understand or accept.

From the above we understand that *change* is the basic feature of *time*, which is the foundation of Einstein-Minkowski's time concept (Reichenbach 1957 [1928]) and we may be even more radical and say that there is no time concept except that produced by change.[7]

When we scrutinize the neoclassical concept of general equilibrium there are indeed difficulties to find a time concept other than what Paul Samuelson (1947) calls *logical time*, thus a set of parameters set by initial conditions and then forming a trajectory completely described at the start as the standard function:

$$x_t = x_0 \cdot e^{\beta \cdot t}$$

According to Einstein-Minkowski this is hardly a dynamic model in their sense. Obviously we can define parts of a model exogenously as developing according to such a logical time model, locally and temporally. But postulating an entire economy to behave like that where time only is related to some exogenous clock and all values are decided at one historical moment, is indeed difficult to characterize as a time process in Einstein-Minkowski's meaning and who is responsible for the clocks is indeed an intriguing question.

As students, not only of economic theory but also of economic reality we know quite well that a dynamic trajectory is more or less in constant change dependent on current events. Paul Samuelson calls this *historical time*. We so to say have a moving x_0 and a changing β in the function above, but still we deal with the problem of parameter values and this has very little to do with Keynes' statement to Harrod which we quoted in the very beginning, and where he dismisses any form of parameterization in order to find a solution with respect to an empirical problem/structure/model.

To understand Keynes fully on this we have to dig in to his early works in philosophy and probability. The central concept is *complexity*. In the two first chapters on Barter and on Keynes' contribution respectively, the concept of complexity will be of central importance and that will also be so in understanding the concept of dynamics and stability.

We will in this book mention several forms of complexity; some attached to the variables themselves, some to the intrinsic dynamic structure of a system and some to the sensibility of perturbations of a system. Sometimes this kind of analysis is said to belong to chaos analysis which is a bit difficult to understand if we analyse basically deterministic systems which sometimes have behave in a surprising way, although this is built into the very logical structure.

Basically the problem of logical/mathematical analysis is a problem of language. Wittgenstein (1921 [1974]) expresses it in Proposition 6.211 where he writes:

> Indeed in real life a mathematical proposition is never what we want. Rather, we make use of mathematical propositions *only* in inferences from propositions that do not belong to mathematics to others that likewise do not belong to mathematics. (In philosophy the question, "What do we actually use this word or this proposition for?" repeatedly leads to valuable insights.)

Let us take an ordinary demand function $q_i^d = a + bp_i$. Given the neoclassical axioms, particularly the axiom of reflexivity, a commodity is identical to itself; $q_i \equiv q_i$. When we analyse this in Chapter 1 we will stress its mathematical importance, although many economists regard it as trivial.

But the problem is that the identity only concerns the physical characteristics of the commodity in question. When we discuss commodities we are not primarily interested in the physical characteristics but in the role of the commodity with respect to its use in the household of the consumer, thus the consumer looks at the technical characteristics of the commodity in relation to an aim created by a set of commodities arranged in a certain structure.

That means that a commodity, as it is understood in household production theory, is input in the production of welfare. But this also means that a commodity is not an atomistic item but a multidimensional complex where the consumer demand is context dependent. This is of fundamental importance because to use mathematics and probability theory properly, all variables have to be defined in an atomistic way. One immediate result of this approach is that reversibility is doubtful and furthermore as we will see additive aggregation is indeed a problem, not only with respect to household production theory but also to all theoretical settings where the axiom of reflexivity is rejected. Furthermore we will have no given price level since the demand of commodities will be contextually dependent.

In many cases we can disregard these aspects for local and temporal analysis but then we also impute another source of uncertainty.

In the more traditional form of stability analysis and sources for instability these are in fact in the deepest sense very dependent on the complex nature of the variables. The two typical sources of catastrophic behaviour of dynamic systems, bifurcations and perturbations are indeed dependent on the degree of precision of the parametric structure, and with respect to differential equation systems truncations become an important issue.

When we discuss Keynes' contributions in Chapter 3 we will go back and follow the rather exciting discussion on atomistic and complex variables.

It is however important to realise that these problems of stability are not linked specifically to the barter economy and neither to the money economy.

Money

When we move to the money economy it appears remarkable that some theoretical structures do not appear in the barter economy. In fact these were, partly at least, discussed by Aristotle and has to do with the specific characteristics of money, medium of exchange, medium of measurement, and medium of conservation of value.

It is instructive to read Aristotle's discussion on wealth-getting and the coin which states the basic contradiction in the money economy.

> When the use of coin had once been discovered, out of the barter of necessary articles arose the other art of wealth-getting, namely, retail trade; which at first probably a simple matter, but became more complicated as soon as men learned by experience whence and by what exchanges the greatest profit might be made. Originating in the use of coin, the art of getting wealth is generally thought to be chiefly concerned with it, and to be the art which produces riches and wealth; having to consider how they may be accumulated. Indeed, riches is assumed by many to be only a quantity of coin, because the art of getting wealth is concerned with coin. Others maintain that coined money is a mere sham, a thing not natural, but conventional only, because if the users substitute another commodity for it, it is worthless and because it is not useful as a means to any of the necessities of life, and, indeed, he who is rich in coin may often be in want of necessary food. But how can that be wealth of which a man may have great abundance and yet perish with hunger, like Midas in the fable, whose insatiable prayer turned everything that was set before him into gold?
>
> (Aristotle (334–324 BC[1990]: 451, B no. 1257^b))

Aristotle points at the intrinsic problem between the commodities of the market exchange and the medium of market exchange. According to Aristotle, and we agree with him, the existence of a medium of market exchange gives rise to an entirely new form of business. Thus when we discuss the neutrality of money, we assume that prices and wages are not affected by a change in the total money stock, but needs a change of production. This is not Aristotle's issue, the coin gives rise to an entirely new market form which is, using more modern terminology, entirely outside the utility aspects of the individual in a neoclassical sense. This is why money feels somewhat uncomfortable and redundant when applied to the neoclassical theory. Furthermore to relate to a neo-classical general equilibrium and add money makes it necessary to pinion money in such a way that it is unrecognizable with respect to the ordinary economy we experience daily.

Arrow and Hahn (1971: 357) tell us that 'If a serious monetary theory comes to be written, the fact that contracts are indeed made in terms of money will be of considerable importance.' We may however ask ourselves if it is by any means possible to develop such a 'serious monetary theory' within the frames of the neoclassical theory and in fact we will deny that.

Jean Baptiste Say is actually one of the very few economists who discusses money as well as price measures in a scientific sense (Say 1834[1803]: 246–7). He frankly denies the existence of a price/money measure persistent in time and space and by that he also rejects the existence of an inter-temporal general equilibrium. With respect to relative prices he says: 'Nor will this measure of relative value, if we may so call it, convey any accurate idea of the ratio of two commodities one to the other, at any considerable distance or place.' Then he discuss the character of the money as a measure of intensity: 'Value may be estimated in the way of price; but it can not be measured that is to say, compared with a known and invariable measure of intensity, for such a measure has not yet been discovered.'

As we mentioned earlier the axioms of the Arrow and Debreu economy is plainly taken from mathematics in order to set up an n-dimensional Euclidian space where the commodities (defined in an atomistic way) are the dimensions and the agents are commodity vectors.[8] When we in Chapter 1 discuss the emergence of the utility theory, Say's words on 'known and invariable measure of intensity' become a key issue.

As Aristotle mentions the introduction of money implies an introduction of a complex. In the neoclassical analysis we see how theoreticians try to find a concept of money free from further connotation than a pure medium of exchange. The early discussion between Smith's Real bill concept (banking school) and Ricardo's bullionist approach (currency school) is a good example. The former claimed that banks should be free to issue paper money as long as the outstanding value of paper money exactly corresponded to the gold holdings but irrespective of any relation to the performance of the real economy. With respect to inflation the issuing policy was of no importance since inflation was due to real factors like variations in harvests, raw material for the manufacturing industry, wages and similar things.

On the other hand, the bullionists followed the Friars of Salamanca and Hume and looked upon money as a kind of dual to real commodities with respect to price-variations. Thus we can clearly trace back the roots of the Quantity equation to a certain extent, and also Aristotle was to some degree aware of the dual relationship between prices of real commodities and the implicit price of money.

However the early theorists were not doctrinaire in the way that modern monetarists tend to be. Inflation was regarded both as a real and a monetary phenomenon. My guess is that the reason for the modern orthodoxy has to do with the underlying theoretical and methodological reference to the general equilibrium theory. If we have a state of general equilibrium the relative prices are locked up in precise relations and thus there cannot exist inflation due to real factors.

The early economists like the Salamanca Friars, Hume and Say rejected the existence of a general equilibrium, Salamanca Friars and Hume implicitly, while Say explicitly rejected its existence.

When we reject the general equilibrium and stick to only local and temporal equilibria the Fisher equation becomes spurious since it will hide distribution and allocation structures which will affect the performance of the economy. It is instructive to read Say on this matter:

> It has been already remarked, that the total value of money of any country, even with the addition to the value of all the precious metals contained in the nation under any other shape, is but an atom, compared with the gross amount of other values. Wherefore, the thing represented would exceed in value the representative; and the latter could not command the present or possession of the former.
>
> Nor is the position of Montesquieu, that money-prices depend upon the relative of the total commodities to that of the total money of the nation at all better founded. What do sellers and buyers know of the existence of any other commodities, but those that are the objects of their dealing? And what difference could such knowledge make demand and supply in respect to those particular commodities? These opinions have originated in the ignorance at once of fact and of principle.
>
> (Ibid.: 246)

Thus with respect to the neoclassical axiomatic structure there exists an index of relative prices, unique for the specific equilibrium. This index possesses none of the features we attach to money in the daily business. By defining one of the commodities as a numeraire we might have some sort of physical appearance of the rather abstract index we arrive at in general equilibrium although such a manipulation to me seems even more abstract. Anyway as we said above, this kind of money can by definition not deal with anything else except for the choice of basis for the numeraire. If the relative prices change we are obviously entering another state of equilibrium and we then have to start from the beginning again. Thus the theoretical content, if taken seriously, of the quantity equation: $M \cdot V = P \cdot Y$, only deals with a nominal mark up of prices. If we uses the equation in a non-equilibrium context important structural features of the economy will be hidden which might affect the performance of the economy in the future.

Linking the quantity equation to the Fisher equation: *nominal interest – inflation ≈ real interest*, gives us an analogue reasoning of distributional and structural effects.

If we think of a non-equilibrium situation, money, as Say also mentions, is to be seen as a local and temporal measure where the context of the market exchange affects both the relative and the nominal level. For an economy as a whole over a certain time spans the relative prices is created by social patterns and restrictions as well as their eventual stabilising factors.

There are, however, two other features appearing when money is introduced: the first one liquidity exists also in a barter economy, but then only in relation to specific commodities. In the money economy liquidity becomes a more general problem for the agents and the reason for eventual problems is due to many different aspects. We have in earlier books (Ekstedt Fusari, 2010 and Ekstedt

2012), used the concept of lexicographic preference to illustrate the problem of liquidity and we are going to discuss it more comprehensively when we come to the problem of inflation, unemployment and growth in Chapter 5.

The second one is directly linked to the quote from Arrow and Hahn above. *Contracts are made in money.*

What we have mentioned before: money as medium of exchange, money as measurement and money as liquidity are aspects which may, at least in principle, occur in a barter economy without involving a money system but when it comes to contracts running over a time period there is a distinct difference between the barter economy and the money economy. A contract in a barter economy must, at least to a certain degree define the relative prices for a relevant commodity basket while in a money economy nothing of the kind is needed. This is probably the most important feature of money. Without going into the neutrality of money in a general sense we can at least say that given certain socioeconomic inertia money is relatively neutral with respect to relative prices. This means that a money contract may concern any sector in the economy but signed it becomes in principle tradable irrespective of sectorial considerations.

This is the virtue and this is the vice. We can illustrate the basic problem with the help of the neoclassical theory. Assume that we start from a particular state of general equilibrium with a uniquely defined price vector. We sign a contract for a future time period in a set of commodities and of a certain value, say 100 index points. When we are going to pay back the loan we however have a different state of equilibrium with another price vector; the question then is the interpretation of the 100 index points and the original commodity basket. Given the new state of equilibrium we have a different price vector which logically speaking has nothing to do with the former commodity basket. This is actually the basic reason why money is impossible to handle in a realistic manner within the neoclassical equilibrium analysis.

In the money economy the flexibility and neutrality of money make such discussions superfluous.

Aggregation

It is important to keep in mind that this book deals with macroeconomics, since it in this regard that we have the most problematic epistemological questions (and may be also ontological). Microeconomics is easier to handle since we may restrict the area of investigation in a way which is impossible for the macroscopic analysis. The concept *ceteris paribus* can be both relevant and suitable for the microscopic analysis due to the possibilities of limiting the analysis to subsystems. This is obviously dependent on observed/assumed inertia. At the macroscopic level *ceteris paribus* has no meaning whatsoever in reality apart from an analytical simplification which has probably no real counterpart. If we assume a macroscopic state as a general equilibrium in the neoclassical sense the *ceteris paribus* expression is obviously meaningless since we cannot change a part of the economy without effects on other parts; either it will throw us out of the equilibrium or we will have stabilizing counter-movements. If we reject the additive aggregation principle it is obvious that the links between economic subsystems may be rather complicated so an assumption of *ceteris paribus* must be scrutinized carefully with respect to implicit effects.

Thus a comparative static analysis is only possible in a dynamic system where we can limit the system to such a degree that the dynamic links to the environment are unimportant with respect to the internal effects of the subsystem. To choose a couple of variables, such as unemployment and inflation and analyse them without taking growth aspects, foreign trade, distribution and allocation effects into consideration may make it more comfortable for the analysis but that is the best which can be said.

In general it can be said that comparative statics work properly when we have a well-defined subsystem with respect to environmental impacts and dynamics.

Basically this is the meaning of Keynes' critique of Tinbergen in his (Keynes') letter to Harrod quoted above.

The new classical economics at the end of the 1960s claimed quite rightly that the macroeconomic theory needs a microscopic underpinning. Their theoretical solution was however not a solution since they basically only added the principle of additive aggregation and they so to say bought the whole package of the neoclassical equilibrium theory, which indeed is not a microscopic underpinning of the macroeconomic level, since it is based on an axiomatic structure which is, at the macroscopic level, subject to the devastating critique underlying Arrow's paradox. This paradox is comprehensively analysed in both Ekstedt and Fusari (2010: 59–62) and Ekstedt (2012: 70–4) so we just include the essentials.

The reason why Arrow's paradox occurs is that the neoclassical agent defined by the six axioms is unable to vote and is thus contradictive to agents which possess this ability. Consequently introducing an agent who is able to vote destroys all possibilities of additive aggregation.

Thus Arrow's paradox is a central issue with respect to economic epistemology since it occurs because of the very axiomatic structure of economic theory in relation to the everyday experience of a working money economy. People care and adapt to the aggregate result, which is also the issue of the so called Lucas critique, and people can form coalitions.

The mistake which is often made is to promote the market result related to the axiomatic structure to something related to democracy which indeed is curious.

As a matter of fact the two Soviet economists Makarov and Rubinov (1977) showed that the Arrow and Debreu setting cannot discriminate between a centrally planned communist economy and a market economy based on the Arrow and Debreu axioms.

Consequently our attitude is that due to the fact that we reject the axiom of reflexivity and due to the correct interpretation of Arrow's paradox we will arrive at a proposition implying that we must separate optimizing decisions on different levels.

But this will drive us into a sharp conflict regarding the interpretation of money values in relation to real values. Thus we can show with respect to the neoclassical theory that for a barter economy with no properly defined money in the ordinary sense, rejecting additive aggregation implies that there is no logical link between individual and aggregate optimization. However when we have forced the theory into a state of non-equilibrium and then introduce money in the ordinary sense we are free to aggregate additively the money values even if these are non-equilibrium values and furthermore using money values implies a complete confusion of general equilibrium as a neoclassical concept with equilibrium of a dynamic model with any parametric structure. Thus what can be called an equilibrium model and what can be called a Keynesian model with temporary equilibrium is to be explained outside the model and at the pleasure of the respective researcher. This follows from the fact that any level of employment can be defined as the relevant labour. The so called NAIRU is for example a set of values on unemployment and inflation, with the latter variables specified in a particular way not shared by the whole economic profession; furthermore the definition of unemployment is structurally dependent where the economic structure is not a static variable but dependent on short run economic activities but due to that money values cannot mirror underlying real disequilibria and any kind of model almost can be true in some sense/interpretation. This reasoning goes for both neoclassical and Keynesian modelling although one should expect Keynesians to have a higher awareness of this problem as Keynes had.

Growth

This problem just discussed is also prevalent in the analysis of growth. If we stick to a barter economy we can describe growth pretty well using a simple production possibility curve and enlarging the two-dimensional curve on the blackboard to n-dimensions which gives principally the same picture. This picture of growth is very good; we can discuss different types of growth, changed relations between production factors, non-asymmetric efficiency growth, effects of growth with respect to non-asymmetric distribution of incomes and wealth. I think those readers who are (have been) academic teachers bless the clarity of this eminent tool of description.

With respect to measurement of growth however particularly non-asymmetric growth we become more careful; the measure cannot be entirely found in the curves we have drawn on the blackboard but also requires discussion of the underlying distribution of incomes and wealth; but it can be discussed.

However all these, hopefully, interesting discussions presuppose that the figure we draw is basically of constant dimensionality. Thus the growth concept in the neoclassical theory presupposes constant dimensionality of the commodity basket. This is a direct consequence of the very axiomatic structure which implies that Brouwer's Dimension Invariance Theorem holds. This tells us that a function from one space to another can be unique if and only if the dimensionality of the two spaces are the same.

This means that if we introduce a new commodity to the commodity basket of an economy there will be an almost infinite number of possible equilibrium price vectors. Thus if we go through a trajectory of commodity baskets of different dimensionalities we thereby pass through different equilibria and the price vectors of these equilibria are not commensurable.

This holds for the barter economy but when introducing money in an ordinary sense this problem does not even occur since you can add price values of ten commodities as well as of one thousand commodities if they are expressed in money terms.

However this problem introduces one clear problem into the money economy and that is if changes in the dimension of the commodity basket cause changes in the measured inflation.

Negative Commodities and Negative Utilities

The neoclassical axiomatic structure is defined on the positive orthant which is quite natural if we regard the 'thingness' of commodities but as we also stated when we rejected the axiom of reflexivity, agents actually do not demand 'things' as such but 'things' for use in relation to other 'things'. That means that we may think of a set of usages with respect to a particular commodity. Fertilizers used in cultivation is probably to be seen as good; on the other hand we have the environmental effects which might affect the judgement but fertilizer used for making bombs are for most people defined on the strict negative orthant.

When considering aggregation with respect to money values it is however always defined on the positive orthant. That means that any model defined in money values fails to mirror these aspects.

In economic discussions we usually talk about external effects but there is instead a defunct economic analysis behind it.

Modelling the Economy

We have said that a rather natural consequence of economic theorizing is economic modelling. On the other hand our discussion of the character of economic models in relation to the real world and our quote from Keynes' question any kind of numerical solution for models which are said to mirror the reality. So why bother about modelling? The only way to attach numerical values to the parameters is by somehow linking them to historical data, either through traditional statistical studies or through different kinds of simulation techniques. Whatever we choose there is one step which is compulsory if we want the numerical values to be relevant for decisions of the future, and that is to grant the inertia of *the reality* within the framework of the model. If we cannot do so Keynes' critique of Tinbergen in the quote above is viable.

This implies that modelling must have a different purpose in economics compared to natural sciences. We said above that the research objects of economics were subjects and to be seen as *final causes*. By that we mean that the individual in any capacity up to *now* has been unable to fully know what goes on in another human being's mind. This means that only actual actions of other people can be subject to analysis. Thus the neoclassical analysis based on utility theory is an effort to bridge the gap between the interior reflexion and the observable action of the agent. Unfortunately as we will see this implies that some assumptions must be taken in order to achieve a consistent logical *model* of the human mind which severely limits the working of the human mind. Nevertheless the neoclassical model of rational market action shows us another purpose of modelling, namely illustrative purpose of a logical structure. Although we cannot use the neoclassical model for the exact description of the reality we may think that its structure describes the central feature of market behaviour in such a way that we get a qualitative knowledge of the logics involved. Other models in economics serve to a great extent the same purpose. This is obviously both a strength and a weakness of economic modelling. It is a strength since we may use the modelling for political purpose and then the analysis of a certain set of problems gives rise to prescriptions on how to avoid those problems which also means that we recommend measures which in strict sense must change the structure of the model. It is a weakness in the sense that we do not have any empirical results for judging the relevance of our models and eventual changes, particularly not at the macroscopic level.

It is sometimes said that in order to test the pudding you must eat it, meaning that using a model for practical policy work is the only way to see its quality. This is from a scientific point of view a deceitful claim. The reason for this can be found on several analytical levels but one important reason which also touches on the quote from Keynes above is the fact that any economic model defines and carries its own measurability.

It is interesting to see a historical shift in the attitudes towards economics taking place form the middle of the 18th century to the late 19th century. From Aristotle to David Hume and Adam Smith, economics was a part of ethical and social analysis. Aristotle's writing on economics is partly to be found in *Politics* and partly in *Nicomachean Ethics*. Both David Hume and Adam Smith treated economics from an ethical point of view. This line of thought continued with Marx, Mill and to a great extent Wicksell. In later times Amartya Sen is a good representative not to mention Keynes who from his very first moment in Cambridge came into contact with G.E. Moore and was deeply affected by him. We will return to this in the Chapter 2.

The other attitude which we meet, from the late 18th century to our days, is an intention to create a solid science based upon the same criteria as natural science, a sort of social engineering. It seems that Ricardo was one of the key figures in this development. Furthermore Mill's philosophical discussions on utility and utilitarianism were technically developed by Jevons into a logically consistent mathematical picture. A sort of radical form of this attitude is the extreme monetarism which tries to lump the entire macroscopic theory of the economy into a single equation.

The mathematical refinement of economic theory has been a temptation to see mathematical models in economics as parallel to models in natural science. For this purpose, econometrics has been developed as a branch of statistical science and has reached a high level of sophistication. Unfortunately this sophistication cannot escape the fundamental problem that economic data are historical and non-experimental.

As indicated above, in economic theory we only have one thoroughly consistent model for illustrating the economy, the neoclassical economic theory. We can of course say that Keynesianism and other so called heterodox theories are alternatives but these are only partly logically consistent and their concepts are generally rather poorly defined compared with the neoclassical theory. The latter is based on a closed axiomatic universe with no environment. Alternative approaches are open and their relevant environment to a large extent is undefined and probably shifting over time. That makes the approaches methodologically and conceptually obscure.

Although almost no one today thinks of the neoclassical theory as theory in the sense of true description of the empirical economy; it is often assumed that it mirrors the central logical structure of the market economy. The economy as outlined in the neoclassical theory is a *barter economy*, although this is a rather late development in economic theory. Aristotle, the Dominican Friars of the Salamanca school, Hume, Smith and Say were all clearly aware of the huge difference between the money economy and the barter economy and their main scope was to analyse the *money economy*. The theory of the pure barter economy was developed in the late 19th century to a great extent as a consequence of the development of utility theory and the alleged relation between the utility/preferences of the individual and the economic behaviour of the individual. We will later consider this link more in depth, suffice to say here that it seems as if it was an effort to make a closed logical system, and it has probably its roots in a dream of creating a closed Newtonian universe. A central feature is the postulated human rationality and then a natural conclusion could be that it is possible to create a rational society where economic policy is a sort of social engineering. Such thoughts are expressed by John Stewart Mill in his little pamphlet on *Utilitarianism* from 1863. It was however only partly the belief of Wilfred Pareto since he thought that the more fundamental forces of dynamics were of broad social and cultural character, the economy was only a social subsystem.

Regarding rationality per se it is however important to spell out clearly at this stage that we will not dispute that humans are rational, except for pathological cases, and we do not dispute optimizing economic behaviour, which we will discuss later. The point, which we will advocate, is that the axiomatic definition of rationality is only a *necessary* condition for human rationality but not a *sufficient* one. It seems à la mode for the moment to question human rationality *in toto* which leads nowhere analytically. We will come back to this of course.

The modern use of neoclassical analysis takes its stance in the Pareto Optimum/ Pareto criteria which is used as an overall efficiency criterion and is said to make it possible to deal with the effects of conform and non-conform interferences in the market with respect to prices and distribution. This also leads to the establishment of the *Second Best Analysis*, which seems a bit awkward from a strict mathematical point of view, but that depends on the kind of political norm created by using the Pareto criterion as an aggregate efficient criterion.[9] When we discuss Arrow's paradox we will come back to the peculiarity of the second best analysis.

Furthermore it is the basis of the cost-benefit analysis, which is actually based on money values. Modern studies, however, tend to favour cost-effectiveness studies where only the cost side is measured in money.

Microeconomic studies are often linked to the neoclassical concepts although the theoretical development sometimes is completely outside the realm of the axiomatic structure. Consumer analysis as long as it deals with preferences and indifference curves is linked to basic neoclassical axioms but modern consumer analysis, Becker's household production theory is definitely outside the neoclassical spheres. Standard production theory is mostly to be characterized as a mixture of engineering economics and accounting. In market analysis we look at different market forms where only perfect competition fits into the neoclassical approach. The only part of microscopic analysis which is neoclassical, save from distributional analysis, is welfare theory and it is precisely here where neoclassical theory is most normative.

When it comes to aggregate studies the use of neoclassical theory is more obscure. In the early 1970s there was severe criticism of Keynesian modelling, particularly the lack of a microscopic underpinning. This critique was already then difficult to understand since it never touched on new consumer theory, structural/industrial analysis, relations between the external and internal economy and so on, but only introduced the neoclassical theory as a microscopic base in its most abstract form.

The critique turned out to focus on three aspects: the concepts of labour market and of unemployment which were elaborated on with respect to the incitement structures; the (non) effectiveness of public stabilization policy, which was emphasized through Lucas' critique; and finally the concept of expectations which was assumed to be based on so called *rational expectations*, which is an elaboration of the perfect expectation hypothesis and an extension of the expected utility approach.

During the 1980s and 1990s and the beginning of the 21st century many economists held it to be true that completing the neoclassical foundation with the rational expectation hypothesis was a final step in integrating the microscopic and the macroscopic levels and the quote from Lucas in the introduction was in line with this belief.

The rational expectation hypothesis is indeed important from a methodological point of view since its macroscopic use is an important link from the axiomatic structure, which concerns the individual, to the macroscopic level and it has also bearing on inter-temporal issues. The original Arrow and Debreu contribution actually lacks both these features. According to Debreu, an equilibrium must be interpreted as momentary with no extension in time and he claims that commodities must be spatially and temporally indexed (Debreu 1988[1959]: 29–30). The rational expectation hypothesis is then an addition to the expected utility hypothesis, which only regards the so called state space, and forms a theory of the agents' actions and reactions. Implicitly we can regard it as an answer to Arrow's paradox and we will come back to it when we have discussed that paradox.

Modelling within mainstream economic theory today is a mixture of traditional Keynesian modelling, accepting the multiplier/accelerator reasoning, liquidity demand, and neoclassical elements particularly with respect to labour market/ wages and expectation formation as well as a part covering the production conditions. Elements like the Phillips curve and NAIRU, which are viewed more in conjunction with empirical findings are added to the analysis with small if any efforts to explain or integrate them theoretically.

There are some other peculiarities with current modelling with respect to money but we will come back to those in later chapters when we deal more in detail with money matters.

Although we seldom see a 'clean' neoclassical model in use, its basic concepts of equilibrium, price behaviour and incitement structures are to be seen as common understanding.[10] Furthermore the division between the market space and the state space of the environment underpins the understanding of the risk concept and uncertainty is often interpreted as volatility of variance following Allais' discussion from 1953. Even Keynesian models are strongly affected by the neoclassical concepts and it is sometimes hard to see the difference between Keynesian and neoclassical equilibria due to the mixture of concepts and substructures in the models.

Keynesian models are dealing with somehow aggregated variables, which Keynes assumes a sort of generic behaviour, but we may also look at the economy in a neoclassical way and transform the economy to additively aggregated sectors of virtually the same kind. Although in the consumption case it has nothing in common with Keynes' assumption of a generic behaviour, since additive aggregation transforms the analysis of aggregated economy to the same quality as the microeconomic analysis. We will later give an example of this from Lucas' writings.

A Keynesian model dealing with labour market but dismissing the heterogeneity of the labour market and inertia of capital is sometimes hard to separate from a neoclassical approach.

Many claims that Keynesian models deal with non-equilibrium, or more correct temporary and local equilibria, but neoclassical models can easily be restricted to the current volume of activities and then it is hard to see any big difference. One distinct point where a difference is said to be detectable is that Keynesian models introduce some sort of socially preferable level of employment and then assume rigidities of varying character of prices/wages but that is natural to do also in neoclassical models and the rigidities are indeed disputable.

When it comes to the fundamental questions of money, finance and uncertainty, few Keynesian models seem to penetrate this rather difficult problem and neoclassical models and Keynesian models seem to be rather similar.

In fact when it comes to defining structures of a very mathematical nature neoclassical and Keynesian modelling may be restricted and completed in such a way that it is almost impossible to discriminate between them, and when it comes to the fundamental matters of the money economy these are normally left to financial theorists with few if any efforts of integration with respect to the real sector.

Another aspect which makes the neoclassical theory of the barter economy important is that the basic conceptualization of economy, which students learn, comes from barter; relative prices, growth concepts and price formation. All this is based on the barter economy and most of all on the relative social independence of the market economy which also makes additive aggregation something quite natural even for many Keynesians since they actually work on money aggregates without noting the difference between money value aggregation and real aggregation.

Notes

1 Isaac Newton was actually head of the British Mint from 1996 until his death in 1717 and reformed the British monetary system. He was much admired by Smith and Ricardo for his scientific brilliance and particularly the latter aimed to construct a system à la Newton in economics; contemporary philosophers and economists like Hume and Say were however skeptical of that. Today we might say that Ricardo succeeded in some aspects although its principle of general equilibrium, basic to the system, is heavy criticized.

2 The study of waves has been brought to a high degree of perfection in analysing stable, unstable and catastrophic forms. This also goes for meteorology with respect to their analytical patterns. Still there is no student of oceanography who can tell us about exact wave behaviour of a gulf like the Biscayan. It is not the theoretical knowledge and modelling that is insufficient but the complexity of the particular case is too high. The same goes for meteorology. Meteorologists are sophisticated modellers but unfortunately when there are several weather systems they are lost in the complexity only after some days, sometimes hours. This of course also depends on the local/regional particulars.

3 Good logical paradoxes are not a sign of scientific deficiencies but a sign of a kind of exhaustion of the used axiomatic structure in the sense that we use it in circumstances where the axioms are insufficient or irrelevant.

4 As we are parts of the system we cannot objectively analyse the consistency and the purposes of the universal system of which we are members.

5 Angelo Fusari has recently published a book which discusses these matters in a very stimulating way. Fusari, A. (2014), *Methodological Misconceptions in the Social Sciences – Rethinking Social Thought and Social Processes*, Dordrech, Heidelberg, New York, London: Springer.

6 Ekstedt and Fusari (2010) discuss this more comprehensively in chapter four: 'On Time and Ethics'.

7 For a more comprehensive analysis see Ekstedt and Fusari (2010) chapter four, where also the concept of social time is discussed as an extension of the Einstein-Minkowski time-concept.

8 The invisible hand is not explicitly present but might be hovering somewhere, but where is a difficult question since the axioms form a space which has no environment so it cannot be there. Furthermore the axioms do not allow it to exist intrinsically so any discussion leaving unexplained factors outside the discussion takes economic analysis into the realm of metaphysics.

9 The Second Best Analysis goes back to Lipsey and Lancaster (1957) and is in its original form not particularly interesting and almost tautological when telling us that

if we change the restriction set in an optimization problem the optimal solution will change.
10 It is interesting to see that some economists seldom blame explicit or implicit assumptions of individual behaviour in economic models for poor results although the political instability can be quite substantial, but blame 'politics'.

Bibliography

Allais, M. (1953) 'Le comportement de l'homme rationel devant le risque: Critique des postulates et axiomes de l'ecole Américaine', *Econometrica*, vol. 21, 503–546.

Aristole (1990 [original around 334–324 BC]) Politics Bno. (1257ᵃ), in *The Works of Aristotle vol II*, Encyclopædia Britannica, Inc. Chicago, London, p. 452, Bno. 1258ᵇ (Bno refers to the Berlin enumeration).

Arrow, K.J and Hahn, F.H. (1971) *General Competitive Analysis*. San Francisco: Holden Day Inc.

Debreu, G. (1998 [1959]) *Theory of Value*. New York: Wiley.

Ekstedt, H. (2012) *Money in Economic Theory*. London and New York: Routledge.

Ekstedt, H. and Fusari, A. (2010) *Economic Theory and Social Change Problems and Revisions*. London and New York: Routledge.

Fusari, A. (2014) *Methodological Misconceptions in the Social Sciences – Rethinking Social Thought and Social Processes*. Dordrech, Heidelberg, New York, London: Springer.

Keynes, J. M. (1973 [1936]) *The General Theory of Employment Interest and Money*. Cambridge: MacMillan, Cambridge University Press.

Keynes, J. M. (1938) Letter to Roy Harrod 10th of July, Collected Works of Keynes. http://economia.unipv.it/harrod/edition/editionstuff/rfh.34a.htm

Lipsey, R. G. and Lancaster, K. (1956) 'The general theory of second best', *The Review of Economic Studies*, vol. 24, no 1, 11–32.

Lucas, R. E. Jr. (2003) 'Macroeconomic priorities', *American Economic Review*, vol. 93, no. 1: 1.

Makarov, V. L. and Rubinov, A. M. (1977) *Economic Dynamics and Equilibria*. Heidelberg, Berlin: Springer Verlag.

Mill, J. S. (1990 [1863]) 'Utilitarianism', in *Great Books of the Western World*, no. 40. Chicago, London, New Delhi, Paris, Seoul, Taipei, Tokyo: Encyclopædia Britannica, Inc.

Reichenbach, H. (1957 [1928]) *The Philosophy of Space and Time*. New York: Dover Publications.

Samuelson, P.A. (1947) *The Foundations of Economic Analysis*, Cambridge, MA: Harvard University Press.

Say, J.B. (1834 [1803]) *A Treatise on Political Economy; or the Production, Distribution, and Consumption of Wealth*. Philadelphia: Grigg & Elliot, 9, North Fourt Street.

Wittgenstein, L. (1974 [1921]), *Tractatus Logico-Philosophicus*, London: Routledge & Kegan Paul.

1 Neoclassical Theory and Rational Expectations

Theoretical Deficiencies

Abstract

The scope of this chapter is to discuss some methodological aspects with respect to barter economy as it appears in neoclassical theory. Basic to this theory is that it starts from an a priori axiomatic structure which implies theoretical restrictions vis-à-vis the money economy.

We will specifically discuss three aspects: rationality, aggregation and the handling of expectations within the theory. Of primary importance in our discussion is the mathematical foundation of the neoclassical axiomatic structure which implies that the concepts used must be atomistic. Furthermore the axiomatic structure defines a 'universe' of the barter economy which does not have a complement. Thus the axiomatic structure either holds or not, it has no neighbourhood. However when scrutinizing the temporal extension of the theory within the rational expectation approach as in Lucas (1966) and Lucas and Prescott's (1981) treatment of the rational expectation hypothesis we surprisingly come close to the most radical form of Moore's paradox: $\neg a \wedge a$, which will be discussed in Chapter 2.

Barter and the Temptation of Generalization

An interesting feature in the development of analytical patterns is the step between Aristotle and the Dominican Friars of Salamanca. Aristotle stresses that the foundation of a just price is the valuation of the work, salaries which constituted a just price. This attitude was taken by the classical economists to a great extent, the School of Salamanca however assigned a higher importance to the precise conditions of the very exchange, and Luís Saravia de la Calle tells us:

> Excluding all deceit and malice, the just price of a thing is the price which it commonly fetches at the time and place of the deal, in cash, and bearing in mind the particular circumstances and manner of sale, the abundance of goods and money, the number of buyers and sellers, the difficulty of procuring the goods, and the benefit to be enjoyed by their use, according to the judgement of an honest man.

> (Grice-Hutchinson 1952: 79)

Obviously we may imagine some converging process but this is not discussed by any of the Friars.

Thus Aristotle and later the classics place the value within production conditions and social frames partly to explain the relative inertia of the prices and they also discuss communities with substantial production. De la Calle however discusses the Spanish economy during the late 16th century where the great inflow of gold made/forced Spain to have a 'trade deficit' of a more voluminous character but since the payment in gold is just the difference between import and export one could think that de la Calle overestimated the importance of the moment of exchange, but in fact de la Calle rules out the Aristotelian thinking all together:

> Those who measure the just price by the labour, costs, and risk incurred by the person who deals in the merchandise or produces it, or by the cost of transport or expense of travelling to the fair, or by what he has to pay the factors of industry, risk and labour, are greatly in error, and still more so are those who allow a certain profit of a fifth or a tenth. For the just price arises from the abundance or scarcity of goods, merchants, and money, as had been said, and not from costs, labour, and risk. If we had to consider labour and risk in order to assess the just price, no merchant would ever suffer loss, nor would abundance or scarcity of goods and money enter into the question.
>
> (ibid. p. 82)

Thus seen from the points of view of the coming marginal revolution this had been 'announced' already in the 16th century, but not only that: the Keynesian attitude of looking at profits as residuals also appears.[1] However de la Calle is not trying to form a general rule but hint at the leading principles which are mixed in the precise context of the trade. Close to de la Calle are both Hume and Say. Say is interesting since he describes the context around the particular trade as de la Calle and he directly reject the existence of sort of psychological ground for value:

> Money or specie has with more plausibility, but in reality with no better ground for truth, been pronounced to be a *measure* of value. Value may be estimated in the way of price; but it can not be measured, that is to say, compared with a known and invariable measure of intensity, for no such measure has yet been discovered.
>
> (Say 1834 [1803]: 246)

By that implies that Say rules out any possibility of a general equilibrium. So Jean Baptise Say claims that there are only local and temporal equilibria where prices are due to contextual conditions.

However the early economists do not try to integrate the macroscopic and the microscopic levels but discussed them with respect to different frames. Furthermore they did not discuss a barter economy but a money economy and moreover they specifically point out the difference between the barter and the money economy.

It is when the discussions on utility and the formalization of the concept of rational man emerged that the analysis moved back to the barter economy and in reality also lost contact with the monetary world. The utility theory performs what Jean Baptiste Say explicitly claims could not be done, namely it developed a measure of intensity. The crux is that it is not 'compared with a known and invariable measure of intensity' (ibid: 246) since the relative prices, which are the measure, only hold in equilibrium. So already here the conflicting views on a persistent general equilibrium are founded.

Going back to Hume, Smith and Say the generalization of economic analysis into some abstract general equilibrium is of no importance but maybe we have to seek the temptation of generalization in Ricardo's efforts to formalize economic science in a similar way as Newton's Principia formalized physical science. The development of the utility theory becomes then the basic tool for this effort and we will see how Jevons struggled to overcome Say's doubts.

Utilitarianism, Utility Theory and Consumption

At the end of the 19th century the natural sciences had a period of unprecedented scientific success. Social sciences on the other hand struggled with finding relevant approaches to reality and finding adequate concepts for their analysis. Economics was in the same predicament but in a different way than other social sciences. Ricardo particularly had started to explore a formal path of generalization built on axioms/assumptions which were seen as generic with respect to the agents' behaviour. Economics had a distinct point which was unique namely that the market exchange implied a moment where a commodity was exchanged for a sum of money and this was actually measureable. At the same time, Jean Baptiste Say's analysis was hard to get around. Say was a French liberal economist who wrote his *magnum opus* in 1803 *A Treatise of Political Economy*, which was particularly well received in the US.[2]

As seen in the earlier quote, Say clearly rejected the thought of general equilibrium and claimed that money/prices could only be measures locally and temporally and he definitely rejected the idea of a measure as in natural sciences (Say 1834 [1803]: 244–252). The basic point in his rejection is that a measure is independent of what it measures. Thus measuring a distance between Paris and Marseilles is not affected by using the measure in measuring the distance between Melbourne and Sidney:

> When I am told that the great pyramid of Ghaize is 656 feet square at the base, I can measure a space of 656 feet square at Paris or elsewhere, and form an exact notion of the space the pyramid will cover; but when I am told that a camel is at Cairo worth 50 *sequins*, that is to say, about 90 ounces of silver, or 100 dollars in coin, I can form no precise notion of the value of the camel; because, although I may have every reason to believe that 100 dollars are

worth less at Paris than at Cairo, I can not tell what may be the difference of value.

Say (1834 [1803]: 247)

Say's analysis is very precise and states the problem which has to be overcome in using prices as a uniform measure and money as a medium of measurement.

The introduction of the concept of utility became however a welcome step in the development of economic analysis into a measurable science. The utility analysis presents a link between the inner mind of the agent and the outer commodity space and thus we might use prices as a consistent measure.

Utility is a concept stemming from the 18th century utilitarianism with Jeremy Bentham as a portal figure. Jeremy Bentham was in close contact with the leading persons of the French revolution, particularly Mirabeau. He was also made an honorary citizen of France. Smith was affected by Bentham in many aspects; it is often mentioned that Smith's view on interest rates was changed as a result of his correspondence with Bentham. There are nevertheless also differences between Bentham and Smith.

Bentham and Smith were both to be regarded as moral philosophers and thus when we use the word utility in economics it is worth remembering that it has its roots in moral philosophy. This is particularly clear when we make a histori-cal jump to John Stuart Mill and read his little pamphlet on Utilitarianism published 1863, which is mainly an ethical analysis. Mill is often seen as a portal figure for modern liberalism and utilitarianism and as an economist he had a substantial influence on the legitimacy of the utility theory although Jevons took the decisive step into the neoclassical version of marginal utility analysis. It is therefore interesting to look a bit at Mill and Jevons with respect to their attitudes to utility, the first a utilitarian philosopher and the second a mathemati-cal economist. The reason why it is interesting is that Jevons actually starts in utilitarianism when he in his book *The Theory of Political Economy*, Chapter Two, analyses 'Theory of Pleasure and Pain' which has close links to Mill's analysis in his pamphlet *Utilitarianism* but Jevons prefers to base his reasoning directly on Bentham, which implies that he can avoid a trap which Mill falls into, but on the other hand he lays the ground for Arrow's paradox which appeared some 80 years later.

Mill's version of utilitarianism goes back to Plato's dialogue *Protagoras* where Socrates presents a version of Epicureanism where the highest good is to seek pleasure and avoid pain not like the swine but honourable pleasures which may *cost* pain but then lead to higher pleasures where the achievement of wisdom is central. Thus the achievement of pleasure implies costs in form of displeasures.[3]

From a measuring point of view Mill regards utility as two-dimensional; a quantitative dimension and a qualitative: 'It is quite compatible with the principle of utility to recognize the fact, that some *kinds* [original emphasis] of pleasures are more desirable and more valuable than others' Mill (1863 [1990]: 448]. More precisely he says:

Neither pains nor pleasures are homogenous, and pain is always heterogeneous with pleasure. What is there to decide whether a particular pleasure is worth purchasing at the cost of a particular pain, except the feelings and judgment of the experienced?

(Ibid.: 450)

First of all it is easy to see links to a marginal utility theory but the problem is of course that neither pains nor pleasures are homogenous, which indeed makes substitution difficult. This is of course due to the two-dimensional character of utility. Furthermore the agent filled with the spirit of utilitarianism is impartial between their own happiness and that of others:

I have dwelt on this point, as being a necessary part of a perfectly just conception of Utility of Happiness, considered as the directive rule of human conduct. But it is by no means an indispensable condition to the acceptance of utilitarian standard; for that standard is not the agent's own greatest happiness but the greatest amount of happiness altogether.

(Ibid.: 450)

This altruistic sentiment of the individual agent is a function of knowledge and wisdom so it is measured along the quality axes. With respect to aggregation the quote is of course most unfortunate since the individuals who are truly utilitarian take the aggregate state into consideration and thus we end up in an interaction between the aggregate state and the individual one with respect to the individual experience of pleasure, which prohibits additive aggregation. This is the same kind of problem which we meet in Arrow's paradox. This is a trap which Mill forgets to analyse in the rest of the text with respect to its solution.

However the quote is difficult from several perspectives. First of all: we can, to my understanding, interpret the optimum pleasure given displeasure as a degree of happiness. Still however Mill speaks of the *utility of happiness* which makes the text nonsensical. Second: he speaks of utilitarian standard which gives the impression that happiness is a standardized concept outside the agent. Third: one gets the impression that what is pleasure for any agent brings zero or positive pleasure to all other agents. This feature is adopted in the neoclassical axiomatic structure save for the case when strict positive pleasures are assumed.

The difficulty with respect to Mill's text is whether it refers to people in general or it is a normative programme for utilitarian missionaries in converting others to become fellows of the true spirit.

With respect to measurement of utility one gets the firm opinion that Mill claims that it is possible and he concludes: 'This, being, according to the utilitarian opinion, the end of human action, is necessarily also the standard of morality' (ibid.: 450). Thus there is a direct link between the agent's action and the enjoyed utility and this can obviously be observed. In relation to the problem we mentioned above that Mill's disciple should not only take his own pleasure/pain into consideration but also the pleasure/pain of other individuals as well as the aggregate utility which is not a simple additive function of the individuals' utilities.

Mill's writings on utilitarianism concern the whole of life and all kind of actions, not only market actions. However it is not unreasonable to see the market actions as a proper subset to the whole set of actions by the agent and so far it is possible to assume that the utilitarian principles hold also for this subset. This brings us to the question of measurability of utility (as well as of pleasure and pain). The problem with the intrinsic link between the aggregate utility and the individual is in fact jeopardizing the whole measurement so we have to dismiss it from our considerations. Thus we only regard utility in a strictly individual way, which actually can give a non-contradictive solution provided that all commodities imply strictly positive utility for all agents, non-negativity may work provided that all commodities are traded. But this possibility is severely limited when we then have the two dimensions of quantity and quality.

For my own part I have to confess that I am unable to interpret Mill with respect to quantity; quality is a different since it can be interpreted as intensity of pleasure and pain. This intensity is a function of intellectual ability, partly brought about by education, so we may assume that given a mental state of wisdom a piece of utility, composed by pleasure and pain, is constant irrespective of what brings it. However different 'commodities' bring a different quantum of utility, so if I am low on the wisdom scale an ice-cream gives me much pleasure while reading a book of Saint Bonaventura but hardly means any utility. In contrast when I am in the strong end of the wisdom scale the opposite may hold, but not necessarily (with respect to the author's own experiences). Thus given a particular person the different commodities should be able to be ordered by an intensity index depending of mental heritage combined with educative efforts.

We must then come back to the question of quantity. In a paper published 1985 on Mill's *Theory of Utility*, Lenny Ebenstein (1985) tries to solve the problem. He confesses his difficulties in understanding Mill's text but his interpretation, not supported by a clear statement from Mill, is that by quantity Mill simply means *duration* of pleasure or pain. If so we have to interpret duration in form of the duration of the effects of a certain action or commodity, not the duration of the action/commodity in itself.

Consequently we have a two-dimensional problem where an individual may form a utility unit based on intensity per time unit. Thus an ice-cream gives me a certain intensity of pleasure, depending on my wisdom, but it is of relatively short duration, while reading a book of Saint Bonaventura gives me intensity of pleasure but of longer duration, still given my degree of wisdom.

When we come to Jevons things are easier from a technical point of view but at the same time more obscure.[4] Mill tries to keep his discussion as close to the real world as possible while Jevons makes a sort of logical atomism as a priori true. He only considers the individual as an atom. He quotes Bentham on the aspects affecting the valuation of pleasure and pain of an action or choice, which are:

i its intensity
ii its duration
iii its certainty or uncertainty
iv its propinquity or remoteness

These factors are, according to Jevons suitable to bring into an economic analysis, which is more limited than the Mill's philosophical analysis. He however quotes Bentham on three other factors:

v fecundity, or the chance a feeling has to be followed by feelings of the same kind: that is, pleasures if it be a pleasure; pains, if it be pain.
vi purity, or the chance it has of not being followed by feelings of an opposite kind.
vii extent, or the number of persons to whom it extends, and who are affected by it.

The last three aspects Jevons dismisses for the simplicity of analysis which is understandable but we see that here is the foundation of Arrow's paradox. The factors i) to iii) are straightforward with respect to our considerations concerning Mill while iv) is understandable but difficult to discriminate between people. Anyway these considerations underpin Jevons' *Theory of Utility* in chapter III which he starts by writing:

Pleasure and pain are undoubtedly the ultimate objects of the Calculus of Economics. To satisfy our wants to the utmost with the least effort – to procure the greatest amount of what is desirable at the expense of the least that is undesirable – in other words, to *maximize pleasure*, is the problem of economics. [original emphasis]

(Jevons 1871 [1888]: iii.1)

Thus utility theory as Jevons explains it, is firmly rooted in utilitarianism and the pleasure and pain problem. However when we look at Bentham's seven aspects of pleasure and pain and particularly if we add Mill's moral analysis the very meaning of pleasure and pain is rather complex, particularly when it comes to linking it to commodities. Above we said that it is appropriate to regard Mill's analysis in such a way that the market actions of the agent are a subset of the entire actions of the agent, thus there is no reason to assume a separate treatment of the market actions. Consequently the concept of commodity is to be seen as an input in the agents' actions and this is what Mill also claims. Consequently Jevons concludes:

In the first place, utility, though a quality of things, is *no inherent quality*. It is better described as a *circumstance of things* arising out of their relation to man's requirements. [original emphasis]

(Ibid.: III.13)

This quote is indeed interesting since it might be interpreted as if commodities were contextually dependent, and subject to our coming discussion of the Axiom of Reflexivity in the Arrow and Debreu model. However Jevons does not advance this track but links it to the technical aspect of *Law of Variation of Utility*, i.e. marginal utility. From our earlier discussed problem of translating causal structures of reality into mathematical/logical models, Jevons more or less consciously limits the problem into a mathematically more simplistic setting. Thus in the rest of the chapter Jevons forms the problem in such a way that rather simple mathematics may be used, which also implies that utility as well as marginal utility, which according to Jevons' own text belong to the agent's internal considerations and he explains: 'The degree of *utility is* [original emphasis], in mathematical language, *the differential coefficient of u considered as a function of x*, [original emphasis] and will itself be another function of x.'

With the concept *final degree of utility* Jevons means the marginal increase of utility with respect to the last addition of the quantity of the existing stock. An elementary problem with Jevons' text, with respect to an agent, is however that it is clear that we may write:

$$u_1 = f_1(x_1) \text{ where } u_1 \text{ is the utility arising from the commodity}$$
$$x_1 \text{ and analogously} \qquad\qquad \text{E.1.1}$$

$$u_2 = f_2(x_2) \text{ and both functions are differentiable.} \qquad\qquad \text{E.1.2}$$

What is not particularly clear is if we can write

$$u = f_1 + f_2 \qquad\qquad \text{E.1.3}$$

Hence we approach the problem of whether or not utility is homogenous. As Mill expresses the matter of pleasure and pain utility as such seems to be a rather complicated function of education and mental dispositions; thus although he is not particularly clear it seems that simpler pleasure is of a different quality compared with more noble ones, thus we run into the problem whether two persons' happiness can be added and if so will the sum of happiness for both persons be greater than the happiness of any of the individual's happiness. Consequently we may run into a problem if utilities of different agents can be contradictory, which would be a sort of parallel to Russell's problem of negative facts, an analysis which we will touch on in the next chapter.

Jevons in fact mentions the same kind of problem. Obviously this problem is important since the aspect of commodity substitution is dependent on the answer. Jevons however choses a different way from Mill when he follows Richard Jennings, who published a book 1855, *Natural Element of Political Economy*, where he treats this problem in a different way than Mill and others which Jevons discusses.[5] Jennings links the utility of a random commodity to sensations on a scale from *inanition* to *satiation*. The very sensation is then seen as independent from the qualitative aspects which Mill discusses and can, in principle at least, be measurable and since Jevons only deals with agents as independent atoms, we will not have any problem with *inanition/satiation* in the individual perspective. With this formulation, E.1.3 above holds and we may have a sort of utility concept which is homogenous. We can obviously write

$$u = g[S_1(x_1), S_2(x_2)] \qquad\qquad\qquad \text{E.1.4}$$

where S_1 and S_2 might be assumed to belong to a set $\hat{S}$ over which we may define a σ-algebra, as Mark Twain expresses it in Tom Sawyer: the happiness of a boy who has learnt a new way of whistling is probably deeper than that of an astronomer who has detected a new planet. So we may actually assume that pleasure might be measured along a one-dimensional axis. The problem lies in the first step: the character of the S_i-functions. The happiness of a boy having found a dead rat with a peculiar tail, while the observation of a particular 'dust' circulating around our sun affects the astronomer in much the same way says nothing of substitutability conditions between the two aspects and this is actually the fundamental problem of Jevons' analysis. Thus we want the market prices somehow to be linked to the interior sensations of the agent but a function like E.1.4 might well be describing very limited substitutability conditions as well as perfect substitutability. In the former case the economic development will be dependent on changes in social class and income distribution in conjunction with inertia of the production structure, while in the latter case such problems are of minor, and even of no importance.

Jevons seems to choose the latter way of analysis although his preceding discussion indicates his awareness of the former problem.

Subsequently we may express the link between the interior minds of the consumers and the commodity set as a function:

$$U_i = U_i(x_1 - - - x_n) \qquad\qquad\qquad \text{E.1.5}$$

Furthermore we have a set W where U_1 --- U_m are subsets and we may over W define a σ-algebra.

This implies that any union of W let us say $U_i^j u_k \in W$ and consequently for i = 1 and j is any finite integer. Thus we have granted that the aggregate utility belongs to the set W and is consequently measureable on the same logical premises as the utility of the single agent since W ∈ W.[6] We may thus write:

$$W = W(x_1 - - - x_n) \qquad\qquad\qquad \text{E.1.6}$$

A central problem with E.1.5 and E.1.6 is their consistency in time. Both Mill and Jevons are quite clear about the fact that the commodities in themselves carry no intrinsic utility value and that the experienced pleasure by the agent is contextually affected. In the very act of choice it can thus be assumed that E.1.5 and E.1.6 exist under suitable conditions, however it is difficult to say whether Mill or Jevons took the temporal aspect into consideration. Debreu (1987 [1959]) for example claims, as we noted above, that a commodity must be defined according to its physical characteristics but also according to its temporal and spatial co-ordinates.

The key problem with the marginal theory by Jevons lies in the aggregation problem. Jevons had in fact a more minor problem than modern neoclassical theory with this since he dealt primarily with the microscopic level and the individual behaviour. Hence he was dealing with purposeful and rational behaviour of the individual which is separate from the problem of aggregation. Thus in a society which is in principle chaotic there is nothing which prevents the individual to be both purposeful and rational but in the later development of economic theory there is a most unfortunate juxtaposition of aggregate levels which reaches its paradoxical peak in Arrow's paradox.

The shift from utility theory to preference theory was a generalization but with respect to our discussions on aggregation and measurability it meant little. True that we got rid of the discussion of cardinal utilities and discussed the individual measurement of the individual according to an ordinal scale but that is only true as long as we do not try to aggregate the individual optima. If the correlate of revealed preferences holds the social optimum must be possible to be ranked among the individuals in cardinal terms. True however that on the individual level this is not necessary.

Irrespective of if we use utility theory or preference theory we still must link something which is going on in the brains of people to the outer world, to a commodity space.

Thus when the preference theory achieved, through Arrow and Debreu, its present form based on six fundamental axioms, it implied that there was an *equivalence relation* between the interior mind of the individual and the outer commodity space.

The result of this was that as long we deal with the momentary choice the mathematical form is OK but when we enter an inter-temporal analysis the specific axiomatic structure imposes peculiarities in the economic analysis. The above mentioned equivalence relation is necessary to make a mathematically stable relation between the interior mind and the exterior commodity space which makes it possible to measure the commodities and the preference relations equivalently and an optimal state corresponds exactly with respect to the two spaces, the interior and the exterior. This is by the way why Say's precise analysis, some 80 years earlier, about measuring a pyramid in relation to comparing prices of a camel in Cairo and Paris is indeed an ingenious counterexample.

This equivalence relation is the basic condition for aggregation but it also transforms the interior mind of the individual agent to be equivalent to the outer world, thus the axioms squeezed the individual into the form of a Euclidian space and alluding to the Polish logician Tarski's analysis of the Geometry of the Solids, the mind becomes a sort of n-dimensional rigid body.[7]

Conclusion: The utility theory/preference theory in fact presented a logical setting which gave a systematic link between the interior mind of the individual and the outer commodity space. Interpreting this link as it holds inter-temporally gives us the theoretical means to create the mathematical tools to produce a measure which might be called prices. The drawback of this tool, however, is that it only holds in general equilibrium which is a bit difficult to explain inter-temporally.

The Axiomatic Structure of the Barter Economy

The axiomatic foundation of the neoclassical theory is of a relatively late datum. The Walrasian counting of equations was until the 1950s the proof of the existence of general equilibrium. From the analysis of Arrow and Debreu (A&D) we however got a fully fledged mathematical proof of the existence of *an* economic general equilibrium. The reason why we emphasize '*an*' by italics is that we actually cannot say whether the A&D axiomatic structure mirrors the thoughts of Jevons, Mill and particularly Jennings or not. The A&D axioms are purely technical and tell us that there is a correspondence between the interior mind of the agent and the commodity space. That there exists such a correspondence is evident and not much to fuss about but the very character of the correspondence is a different matter and that is what we shall discuss.

The A&D approach concerns a barter economy and prices appears only as an index of the relative valuation which is set in a market exchange of commodities. The theory of the barter economy is strongly linked to rational choice, methodological individualism and purposeful action.[8]

There are six basic axioms. In the Appendix to this chapter they are given in their technical form: completeness, reflexivity, transitivity, continuity, convexity and local non-satiation. The first three are usually addressed as rational behaviour but from a mathematical point of view they define an *equivalence relation*, (given symmetry). The equivalence relation, which is a very strong condition, makes it possible to form a homomorphism between the preference space and the commodity space. The two axioms continuity and convexity form together with the first three an n-dimensional Euclidian space and the last axiom guarantees the utility maximization and is the modern variant of Say's law.[9]

The proof of the existence of general equilibrium is pursued as in Figure 1.1.

As is seen from the structure of the proof, economic and social/psychological arguments are not used whatsoever and that is a result of the fact that the axioms are purely mathematical propositions, the first five axioms are ordinary requirements to define a measurable Euclidian space. Thus the first five axioms tell us that the mind of the individual is a Euclidian space.

Squeezing the individual mind into a mathematical setting implies a lot of implicit assumptions concerning the individual as well as the commodities. One evident thing is that the individual is not able to choose. That is what we always get when we transform individual actions into deterministic logic but mostly the form of the analysis is local and temporal and also reflects an assumed inertia. The general equilibrium as proved in Figure 1.1 is a different thing because either the analysis holds inter-temporally or we have a new state of equilibrium each moment of time for which we have no theory of how prices are created or relate to earlier moments. This is an important feature of our proceeding analysis.

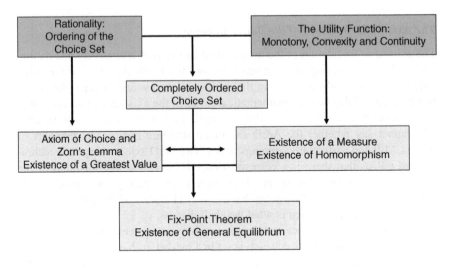

Figure 1.1 The Skeleton of the Proof of the Existence of General Equilibrium

However since the axioms, save for the local non-satiation, are purely mathematical and define a measurable space the question is how are we going to separate a neoclassical equilibrium from a Keynesian one? A Keynesian model must be defined on exactly the same space, that means that we have some assumptions of inter-temporal inertia. Hicks, for example makes a very interesting mistake or at least non-commensurable assumption with standard general equilibrium theory. In his famous paper from 1937, *Mr Keynes and the Classics* Hicks define a model economy consisting of two sectors: consumption and investment industry respectively:[10]

$$Y^c = w \cdot C \cdot \frac{dN_c}{dC} \qquad \begin{array}{l} \text{w-wages} \\ \text{N-employment} \end{array}$$

$$Y^I = w \cdot I \cdot \frac{dN_I}{dI}$$

$$Y = Y^C + Y^I \qquad\qquad\qquad\qquad\qquad\qquad \text{E.1.7}$$

Using the Cambridge equation: $M = kY$ he can derive the model:

$$M = kY$$
$$Y^I = K(i) \qquad\qquad \text{Investments dependent on interest}$$
$$Y^I = S(i, Y) \qquad\qquad \text{rate and equal to saving.} \qquad\qquad \text{E.1.8}$$

Hicks then makes a rather curious assumption that elasticity of supply is different for the two sectors; it is greater for the investment sector than for the consumption sector. If we here express the production functions as Cobb-Douglas, the difference in elasticity between the two sectors will obviously produce different levels of employment due to the price vector and assuming some sort of dynamics in the price formation it is easy to get a cyclical employment. But then we also have changing endowments which implies a shift in equilibrium and Hicks does not advise any path from one to another so we have a rather dubious general equilibrium model and it seems more to be a sort of Keynesian model.

What we mean here is that for any kind of mathematical model where we apply standard ordinary differential equations and we have some sort of equilibrium the neoclassical assumptions concerning the topological space have to be fulfilled, save for the axiom of local non-satiation. With respect to the latter axiom we will have a most interesting conflict if we, as Keynes did, claim that the profit is a residual. Then a standard model will be open although we can close it if we stubbornly claim the axiom of local non-satiation. Below we discuss the dynamics more carefully and show the basic problem of general equilibrium.

However it is important that we cannot claim that a certain model is a general equilibrium or a Keynesian model without specifying the exact mathematical restrictions and conditions with respect to the individual market behaviour.

The axioms of general equilibrium theory transform each good to an axis in the commodity space and each agent to a commodity vector. Given the axioms aggregation is just a simple vector aggregation as in Figure 1.2; thus aggregation is additive. But it is only an aggregate for the precise price vector linked to the specific general equilibrium which is not true for any other price vector.

Thus general equilibrium is the only state where real aggregation of utilities/ preferences coincide with aggregation of their attached values. This is evident but later on when we introduce money we will have an interesting contradiction.

Two important corollaries relative to the existence of general equilibrium is that of *independence of irrelevant alternatives*, which says that any binary choice is independent of other commodities in the basket and the so called *revealed preference hypothesis*, implying, on the aggregate level, that if we know the income distribution and the price vector we can depict the preference structure.

It is important to understand that this is a theory of the barter economy and that money in its daily meaning does not exist and cannot exist. The obtained price vector is equivalent to an index and a *measure*; thus adding money to the model implies that we add a *medium of measurement*, related to relevant supply and demand of commodities and consequently also measures itself, but if so we destroy the measure itself. Furthermore this measure does not hold for any equilibrium but the particular one for the adequate price vector, so if we think of a trajectory of temporary general equilibria we also think of a trajectory of different price vectors. If we believe in the existence of a constant market price vector this is equivalent with the assumption of a constant inter-temporal general equilibrium. This will be important when we later discuss the effects of inflation policy.

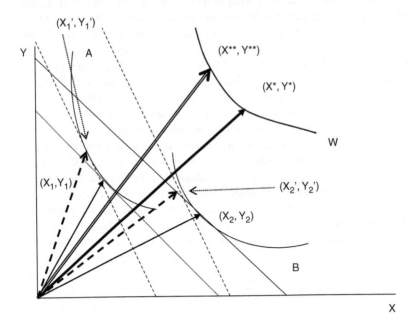

Figure 1.2 Aggregate level through Additive Aggregation

Source: Ekstedt (2012): 69

If the agents are supposed to have a constant preference structure the choice of the commodity basket is made by those controlling the price vector.[11]

The rational choice aspect is indeed interesting since it also is a ground for logical consistency in choice. It is very hard to oppose that type of rationality if we look at the agent in the very moment of choice. It is a kind of animal rationality and people lacking this are normally not able to take care of themselves.

Equilibrium and Dynamics

When it comes to eventual dynamics given the axioms, it is a bit tricky, since there are in principle two different interpretations of the axioms. One says that the axioms only deal with the situation when the agent has premeditated the precise context of the choice and only the very act of choosing is governed by the axioms. We are going to advocate this interpretation in this book, which also, as mentioned earlier, is in line with Debreu (1959). The other interpretation is that a precise general equilibrium has an extension in time. The two interpretations lead us into two different kinds of difficulties with respect to dynamics.

The first kind of interpretation leaves us with a trajectory of different temporal and local equilibria where there are multiple price vectors which also are varying. The second interpretation prescribes a unique inter-temporal price vector and an everlasting equilibrium although this interpretation is seldom expressed explicitly as a postulate but is somehow inserted implicitly.

Our position is that the first interpretation is the best deal we can get. The second interpretation seems a bit naïve but it nevertheless seems hovering in the background and there are some principal well-known conditions which we then need to bear in mind. First it is important to establish that if you have a set of a priori axioms as a foundation for your analysis, all derived propositions are true if and only if *all* axioms hold. Second: the axioms create an analytical space which has no contradictive environment, since it only concerns the positive orthant. This means that if we regard the axioms as creating a space, this space is universal and the complement to that space is empty. This also means that if we can prove that there exists spaces where the axioms do not hold, anything but local and temporal cases exist where the axioms are relevant and the extension in time is dependent on inertia.[12] There does not exist an on/off button to help us decide when the axioms shall hold or not and no approximations. Furthermore the axioms do not tell anything about out of equilibrium trading. Third: since the *economy*, in which the axioms are said to hold, in the expected utility approach, has a physical environment, *state space*, either perfect knowledge of the future development of the state space must prevail or all agents must act according to the same space of outcome and with respect to the same joint probability distribution for the different states and to avoid the problems inserted by Allais' paradox, all agents are supposed to be risk averse. Furthermore any change of the state space, with respect to the space of outcomes or probability distribution, will change the equilibrium. Some analysts discuss the matter of convergence in case of expectation errors. If so we run into the rather intricate problem of *false trading* which rejects the assumption of an inter-temporal equilibrium. Consequently we can conclude that the general equilibrium is *nowhere dense*.

The first interpretation of equilibrium is in comparison to the second a rather sloppy one and it leaves us with the question of what happens between local and temporal equilibria. Thus when we have events affecting the economy these are bound to get distribution and allocation effects and subsequently this will have secondary, and so on, effects. In such analysis we may use the mathematical concept of equilibrium but that is with respect to a particular set of variables and parameters and has the role of an analytical tool, with no normative value. Furthermore the kind of analysis in which Jennings was involved, seems a possible approach in this case and is in principle possible to study.

For those aiming at logical/mathematical studies of dynamics, the equilibrium concept of the second kind is indeed necessary in order to study convergence/divergence processes in the neighbourhood of the equilibrium, relevant to the variable/parameter structure, and to define rules for the convergence which if added to the axiomatic structure, allows only for auctioneer/tâtonnement solution or similar. Thus real trading never takes place other than in equilibrium under appropriate assumptions. Since the neoclassical theory is built on an a priori axiomatic structure *these axioms must always hold* otherwise we must pass over to empirically induced assumptions which also impose a whole set of inconvenient questions which we will discuss with respect to Keynes.

There are studies aiming at chaos analysis but then the question is what we precisely mean with the chaos concept, which per se can be regarded as a kind of general equilibrium, with respect to an economic and social structure. Mathematical chaos is rather strict with respect to parametrical structures. We will come back to these complex questions in later chapters on stability.

Stability Matters and Community Excess Demand Curves

The proof of existence of a general equilibrium given the neoclassical axiomatic structure says nothing on the stability of this equilibrium. On one hand we have stability of the individual optima and on the other we have the stability of the aggregate equilibrium.

Thus if GE is perturbed the question is does it then returns due to intrinsic forces? At the microscopic state we may believe in a certain reversibility given some inertia, but the essential problem concerns the macroscopic state where it is more doubtful. Wicksell (1922 [1937]: 222), for example, is rather explicit about this when describing the microscopic stability as a pendulum and the macroscopic stability as a ball lying on a horizontal table.

During the 1970s the problem of maintaining the characteristics when aggregating microscopic functions into a macroscopic function was discussed intensively with respect to the existence of the community demand curve in the so called SMD (Sonnenshein, Mantel, Debreu) discussion, where others like McFadden and Mas-Collell also participated. The discussion concerned the necessary requirements for creating an aggregate excess demand function fulfilling the conditions of general equilibrium based on individual excess demand functions. Basically it was asked if the revealed preference condition is fulfilled also for an environment to the general equilibrium.[13] We will review this discussion and its conclusions but let us start with some elementary comments on stability matters.

Fundamental to the stability analysis of GE is that there exists a general optimum for the aggregate community for the same price vector as each and all the individual agents have an individual optimum. Furthermore the axiomatic structure applies both to the community as well as the individual agent. We thus have the so called heredity principle implying that for a set S where certain conditions hold, heredity means that these conditions also hold for all the subsets s_i, $i = 1...n$. Consequently the stability analysis also concerns the principle of revealed preferences.

A particular GE, let us call it E*, is perturbed and tautologically so is the price vector P*; we may thus ask whether the market actions force the non-equilibrium price vector P back to P* and restore the equilibrium E*.

In the state of non-equilibrium, excess demand, positive or negative, has appeared and the market behaviour must display, for the community as well as for the individuals, that when excess demand is positive there will be an upward price pressure and when excess demand is negative we will have a downward price pressure. If excess demand is zero there is no price pressure. All quantities and prices are assumed non-negative.[14]

A simple two-goods example will help us to see the essentials. Let us define the excess demand functions where we have two commodities, x_1 and x_2, and since we only are interested in relative prices we set the price of commodity x_1 to 1. We thus have:

$$dx_1 = f(p)$$
$$dx_2 = g(p)$$
$$dp = h(dx_1 - dx_2)$$

E.1.9

To simplify we can assume that the functions are linear in a neighbourhood of the equilibrium so we get:

$$dx_1 = a + \alpha \cdot p$$
$$dx_2 = b + \beta \cdot p$$
$$dp = \gamma \cdot (dx_1 - dx_2)$$

E.1.10

Solving E.1.10 gives us the equilibrium price p*

$$p^* = \gamma \cdot \frac{a+b}{\alpha + \beta}$$

E.1.11

And we get the dynamic solution, since γ is just a scalar we set it to 1.

$$p = (a+b) \cdot e^{(\alpha+\beta) \cdot t}$$

E.1.12

Equations E.1.11 and E.1.12 thus give a general parametric solution the form of which must be the same both for the community excess demand functions as well as for the individual ones. The heredity condition now raises the question whether the individual convergent processes will add up to the community process. We may as usual take a number of assumptions to grant this and these assumptions must then eliminate eventual asymmetries among the excess demand functions. We have two basic groups, positive and negative excess demand, and basically added assumptions must grant that these two groups cancel out each other. To claim any empirical value of such manipulation may be somewhat difficult though we equally well may assume contradictory structures. Our survey below of the debate during the 1970s will show the difficulties.

There is however a deeper problem concerning the concept of general equilibrium and our particular equilibrium E*. In the proof of the existence of that equilibrium we have to represent the ith individual agents as $(\lesssim_i, e_i)$, a preference relation and a set of endowments and we know that to each set of preference orders in the economy in conjunction with a certain distribution of endowments there is a unique equilibrium. Consequently our chosen equilibrium E* is based on a certain set of agents whose individual optima we may write $(\lesssim_i, e_i)$* and where the community optima is the union of these agents: $(\lesssim^*, E) = U_i(\lesssim_i, e_i)^*$. In equilibrium E* there exists one and only one price vector P*. Consequently a particular distribution in the society of preferences and endowments will end up in one and only one particular equilibrium which relates the price vector P* to the particular distribution of preferences and endowments. Since the existence of equilibrium is based on the axiomatic structure we have reversibility of the logics which often is called the *principle of revealed preferences*.

Thus any perturbation of E* results in a new price vector P^p where P* $\neq$ P^p but that also implies that by logical necessity we will have a new price vector which revaluate the individuals' as well as the community's endowment vectors. That means that we must now start the exchange from a new set of endowment vectors which imply an equilibrium, given the distribution of preferences, E^p, and by necessity we have E* $\neq$ E^p.

Consequently the stability analysis above implying a convergent process as in E.1.9 – E.1.12 *does not exist*.

Technically speaking we can say that the set of feasible general equilibria in a community, S^E is nowhere dense.

In Figure 1.3 we show the principle of a dense set, which is necessary for continuity.

Let us think of an environment in form of a sphere around GE with a radius of λ. Within this sphere we may define a point ε with an environment with a radius of $\lambda/5$, and we may go on decreasing the distance between ε and GE. In order to be a dense set this environment around ε must contain GE and points belonging to the complement of GE. Thus the closure of GE must belong to GE.

However when an element is nowhere dense this not hold. Thus an element Y which is nowhere dense has a closure with no interior, consequently the complement of Y is open and dense. This implies that the interior of a nowhere dense set is dense.

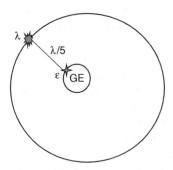

Figure 1.3 Dense Set

Consequently General Equilibrium belongs to a set defined in a Euclidian space which is dense but its closure does not belong to it.

Thus the stability analysis fails because the state of general equilibrium has no environment; it is nowhere dense. This very feature is of utmost importance to remember when using general equilibrium analysis for empirical research.

Thus the result of the discussion on the existence of community excess demand curves, which was triggered by Hugo Sonnenshein (1972), was negative. Sonnenshein's answer to this question was negative, as predominantly the whole discussion was, and he points out that according to Arrow and Debreu the community demand is derived by adding the actions of all its individuals, and furthermore that this condition was also necessary for excess demand analysis.

Arrow (1986) made some comments on the discussion but his most interesting contribution in this paper was that he separated rationality concerning self from rationality concerning the community, which indeed is a logical step forward and consistent with his own paradox.

First Sonnenshein stated that a *hereditary principle* namely that the macroscopic state was seen as a universal set where all individual subsets were obeying exactly the same conditions as the universal set, which implies that the aggregate state behaves like an individual and with respect to Russell's paradox we then transform the individuals and the universal set to non-proper sets.

Second, with respect to the excess demand functions the consumers are seen as 'Cobb-Douglas' – consumers these were divided into two groups 'positive' and 'negative' depending on the sign of the individual excess demand. However there are also some macroscopic excess demand functions which can be of either sign.

Let us look at this second aspect a bit more carefully since this is in line with the fact that general equilibrium is nowhere dense. The general scenario is that the general equilibrium has been perturbed by some exogenous event. Our primary problem to answer given this, is whether we expect a process where the macroscopic excess demand function does the job alone or we allow the agents to take responsibility of their own excess demand function. In the first case we realize that the macroscopic excess demand has to be an average of the individual agents and thus we can only get the desired convergence if all the individual excess demand functions are the same as the macroscopic ones proportionally to the relative initial endowments. The most efficient assumption is of course that all agents are alike with respect to preferences and initial endowments. But if so how could we have an excess demand function as a result of the perturbation? It certainly seems like a new general equilibrium.

In the second case we may assume that the perturbation of the original equilibrium is distributed over the agents, but if the agents have different initial endowments the perturbation obviously changes the valuations of the initial endowments and thus we arrive to a new general equilibrium. The only case which does not have this effect is when the initial distribution of endowments is exactly the same for all agents and equal preferences. Then we will have a convergence back to the same equilibrium and thus the heredity principle must hold.

In all other cases we will have no convergence since trading out of equilibrium changes the distribution of the initial endowments. A price change results in an income effect and a substitution effect which imply, particularly the latter effect, that the two groups will act differently and create asymmetries.

In the case we assume that all agents are alike with respect to preferences and endowments we will have the two groups, positive and negative Cobb-Douglas and these will navigate separately and thus will create asymmetries, consequently our assumption will not help us to have a converging process since the price movements will affect the valuation of the involved endowment vectors and consequently the macroscopic distribution.

McFadden et al. express the conclusion:

> This paper has established that candidate community excess demand functions in an economy with l commodities can be decomposed into the sum of l individual excess demand functions, each consistent with preference maximization. This conclusion has been shown not to hold universally when consideration is extended to candidate community total demand functions or excess demand correspondences.
>
> (McFadden et al. 1974: 372)

Rizvi having scrutinized the 30-year-old debate in a provoking way, discusses the ability of the general equilibrium theory to produce refutable propositions. He ends his paper:

> Matters are even clearer on qualitative features of equilibrium such as local uniqueness, stability, and comparative statics. The equilibrium manifold approach employing a finite set of observations does not allow us to refute statements on these features of equilibrium. Thus many of the problematic outcomes from SMD theory remain entrenched. Not only are there no results for general configurations of the data in these areas (Nachbar 2002, 2004), we still cannot test to see if the economy is poorly behaved. So we have no progress on these aspects of the theory. In this important area, then, the intuition that general equilibrium theory is devoid of meaningfully general results remains true. It turns out that Arrow was correct to conclude that "if agents are different in unspecifiable ways, then ... very little, if any, inferences can be made".
>
> (Rizvi 2006: 242)

The reason for this harsh conclusion, as we have pointed out in the introductory remarks, is that for all sets of a priori axiomatic structures holds, that they are nowhere dense.

However there are more principle conclusions we can make, which link the present discussion to our coming discussions. As we have seen the related discussion deals with a mathematical concept named the heredity principle which tells us that a property of a Space S holds for all its subspace s_i, $i - 1 - - - n$. This property of Heredity is link to Russell's paradox which tells us that:

Russell's paradox: *If for a set S of elements, all possible subsets as well as the universal set belongs to S we may say that S belongs to a non-proper class of sets. If however we have a set S where the universal set of possible subsets does not belong to S then S belong to a proper class of sets.*

Correlate: *The heredity principle only holds for sets belonging to non-proper classes.*

The axiomatic structure of the neoclassical theory transforms commodities and agents to variables in a Euclidian space. That means that with respect to general equilibrium all sets of agents and commodities belong to non-proper classes. Thus the heredity principle also holds. Furthermore we can state that a general equilibrium has a unique price vector and this price vector is independent of the agents. Consequently any change of the price vector also changes the general equilibrium and as a consequence of that general equilibrium is nowhere dense different general equilibria have no connection.

This leads to a general conclusion that for a given economy defined by the neoclassical axiomatic structure that there exist an infinite number of equilibria but they are each and all nowhere dense.

Growth

With respect to the general growth of the economy there is a basic problem which we will return to later but it is suitable to mention it here. As we see from Figure 1.2 the commodities are forming a space where the commodities are the actual dimensions and the agents are vectors. As long as we consider growth as a multidimensional production possibility curve which expands, we have a constant dimensionality of the commodity space and we can handle it within the realm of the barter economy. In the case of symmetric growth we will have a constant price vector given the population. A growth in population probably can change the distribution of preferences so we will have a new equilibrium which changes the price vector. If we have an asymmetric growth there will be a new price vector but if we assume the agents' initial endowments to be productive capacity and assume perfect substitutability we will be able to speak about general growth as in the case of constant population and symmetric growth.

However there is a nastier case, and that is when part of the growth means that the dimensionality of the commodity space changes and increases. In the former case we could in all subcases analyse the substitutability conditions and have a picture of the possible changes in the price vector. But in this case no such possibility exists, save for brave assumptions of course.

In principle there are two ways of looking at equilibrium growth in neoclassical tradition: the Solowian approach and the Neumann-Gale approach. Both of them basically analyse the production side and implicitly assume that the consumer market works smoothly with respect to the axioms. Solow's model (1956) is a one-sector model of the economy which can be given the interpretation that if all sectors/agents behave according to the axiomatic structure then we might handle the economy as one-sector, a perfectly legitimate assumption given the assumptions of the axiomatic structure. However one feels a bit concerned as to question whether false trading is allowed or not during the converging process.

Efforts have been made to close the Solowian model in a so called endogenous growth model. The multitude of explicit and implicit assumptions and the, in many cases missing, analysis of the consistency of the assumptions make these efforts more like rather loose ideas for further research, which of course is legitimate but at this stage we will not discuss it.[15]

The Neumann-Gale model (Makarov and Rubinov 1977) concerns multiple sectors, but perfectly substitutability of labour and capital. Basically it starts from the same assumptions as Solow's model but the multi-sectorial approach will allow for the appearance of changing trajectories depending on asymmetrical exogenous events.

Both the approaches have in reality no growth in the sense we normally attach to the word, but show a convergence to an optimizing combination of production factors. The basic difference between the two approaches is that technical improvements may have different effects. In the Solowian case there will be an augmented development of the converging curve and the per capita income will increase in optimum. The Neumann-Gale model in principle allows for asymmetric technical changes but then we will have a new price vector, thus a new general equilibrium, but the optimal production will increase also with the new price vector and given an Arrow and Debreu setting the optimal price vector will be set by the production side since the technology is exogenous to the production. Consequently the Neumann-Gale model can be attached to changing equilibrium paths, which are equivalent to changes in the price vector or the distribution of the initial vector. A parallel case may be achieved when we impose a consumption path, which puts a restriction on the production sector, which affect the input prices. It is shown by Rubinov and Makarov (1977: 211–233), that starting from the interior of the consumption set there exists an optimal trajectory, à la Solow, but multi-sectorial. That implies that for example, given a set of innovations, i.e. new products, and a potential demand, the production sector will converge towards a new equilibrium and subsequently a new price vector. In fact we have switched to a setting where the production sector is the governing sector for the price vector.

Maurice Allais (1987) has developed the *equimarginal principle* which takes its start in the search behaviour of entrepreneurs making inventions leading to local concavities but these are eliminated as time goes by through imitation and innovation of substitutes which affects prices for the adequate sector, thus eliminating concavities and reaching local sectorial optima. It is also important to realize that Allais rejects the idea of the existence of a general equilibrium since innovations and the subsequent equimarginal process is an ever ongoing process. Figure 1.4 illustrates the rough principles of Allais' discussion; in Ekstedt (2012: 95–103) there is a more comprehensive discussion of Allais' contribution.

Thus when it comes to modelling growth we can in principle model multi-sectorial production, technological asymmetries and changing consumption patterns.

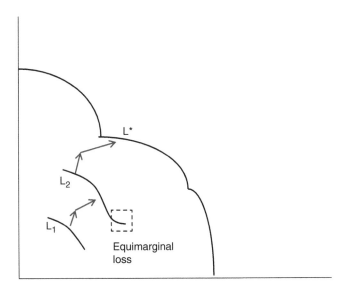

Figure 1.4 Approximation á la Equimarginal Process

However these are exogenously imputed and imply new price vectors so the consumption side has to run smoothly with no kick-backs on the production sector due to changed allocation. We have to add homogeneity of production factors as a central postulate to clear things properly.[16]

However when we look at growth theories in the sense of a barter economy it seems a bit awkward. If we look at analysts like Hume and Say they paid much attention to the very qualitative difference between a barter economy and the money economy with respect to the growth potential immanent in the social change. From that point of view the deterministic models which we handle in modern theory apart from working only under rather unrealistic assumptions also avoid the underlying growth dynamics of the social structure. Furthermore if we look from some kind of social/historic perspective it is hard to see that there exists any kind of barter economy with a process which we are apt to call growth.

Measuring growth is a most complicated thing since it has technical mathematical aspects and distribution as well as allocation problems, which we will discuss later. It is however important to look at the already discussed matters in the light of this measurement problem since it is juxtaposed with the inflation measurement.

If we lived in a sustainable general equilibrium according to the neoclassical axioms we would have no such problems. But the change of interpretation of the axioms, which is in a way one way out of the Sonnenshein, Debreu, Mantel discussion, that they hold only in the precise moment of choice and adding Debreu's precise (1987 [1959]) definition of a commodity it has to be temporally and spatially indexed we arrive at a trajectory of successive equilibria, where we have no theoretical hint about whether the price formation is in any way measurable. It is true that this problem will be dealt with in relation to the expected utility approach by assuming that the agents are contemplating the same space of outcome of the state space and the same distribution of the joint probability distribution, but it feels a bit awkward to make these assumptions for the macroscopic world, although they may be accepted for a strictly limited problem.[17] In all other cases we either have to look at some real aspects of wellbeing, as the different measures the UN uses, or we have to manipulate money measures with respect to nominal values. We will come back to these aspects later.

Aggregation and Arrow's Paradox

From Figure 1.2 we see that aggregation with respect to the axiomatic structure is additive. In nature additive aggregation exists as when half a litre of beer is added to another half a litre and we get one litre of beer. But if we for example make a French omelette we add three eggs, some cheese, butter, salt, some drops of water, electricity when using a stove, a frying pan plus a fork to stir, and thus we may get a French omelette as an aggregate but it is not an additive aggregation and the used components do not span a Euclidian space.

We will in the next chapter discuss Keynes' work on probability and induction and the contrasting opinions it caused and much of these have their roots in the problem of aggregation with respect to atomic facts versus complexes. The two rather trivial examples of aggregation above illustrate the basic problem in the discussions. They also illustrate the difference between *set theory in atomistic logic* and *mereology*, where the latter stands for a more complex relation between the whole and the parts.[18]

Thus when we look at beer molecules (or whatever we shall call them) in a certain quantity of beer, B, you can name the certain quantities of the smallest molecules into sets $x_1 - x_n$ and add them randomly into quantities $y_1 - y_m$ which you can add randomly to other quantities $z_1 - z_k$ and so on. All the different sets are thus subsets and belong to themselves so also the universal set B, which belongs to itself.

When we come to the French omelette things start to become difficult. Let us start with the word *stir*, if you stir the forthcoming omelette in a particular way and too much you get scrambled eggs. Thus the word stir is structurally defined. Furthermore what is *one* omelette? Obviously you can change the number of eggs but then you ran into the problem of scale in relation to structural relationships and adding different omelettes is just adding different omelettes.[19]

Thus one of the problems which occupy Keynes, Whitehead, Russell and others concerns the aggregation of pieces of different substances into a structural whole. This discussion is important because the foundation for the additive aggregation is that we transform the commodities into items with no structures which are to be represented by variables, numbers etc., while in the example of French omelette above the components have a very distinct structure. Thus aggregation may take many forms. The most well-known critique of additive aggregation is, implicitly at least, *Arrow's paradox* but the roots of the problem lies in the a*xiom of reflexivity*.

The axiom of reflexivity tells us that a commodity is equivalent to itself. Many textbooks consider this as an evident fact, but it is not. If we look at the commodities as physical items the axiom is obviously true but when we see them as commodities which are valued in the mind of the consumer one becomes doubtful. When we look at commodities as independent dimensions of the commodity space and each commodity is consumed independently of every other, (remember the correlate of independency of irrelevant alternatives), the axiom is relevant, although it transforms the agents into passive commodity vectors, slaves to the one who controls the price vector, which as we earlier discussed could well be the production sector, which may be some sort of invisible hand but not of the same kind as the one Smith (1952 [1776]) discussed.[20] But when we look at the consumption process, as in the modern consumption theory, *household production theory*, the commodities are a kind of inputs where we may think of different production techniques, then we realize that the postulated independency is doubtful. A commodity has to be seen as a multidimensional complex to a lower or higher degree. In such a case it is hard to advocate a unique price relation to other goods and with that follows also the rejection of the existence of unique general equilibrium. The point is that the role of an axiomatic structure with respect to empirical induction is not to make mathematical calculus more efficient but to make deductions possible within the adequate empirical context.

Aggregation is in a way the central issue of economics since it deals in the deepest sense with the question whether aggregate measures have any links to the individual. If this is questioned we also lose the link between microscopic and macroscopic efficiency, the equivalence between Pareto-optimum and general equilibrium. Mostly Pareto-optimum is interpreted within the realms of the economic frames and the social links to efficiency are either outside or implicitly assumed to be always true. Pareto-optimum does not need to be an economic concept *per se* but may as well work as a sociological concept, obviously more complex then but given the neoclassical structure and its definition of the agent ($\leq_i$, e_i) in Debreu's notation, the two sides happen to coincide in general equilibrium.

However the message of Arrow's paradox is that allowing agents who are able to consider the aggregate results of the market process and to form majorities for voting, makes the economic 'branch' of the Pareto concept disappear and we are left with the extremely difficult task of finding an acceptable social meaning of the concept of Pareto-optimum.

The problem of additive aggregation is also central from a philosophical point of view since it partly deals with the problem of Wittgenstein about whether mathematical/logical models can be a tool for social sciences and if so to what extent and partly with the central problem of atomistic set logics.

Thus if we reject the axiom of reflexivity we are not in the position to use mathematics which presuppose a Euclidian space and subsequently we will have difficulties to motivate any general forms of measures. Furthermore we will have difficulties to relate an aggregate of items to the items themselves which may lead to various problems of reversibility depending on the character of the problem. Mashed potatoes is obviously irreversible with respect to the different use of potatoes while a specific car is reversible, at least in principle if we disregard any eventual damages during the process.

Mereology is about the relations between the whole and its parts which is 'softer' than the set logics in atomistic terms and particularly we may discuss problems created by Russell's paradox. Be as it can with this but whatever we call the logical technique in question and its analytical qualities we obviously have a problem when the agents form complexes which are linked to utilities and the single commodities are just a kind of inputs, we then have no simple relation between the microscopic and macroscopic efficiency.

When reading Keynes' *General Theory*, he obviously rejects the principles of additive aggregation. In fact he already in 1903, at the age of 20, rejected additive aggregation. In an unpublished paper, 'Ethics in Relation to Conduct', read to the Apostles on 23 January 2003, the 20-year-old Keynes says the following:

> ...the unpopularity of the principle of organic unities shows very clearly how great is the danger of the assumption of unproved additive formulas. The fallacy, of which ignorance of organic unity is a particular instance, may perhaps be mathematically represented thus: suppose $f(x)$ is the goodness of x and $f(y)$. It is then assumed that the goodness of x and y together is $f(x)+f(y)$ when it is clearly $f(x+y)$ and only in special cases will it be true that $f(x+y) = f(x)+f(y)$. It is plain that it is never legitimate to assume this property in the case of any given function without proof.[21]
>
> (Mail from Robert Skidelsky July 2013)

As it stands, Keynes' rejection is more directed towards utility theory and with respect to Jevons' construction of a theory of utilities Keynes' critique is hard to neglect. As we will discuss in the next chapter Keynes was concerned with the logical dealing with atomistic variables contra complexes and the quote above should also be seen in relation to that. The quote also covers the case of aggregation of microscopic conditions to macroscopic, irrespective of whether it concerns commodity volumes or agents. As we already have touched on in our analysis of the axiomatic structure agents and commodities are atomistically defined. However when we reject the axiom of reflexivity and consider the message of Arrow's paradox which makes both agents and commodities into complexes. On one hand this disqualifies additive aggregation and on the hand makes all kinds of logical analysis difficult, since logic in its mathematical form requires atomistic variables. Thus we have to limit the dimensionality of variables, in our cases commodities, to one and only one dimension which is then to be seen as an atomistic fact. In our earlier discussion of the utility theory we saw how both Mill and Jevons struggled with this problem although expressed in non-technical terms.

The neoclassical aggregation takes the liberty of aggregating both commodities and agents, two aspects of the same problem, which is due to the assumed axiomatic structure and particularly the axiom of reflexivity.

The most precise formulation of the aggregation problem in economics is Arrow's paradox. Unfortunately Arrow's paradox is often interpreted as dealing with a sort of discussion of political democracy versus market efficiency where the latter seems to be the norm. This is obviously a very loose and superficial, not to say wrong interpretation. Theoretical paradoxes appearing in well-structured logical/mathematical theories almost always concern the very axiomatic structures and their limits, so also Arrow's paradox. The reason is of course that the axiomatic structure *per se* defines a world with no exterior, thus you are either inside the axiomatic world or the axioms do not hold. With respect to popular/political interpretations of Arrow's paradox we must remind ourselves of the fact that concepts like democracy and voting are not actually defined within the neoclassical axiomatic structure, so in Arrow's paradox we sort of compare agents of an intra-axiomatic kind with agents whose behaviour is exterior to the axioms. Obviously it might be interesting to discuss the results with respect to eventual (far-reaching) interpretations of the axiomatic structure but being aware of the limitations of such a structure the paradox only enlightens a particular feature which is not possible to analyse within the structure.

The very axioms of the neoclassical theory of the market economy tell us that given preferences the consumer in a strict interpretation does not choose but is the 'slave' of the price vector.[22] It is a pure deterministic theory. The agents are furthermore completely *unaware* of the aggregate result since that is created as an additive function outside the choice mechanisms defined by the axioms. In order to get the paradoxical result Arrow therefore introduces an agent who is not only aware of the aggregate result but can also affect it. Thus Arrow's result shows that the additive aggregation is unlikely to appear in an economy of agents who have the ability to vote. Whether or not this is comfortable is not a theoretical question but a metaphysical one. So if we claim that the agents in an economy are able to affect the aggregate structures then we must obviously reject general equilibrium a priori and consequently reject the axiomatic structure of the neoclassical theory. Milton Friedman once claimed that the market economy is a necessary prerequisite for democracy and we in principle do not object to that, but what is then the definition of a market economy? It can hardly be a system based on the axiomatic structure which is analysed with respect to Arrow's impossibility theorem and breaks down when we allow the agents to vote. To analyse Friedman's claim quite a different kind of analysis is required in comparison with Arrow's paradox.

Furthermore we may consider the theory of second best which tells us that if we change a restriction or impose a new one the optimal solution will change and if we have a unique measure (which is hard to think of, since we then obviously must allow for false trading) it will have a lower value that the first best which is assumed to be the pure market solution. Given a ruling general equilibrium the theory of second best is always true apart from the fact that there does not exist a unique measure for valuation covering the so called second best solution, because it is simply not a concept of the axiomatic structure. However if we apply the theory of second best to a situation where we have agents whose behaviour is affected by the macroscopic situation and who are also able to affect the macroscopic situation, this theory is at best nonsensical and just a mathematical result due to manipulations of parameters.

Expectations

There are many ways of modelling expectations; adaptive, extrapolative, constant, and rational are the most frequently used. Expectations usually concern future prices and the different forms of expectations often depend on differences in structural inertia. Constant expectation means then that the agents expect prices to remain at the current level, thus we have a high degree of inertia. Adaptive expectations describe a sort of learning process where the agents are supposed to systematically observe the historical deviances between expected and actual values and impute a form of correction factor in the current expectations. Thus the change in expectation for a certain market price can be written

$$\dot{p}_t^e = \alpha \cdot \left(p_t - p_{t-1} \right) - \beta \cdot \left(p_t^e - p_t \right)$$

From a stability point of view we have convergence when $\beta \geq 0$ and static expectations when $\beta = 0$. Thus β is a kind of expectation elasticity with respect to the correction factor.

Thus adaptive expectations build on a hypothesis which says that changes are basically stable in their movements and larger changes are normally dampened over time. If we try to imagine where this approach will work, stable market structures with basically balanced demand and supply save for minor fluctuations come to mind like complex inputs in other productions like special variants of steel, implying both highly specialized workers as well as production capital.

Extrapolative expectations are different in the respect that the new and present development plays a more distinct role, and as already in the name it deals with extrapolating that development. Normally they do not contain the element where the degree of success in historical expectations affects the extrapolation. While the adaptive expectations are symptomatic for the real markets where reactions are more attached to changes in the environment of the market, that state space, which set the basic conditions forms supply and demand and consumers are rather inert, the extrapolative expectations are more used when it comes to the actual price-formation at a market which is very volatile, like the financial market. Theoretically it starts from the assumption that the prices contain all information which implies that an event which you do not know but which have effect at the prices gives you the information that someone has such information that prices are changed and that forces you to reconsider your actions at the market. Thus if you see a substantial price change outside the frame of what we might call it white noise you are apt (or at least think so) to react on the price change in itself.

This means often that a large price change tends to create expectations of large successive changes while small changes are assumed to fade out. Typically these kinds of expectations are often used to describe the behaviour on the financial asset markets, (Vega-Redondo 1989, Choi 2005, Lansing 2005 and Hirshleifer and Yu 2012).

Typically we would write for these kinds of expectations

$$p^e = \alpha \cdot p + \gamma \cdot \dot{p}$$

The stability problems of these kinds of expectations are obvious and if you think of a set of such functions in a demand system the stability conditions are rather demanding as Arrow and Enthoven show in their famous 1956 paper. In general if we can grant gross-substitutability in the demand system, we will have overall stability, but precisely for the asset market this is not evident as shown in Blanchard and Plantes (1977) and partly also Rader (1968). The gross substitutability implies that all asset returns should be positively correlated while rational portfolio selection implies that this is doubtful.

Characteristic for these kinds of expectation hypotheses is that they have nothing per se to do with an eventual existence of general equilibrium. The equilibrium concept they use is an ordinary equilibrium in mathematical dynamics; it reflects a certain parameter structure and is used for partial analysis. The expectations are based on characteristics of local and temporal excess demand functions and the parameters, expectation elasticities, are in principle due to empirical judgements.

This is not so for the *rational expectation* hypothesis.

Rational Expectations

When we look at the use of rational expectation hypothesis at the microscopic level it has partially a certain realism. Well organized markets like oil, transcontinental transports, and primary commodities are pretty efficient and a perturbation in the state space upsetting markets will create a foreseeable process of price convergence to the same or a new equilibrium. The actors are generally big and well informed and furthermore the products are well defined, almost atomistically, a certain quality of diesel for example can be controlled equally well on both sides of the trade.

When we however use the hypothesis for the macroscopic levels we are entering a complex world where action alternatives are not atomistically defined. An aggregate state consists of many dimensions which may be subject to priority ordering. Thus an increase in the tax rate is certainly unpleasant from one point of view but may still be accepted because of its purpose. Any important aggregate variable like inflation, growth and unemployment is complex and has to be interpreted structurally. We will come back to these matters particularly when such complexes are related to simplistic variables like budget or current account balances.

Anyway using the rational expectation hypothesis as it is formed for the microscopic level requires that aggregate variables are atomistically definable and subject to additive aggregation otherwise we would end up in a logical mess. Furthermore a ruling general equilibrium is the only possible realm of the hypothesis which as we will see would be meaningless otherwise.

The only reason why prices should deviate from their equilibrium values is that some events in the surrounding state space create some sort of perturbation. The occurred deviation would then trigger expectations of a future price vector. This indeed creates some logical difficulties which we will come back to.

If we first look at the very name of the hypothesis, rational expectation, our first reaction is maybe that the two approaches we previously analysed seems rather rational, at least in a proper context, so it is a bit hard to understand the word rational. Although, as we shall see, the hypothesis is linked to a broader social context. It has been used exclusively as a tool under the postulate that general equilibrium prevails both currently and in the future, save for the moment of perturbation. With respect to the earlier analysis of general equilibrium as nowhere dense we are indeed a bit doubtful from start.

The rational expectation hypothesis is said to be the single most commonly used outcome from the neoclassical economic theory with respect to politics. We are told by the Nobel Laureate Thomas Sargent in an article for Library for Economics and Liberty (http://www.econlib.org/library/Enc/Rational Expectations.html) that:

> While rational expectations is often thought of as a school of economic thought, it is better regarded as a ubiquitous modelling technique used widely throughout economics.

It is interesting in the sense that it introduces a new feature to the neoclassical theory in a statement about the behaviour of an agent which must be exogenous and work like an additional axiom, which tells us what people *believe*. As seen in the opening paragraph of this chapter we touch on Moore's paradox which might be seen in its most radical form as a clash between beliefs and known facts.[23]

If everybody believes in the neoclassical model and is convinced that everybody does the same we have seemingly inserting a dynamic element into the neoclassical model. Arrow's paradox tells us that people are able not only to vote but also to consider and affect the aggregate level which obviously implies that we have to reject the axiomatic structure *in toto*. However if we postulate the belief of the agent it incapacitates the effects of Arrow's paradox and then we are back to the neoclassical axioms again, (save for the problem with reflexivity which we can assume to have negligible effects).

The hypothesis tells about a precise behaviour with respect to expectation and if all the agents subordinate to that principle we will be back into the realms of the general equilibrium setting again. The problem is that this only tells us that if people are willing to refrain from the behaviour Arrow allowed them, and then we may ask if the agents are completely unaware that an aggregate level might be affected through their behaviour, which at least in the author's country seems very strange.

The rational expectation theory, if we interpret rational in a broad sense according to the context of the agent is not particularly demanding, when commodities are indexed spatially and temporally, and has thus no extension in time, which means that we have to assume a certain inertia, which is possible in certain well defined markets as we mentioned above. But interpreting expectations at the macroscopic level and inserting a temporal extension is quite a different thing.

The rational expectation hypothesis is often seen in relation to the Lucas critique (1976: 41) which tells us:

> Given that the structure of an econometric model consists of optimal decision rules vary systematically with changes in the structure of series relevant to the decision maker, it follows that any change in policy will systematically alter the structure of econometric models.

If we disregard the word *systematically* in the quote for a moment, the critique in relation to our discussion of Arrow's paradox seems adequate and trivially so. The word *systematically* is however a bit worrying. One interpretation is of course that it can be replaced with the word *often* and then the conclusions are acceptable. The other interpretation is that the effects of the changes, irrespective which, vary according to a certain theory or model and then things become interesting, and it is here that the rational expectation hypothesis comes in.

The rational expectation hypothesis originates from Muth (1961) and in the original form it dealt with a specific and well defined market. It is interesting since it partly alludes to Keynes' famous words on 'Madmen in authority' in his concluding notes (1973[1936]: 383) which implies that decision makers are affected by theories and models, and partly it alludes to the so called Campbell's law, which goes:

> The more any quantitative social indicator (or even some qualitative indicator) is used for social decision-making, the more subject it will be to corruption pressures and the more apt it will be to distort and corrupt the social processes it is intended to monitor.
>
> (Campbell 1976: 49)

With respect to rational expectation hypothesis there might be a snag as it is hard to understand why the rational expectation hypothesis should be an exempt from Campbell's law. This is however overcome by assuming that the rational expectations are true expectations since they are based on an equilibrium and deals with a stable converging process.

Considering Campbell's law, which is at the bottom of Lucas' critique, it is almost tautologically true. It is open in the sense that it does not say anything of the direction of the distortions. Thus it does not say for example that reaction of the agents to a certain decision will just make the decision meaningless. It tells us that the social reaction will give rise to a distortion of an undefined character, which is easy to agree with.

But given that agents are subjects of the kind Arrow discusses, who can vote and consider the effects of actions on the macroscopic level and the counter-reactions on the individual level, given the particular context of the individual agent we will in fact start many different causal chains on the microscopic level of which some will be relevant to the macroscopic level but some not. Thus it is not unreasonable that Campbell's law from individual perspective creates partly contradictive effects, which on the aggregate level generates an increase in uncertainty for collective decision bodies and thus also for the individual agents.

Still however, coming back to the word rational it is a bit curious since the neoclassical equilibrium model is rather restrictive as we have seen in our earlier analysis and for example a piece of asymmetric information would be disastrous one might think and it surely is since a general equilibrium is nowhere dense. But if we loosely think of a microscopic, well defined market in terms of sequential market solutions the prices are quite naturally to be seen as information carriers. Thus asymmetric information may have initial effects but sooner or later the correct information on the state space is 'packed' into the price behaviour so we converge towards a uniform behaviour. But when we handle macroscopic varia-bles which are to be seen as complexes the efficiency of prices as information carriers will diminish and if we have actual trade during these circumstances we run into the problem of non-equilibrium pricing which makes the information value of the price formation at best local and temporal. This is to be classified as 'false trading'.

Muth's hypothesis was however formulated:

> expectations of firms (or more generally, the subjective probability distribu-tion of outcomes) tend to be distributed, for the same information set, about the prediction of the theory (or the 'objective' probability distribution of outcomes).

(Muth 1961: 316)

Thus we assume that agents are uniform in their beliefs of the working of the market. Muth uses three assumptions for his analysis: i) random disturbances are normally distributed, ii) certain equivalents exist for the variables to be predicted, and iii) the equations of the system, also the expectations, are linear. The latter iii) normally rules out extrapolative expectations.

Muth discusses two specific problems: *price fluctuations in an isolated market* and *effects on inventory speculation* and he finishes with some comparisons of some expectation hypotheses with respect to cobweb theorems.

Muth however interprets his model to be based on three fundamental postulates:

... (1) Information is scarce and the economic system generally does not waste it. (2) The way expectations are formed depends specifically on the structure of the relevant system describing the economy. (3) A 'public prediction', in the sense of Grunberg and Modigliani will have no substantial effect on the operation of the economic system (unless it is based on inside information).[24]

(Ibid.: 316)

Muth's discussion of rational expectations is on the whole within proper postulates and assumptions and applies to a microscopic problem with a properly defined context. What is left to do is to go on establishing the principle for well-defined markets/problems and then try to specify the precise empirical context where the theory is working. We can agree with almost all steps in the quotes from Muth but only with respect to partial markets at the microscopic level. In the above discussion we saw that adaptive and extrapolative expectations although starting from the same basis have fundamentally different stability conditions. That means that we must interpret Muth in such a way that the hypothesis works if the agents agree on what is 'the structure of the relevant economy'. If they do not agree on that we will probably have a dynamic process with continuous revisions of behaviour. This is the key point if we want to aggregate the hypothesis to the macroscopic level.

The hypothesis was transformed to a macroscopic usage which means that the postulates and assumptions must be considered with respect to a different economic space where the structure is vaguer according to our interpretation of Arrow's paradox and to the problem of the variables generically being complexes.

Thus evidently we must assume that we start from a state of general equilibrium and that the agents behave according to the axiomatic structure and then there is no problem to aggregate the hypothesis. If we however only think of local and temporal equilibria, aggregation is rather doubtful.

To our understanding the rational expectation hypothesis makes a bold assumption as it links a certain theoretical approach, the neoclassical, to the agents' expectations of the future, and it is not something entirely wrong *per se*, particularly not when we analyse well-defined markets manipulated by professional agents. The problem in such a case is the question of inert/dissipative structures, but that is an empirical question.

However if we go back to Campbell's law above, which we wholeheartedly can accept as a lesson we are taught from history, we may ask if we can apply the rational expectation in all kinds of thinking as it is expressed by Muth. The generalizations are creating questions if we accept the assumption that *all* information is uniform and correct, can we assume that *all* agents behave precisely predictably, can we assume that the agents' behaviour is *always* either independent of context or that *all* contexts are known to all agents? If any of these questions are answered with 'no' then the rational expectation hypothesis is subject to Campbell's law itself.

It is obvious that if we restrict the analysed problem enough we may well find empirical markets which can use the rational expectation hypothesis but the higher the level of aggregation, the more difficult this seems to be.

We mentioned above Maurice Allais' (1987) discussions of the equimarginal principle. These discussions deal on one hand with innovations – concavities – competitive innovations and on the other hand with structural change. Allais' discussions strictly concern the microscopic level although the equimarginal process leads to macroscopic effects, but these are outside his scope. He also dismisses the existence of a global equilibrium since the innovations and the subsequent equimarginal process is an ever ongoing process.

We mentioned also above the content of Lucas' critique, which makes sense with respect to policy measures. The problem is that if we, according to Allais, allow for innovations and concavities then we are actually thrown out of any general equilibrium and although we may assume that the agents can handle policy changes and make them inefficient the factors which Allais imposes are somewhat worse to handle for the market and we will in later chapters add some more disturbing matters.

When we use the hypothesis of rational expectation on the macroscopic level it is obvious that, if all agents fulfil the neoclassical axiomatic structure in their behaviour, the hypothesis is always true but in that case it is hard to see that the rational expectation theory adds any substance to the traditional perfect informa-tion assumption. It is also *seemingly obvious* that forecasting errors will converge in some long run, whatever that can be, since a *true* model is assumed and fore-casting errors are randomly distributed, the true result should indeed converge. But here the theoretical question of false trading comes into the analysis and there is, to my understanding, not a clear-cut link from randomly distributed forecast-ing errors to randomly distributed results of false trading on a macroscopic scale since variables are complexes.[25]

If the agents apply the rational expectation hypothesis when the current situa-tion is out of general equilibrium then we logically cannot say anything of the future result. One obvious question is for example what we shall judge as an expectation error. The hypothesis so to say stops at the first step and given basi-cally an overall disequilibrium with only temporal and local equilibria we cannot say whether the result is converging to something or diverging. This was discussed already by Roy Radner (1982).

When it comes to the specific question of inflation and monetary policy the rational expectation hypothesis is interesting from a more specific perspective with respect to money and the money economy. So we will wait to discuss this until we have discussed the matter of money more carefully.

Lucas empirical use of the theory with respect to aggregate investment is found in Lucas (1981 [1966]) on optimal investment and in Lucas and Prescott (1981 [1971]) on investment under uncertainty. His aggregation technique from single firms to industry goes through the assumption of a competitive economy in the theoretical sense. In this paper he starts from a basic case of static expectations:

The argument of this section proceeds in what would seem to be a natural 'two-step' fashion: first, the supply response of an individual firm to changing current and expected prices is obtained; secondly, these supply functions are aggregated over firms and combined with a demand function to determine price and industry output.

   To conduct an analysis of this sort, it is necessary to make some assumption about the way in which firms form price expectations. For simplicity, I have assumed that firms' expectations are *static* in the sense that current price is believed to be permanent.

(Lucas, 1981 [1966]: 55)

Lucas' conclusions are that the results are in support of the assumed constant returns to scale hypothesis, but does not distinguish between short- and long-run matters which the second case about the competitive model under rational expectations is said to do. Concerning aggregation it seems that he uses ordinary additive aggregation.

   In this part II he makes the following assumptions:

In the preceding section, firms were assumed to regard the current price at each moment of time as a 'permanent' price, yet this expectation proved valid at one price only: the industry's long-run equilibrium price. In this section, it is assumed that the output price expectations of each firm are *rational*, or that the entire future price pattern, $p(t, \ t > 0$, is correctly anticipated? All other assumptions made in Section I will be maintained, including the assumption that expectations on prices other than $p(t)(q$ and $r)$ are static.

(ibid.: 61)

Furthermore Lucas has specified the difference between the base case I and case II in an important aspect:

In Section II, an industry with the characteristics postulated in Section I is analyzed again, this time under the assumption that firms' expectations are *rational* (i.e., correct). In this context, the optimal supply response of firms and the industry as a whole must be determined simultaneously rather than sequentially as in Section I.

(ibid.: 55)

It is interesting that for the case of static expectations he works with a sequential implementation of the investment plan, which might actually leave room for at least mentioning of eventual later shocks but in the asserted more interesting case he goes back to a simultaneous global solution. Thus the supply curve is fixed and known and the consumer side is assumed to work according to the neoclassical axioms.

Lucas then introduces expectation errors in the analysis and arrives at the following comparison between the two cases:

> Under static expectations, condition (7) holds at each point in time, which implies that the industry remains continuously on the $\lambda = 0$ curve of this diagram. Under rational expectations, the industry will move on a path to the left of this curve for $x(t)$ less than its equilibrium value, x^*, and on a path to the right of this curve for $x > x^*$. In other words, for any x, λ will be closer to its equilibrium value under rational than under static expectations. From (15), this implies that the industry will approach equilibrium *less* rapidly if expectations are rational.
>
> (Ibid.: 64)

The quote is very interesting since if the expectation errors imply that the economy obtains a state *near* equilibrium, which obviously is not in equilibrium. Lucas seems implicitly to assume that there exists a dynamic process for states *outside* the initially assumed equilibrium state such that the economy converges to the equilibrium for which it 'aimed' in the first state. And we have to remember that since we have a *simultaneous solution* given all the assumptions, we obviously must land in a different general equilibrium but obviously the 'stubborn' agents are not satisfied with that, so they revise their expectations and make a new try to go for the desired equilibrium. But if there exists such a dynamic process it is the information given in the paper as:

> The stationary solutions of the system (15)–(18) must also be stationary solutions of the system with static expectations treated in Section I, and conversely. The system under rational expectations thus also has either one stationary solution or none. ...
>
> If the system does have a stationary solution, its stability may be determined by examining the linear system which is approximately valid near the stationary solution.
>
> (Ibid.: 64)

Lucas makes a provision for no stationary solution, which is interesting, but that is actually not an answer to our questions, although the character of the non-stationary solution would have been interesting to scrutinize. Lucas also offers the possibility that a general equilibrium can be extended in time after some process of convergence which rejects our principle position which we have hereto been rather explicit about namely that the existence of uncertainty, in the meaning that the set of outcomes is unknown, in neoclassical theory within the axiomatic frames cannot exist without producing different equilibria if we extend the theory in the time dimension. So let us look more closely at some aspects.

First we must make a very strong assumption that the commodity space is constant over time. We noted in our discussion of the axiomatic structure that the different commodities spanned a space where the commodities were the dimensions and that the agent was to be seen as a commodity vector (see Figure 1.2 above). Thus if we think of an expectation function over time based on the current general equilibrium of the character which Lucas suggests, the only possibility to get a unique solution is to assume the dimensionality of the commodity space constant.[26]

Second we have the problem of Allais' paradox which can be overcome by assuming strict risk aversion. But looking at the macroeconomic landscape which implies a lot of interdependencies the implementation of risk aversion means on one hand that we have a joint distribution function, a *copula*, and on the other hand the error term must be organised as a joint error term. Lucas obviously solves this problem by assuming that the agents are expecting the true result.

The second paper from 1971 by Lucas and Prescott deals explicitly with the concept of uncertainty:

> In the present paper, an uncertain future is introduced into an adjustment-cost type model of the firm, and the optimal response to this uncertainty is studied in an attempt to integrate variables of the first category into the existing theory. Briefly, we shall be concerned with a competitive industry in which product demand shifts randomly each period, and where factor costs remain stable. In this context, we attempt to determine the competitive equilibrium time paths of capital stock, investment rates, output, and output price for the industry as a whole and for the component firms. From the viewpoint of firms in this industry, forecasting future demand means simply forecasting future output prices.
>
> (Lucas and Prescott 1981 [1971]: 67)

The last sentence is indicating that they assume implicitly a constant commodity space. Thus *uncertainty* may refer either to the problem of the error term which may lead to Allais' problem or to the case when the assumed distribution function differs among the agents.[27] Lucas and Prescott find a way out of this which is theoretically possible but a bit problematic from an empirical point of view.

> Typically the forecasting rule postulated takes the form of anticipated prices being a fixed function of past prices—'adaptive expectations.' But it is clear that if the underlying disturbance (in our case, the demand shift) has a regular stochastic character (such as a Markov process), forecasting in this manner is adaptive only in a restrictive and not very interesting sense. Except for an unlikely coincidence, price forecasts and actual prices will have different probability distributions, and this difference will be persistent, costly to forecasters, and readily correctible.
>
> To avoid this difficulty, we shall, in this paper, go to the opposite extreme, assuming that the actual and anticipated prices have the *same* probability distribution, or that price expectations are *rational*. Thus we surrender, in advance, any hope of shedding light on the *process* by which firms translate current information into price forecasts. In return, we obtain an operational

investment theory linking current investment to observable current and past explanatory variables, rather than to 'expected' future variables which must, in practice, be replaced by various 'proxy variables.'

(Ibid.: 68)

This quote is very important from a couple of different angles. Lucas and Prescott are well aware of the problem that agents generically have different probability functions 'and that this difference is persistent'. The role of the rational expectation is in fact to avoid this difficulty, furthermore the authors 'surrender in advance' with respect to the problem of how the firms manage to make such a forecast based on currently existent information.

The assumption of rational expectation is rewarding in the sense that the investment theory becomes operational. One certainly gets some associations to the provoking Hoffman/de Niro/Heche film *Wag the Dog*, from many perspectives: 'If they don't behave like our assumptions, we had better teach them to do so', is certainly one type of association. Anyway for empirical research the quote is indeed problematic.

With respect to the basics Lucas and Prescott obviously assume a competitive economy and although nothing is said it seems natural to think according to the rest of the assumptions that the economy starts from a state of general equilibrium in which 'it' likes to remain. We then assume that the supply prices are correctly anticipated for the entire future; thus the supply curve is given for all future.

Let us now sum up our discussions on the rational expectation theory/hypothesis and look at a precise formulation of the rational expectation hypothesis as it appears in Tesfatsion [2]014: 2–4. The author has two definitions one is called the Weak Form (WF) and the Strong Form (SF).

Definition Weak Form:

The agent i is said to have a WF rational expectation
If

$$E_{t-1,i} v_{t+k} = E\left\{ v_{t+k} \mid I_{t-1,i} \right\} + \mu_{t,i}$$

Where the Left side denotes the individual expectation at the beginning of t and the Right side denotes the objectively true expectation and an error term.

The Strong Form adds restrictions/conditions for the information set.

Definition Strong Form:

The additional information set includes: (We add point i which appears earlier in the text.)

i.   The WF rational expectation holds;
ii.   The structural equations and classification of the model, *including the actual decision rules used by any **other** agent (private or public) appearing in the model to generate their actions and/or expectations*; [original emphasis]

iii.   The true values for all deterministic exogenous variables for the model;
iv.   All properties of the probability distributions governing stochastic exogenous variables are known by the modeller at the beginning of period t;
v.   Realized values for all endogenous variables and stochastic exogenous variables as observed by the modeller through the beginning of period t.

The *strong form* of rational expectation is really demanding and tells us in principle that any agent should be able to repeat the model analysis. The *weak form*
is based on two conditions: the agents know the principle structure of the model
and the prices carry all the relevant information. Given these conditions we
have that for a change in public politics the agents are able to forecast the principle result for the price vector subject to a statistical error term since they do
not know the objectively true distributions. The error term can however be
assumed to be randomly distributed, but it becomes subject to more assumptions than there already are in the hypothesis concerning the dynamic process
of convergence. We then remind of the fact that a non-successful outcome at
any period t_i so to say stops the whole game according to Radner (1982), since
we then have to 'start' our expectations in non-equilibrium or another
equilibrium.

   Thus the rational expectation hypothesis is most probably true for most kinds
of models of reality in the sense of Keynes' wording of 'Madmen in authority ...'
and Campbell's law. However with respect to rational expectation in the setting
of Sargent/Lucas/Prescott requires very substantial empirical proofs that it is
rational to apply the rational expectation hypothesis in its weak or strong form is
rational. Does it really add anything with respect to the empirical economy
particularly to the macroscopic analysis apart from the more general formulation
by Campbell? In Keynes' wording we thus ask if the belief in the rational expectation model with respect to Sargent/Lucas/Prescott is *a rational belief.*

   G.E. Moore wrote:

> In short, where there is belief in the sense in which we *do* believe the exist-
> ence of Nature and horses and do *not* believe in the existence of an ideal
> landscape and unicorns, the *truth* of what is believed does make a great
> difference to the value of the organic whole.
>
> (1993 [1903]: 243)

However when we come to the question of using the rational expectation hypothesis with respect to money matters like inflation and inflation policy and the
financial sector things are a bit different because of the peculiarities of money,
but we will return to these questions later in the book.

Final Comments

As we have noticed in our analysis of the neoclassical analysis of the barter
economy there are several difficulties with respect to the conceptualizations

which ultimately leads to Arrow's paradox which in practical terms reduce the axiomatic structure to just deal with the actual choice situation and has no extension either in space or time, which is also consistent with Debreu's position in *Theory of Value* (1959: 29–30). The rational expectation theory however postulates its extension in time and space. That does not mean that most economists agree that neoclassical theory is of any empirical relevance but still it is often said that the theory induces some sort of norm, efficiency norm, into economic analysis. So a relevant question to ask could be how a theory, which not only lacks important empirical features as money but also contradicts the daily experiences that people can vote and affect different aggregate levels in different degrees, can have any normative value whatsoever, and how comes that the rational expectation hypothesis has gained the status it has, if General Equilibrium theorists of any rank are aware that general equilibrium theory has little resemblance with the economy we experience daily.

It is sometimes claimed that the status of general equilibrium theory is that of a model constructed to demonstrate the existence, uniqueness and stability of equilibrium in a stylized market economy.

Such a statement goes in principle for any model and the scientific task is to scrutinize such models with respect to their axiomatic structure, empirical and social relevance and of course the logical consistence of derived propositions. What is notable immediately is the lack of money and our question is of course why money is excluded from a 'stylized market economy' and we cannot discuss money with respect to general equilibrium theory since it is simply not there.

With respect to the dynamic element of expectations these normally deal with partial and sequential markets like adaptive and extrapolative expectations. Generally different kinds of expectation formation relates to different kinds of markets. Obviously it is often a rather substantial difference between expectations on the financial asset markets and the real commodity markets.

We have however one approach to expectations which claims to take the total working, even at the aggregate level, of the economy into consideration and that is the rational expectation hypothesis. As we have seen however this is done only through an excessive amount of extra assumptions concerning the character of beliefs of the agents and also by postulating the correct expectation and the correct information must be in line with the neoclassical general equilibrium theory. But since the theory is based on rather restrictive axioms, this will impute contradictions into the hypothesis in trying to squeeze the real economy into the set of axioms, most of all the problem of false trading.

As a matter of fact one can say that the rational expectation hypothesis looks similar to Moore's paradox, which we will discuss in the next chapter, at least in its weak form

$$\neg p \wedge a(p)$$

Which should be read: not p is but p is believed.

Appendix: The Neoclassical Axiomatic Structure in a Technical Form[28]

Algebraic fundamentals

Definition 1: Partial order relation

Let $\mathbb{C}$ be a non-empty set (choice set). A partial order relation in $\mathbb{C}$, denoted $\lesssim$, have the following properties:

1. $x \lesssim x; \forall x \in \mathbb{C}$
2. $x \lesssim y \wedge y \lesssim x \Rightarrow x \sim y; \forall x, y \in \mathbb{C}$
3. $x \lesssim y \wedge y \lesssim z \Rightarrow x \lesssim z; \forall x, y, z \in \mathbb{C}$

Definition 2: Equivalence relation

Let $\mathbb{C}$ be a set. For any relation $\lesssim \subset R^2$ ($\mathbb{C} \times \mathbb{C}$) such that $\forall x, y, z \in X$

1. $x \sim x;$ (reflexive)
2. $x \sim y; \wedge y \sim x;) x = y;$ (symmetric)
3. $x \sim y; \wedge y \sim z; \Rightarrow x \sim z;$ (transitive)

The Neoclassical Axioms (Economics)

Axiom 1: Completeness

$x \lesssim y \vee y \lesssim x; \forall x, y \in \mathbb{C}$

Axiom 2: Reflexivity

$x \sim x; \forall x \in \mathbb{C}$

Axiom 3: Transitivity

$x \lesssim y \wedge y \lesssim z \Rightarrow x \lesssim z; \forall x, y, z \in \mathbb{C}$

Axiom 4: Local non-satiation

$\forall x, y \in \mathbb{C}$ then $\exists \varepsilon > 0 \Rightarrow y < x \wedge \| y - x \| < \varepsilon$

Axiom 5: Continuity

Let $\mathbb{F}$ be defined onto $\mathbb{C}$ and continuous. Furthermore define two distance functions d_1 and d_2. Given $\forall x, y \in \mathbb{C} \wedge \delta > 0 \wedge \varepsilon > 0$; then $d_1[x; y] < \delta \Rightarrow d_2[\mathbb{F}(x); \mathbb{F}(y)] < \varepsilon$

Axiom 6: Convexity

$\forall x, y \in \mathbb{C}; x \lesssim y \wedge x \neq y \Rightarrow \alpha x + (1 - \alpha)y \lesssim y;$
$1 \geqslant \alpha > 0.$

Strict convexity implies $x \lesssim y \wedge x \neq y \Rightarrow \alpha x + (1 - \alpha)y < y; 1 \geq \alpha > 0$

Notes

1 For a more comprehensive historical review see Ekstedt (2012), Chapter 2.
2 Unfortunately he is nowadays remembered as the father of Say's law which is a complete misconception and Keynes who criticised this law ought to have realised that the actual analysis that Say performed in its context was more like Keynes' concept of marginal propensity to consume and his multiplier discussion than Keynes' interpretation of Say's law.
     Say does not mention the multiplier explicitly but discusses the importance of the dispersion of money as a growth factor both in quantitative as well as qualitative aspects, which follows the discussion by Hume quite well.
3 Some philosophers actually claim that also Jesus Christ was an epicurean.
4 All references to Jevons are taken from chapters II and III in: Jevons, W.S. (1888) *The Theory of Political Economy*. Library of Economics and Liberty. Accessed 3 September 2014 at http://www.econlib.org/library/YPDBooks/Jevons/jvnPE2.html
5 Richard Jennings is a very interesting economist and discusses economics from a psychological and moral point of view. We will come back to him in the Epilogue.
6 Which indeed could be as strong an assumption as we have seen.
7 Tarski (1955[1983]), Chapter II: Foundations of the Geometry of Solids.
8 A comprehensive discussion of the mechanisms of the neoclassical theory is found in Ekstedt and Fusari (2010) Chapter 2.
9 The old-fashion marginal decreasing utility is thus replaced with a commodity basket that can always be improved in some dimension.
10 See the discussion in Ekstedt (2012:113–15).
11 Makarov and Rubinov (1977: 201–205) has some interesting notes on this aspect.
12 This is parallel to one aspect of Leibnitz proof of God's omnipotence. If God exists there is no complement but non-existence.
13 Our discussion is based on McFadden et al. (1974). This paper can be seen as a conclusion of the discussions which contained Debreu (1974), Mantel (1974), Sonnenshein (1973). Later on Mantel (1976) discusses homothetic preferences in the same context and arrive to some interesting results although negative. Arrow (1986) makes some comments on the discussion and use the predominantly negative answers in his discussion on rationality. But he then also separates rationality of self and the community so it is to be seen as a further step of the analysis. Rizvi, S.A.T (2006) makes a very interesting analysis in retrospect of the discussion.
14 The assumption that all quantities are non-negative implies that we allow some quantities to be zero; according to the axiomatic structure it would be more natural to assume that quantities are strictly positive. We will discuss this later but for our present purpose the non-negativeness is sufficient.
15 In Ekstedt and Fusari (2010) some comments are made on the endogenous growth model in Chapter 5.
16 It is interesting to read old economists like Hume, Ricardo and Say who are perfectly well aware of existing differences in quality and for example Say (ibid. ch. VII: Of the labour of mankind, of nature, and of machinery respectively) discusses a kind of unemployment which is impossible to avoid within current production structure. Economic modelling in, let us say, the last 50 years, has often taken the explicit/implicit

assumption of homogeneity without noticing the intrinsic links to the production structure with which such an assumption must be underpinned. Instead the defence of the assumption often is explained by simplifying mathematics thus revealing other important aspects, which indeed is dubious.

17 A more comprehensive discussion of these matters can be found in Ekstedt (2012: 90–103)

18 Mereology is not new as an analytical approach and as such it goes back at least to Aristotle. As a concept however it was an attempt by the Polish logician Leśniewski to develop a logic at variance with set theory and particularly an attempt to escape the problems of Russell's paradox. Since we are going to use Russell's paradox rather extensively it is of some importance to look at the logical foundations.

19 This problem in particular is analysed by D'Arcy Thompson more or less contemporary with Keynes and Russell. He wrote the famous *book On Growth and Form* which we will discuss later in this book.

20 This is in line with Makarov and Rubinov (1977: ch 5) who actually show that the neoclassical theory as a logical system cannot discriminate between a market economy and a centralized command economy but that has to be set exogenously and then the capital market will set the price vector in the end.

21 I am grateful to Lord Robert Skidelsky who called my attention to Keynes' very early awareness of the problems of aggregation and his kindness to send me this quote in July 2013.

22 Makarov and Rubinov (1977:202–5) have a very precise interpretation when we link the Arrow and Debreu model to the Newman and Gale model.

23 In a way the trial of Galileo was built on such a clash. The church representatives who judged him were most probably aware of Kepler's work, which was accepted within the church. But Galileo's work had wider consequences at the philosophical level and thus the whole set of ideas by Galileo was rejected.

24 Grunberg and Modigliani (1954) deal with the different effects of public and private predictions. A prediction which is public will alter the behaviour of agents in such a way that the prediction is falsified while a private prediction even if correct will be falsified on the opposite grounds. However if it is generally accepted that a private prediction might be right, it is possible that public predictions might turn out to be right.

   It is interesting that this paper never includes prices as information bearers in consecutive market solutions as is done in adaptive and extrapolative expectations approaches.

25 Ekstedt (2012: 90–103) has a comprehensive discussion on forecasting errors and convergence to a 'correct' forecast, if such exist.

26 This follows from the dimension invariance theorem by the Dutch mathematician Brouwer which tells us that R^n is homeomorphic to R^m *if and only if* $n = m$

27 The broad concept of uncertainty and different attitudes to it are discussed in Ekstedt (2012: 194–203).

28 This is mainly based on Ekstedt and Fusari (2010: 49–56).

Bibliography

Allais, M. (1987) 'The Equimarginal Principle: Meaning, Limits and Generalization', *Rivista Internazionale di Scienza Economica e Commerciale*, Vol. 34, No. 8: 689-750.

Arrow, K.J. (1986) 'Rationality of Self and Others in an Economic System', *The Journal of Business*, Vol. 59, No. 4, Part 2: The Behavioral Foundations of Economic Theory. (Oct.): S385–S399.

Blanchard, O.J. & Plantes, M.K., (1977), A Note on Gross Substitutability of Financial Assets, *Econometrica*, vol. 45(3), pages 769-71, April.

Campbell, D.T., (1976) *Assessing the Impact of Planned Social Change*, Paper 8, Occantional Paper Series, The Public Affairs Center, Dartmouth College. Available at https://www.globalhivmeinfo.org/

Choi, J.J. (2005) *Extrapolative Expectations and the Equity Premium*. Harvard University Accessed at http://www.stanford.edu/group/SITE/papers2005/Choi.05.pdf

Debreu, G. (1987[1959]) *Theory of Value*. New York: Wiley.

Ebenstein, L. (1985) 'Mill's Theory of Utility', *Philosophy*, Vol. 60, No. 234: 539–543.

Ekstedt, H. (2012) *Money in Economic Theory*. London and New York: Routledge.

Ekstedt, H. and Fusari, A. (2010) *Economic Theory and Social Change Problems and Revisions*. London and New York: Routledge.

Enthoven, A. C. and Arrow, K. J. (1956) 'A Theorem on Expectations and the Stability of Equilibrium', *Econometrica* Vol. 24. No. 3: 288–293.

Grice-Hutchinson, M. (1952) *The School of Salamanca*. Oxford: Clarendon Press.

Grunberg, E. and Modigliani, F. (1954) 'The Predictability of Social Events', *Journal of Political Economy*, Vol. 62: 465–478.

Hirshleifer, D. and Yu, J. (2012) *Asset Pricing in Production Economies with Extrapolative Expectations*. Accessed at http://papers.ssrn.com/sol3/papers.cfm?abstract_id=1785961

Jennings, R. (1855) *Natural Elements of Political Economy*. London: Longman, Brown, Green, and Longmans.

Jevons, W.S. (1888[1871]) *The Theory of Political Economy*, London: Macmillan & Co. Accessed at: http://www.econlib.org/library/YPDBooks/Jevons/jvnPE3.html#

Keynes, J. M. (1973[1936]). *The General Theory of Employment Interest and Money*. Cambridge: MacMillan, Cambridge University Press.

Lansing, K.J. (2005) *Lock-in of Extrapolative Expectations in an Asset Pricing Model*. Federal Reserve Bank of San Francisco working paper 2004–06. Accessed at http://www.frbsf.org/publications/economics/papers/2004/wp04-06bk.pdf

Lucas, R.E. Jr. (1976) *Econometric Policy Evaluation: A Critique*. Accessed at http://www.econ.umn.edu/~longw011/teaching/Lucas%20Critique.pdf

Lucas, R.E. Jr. (1981[1966]) 'Optimal Investment with Rational Expectations', in *Rational Expectations and Economic Practice* Vol. 1, Lucas, R.E. Jr. and Sargent, T.J. (eds). Minneapolis: The University of Minnesota Press.

Lucas, R.E. and Prescott, E.C., (1981[1971]), 'Investment under Uncertainty', in *Rational Expectations and Economic Practice* Vol. 1, Lucas, R.E. Jr. and Sargent, T.J. (eds). Minneapolis: The University of Minnesota Press.

McFadden, D., Mas-Colell, A., Mantel, R., and Richter, M.K. (1974), 'A Characterization of Community Excess Demand Functions', *Journal of Economic Theory*, Vol. 9, No. 4, 361–374.

Makarov, V.L. and Rubinov, A.M. (1977) *Economic Dynamics and Equilibria*. Heidelberg, Berlin: Springer Verlag.

Mantel, R. (1974) 'On the characterization of aggregate excess-demand', *Journal of Economic Theory* 7: 348–353.

Mill, J.S. (1990 [1863]) *Utilitarianism*, in Great Books of the Western World no. 40, Chicago, London, New Delhi, Paris, Seoul, Taipei, Tokyo: Encyclopædia Britannica, Inc.

Moore, G.E. (1993 [1903]) *Principia Ethica*. Cambridge: Cambridge University Press.

Muth, J.F. (1961) 'Rational Expectations and the Theory of Price Movements', *Econometrica*, Vol. 29, No. 3, July: 315–335.

Rader, T., (1968) 'Normally, factor inputs are never gross substitutes', *Journal of Political Economy*, 76: 38–43

Radner, R. (1982) 'Equilibrium under Uncertainty', in K.J. Arrow and M.D. Intrilligator (eds), *Handbook of Mathematical Economics*, Vol. 2. Amsterdam, New York, Oxford: North-Holland Publishing Company. pp. 923–1006.

Rizvi Abu Turab, S. (2006) 'The Sonnenschein-Mantel-Debreu Results after Thirty Years', *History of Political Economy*, 38 (annual suppl.).

Say, J.B. (1834 [1803]) *A Treatise on Political Economy; or the Production, Distribution, and Consumption of Wealth*. Philadelphia: Grigg & Elliot, 9, North Fourt Street.

Smith, A. (1952 [1776]) *An Inquiry Into the Nature and Causes of the Wealth of Nations*. Chicago, London, Toronto: Encyclopedia Britannica INC.

Solow, R.M. (1956) 'A Contribution to the Theory of Economic Growth', *The Quarterly Journal of Economics*, Vol. 70, No. 1: 65–94.

Sonnenschein, H. (1972) 'Market Excess Demand Functions', *Econometrica*, Vol. 40, No. 3: 549–563.

Tarski, A. (1955 [1983]) *Logic, Semantic, Meta-Mathematics*. Indianapolis: Hackett Publishing Company.

Tesfatsion, L. (2014) Introductory Notes on Rational Expectations. Accessed at http://www2.econ.iastate.edu/tesfatsi/reintro.pdf

Vega-Redondo, F. (1989) 'Extrapolative Expectations and Market Stability', *International Economic Review*, Vol. 30, No. 3: 513–517.

Wicksell, K., (1937 [1922]) *Lectures on Political Economy*. London: Routledge.

2 Aggregation, Money and Keynes' Epistemology

Abstract

In Chapter 2 we reject the neoclassical axiomatic structure on two grounds: rejection of the axiom of reflexivity and the interpretation of Arrow's paradox. However we do not reject the postulate that the agents are rational in the sense of the neoclassical definition, but this is only a necessary but not sufficient condition for rationality. By introducing the concept of epistemic cycles we save the rational and optimizing agent as a meaningful concept in a non-equilibrium analysis.

Furthermore our main criticism against the rational expectation approach as a theoretical tool in the macroscopic analysis was that using a precise mathematical structure in the analysis of reality requires almost atomistic definitions of variables. This leads to contradictions and anomalies.

The concept of *epistemic cycles* implies that the agents are rational with respect to a set of epistemic cycles consisting of purposes and contextual apprehensions. We will then be able to show that on one hand there does not exist a general equilibrium in this setting and on the other hand that optimization on different aggregate levels is possible although the optimization on different aggregate levels are not logically dependent on each other. These results however hold only for a barter economy. The role of money will be curious: on one hand money will work as a medium of exchange in spite of no general equilibrium but it is also possible to aggregate money values additively. We thus have an anomaly in relation to the barter economy.

We formulate Proposition 2.1 implying that in a barter economy the different aggregate levels optimize independently of each other. We will link these aspects to Keynes philosophical contribution with respect to theoretical conceptualization, particularly the problem of atomistic variables versus complexes. We will also compare Keynes' social analysis with the analysis of natural sciences with respect to probability and induction.

Rationality, Equilibrium and Epistemic Cycles

As we have discussed earlier and which was obvious in our analysis of the rational expectation theory, an *a priori* axiomatic theory is indeed demanding. It has no environment since either the axioms hold or not. Thus any reference to a general equilibrium in a dynamic sense implies that the obtained general equilibrium is extended in the time dimension and since the agents must behave according to the axioms there is no room for discussing any future disequilibrium. As we said earlier there is no on/off button such that the agents outside equilibrium behave in one way but when they reach a general equilibrium they start to behave according to the axioms.

This implies that we must ask what researchers refer to when they use the word equilibrium in general and general equilibrium in particular. If they refer to the equilibrium implied by the axiomatic structure as some kind of norm they obviously run into considerable logical difficulties if they at the same time accept an out-of-equilibrium behaviour by any agent, also including collective agents. If however they refer to equilibrium merely as a mathematical solution given a particular variable/parameter structure, the concept of equilibrium has no intrinsic normative value since such a value has to be imposed exogenously, as political preferences for example. If we thus go for the later interpretation of the word equilibrium, the whole scientific business is to come up with local and temporal theoretical structures which are more or less appropriate given the apprehended empirical structure. Eventual extension in time of the theory must then depend on inertia which must then be discussed explicitly in the theoretical approach since such inertia is not intrinsic to the variables *per se* but to exogenous structural patterns.

This also, as we mentioned in our discussion of rational expectation hypothesis in Chapter 1, concerns stability analysis. If, in a dynamic model, we find an equilibrium it is natural to study its stability properties, like in a simple system below where we discuss the demand for two commodities X_1 and X_2 and the stability of a price with respect to imposed excess demand functions. We normalize the prices in letting $P_1 = 1$ thus we set $P_2 = P$

$$\dot{X}_1 = f_1(P)$$
$$\dot{X}_2 = f_2(P)$$
$$\dot{P} = g(X_1 - X_2) \tag{E.2.1}$$

Given a sufficiently small neighbourhood of the equilibrium we may linearize the functions so we get the linear system

$$\dot{X}_1 = a_0 + a_1 P$$
$$\dot{X}_2 = b_0 + b_1 P$$
$$\dot{P} = c \cdot (dX_1 - dX_2); \tag{E.2.2}$$

(Since c is a scalar we may simplify and set it to 1.)
We thus get the equilibrium price

$$P^* = \frac{a_0 + b_0}{a_1 + b_1} \tag{E.2.3}$$

And we will get the dynamic solution:

$$P = \left(a_0 - b_0\right) \cdot e^{(a_1 + b_1) \cdot t}$$

E.2.4

First of all we have made the process time consuming and this also goes for auctions. But the point here, with respect to general equilibrium theory, is that the stabilization process must always be dealt with in auctions and there exists no market price until the general equilibrium is reached when all the exchange takes place. But this does not concern only one commodity but all commodities in the economy.

We have no false trading. This means that behavioural functions in E.2.1 and E.2.3 are very mysterious with respect to their very existence and eventual measurement. Obviously we see that the relative size of the parameters is of central importance but how do we impose them, otherwise than as postulates? That means that any attempt to measurement fails as a consequence of the fact that the neoclassical equilibrium fulfilling the axiomatic structure has no environment, thus false trading does not exist.

For ordinary dynamic equilibria the stability analysis singles out from the very specification of the dynamic model and will initiate the discussion of the relative inertia of the parameter structure and will usually take social, political and cultural/habitual factors into consideration, which is exogenous to the model.

A change in attitude as described above will also affect the practical econometrical work. Any kind of econometric study has a form of parametric solution which is to be seen as a multivariate average, either from a cross-section view or from a temporal view. If we look at this from the point of view of the neoclassical axiomatic structure implying additive aggregation we obviously have a sort of 'average' but that is trivial since the variance must be zero. Thus for normal studies we must realize that the 'average' parameter structure is only relevant if we pay the utmost attention to the variance and also higher moments, not in the sense that we need to investigate the characteristics of the average but that it provides us with information of the posed problems as such.

The weakness of macroscopic models often depends on the fact that they implicitly work with additive aggregation which we reject with respect to the barter economy. But if we reject the neoclassical picture of the empirical economy this also goes for the definition of the agent. In Chapter 1 we stated rather promptly that we accept that the agent is rational and optimizing, and we stated that the neoclassical rationality in the sense of the three axioms of choice (given the assumption of symmetry) is a necessary feature but not a sufficient one. The reason is that we apply systematically Debreu's setting of an agent $\left(\precsim_i, e_i\right)_t^s$, a preference relation and an endowment vector specified spatially, s, and temporally, t. Thus we here interpret the neoclassical equilibrium as dealing with the very choice given the premeditated contextual environment.

However since we also assume the individual agent as a subject and thus a final cause, the fellow agents are a part of the agent's context in the sense of Arrow's paradox and by all means the Lucas' critique. Thus we cannot as in an ordinary neoclassical analysis see an agent as an independent atom but, as Donne claims, that 'no man is an island'.

When we reject the existence of equilibrium with any extension in time and space, we obviously lose any possibility to create a unique index of measurement as we do in neoclassical theory. The question then is what happens to the concept of money as a medium of exchange/valuation? Obviously nothing – since it is non-existent in neoclassical theory. Money price as valuation is only relevant at local and temporal markets when the agents compare different specifications of frying pans for example relative to their specific use and relative to the prices. But the real systematic valuation is with respect to the specific budget and liquidity condition of the particular agent; thus stability of demand is a matter of social inertia and not of an assumed equilibrium. Thus a condition as *gross-substitutability* is reasonable to assume although we do not derive it from a set of axioms, but due to the existence of limited budgets. The same goes for the economy as a whole but is then due to the lack of intermediate and primary commodities and limited competitiveness in international trade.

However if this is our principle attitude we indeed need to define the characteristics of the agents with which we equip this non-equilibrium economy. They are said to be rational without being rational as we know the concept of rationality which in loose terms may be described as *methodological individualism* and *purposeful action*. The somewhat difficult aspect is methodological individualism which has to be interpreted differently when we allow people to affect and be affected by the macroscopic levels and also to form coalitions, this is of course the result of Arrow's paradox. We must thus postulate that the individuals are free to choose given eventual explicit or implicit social and cultural restrictions.

Debreu's definition of an agent is rather rudimentary; thus given market rationality and the same state space for all agents who all know the true space of outcome and have the same subjective probability distribution, we logically end up in the traditional general equilibrium which also may be extended in space and time. Consequently we need to be a bit more explicit about the characteristics of the agent. Since we are not psychologists we cannot discuss generic psychological behaviour which also is implied by our claim that the agent is a subject. We may however safely drop any assumption that the agent is perfectly informed and furthermore we may add that the agent is sensitive to both the social and physical environment in the consumption decision. We also maintain what we earlier have discussed namely that the rationality only deals with the choice *after* the current context is premeditated.

Epistemic Cycles

Tomas Brody (1994) developed a concept *epistemic cycles* to describe how different researchers in physics could reach different results with respect to experiments and the design of experiments. In Ekstedt and Fusari (2010) this concept is developed more generally.

We claim that agents are rational in the sense of the axioms of choice in the neoclassical theory but also that this is not sufficient to describe human rationality.[1] Human rationality also includes contextual considerations. That means that the context of an agent beside the relevant state space also includes relevant fellow agents and relevant macroscopic structures; thus we define an agent at t as:
Epistemic cycle:

> All agents act with respect to purposes, beliefs, contextual apprehensions at a moment t. Furthermore the agent acts with respect to a preference order at t, concerning purposes at different levels and an assumed endowment vector e_t at t.

Alluding to Debreu's definition of an agent we can define an agent as

$$(C_t, \precsim_t, e_t)$$

The agent is important with respect to an outcome of an action/choice which means that the consumption act might be that the commodity per se is not the purpose but a means to obtain a purpose. This also implies that the preference order is not necessarily linked to a commodity but to a wider purpose. The market rationality related to the very consumption decision may thus be derived from a set of primary decisions related to the ultimate purpose.

The epistemic cycle is in a sense related to the modern household production theory. Consequently the concept of epistemic cycle contains anything that affects the decisions and the actions of an agent. Thus it does not restrict the problem one bit. This is to emphasize that there is no possible way for economists to do research by recreating humans or the world. Our empirical studies have to detect social and cultural inertia which explains the existence of certain inertia.

We may illustrate the concept of epistemic cycle as in Figure 2.1.

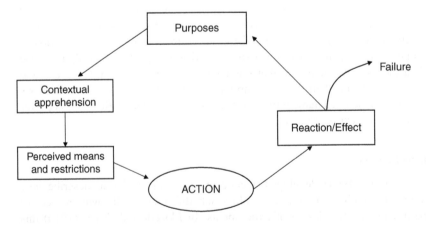

Figure 2.1 Epistemic Cycle

Thus the agent is rational within the realm of an epistemic cycle. This means that we regard the agent as rational in the neoclassical sense, save for pathological cases. Contradicting this would mean that we make some form of normative statement.

The concept of epistemic cycles is important since we then can keep the concept of a rational agent. There are many social scientists claiming that humans are not to be regarded as rational. It is hard to understand that either of the two statements 'human are rational beings' and 'humans are not rational beings' can be finally proved, either by logical reasoning, or by empirical investigations. In fact the very concept of epistemic cycles shows the difficulties. In claiming that humans are rational given a set of epistemic cycles we allow for differences in purposes and contextual apprehensions which might well explain a seemingly irrational behaviour.

The trial of the Norwegian mass-murderer Anders Breivik, a couple of years ago, brought the problem to its edge. One group of psychiatrists and psychologists claimed that Breivik was not rational, which means that he was not responsible for his actions. The reason for this was mainly his bizarre interpretation of the society.

The other group of psychiatrists and psychologists claimed that Breivik's apprehension of the society was not limited to him only but could be found in written texts both on internet and in other sources. Thus he could have deliberately chosen a set of available apprehensions, and given these apprehensions his actions were perfectly rational given his purpose to kill as many people as possible. Consequently he was found guilty of the mass murder and could not be seen as mentally sick to the extent that he was not responsible for his actions. The verdict was clearly in line with the Nürnberg trials and the work of the International Court for War Crimes in Den Haag.

Our attitude here is in line with this latter opinion and regard irrationality as a state of the individual where even the most elementary logic is lacking; thus the individual is inconsistent in analysis and also in action in relation to an eventual analysis.

It is important to note that given an agent the epistemic cycles are attached to actions to achieve some goals. That means that an agent may behave in a seemingly contradictory manner given different purposes/apprehensions; a wish to give help to poor countries may result in work for non-governmental organisations and voting against increasing the public help since such support is believed to be linked to unfavourable conditions for the poor countries, while other agents may choose other solutions depending on different information/ analysis.

Philosophically this means that we break with the Kantian analysis, built on Laplace, in which, given the a priori definitions of the apprehended empirical world and its intrinsic relations, it is possible to reach a unanimous result of the logical analysis. Instead we apply Hume's approach that passion and will (in Hume's sense) are the main determinants and the logical reasoning (reason) is just a mean.

Furthermore choices concerning different aggregate levels may be linked to different epistemic cycles which also might be contradictive. If the cycle is closed, the action has fulfilled the purposes but if the action fails to close the cycle we might reconsider the purposes and contextual interpretations which affect future behaviour. It is also important to note that if the cycle is closed this does not imply that the agent's analysis is correct in an objective sense; it might be completely wrong but the cycle is still occasionally closed. It is then possible that the agent is reinforced in the belief of the preceding analysis which of course is unlucky.

A very important feature of this approach is that the epistemic cycle is attached to the very action, which has a more or less precise position in space-time; thus the prices relevant to the agent are only relevant for actions with respect to the very epistemic cycle. Furthermore, contrary to the division of a state space and the market space in the neoclassical theory, where all the judgements are dependent on the information of the state space which makes the agents objective vectors in the market space, our approach implies that fellow agents and aggregate structures belong *to the apprehended context which affects the agent's decision* and this is congruent with our interpretation of Arrow's paradox.

Obviously we might observe spatial and temporal inertia which might induce us to simplify our analysis to a neoclassical setting but then the adequate inertia is to be argued/proven.

The introduction of epistemic cycles provides us with a primary concept of agents which is attached to the very actions. Furthermore we have a precise abstract structure attached to the action and can thus be used as a logical concept but, and this is important, *epistemic cycles are to be regarded as complexes* with respect to our discussion of Keynes' philosophical position and *not an atomistic variable*. Thus in the neoclassical theory the agents are transformed to vectors in a commodity space where their choice is subject to the manipulator of the price vector. In our setting agents are complex subjects.

Summing up on epistemic cycles:

- An Epistemic Cycle (EC) is a set of concepts and axioms in a certain epistemology which creates a proper logical structure.
- An EC may be inert or dissipative in the sense that influences from the environment may change the epistemology as well as the axioms.
- An EC may be created by a set of systematic observations as well as by scientific traditions.
- An EC may be formed by ethical, historical, religious and cultural traditions.
- An EC may be formed by ignorance, prejudices and lack of information.

Given an EC we may now rather safely assume that the agents are rational and that they are optimizing but now specified by the EC, which, as said before, does not imply that a certain action is a part of an inter-spatial and inter-temporal global optimization.[2]

The concept of epistemic cycles may also be extended to aggregate organizations in the meaning that the organization in question has a formal body which makes decisions. Examples of such formal bodies are public organizations at local, regional, national and international levels but also companies and non-governmental organizations. The made decisions express the relations between the organization and consequently all the people of within the dimensions of responsibility of the organizations and its environment in adequate dimensions.[3]

When it comes to informal aggregate levels as customs, ethical conventions and similar we obviously cannot speak of epistemic cycles, but these are underlying any agreement between groups of individuals and a break of an agreement may affect the agent in question by for example bad reputation and moral stigma.

Thus we can most probably dismiss the idea of a global rationality and optimality. The aggregate rationality is not necessarily contradictive to the contained individual agents' rationality, this also follows as we have seen from the discussion of Arrow's paradox, but the aggregate optimality does not follow from any additive aggregation of individual optimization. Thus an aggregate decision may well be optimal given an appropriate epistemic cycle which is involved in the decision of an eventual aggregate body or a group of agents, but the condition is of course that the concerned individual agents contained in the aggregate are willing (or forced) to accept the aggregate decision. Thus if I object to the implicit ethics involved in the decisions of the company in which I work, I can always quit, but if I stay it is a sign that the reasons for staying are obviously stronger than the degree of my ethical irritation.

So the voting agent, which Arrow left us with in his paradox, must have a willingness to subordinate to a coalition. However since the epistemic cycles governing their 'voting' behaviour with respect to aggregate matters are most probably different among the agents since they are *subjects*, aggregation may appear in many forms.

Epistemic Cycles in Relation to Aggregation

When using preference theory as it appears in the neoclassical theory given an *epistemic cycle* the result is not in any sense related to those we would have in the neoclassical world; it is different but in what way it is hard to tell.

We described an epistemic cycle as a set of purposes, means and contextual apprehensions which lead to actions. The cycle is completed when purposes are fulfilled, and not completed when that is not the case. From the individual agent's point of view an epistemic cycle may be regarded as fulfilled even if the foregoing analysis was entirely wrong but the purposes still were fulfilled by chance and the contrary case may also appear. This means that the agent might be strengthened in the apprehension of the environment as well as the analysis although it is basically wrong from some point of view. Furthermore a non-closed epistemic cycle gives rise to a reconsideration of contextual apprehensions and/or purposes and means. Thus this kind of partial analysis is similar to an ex post/ex ante analysis and is by its very character open to learning and reconsiderations and consequently dynamic.

It also brings another feature, thoroughly discussed in Ekstedt and Fusari (2010), that concerns the very concept of social time and we will discuss it later on. In a social time-space causality, in Hume's sense, one of the central issues is that a change in behaviour of surrounding individuals creates new kinds of logical structures for an individual. The neoclassical theory has in fact given rise to a risk analysis which is static and devastating with respect to dynamic analysis; its fundamental risk-creating factor is the surrounding state space, which is possible to analyse in probability terms. This has in its turn given rise to analysis of so called decision trees, which may be of value given the appropriate context but it is a completely static risk analysis. With respect to *uncertainty* in Keynes' meaning such analysis completely misses the point. The fundamental risk-creating factor in the market economy is the individuals themselves and their very ability to perform analysis right or wrong of the market structure, the state space and of the aggregate levels, and also that these misjudgements both affect and are affected by aggregate levels.[4]

There is a kind of 'softer' logic concerning the whole and its parts compared with the traditional set theory, *mereology*. The author is not frightfully fond of it although it has a point that analysing complexes is different from analysing atomistic facts. Mereology was initially developed by the Polish logician Leśnievsky as some kind of escape from Russell's paradox. However here we must dive into this latter paradox to see its relation to our problem of aggregation.

In relation to probability we mentioned in Chapter 1 when we deal with complexes these must be very carefully analysed with respect to their structural connotations in order to be transformed to atomistic variables. The important thing about atomistic variables is that they can safely be replaced by abstract algebraic denotations and thus can be treated mathematically. This is exactly what Wittgenstein means in proposition 6.211 where he writes:

> In real life a mathematical proposition is never what we want. Rather, we make use of mathematical propositions only in inferences from propositions that do not belong to mathematics to others that likewise do not belong to mathematics. (In philosophy the question, 'What do we actually use this word or this proposition for?' repeatedly leads to valuable insight.)
>
> (Wittgenstein 1974[1921]: 65)

Atomistic variables are defined independent of context while complexes are context dependent.

The agents produced by the neoclassical axiomatic structure are defined as vectors in the commodity space which is a measurable Euclidian space. To do so we must be able to treat both commodities and agents as atomistic variables. That implicitly means that all agents are facing the same context and for all commodities it holds that the physical entities are defining their role as commodities, thus either all items of commodity x_i have exactly the same physical features or all items of commodity x_i possess a substance which is the same for all items of x_i and which is desired by the agents.

So defined we may look at two sets of agents, s_i and s_j, which we may obtain by enumerating the different vectors. Let these sets of agents belong to an aggregate set $[s_i, s_j] \subseteq S_i$, and we can go on proceeding with the creation of new sets.

Thus for the universal set S* we find that the set $[s_1, ..., s_i, ..., s_n, S_1 ..., S_m]$ $\subseteq S^* \wedge S^* \subseteq [s_1, ..., s_i, ..., s_n, S_1 ..., S_m]$, which implies that the universal set of agents is a set of agents. Consequently in Russell's terms neoclassical sets of agents belong to *non-proper sets*.

> Russell's paradox: *Let S* denote the set of all sets which are not members of themselves. Then S* neither belongs to itself nor not belongs to itself.*
> *Formally we thus have*
>
> $$S^* = \{x \mid x \notin x\} \, then \, S^* \in S^* \, if \, f \, S^* \notin S^*.$$

We have an example of nonproper sets above. Characteristic of these is that we may switch names and enumerations without affecting the logical structure and analysis. This does not hold for a proper set. A simple example is brands of cars: we can form a set C* of all BMWs and all Fiats but the set C* does not belong to itself since it is not a brand. But since the concept of car is a complex which is structurally defined both BMW and Fiat it may fulfil the basic structural definition but still be completely different in other structural dimensions than those appearing in the definition of the concept car. Thus proper classes are equipped with complex elements.

If we then transform the agents to be represented by the epistemic cycles, which actually Debreu is on his way to do in his definition of an agent $(\precsim_i, e_i)^s_t$, which is indexed spatially and temporally, we find that the agents 'equipped' with epistemic cycles contain theoretically all other agents' actual and potential actions. Thus any agent a_i belongs to the context of all other agents $a_1, \ldots, a_{i-1}$, $a_{i+1}, \ldots a_n$ but then the universal class $A^* \supseteq [a_1, \ldots, a_{i-1}, a_i, a_{i+1}, \ldots a_n]$ does not belong to itself and thus a class of agents defined as earlier belongs to proper classes in Russell's terminology.

Subsequently any aggregate deciding body, formal or informal, does not belong to the class of agents it concerns consequently any decision in the meaning of additive aggregation is independent of the individual agents with respect to simple addition.

We can then state the following proposition:

Proposition 2.1:

> Assume a system A* consisting of a finite number of subsystems, which are to be regarded as proper classes, $s_1 \, \text{---} \, s_n$. If then we have a measure allowing us to define an optimizing rule both on A* as well as $s_1 \, \text{---} \, s_n$; optimization of the global system A* must imply that at least one of the subsystems s_i must sub-optimize.

> If on the other hand all the subsystems, s_1 --- s_n are optimized according to the same optimizing process the global system A^* must sub-optimize.
>
> (Ekstedt 2012: 83)

Given Proposition 2.1 we realize that optimum is possible for organizations on any aggregate level independently of eventual optimum on any other level. That does not mean that the different aggregate decision levels of a system are independent of each other but this is more connected to the question whether the organization *per se* is accepted. Second, following the technique in Arrow's paradox, no epistemic cycle can be formed by an abstract organizational entity on any aggregate level but is formed by its individual members of the deciding body relative to its institutional and/or hierarchical form. That means that we do not accept any organisational metaphysics as maintained by the 19th century bureaucratic philosophers like von Treitschke's 'Welt Geist'. The humans and the peculiarities in their relations form all kind of institutional decisions.

The third aspect implicit in the concept of epistemic cycles and the derived proposition is that the factor which is most important for the stability of the existence of epistemic cycles and decision entities on higher aggregate levels (if it is not stabilized with sheer repressive power) is the relation between the aggregate structures and its contained individual epistemic cycles. So what was a problem in the analysis of Arrow's paradox becomes now something very important for aggregate stability.

Fundamental for the use of the concept epistemic cycle is that we focus of the agents' actions and the inertia of behaviour. Theoretically however we cannot derive any link from action to the purposes of the agents like we do according to the *correlate of revealed preferences* with respect to the axioms of the neoclassical theory, since we cannot say anything of the agents' apprehension of the context.

In the analysis of Arrow's paradox we pointed out that the agents have the ability to act on information of the aggregate results which means that some epistemic cycles of an agent may involve apprehensions of different aggregate levels depending on the actual purposes of the agent, thus the agent is actually defining the appropriate context which means that agents with the same purposes may apprehend different contexts and thus arrive at different conclusions with respect to actions on the aggregate levels.

Furthermore we have achieved to derive a logical rational for Wicksell's differentiation of stability on the microscopic level and stability on the macroscopic level. But before we can discuss this we have a gigantic logical/semantical problem to deal with, which also links us to Keynes' discussions on atomistic and complex variables.

Keynes' Philosophical Contribution

There has been much ado about whether Keynes really developed a theory of a similar kind as the neoclassical theory or what he really was up to.

The multiplier and the marginal propensity to consume was discussed already by both Hume and Smith although not as explicit concepts and the famous Say's law, put into relation to what Say actually has written, is nothing else but a discussion of a multiplier process. Since Say rejected general price vectors and prices as general measures it is indeed hard to claim that he invented a 'law' in the meaning used by neoclassical economists and which also Keynes thought.

Disequilibrium of the economy was thoroughly discussed by Knut Wicksell when he discriminated between the bank rate and the growth rate. Moreover he made a clear difference between microscopic and macroscopic equilibrium (Wicksell 1937 [1922]: 222).

Often Keynes is interpreted only with respect to small parts of his General Theory of Employment, Interest and Money (GT), which also is the foundation for Hicks' famous interpretation from 1937.[5] If we start with the latter, Hicks in his article from 1980 admits that he did not really understood Keynes' approach to money and uncertainty in his paper from 1937. He also looks at Keynes' contribution in GT from a much broader perspective.

It is important to realize that Keynes when he wrote GT on one hand had written two volumes on money: *Treatise on Money* (1929), where he discusses the concept of liquidity and *Indian Currency* (1908) where he thoroughly discusses the principle of prime and secondary currencies with respect to pricing and trade in the involved countries. The later volume it is very valuable for those who want to understand Keynes' position in the Bretton Woods negotiations.[6] In *The Economic Consequences of the Peace* (1920), which he wrote as a critique of the Versailles Peace Treaty, and where he shows fundamental awareness of the economy as a social and cultural subsystem and that economic factors interrelate with social and cultural factors. In the last chapter he forecasts the future in a dreary way and it showed up that he unfortunately was right. Perhaps the most important contribution from a scientific point of view is *Treatise on Probability* (1921).

The latter is particularly important since it is not a textbook in statistical theory but a philosophical discussion of the concepts of induction and probability in the tradition of Moore, Russell and Hume. It seems however that he is more close to Hume than to Russell since Hume more treats the psychological and the social concepts of knowledge and observation and thus is nearer the social sciences, while Russell discusses from a formal view of logical atomism.

Keynes' link between money and uncertainty is well known but unfortunately the roots of uncertainty in considerations on empirical induction have come to be rather obscure. Kolmogorov's Strong and Weak Laws of large numbers and the formal apparatus which has grown around them are of course a standard tool of the researcher and as long the relevant problem fulfils the mathematical conditions stochastic problems imply no difficulty for very limited problems.

It is exactly here that the difference between science of objects and science of subjects enters. Norbert Wiener (1950) claimed that natural scientists have an honourable opponent since the nature does not consciously adapt to human research while the social scientist cannot assume this and furthermore the social scientist is also an acting subject beside the role of being a scientist. A problem in natural sciences can often be assumed to be closed due to observed inertia while in social sciences where the research object is a subject and a final cause the problem is *per definition* open.

Thus when discussing economic science, particularly on the macroscopic level we are seldom discussing the administration of well organized experiments but more or less well founded axioms/assumptions and observations of which the degree of social and cultural generality are normally difficult to judge.

It is in this very context Keynes' discussion of probability, induction and uncertainty appears. Thus as long as we stick to the earlier discussed neoclassical axioms concerning the individual agent and the aggregate economy there is no reason to apply the laws of large numbers, but Keynes' concept of *insufficient reason* cuts like a knife through our analysis. Thus are there sufficient reasons to assume that the axioms are *bona fide* with respect to our empirical problem? This is actually the underlying fundament in our discussion of the rational expectation hypothesis when formed into an operational model.

In discussing Keynes it is important to realize that he set out in his youth aiming for philosophical research. The atmosphere in Cambridge when Keynes started there was a melting pot for philosophical discussions; Russell and Whitehead were finishing *Principia Mathematica* (1927 [1910]), G.E. Moore had recently, 1903, completed his *Principia Ethica*, the young Wittgenstein made his entrance, just to mention some of the impressive personages. Keynes was, like Smith and Marx, first attracted by philosophy and particularly ethics and Moore's work became the primary source of ideas. But at variance with Smith and Marx he came to become more and more interested in logics and logical atomism, no doubt affected by his intellectual environment, to which he tried to adapt but became more and more doubtful about in certain dimensions.

However we have no intention to go through Keynes' philosophical development but stick to Davis' view:

> The view here is not that Keynes's involvement with economic reasoning caused him to re-select among preferred, traditional concepts and theories, and that this arose from an intention to alter his traditional philosophical affiliations. Rather the view here is more radical in supposing that Keynes's changing concerns and increasing allegiance philosophical reasoning to economic thinking per se disrupted the integrity of philosophical reasoning itself for Keynes so that his philosophical concepts, as they operated in a transformed guise in the language of his economics came to possess different roles for those which were customary for philosophical concepts in pure philosophy.
>
> (Davis 1994: 7)

I think that Davis' approach also at least partially can be reversed; thus Keynes' philosophical and economic thinking were affecting his thoughts in a way which is rather difficult to determine for non-specialists.

We will concentrate on Keynes' approaches to aggregation and probability and the problem of scientific induction with respect to causal structures. It is then important to be reminded of the role Hume's scepticism played in the philosophical discussions in Cambridge for the development of the anti-idealistic attitude and also for Keynes' attitudes to scientific induction and probability. Considering our earlier discussion of the rational expectation hypothesis Davis writes:

> In short, policy recommendation could never flow from positive economic analysis itself, since 'ought to' and 'is' were on two separate, incommunicable planes of discourse, and (following Hume) one could never argue from 'is' to 'ought'.
>
> (Ibid.: 56)

Keynes gives rise to two aspects of how expectations are formed, we then disregard the very content of the expectations and just deal with the forms.

The two aspects are both in GT Chapter 12 and they can be made to coincide. The first aspect deals with the aspects of risk and uncertainty. As a matter of fact if we strain our interpretation a bit we might say that Keynes anticipates to a certain extent the principle content of Allais' paradox. Allais' paradox is of course more precise from a technical aspect but Keynes as an able mathematician and statistician would not have any difficulties in having such associations. We could actually speak of the variance as a sort of uncertainty, thus the arguments of Allais' paradox are *mean value* and the *entropy of the distribution*.[7] In subjective terms we may call a situation with higher entropy, given the mean value, as a situation of less degree of confidence. Keynes writes:

> The state of long-term expectation, upon which our decisions are based, does not solely depend, therefore, on the most probable forecast we can make. It also depends on the *confidence* with which we make this forecast – on how highly we rate the likelihood of our best forecast turning out quite wrong. If we expect large changes but are very uncertain as to what precise form these changes will take, then our confidence will be weak [original emphasis].
>
> (Keynes 1973 [1936]: 148)

The second aspect deals with the nature of forecasts and there he makes some comments which might be seen as similar to rational expectation particularly if we stress an interpretation in the line of Campbell's law, which we quoted in Chapter 1. Keynes writes:

> We are assuming, in effect that the existing market valuation, however arrived at, is uniquely *correct* in relation to our existing knowledge of the facts which will influence the yield of the investment, and that it will only change in proportion to the knowledge; though, philosophically speaking, it

cannot be uniquely correct, since our existing knowledge does not provide a sufficient basis for a calculated mathematical expectation.

(Ibid.: 152)

More specifically Keynes presents his famous beauty contest as a relevant example of market behaviour. The example is indeed relevant in economics since it coincides with the assumption that prices contain all relevant information which is a fundamental correlate to the neoclassical theory of market behaviour, but the problem is that unless there is a 'correct' common opinion, which everybody sticks to, as assumed in the rational expectation hypothesis, we are in for a vicious circle.

Keynes' discussions in chapter twelve of GT deal with the investment problem; thus in principle it deals with a microscopic decision for a supposedly well-defined market sector. If we now assume that the expectations are dealing with the effects of macroscopic decisions covering the whole economy we may very well think that some agents judge the effects in relation to some neoclassical/Keynesian or some Marxist/heterodox theory, but with respect to those who are not convinced that the theory in charge for the moment is fully adequate; what do we do with them? Shall we do like the Chinese authorities during the Cultural Revolution, send people to re-thinking/re-education courses?

When discussing expectations Keynes looked at them from a rational perspective, not that a rational perspective necessarily is rational but anyway it is good to find a slightly more intellectually satisfying way than reading the intestines of a fish or manipulate Tarot cards to form opinions on future events and ways of action. The general forecast 'it will be the same weather tomorrow as today' might be perfectly rational in inland areas due to observed inertia although it is less often so on the coast.

Please note the word *actions*; foreseeing events is one thing but considering relevant actions with respect to an event is something else which Allais' paradox is a simple illustration of. Thus we seldom put intellectual efforts into forecasting the future if the forecast concerns, for us, an irrelevant set of potential events. Having said this we must however consider that events in a broad and general meaning are seldom atomistic but have secondary, tertiary or more side effects, consequently forecasting the economy might involve a rather broad context. Thus strictly speaking the very first rather crude limitation of the problem, more based on passion and less on reason, inserts most probably some of the more serious misapprehensions in our final analysis. It is at this stage that the basic ontological and epistemological idiosyncrasies play the most important role in analysing the society even when it concerns factors that directly influence the individual not to speak of analysing macroscopic events and development. Thus the rational expectation hypothesis seems to be correct even for the macroscopic level although perhaps not in Muth's and Lucas' sense but more in Campbell's and Keynes' sense and furthermore there is probably not one theory hovering in the air but a quite substantial flock of theories combined with dreams.

A rational analysis must actually take these things into consideration even firm believers of forecasting according to Keynes' beauty test must somewhere realise that it leads to a vicious circle and thus breaks down as a tool, irrespective of the degree of information.

Keynes' attitude to probability has thus two sides: one concerns the forecast *per se*, and the other concerns the confidence in the forecast. We must however be aware that the latter factor on one hand concerns the more technical problems discussed within Allais' paradox and on the other the adequacy of the problem formulation *per se* and also the appropriateness of the forecast and subsequent inferences.

Moore's Paradox

Keynes' philosophical interest for probability and induction goes back to the early 20th century when he wrote a paper titled 'Miscellanea ethica' and strongly affected by G.E. Moore's ethics.[8] Alfred Whitehead, who was one of his examiners, was very critical. In Skidelsky (2003:109) we read 'that he [Keynes] raged against Whitehead's incompetence as an examiner, claiming that he had not bothered to try to understand what he was saying.' I am sure that those readers who are academic teachers recognize the type of critique from students. However it is interesting to scrutinize what Whitehead should have understood.

It starts with the so called Moore's paradox in the weak form: $p \wedge A(\neg p)$ where A stands for 'I believe', so we read '*p is and I believe not p*'. It seems as an obvious contradiction but when it comes to the pure logical analysis it is not, since a states about *what is* and A($\neg$p) tells us about what *I believe*.

The most radical form of Moore's paradox is however $a \wedge \neg a$ which is read *p and not p* and here the contradiction is obvious.

The strong form is probably most used by blue-eyed idealists and religious/political activists, who impute a moral dimension and then separate what is with what ought to be. Thus policy recommendations are built on what ought to be, not on what is.

However when looking at Moore's paradox as it stands it is easy to wonder whether philosophers are doing anything but playing around with words and concepts without any purpose but to shock the common sense.

However the way we express the very paradox is indeed deceitful when using the notion p for the matter that is or that we believe. In literature examples are given that p is expressing 'it is raining' which does not meet the case of the hidden problem properly. I can say 'it is raining but not raining since its drizzling' that is in the neighbourhood of an interesting interpretation but drizzling could be seen as a subset of states in a set of states of raining.

The point is that the paradox concerns the difference between atomistic facts and complexes. If we look at the two colours blue and red in the colour circle we have an almost continuous interval where blue turns into red via violet which can be of more reddish or bluish kind. So somewhere in this continuum we have to say 'it is not violet but blue/red'. Thus the statement 'p is red' could be answered

'Yes – but actually not red but more violet'. Furthermore the determination may also be affected by the light conditions.

Moore's paradox thus concerns variables which require contextual determinations of which different interpretations can exist.[9]

We saw for example in the first chapter how Lucas interpreted the neoclassical theory in trying to squeeze it into a context where the equilibrium approximately held, while our approach was that this is not allowed if we shall use logical conclusions based on the axiomatic structure *per se* at the same time since that would imply false trading. Lucas was thus trying to enlarge the possible field for interpretation which certainly is legitimate although a priori axiomatic structures are perhaps not the best start for such enlarging.

Thus Moore's paradox, in its radical form, seems to be a magnificent contradiction and given *p* as defined in an *atomistic sense* it indeed is a contradiction, save for lack of information, emotional agitation and similar things. But if we regard *p* as a complex it does not need to be a contradiction.

Keynes was thus inspired to work on the problem of rational beliefs. He then worked within the realms of atomistic logic for studying the concept of probability with relation to induction in fact his aims were somewhat foreshadowing Popper's discussions on proving/disapproving propositions. To quote Keynes:

> In the ordinary course of thought and argument we are constantly asserting the truth of one statement, while not *proving* another, is nevertheless *some ground* for believing the second. We assert that, with the evidence at our command, we *ought* to hold such and such a belief.... We recognize that *objectively* evidence can be *real* evidence and yet not *conclusive* evidence. [original emphasis]
>
> (Keynes in Skidelsky (2003: 109))

The quote is interesting in the sense that Keynes obviously leaves the world of atomistic logic and discusses complex propositions; thus to answer *no* to a proposition A implies that we should be able to describe the non-A. In atomistic logic non-A is just the complement of A but thinking in complexes and structures implies usually that we may have both A and non-A with characteristics of some kind. In politics this is obvious when we look at referendums where we have a structured alternative X as the YES-alternative and the complement is NO but that is not structured, which may imply that the NO-side might consist of contradictory opinions.[10]

Moore's influence on Keynes is noteworthy in a broader perspective since Moore was one of the front figures in the opposition against idealism. According to Bertrand Russell, Moore led the rebellion against idealism (Copleston 1966: 403). An important step in this rebellion was to deliberate logics from its real content. Thus a logical analysis in itself has no normative value. Copleston expresses it: 'it looks at first sight as though Moore were creating an unbridgeable gulf between the world of propositions, which is the sphere of truth and falsity, and the world of non-propositional reality or facts' (ibid.). Thus the *logical truth* of a proposition is independent of any interpretation/inference in relation to the reality.

In the first chapter we showed that the axiomatic structure of the neoclassical theory is actually copying a logical form, namely that of an equivalence relation. Thus we want to show that if we have two spaces, the commodity space and the preference space, we postulate that the structure of the preference space, which somehow is interior to the agent, is applicable at the commodity space. Consequently the agents are defined in the commodity space by their preference function and their initial endowments. This implies that the logical operations become normative and furthermore the agent so defined have no complement space to be in except the case when we reject the logical structure *in toto*.

As empirical scientists we know however that market behaviour may well be described by neoclassical theory given sufficient inertia but that is a local and temporal equilibrium with no normative role.

From an ethical point of view Moore's approach might imply that we could develop a rational ethics in the sense that the logical structure is consistent and after that conceptualize the real world variables which should/'ought to' be used in the ethical analysis, which implies a closed logical system. This applies rather well as we see to the neoclassical model. The logical system is consistent and thus all propositions based on the axiomatic structure are true, but the intrinsic eventual ethics is just one of at least two possible interpretations. In the case of the neoclassical general equilibrium we can say, in line with the Nash-equilibrium, that if all agents will treat their fellow agents' utility functions as restrictions of their own. Such a formulation is in the neighbourhood of Kant's imperative. Thus we define exogenously how the axiomatic structure should be treated ethically.

There are two caterpillars in this salad and they are the closeness of the system and the definition of the variables. The closeness implies that it dwells within the frames of Gödel's paradox, thus you have to scrutinize the relevance of the axioms and if any is rejected the whole building falls. The definitions of the variables must be atomistic in order to have uniqueness of the propositions. That means that variables which are complex will not do. Thus if you point at a person and say: 'This is John and he is bald-headed' John is an atomistic variable while 'bald-headed' is more complex if we can think of degrees of 'not being bald-headed'. It is a matter of further definitions. In this case the definition of non-baldheadedness also defines the baldheadedness, while if we had taken hair colour instead non-black hair is not defined as a complement to black hair in the sense that it is a colour. Thus to define A, we must define not-A properly. This will be of importance when we discuss Keynes' attitudes to probability when dealing with complex variables.

Bertrand Russell rounds up the discussion when he states:

> Attributes and relations, though they may be not susceptible of analysis, differ from substances by the fact that they suggest structure, and that there can be no significant symbol which symbolizes them in isolation.
>
> (Russell (2007 [1924]: 337)

In our discussion of the neoclassical axiomatic structure we rejected the axiom of reflexivity on these grounds. The commodity as a physical item or defined process is a substance while this very substance as a commodity is part of the momentary consumption structure of the agent. Furthermore our discussions on Arrow's paradox led to a rejection of the neoclassical axiomatic structure when we allowed people who might affect or be affected by the aggregate levels, which then implied an open system which rejects the relevance of the axioms of choice, in particular the axiom of reflexivity, and subsequently the created equivalence relation.

In Chapter 1 we quoted Wittgenstein's proposition 6.211. This proposition is in a way inspired by Moore's paradox and describes the relations between logic and the reality. We repeat the proposition 6.211

> Indeed in real life a mathematical proposition is never what we want. Rather, we make use of mathematical propositions *only* in inferences from propositions that do not belong to mathematics to others that likewise do not belong to mathematics. (In philosophy the question, 'What do we actually use this word or this proposition for?' repeatedly leads to valuable insights.

In Ekstedt and Fusari (2010) this proposition was illustrated as in Figure 2.2.

Anyway Keynes set out to analyse probability and 'rational beliefs' and thus had to deal with the concepts of probability/possibility and inference/implication. I have no access to Keynes' dissertation but from Skidelsky (2003), Davis (1994) and Winslow (1986) I understand that the very foundation of the Whitehead criticism was that Keynes tried to solve this problem using atomistic logical analysis as a tool and this is an impossible task regarding our discussion of complexes

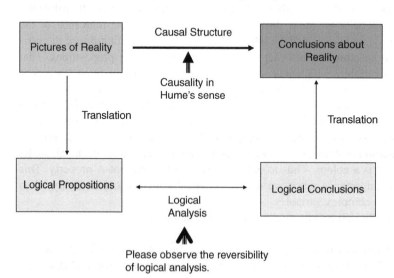

Figure 2.2 Wittgenstein prop. 6.211

above. Whitehead expresses his principle way of reasoning concerning atomistic variables and complexes:

> The notion of 'probability', in the widest sense of that term, presents a puzzling philosophical problem. The mathematical theory of probability is based upon certain statistical assumptions. When these assumptions hold, the meaning of probability is simple; and the only remaining difficulties are concerned with the technical mathematical development. But it is not easy to understand how the statistical theory can apply to all cases to which the notion of more or less probability is habitually applied. For example, when we consider – as we do consider – the probability of some scientific conjecture as to the internal constitution of the stars, or as to the future of human society after some unprecedented convulsion, we seem to be influenced by some analogy which is very difficult to convert into an appeal to any definite statistical fact.
>
> (Whitehead 1978 [1929]: 201)

Thus Whitehead's critique of Keynes' first efforts was in fact rather fundamental and my opinion is that there is not much for Whitehead to understand apart from the very purpose since he dismisses the very foundation of the analysis of this purpose so there is not much to improve as it needed a complete rethink. Keynes' complaints are thus unjustified.

Physics and Social Sciences: Inference and Induction

However Keynes took the critique seriously and revised his approach. Whitehead did support him and when we ten years later meet Keynes in *Treatise on Probability* he shows that he has taken Whitehead's critique to his heart. This book was and is very influential as some kind of watershed. It is instructive to go through some of the most controversial passages and the discussions they have provoked.

When it comes to judging the reliability of an estimation of probability concerning complex arguments Keynes elaborates on the question of sufficient and insufficient reason which also involves a link from subjective probability estimations to uncertainty. In *Treatise on Probability* he writes:

> The question to be raised in this chapter is somewhat novel; after much consideration I remain uncertain as to how much importance to attach to it. The magnitude of the probability of an argument, in the sense discussed in Chapter III, depends upon a balance between what may be termed the favourable and the unfavourable evidence; a new piece of evidence which leaves this balance unchanged, also leaves the probability of the argument unchanged. But it seems that there may be another respect in which some kind of quantitative comparison between arguments is possible. This comparison turns upon a balance not between the favourable and the unfavourable

evidence, but between the absolute amounts of relevant knowledge and of relevant ignorance respectively.

(Keynes 1962 [1921]: 71)

Underlying the whole discussion above is of course the problem of empirical induction. *Mathematical induction* is based on Peano's axiom which states:[11]
Peano's Axiom:

If a Set S of numbers contains zero and also the successor of every number in S, then every number is in S.

Proposition:

Assume any natural number n ρ 3 then proposition A holds

$A:\quad 3^n \geq 2 \cdot n^2 + 3 \cdot n$

Proof:

For n = 3 the proposition obviously holds

$B:\quad 3^n - 2 \cdot n^2 - 3 \cdot n \geq 0$

Developing B with respect to the left part (LP) we get

$$LP = 3 \cdot 3^n - 2 \cdot (n+1)^2 - 3 \cdot (n+1)$$

Inserting $n \geq 3$ gives us

$$LP \geq 3 \cdot (2 \cdot n^2 + 3n) - 2 \cdot (n+1)^2 - 3 \cdot (n+1) =$$
$$= 4 \cdot n^2 + 2 \cdot n - 5 \geq 4 \cdot 3^2 + 2 \cdot 3 - 5 = 37 \geq 0$$

Thus we have proven A for the number 4 and subsequently given Peano's axiom, that if we assume a Set Φ of natural numbers for which the condition A holds; all natural numbers n ρ 3 belong to Set Φ.

Q.E.D.

Thus mathematical induction leads to *implication*, which for the above case is that n ρ 3 $\Rightarrow$ A is true, and the proof only concerned number 3 and the subsequent number 4 and then we applied the axiom.

The links between mathematical and empirical induction are seemingly a natural link but it is a deceitful impression and it is here the whole problem of atomistic logic and complex variable enters. The quote from Whitehead as well as Figure 2.2 and its underlying quote from Wittgenstein state the art of the problem. Thus in order to use any kind of association whatsoever to mathematical induction, we must transform our variables into an atomistic setting where the real variables can be replaced by numbers. Consequently we have the restriction that the real variables should be defined in the relevant dimensions such that they belong to non-proper classes using the terminology of Russell's paradox.[12]

A set of quotes from Keynes, Russell and Brody give a hint of the kind of difference it is between Keynes' more social point of view and the philosophers based in the art of thinking in natural sciences. Keynes criticized Russell mainly on the use of the concepts *inference* in relation to the concept *implication*.

> The distinction between the Relative Logic of Inference and Probability, and Mr. Russell's Universal Logic of Implication, seems to be that the former is concerned with the relations of propositions in general to a particular limited *group*. Inference and Probability depend for their importance upon the fact that in actual reasoning the limitation of our knowledge presents us with a particular set of propositions, to which we must relate any other proposition about which we seek knowledge. The course of an argument and the results of reasoning depend, not simply on what is true, but on the particular body of knowledge from which we have set out.
>
> (Ibid.:118–119)

Keynes seems to claim that the arguments of a propositional function must always be specified as atomistic variables implying that complexes, which are subject to different interpretations, must be brought to a structure meaningful to the propositional function.

Russell seems to answer to this in Chapter 5 in *Human Knowledge*, where he ends his comments on Keynes:

> My conclusion is that the chief *formal* defect in Keynes's theory of probability consists in his regarding probability as a relation between propositions rather than between propositional functions. The application to propositions, I should say, belongs to the *uses* of the theory, not the theory itself.
>
> (Russell 1948: 397)

A precise critique of Keynes comes from Thomas Brody. This critique is also interesting because it implicitly formulates the divorce between social and natural sciences with respect to the nature of the concept of probability and how to deal with complexes. Brody's critique is indeed sensible with respect to natural sciences, particularly physics which is his subject and I certainly agree with him, as long as it concerns physics but Keynes was never a physicist and his philosophical considerations emanated out of knowledge and studies of the society where he treated humans as acting subjects, thus complexes. Brody writes:

> For the subjectivist interpretations probability concerns a proposition and more specifically our view of that proposition, and no experimental component is offered. The link to any observed frequency then poses an insoluble problem. To circumvent it, peculiar abstract principles, such as principles of

insufficient reason (Keynes 1921) or the stability of long run frequencies (Hacking 1966), must be invoked. But they are apt to fail at the critical moment; insufficient reason gives rise to paradoxes, and probability can be meaningfully used even if there are no stable long-term runs. The profound divorce between theory and experiment in the subjectivist conceptions appears again in their inability to incorporate the Kolmogorov axioms in a natural way: indeed, the actual use of the betting quotients that some of them take as a starting point may not even conform to these axioms.

(Brody 1993: 124)

Let us look at a skeleton of an answer from Keynes, thus written already in 1921, so it is in his polemic with Russell:

Ultimately, indeed, Mr. Russell cannot avoid concerning himself with groups. For his aim is to discover the smallest set of propositions which specify our formal knowledge, and then to show that they do in fact specify it. In this enterprise, being human, he must confine himself to that part of formal truth which we know, and the question, how far his axioms compre- hend *all* formal truth, must remain insoluble. But his object, nevertheless, is to establish a train of implications between formal truths; and the character and the justification of rational argument as such is not his subject.

(Keynes 1921: 119)

When we make an inference from a probability analysis, let us think of a perfectly objective probability function; we still have two aspects to consider as Maurice Allais (1953) pointed out: the intrinsic structure of the two moments *mean* and *variance* may change with respect to a binary *choice* when alternatives not involved in the binary *choice* are added to the space of outcomes, but when we handle complexes we have an 'error term' in the very transformation of an aspect of the complex into an atomistic variable.

When pointing out that Keynes deals with the content of the propositional function, the very proposition, it is relevant if the problem is such that the form of the propositional function displays a unique result. Mathematics, as logics of a more general character, is a language directed towards precision and uniqueness of proposition. If we look at a standard conditional frequency function: $(x \mid y) = \dfrac{p(x, y)}{p_y(y)}$, this means that we have to regard the set of outcomes y as defined in an atomistic way or at least near so.

We may take as an example the presidential election in USA in 2008, Obama vs. McCain. According to the polls McCain had a lead up until the bankruptcy of Lehman Brothers after which there was a substantial swing in the opinion (according to polls).

If we want to analyse the causal structure of such a change in opinion there are a couple of principal questions. A standard explanation is that the Lehman

Brothers disaster implied a shift in the focus of the potential voters. But based on ordinary polls this question cannot be answered. Furthermore the assumed change in opinion displays an instability in that very opinion so we do not really know if what is assumed to have happened really happened. We neither know if the Lehman Brothers disaster was important at all but just a coincidence in an ongoing change and at best some sort of catalyst. We know however that extra polls were done in order to test such questions but still the space of outcomes in these polls are complex and apparently unstable; thus using the polls requires a moment of reflexion on the quality in different aspects of the polls and at the bottom of such reflexions we find *the question of the reason for rational belief*.

So, different from these considerations, not in kind but in degrees, are the experimental sciences and there we find the difference between Brody and Keynes and which actually Keynes spelt out in his letter to Harrod in 1937. The very aim of the experimental activity is to refine the definition of the variables, which are almost always complex to a less or higher degree, and bring the definition in line with the scientific purpose. We thus try to single out a minimum structural definition which we hold constant in subsequent experiments, which then will be an almost atomic fact.

The problem with social sciences in the deepest sense, as we have mentioned earlier, is that humans are subjects and thus final causes.

Thus Keynes' answer to Brody is that working with complexes implies that the functional form will be affected by our a priori knowledge of the problem in question.

Torretti (1999) enters the discussion by claiming that 'Research in this area – known as inductive logic, but also more modestly, as confirmation theory – is one of the blindest alleys in twentieth century philosophy.' And he proceeds:

> Keynes (1921) conceived probability as a quantitative relation between statements based on their meanings. A similar idea was adumbrated by Wittgenstein (1922, 5.15-5.156). From this standpoint, given two statements *h* and *e* say, the probability that *h* is true if *e* is true is a real number p(*h*,*e*) in the closed interval [0, 1], which depends solely on what *h* and *e* say. Thus a statement such as '**p**(*h*,*e*) = 0.75' is a logical truth. If *h* is a scientific hypothesis and e is the conjunction of all available evidence, **p**(*h*,*e*) can be regarded as a measure of confirmation of *h* and *e*. Clearly, a relation of this sort can only be made precise for statements couched in a formal language, with fixed, explicit syntactic and semantic rules.
>
> (Toretti 1999: 437)

Thus Keynes' problem is whether a propositional function involving probabilities can display a unique proposition which implies that the statistical concept *inference* can be used as the logical concept of *implication*, and this problem is fundamental for empirical induction. Keynes obviously doubts it, as Hume did. We will come back to Hume and his scepticism below but Russell has an interesting answer to Hume's scepticism in his *History of Western Philosophy*, which actually supports Keynes' criticism of induction:

> If this principle, or any other from which it can be deduced, is true, then the causal inferences which Hume rejects are valid, not indeed as giving certainty, *but as giving a sufficient probability for practical purposes.* If this principle is not true, every attempt to arrive at general scientific laws from particular observations is fallacious, and Hume's scepticism is inescapable for an empiricist. --- What these arguments prove – and I do not think the proof can be controverted – is, that induction is an independent logical principle, incapable of being inferred either from experience or from other logical principles, and that without this principle science is impossible [emphasis added].
>
> (Russell 2000 [1946]: 647)

Russell's words are indeed dramatic and rightly so. Here we have an indirect confession that the problem with the logical links between inference and implication cannot be solved or proved with respect to formal logics, which also show the relevance of Whitehead's criticism of Keynes' dissertation.

We actually need to define groups a posteriori for which the propositional functions may work; thus we get an implicit link between a possible set of propositions and the formal propositional functions. This is actually the role of the experiments but for social sciences, particularly with respect to the macroscopic levels, experiments are seldom possible. Obviously an important concept in this context is that of *inertia*. Brody is in my opinion a bit sanguine with respect to solving unstable frequencies and that probably depends on his background in physics and working with *objects* which may be complex but also of high inertia.

With respect to Brody's criticism of the subjectivist approach he actually refers to an experimental situation where the selection of groups, à la Keynes, has already taken place. This implies that any empirical problem whatsoever when it is transformed to a logical setting must undergo the tests implicit in Figure 2.2 above.

The last part of the quote from Russell about induction as an independent logical principle is therefore rather difficult to understand, since the *reasons* by which we judge the result of the logical analysis are those which we employ in Figure 2.1 in projecting the set of empirical observations to a logical (mathematical) model. These reasons cannot be of a formal logical character but need to be based on a judgement of our observations, and thus subjective in a strict sense.

In the empirical world there does not exist any kind of 'axiom' à la Peano which might finalize a decisive proof as in the above example of mathematical induction, other than if we can translate exactly the empirical picture into a logical/mathematical picture, and it is here that the difference between natural, particularly experimental sciences, and social sciences appears. Obviously not even natural sciences can claim that *implication* and *inference* are the same with respect to their business but as experiments they are becoming more and more repetitive as the two concepts approach each other.

Social sciences are on the contrary more difficult conceptually as well as with respect to the necessary inertia of the variable. It is important to realise that Brody's sanguine position with respect to unstable frequencies concerns experimental sciences. In social sciences the instability of frequencies may appear out of two reasons, on one hand we have the same reason as Brody refers to, namely that frequencies are not stable because of intrinsic instability. On the other hand however we have the subjective, with respect to the researcher, transformation of complex variables into seemingly atomistic ones.

These difficulties in social sciences are in fact fundamental in a scientific perspective since establishing that facts/relations/propositions properly held true through inductive conclusions may be used in deductive logic.[13] But having said this we obviously must scrutinize the basis for empirical induction. Furthermore if probability statements on a set A of causal events give rise to inferences to a larger set of events, B, where A is said to be a proper subset of B, under what conditions are such inferences *bona fide*? This is an important question in Keynes' *Treatise on Probability*.

Obviously our discussions above are central to this question and if we go back to the earlier quote from Whitehead (1978 [1929]: 201), he writes; 'But it is not easy to understand how the statistical theory can apply to all cases to which the notion of more or less probability is habitually applied', we must then judge whether the statistical assumptions are reasonable. We also remember that Russell more or less rules out the possibility of defining an empirical variable so that it can be regarded as a proper variable in atomistic logics, which means that we must find ways of handling complexes, and in this process the reasons for rational belief enters our mind.

Hume on Induction

In discussing induction it is difficult not to consider Hume. His works on causality in the mid-18th century were more or less throwing a bomb into a well-ordered scientific society in the aftermath of Newton. His empirical scepticism is a stumbling block for all empirical scientists and he is underlying all our discussions of induction with respect to causal structures. Figure 2.2 deals with the case where we have established a certain causal structure in an inductive way and are prepared to let these conclusions evolve into a deterministic logical analysis. We have in earlier works dealt with the 'translation' arrows, but now we will take a step back and discuss the very inductive step. Central to this step is the single-directed arrow which means that the reversal analysis is not possible while in the deterministic logical analysis it is. So what is the precise meaning of this difference between the two modes of analysis? Let us quote Hume

> *First,* We may observe, that there is no probability so great as not to allow a contrary possibility; because otherwise 'twou'd cease to be probability, and wou'd be certainty.
>
> (2002 [1740]: 93)

Thus we may state that 'I lit the paper with a match' normally implies that 'the paper burns' but that does not imply the reverse implication that the statement 'the paper burns' implies that it was lit by a match. Thus the reversibility, integrability, postulated in the neoclassical theory implies certainty.

Hume proceeds:

> *Secondly*, The component parts of this possibility and probability are of same nature, and differ in number only, but not in kind. It has been observ'd, that all single chances are entirely equal, and the only circumstance, which can give any event, that is contingent, a superiority over another, is a superior number of chances.
>
> (ibid.: 13)

Paper burns at around 230°C and all processes which cause the fire have to somehow produce that temperature. Thus from a causation point of view all processes fulfilling this criterion are equal but if we see a paper burning maybe we do not think of volcano outburst if we do not have other specific reasons for that belief. This is important to keep in mind when reading the discussion between Keynes/Russell/Brody/Torretti.

Hume proceeds:

> Thirdly we may establish it as a certain maxim, that in all moral as well as natural phænomena, wherever any cause consists of a number of parts, and the effects encreases or diminishes, according to the variation of that number, the effect, properly speaking, is a compounded one, and arises from the union of the several effect, that proceed from each part of the cause.
>
> (ibid.: 13)

Thus a paper may be set on fire, given enough oxygen, by a number of causes, matches, chemical reactions producing heat, a magnifying glass concentrating the sun light and so on, but each 'cause' needs to be explained how it came to be relevant in setting the fire and then each of those causes may have a multitude of alternative causes *and* effects.

When we contemplate the above considerations by Hume in relation to propositional functions, we find that outside mathematical propositions we will almost never find a propositional function where *implication* is equivalent to *inference* but needs to be specified according to a context; thus the formal function conveys no information given imputed abstract variables. The probability of α given β is logically true only given the material content of α and β, but according to Hume's considerations such material contents requires additional information concerning underlying probabilities which form in the end an infinite chain ending in something similar to Gödel's paradox.

It is therefore natural that we take a jump from Kolmogorov's mathematically ordered world to the Bayesian subjective probability based on conditionalization. This means systematic reconsideration with respect to new knowledge given that the new information cannot change the basic structure of the apprehended causality and probability as Keynes discusses with respect to 'black swans' in *Treatise of Probability* (1962[1921]: 222).

A white swan has appeared to the left of the entrance of the house where you work for 999 days. You are then disposed to think that the Swan will be there the 1000th day and that it will be white. So if a black swan appears the 1000th day, what is your forecast for day number 1001?

Thus it is hard to see in what way a Bayesian approach changes the basic problem more than it emphasizes the necessity of accurate information, but that is exogenous to the mathematical/logical analysis and is basically about the problem which Keynes and Wittgenstein emphasize.

The debate between Russell/Brody and Keynes actually reveals the weakness of the logical atomism. This weakness is expressed in Russell's paradox. Abstract variables and functional expressions belong to what we may name non-proper classes while the material content of a variable belongs to proper classes, thus the universal class does not belong to itself; the opposite holds for non-proper classes.[14] We may take an example concerning abstract variables, *Cantor's unaccountability theorem* {Weisstein 2000): the three variables x, y, z can be formed into infinitely many classes: $\{x, y\}$, $\{x, z\}$, $\{x, \{x, z\}\}$, $\{y, \{x, y\}$, $\{x, \{x, y\}$, $\{y, \{x, z\}\}$ and so on, however the universal class of sets always belongs to itself. With respect to abstract functions analogous reasoning is obvious. This means that any empirical content possessing a more or less complex structure must be treated and transformed into abstract variables in order to be handled mathematically but such a transformation violates the content in the meaning that certain aspects of it must be dismissed. With respect to Russell's paradox it means that a real variable with a complex structure is belonging to what Russell names proper classes while the aim of the transformation is to make an abstract variable which belongs to non-proper classes and there we have the deepest problem.

As we will see Russell's paradox will cause us much trouble with respect to economic theory, but looking at the discussion of induction and probability linking it to Hume's considerations above we have the specific problem of the relation between implication and inference. Obvious certainty does not need any inductive analysis, which Hume points out, but then our analysis is bound to make inferences from a set of historical experiences onto a future relation between a set of variables, which are to be seen as complexes and thus require additional structural definitions and postulates. But discussing only abstract variables (or by all means functional expressions) these can never be anything but a priori and empty of material content thus they hold for an abstract mathematical analysis implying that the implication sign will hold a priori if postulated, thus any variable involved in an analysis of inference is void of any time dimension. Furthermore any probability structure involves two aspects: mean and variance which affect any inference onto the future and with respect to the causal structure.

This means that the relation between *inference* and *implication* is bound to be dependent on the very context of reality in which the inference is made. Thus it is true of what Russell and Brody claim, namely that Keynes deals with the *use of propositional functions* but nevertheless *any propositional function concerning probability statements contain two independent statements on mean and variance* which may be interpreted differently with respect to the precise context and that is exactly why Keynes has to operate within the concept of 'insufficient reason'. Modern financial analysis has tried to develop these arguments when developing mathematical methods to specifically analyse the changes in volatility as an argument in the pricing of options for example, particularly the so called Heston model (Arnér and Ekstedt 2008).

Facts, Commodities and Structures

We have noted that the neoclassical theory only defines commodities in the positive orthant. However we have treated commodities as complexes which implies that a certain agent may appreciate some features of a commodity as positive while others are seen as negative, relative to a given context. Thus in this case the commodity as a physical item is defined in the positive orthant but utility connotations are defined in the positive as well as the negative space. 'I want to have this car but unfortunately my garage is too small'. The negative connotations in this case may disappear in a different context. An example like this is interesting since it shows the commodity linked to a certain commodity structure.

Another type of example which is somewhat irritating is the question of *zero*. In a later chapter on dynamics we will see the dominating role of zero which makes some mathematicians talk about zero as a royal number. Zero bananas means we have no bananas but what does 'we have nothing' mean? (Zero means nothing.)

If we now apply this to commodities we may say: i) I have no Ferrari. ii) I have no house. iii) I have no food. iv) I have no water. v) I have no money.

Let us treat the first four different items and imagine a four-dimensional Euclidian space. Shall we then let zero belong to the space or not. Given the neoclassical axiomatic structure general equilibrium only concerns commodities in the strictly positive orthant. The reason is that the community demand is the vector sum of all individuals' demand. If then we allowed zero consumption of some good(s) we would not be able to aggregate the individual demand vectors due to different dimensionality of the vector spaces according to Brower's dimension invariance theorem (Weisstein 2000b).[15]

However since we have rejected the empirical meaningfulness of the neoclassical axiomatic structure we can/must drop the restriction to the strictly positive commodity orthant. Then comes the unavoidable questions of the effects of zero of a commodity are equal for all commodities.

The four commodities above indicate that commodities are parts of a structure which might be physiological, psychological, and social and so on. With respect to the Ferrari most people do not even regard the nonexistence as a problem but still there probably exist groups for which a Ferrari have a great social value for example but lack of it might be compensated with a ruby ring. Thus normally when we consider the lack of a Ferrari a problem we either are collectors or some sort of car fanatics or we want it to emphasize our social position. In the former case there is no possibility of substitution but in the latter case we have plenty of substitutions.

With respect to water the physiological structures are of immense importance for almost all people and lack of water might have consequences for their survival. Normally there are substitutes but when there are not we reach a point of breakdown of substitution possibilities and the only alternative is to pay any price to stay alive.

The four different commodities all possess, to a higher or lower degree, the ability that the lack of the commodity with respect to certain contexts affects the agent since the commodity in question stands in a structural relation to other commodities as well as to the total welfare of the agent.

Concerning money it is a bit more complicated than discussing real commodities since we have both income/wealth aspects and liquidity aspects. But in its extreme interpretation the agent obviously loses its links to the modern society. We will analyse this later in terms of lexicographic preferences.

Anyway, this shows that to limit the analysis to the positive orthant, which happens of we just interpret commodities with respect to their physical existence as we do when we accept the axiom of reflexivity is indeed doubtful. Although commodities have their physical definition which is unalterable, their role for the agents are normally structurally defined which give them an eventual market value which is apart from their physical existence.

Here we have asked about negative effects of the lack of commodities but we may also ask if there exist altogether negative commodities. Such questions take us to the border of the philosophical discussion initiated by Russell during the 1920s about negative facts and we must consider that problem a bit.

The Discussion on Negative Facts

We start with the problem of negative facts since this problem is close to Keynes discussion of atomistic facts and complexes as well as certainty and rational beliefs. Furthermore the discussion of negative facts brings us to consider false beliefs which are central to expectations. Since we have claimed that most, almost all, commodities are to be seen as multidimensional complexes it is of importance that we follow this line of development particularly when the neoclassical axioms presume atomistic definitions of commodities.

The basic start of the discussion is found in Russell (2007: 216–228), a reprint of an article on propositions and facts with more than one verb which was contained in a series of articles on the Philosophy of Logical Atomism published in *The Monist* 1918. Russell discusses here the difference between perceived facts and believed facts. If we look at the proposition 'It is raining' and compare this with 'Jones believes it is raining' the first one is a statement of a fact which can be perceived to be either right or wrong while the second is more complex since the both the content of Jones' belief, 'it is raining', and the proposition that

Jones *believes* it is raining can be right or wrong. Furthermore the eventual truth of either of the two sub-propositions does not affect the other. This problem also underlies Moore's paradox 'He believes it is raining but it isn't'.

The discussion developed and came to involve the very atomistic facts. Let us look at three seemingly atomic propositions i) 'He is bald-headed', ii) 'The carpet is red' and iii) 'My horse is winged'.

Let us see what happens if we negate the three propositions. *Not bald-headed* has a positive meaning which actually becomes defined when we define the concept bald-headed. Obviously with respect to the concept bald-headed there exists a meaningful negative fact which is as well defined as the positive fact.

When we come to proposition ii) the negation of redness is a bit more complex. A carpet not being red has no particular colour via the definition of red. We can say that the negative fact is that the carpet has some colour but not which one. The negative fact is not structured.

Finally when we look at proposition iii) we are in deep trouble. I could claim that winged is to be understood in a symbolic way just indicating that my horse is a very fast runner. However a negation of the proposition can mean that winged horses do not exist, or it can be a rejection of my belief that my horse is a fast runner, or it can also mean that I cannot be so stupid that I believe such a thing. Thus here we have that the atomic proposition actually is not atomic but needs a structural explanation.

The reader may now wonder why on earth we are discussing these things. We are in a different universe with respect to inflation, debt-structures, unemployment and similar things. Let me tell an interesting episode which occurred to me in the early 1980s originating from a conversation during my bus ride commuting to work.

I often talked with a friend, the head of currency business at a bank, during the bus ride. However on a particular day, I think it was the second Thursday each month, on the five o'clock news they reported the change of the US current account deficit, which was seen as decisive for the currency market. The report was however based on the quick statistics with unrevised figures. One such day I noted that the deficit was increased to some 11,5 billions USD while the expectations by the markets had been some 10,5 billions USD and the following day I noted that the markets had been rather much affected. However three months later I checked the revised statistics and the current account deficit was actually below 10 billions USD. I asked my friend how the markets reacted on these revised figures and he answered 'Nobody cares about such revised figures'. Pilate's question to Jesus Christ 'What is truth?' really comes to mind.

So with respect to this example we could say alluding to Keynes' beauty contest that we believe in the quick unrevised statistics even if we know it is probably wrong. What should I have said to my friend: 'Your belief is wrong', 'The figures are wrong', 'Your belief that you must act as the figures are right although you think that the figures are wrong is right/wrong'. All these questions are meaningless because the right question is: 'How will the market react to these figures?' In behaviouristic theory some claim that a fact is true if it causes actions and although not entirely satisfactory, it is in some sense a plausible view. Definitely it is relevant for us when we reject uniform and full information but link actions to the individual set of epistemic cycles.

The discussion of negative facts occurred within the search for the prefect language where we can reduce variables to be defined in an atomistic way. Let us look at a simple syllogism:

P belongs to Q

A belongs to P

A belongs to Q

We then claim: P – all mammals walking on two legs; Q – Apes; A– Socrates. Consequently we find that some individual creature named Socrates is an Ape. As we see, this syllogism is full of not fully self-evident claims. The conclusion is obviously right but what is going on before the conclusion is doubtful. The definitions of P and Q are somewhat problematic. We may say that P has at least two subsets of mammals walking on two legs which are mutually contradictive. The definition of A is unclear: Socrates can actually be my favourite chimpanzee but it can also be a historical or living human.

So using atomistic logic with respect to social sciences implies that we transform humans to machines that from an abstract point of view generates an always true conclusion, and that implies certain qualities of the variable definition as one used to say about computers 'garbage in means garbage out'. It is exactly here where the negative facts enter the problem. Our little example above of the non-existence of certain commodities show that $\varnothing$ may be of some importance for the agents' priorities and actions, but how do we express that? How do we express the non-existence of food/Ferrari in a mathematical model? We must expand the model and define food and Ferrari structurally with respect to effects of eventual non-existence. If we now make a macroeconomic model such an effort is probably almost impossible and in any case expensive so we might dismiss it with a reference to Keynes' expression of what happens in the long run. But what about the eventual importance of food for the risk of social uneasiness? Well we see what we are in for.

Thus the non-existence of one or several commodities we use every day can be perfectly trivial but on the other hand the non-existence of certain commodities may change the entire logics of action. We also noticed above that the non-existence may perfectly define a dual positive contrary fact like bald-headed and non-bald headed. This case we can of course handle even in simple statistical models. But on the other hand a definition of red leaves the question of non-red undefined.

Thus we are now back to our earlier discussion of atomic facts versus complexes. With respect to our little syllogism above we can say that as long as we deal with atomic facts the atomistic logics is close to a perfect language, while if not any logical language will fail if we do not specify the very aspects we are dealing with and grant that these aspects are independent of the environment. Now we see what Norbert Wiener hinted at. In natural sciences this is to a great extent at least almost possible but in social sciences extremely difficult, if not impossible.

We also see that such a state as non-existence is possible to some extent to handle in microscopic cross section studies, and there are many interesting studies already performed but what about macroscopic dynamic modelling? If non-existence of a group of commodities occur for groups of a certain size what will happen? We will in a later chapter discuss chaotic behaviour, bifurcations and perturbations from a technical point of view and that is rather simple. But how can we use such models when we do not even know how to define the adequate variables?

We have P_i and $\neg P_i$, so what is $\neg P_i$? If we use the neoclassical assumption of independence of irrelevant alternatives we can claim that P_i is an atom independent of the rest of the universe. If we go on and claim that all atoms in the universe $i - 1, ..., n$ where $n \to \infty$ defined like P_i, we may ask what will happen if P_i by some reason vanishes and is replaced by $\neg P_i \in \varnothing$. We can re-numerate the subscripts but that's all. So in the new universe, void of P_i, the atom P_j suddenly disappears and is replaced by $\neg P_j \in \varnothing$ and what happens? Obviously nothing since P_j is independent of all other atoms in the universe. We can go on like this and eliminate the entire universe without any consequences.

The point is that when we have to define a variable atomistically in order to be able to treat it in logics/mathematics we must be exactly aware of the structural border for such a definition. It is hard to see any real variables in the real world which are atomistic in their real appearance and particularly if we add the postulate of independence of irrelevant alternatives and if so when translating into a logical language the boundaries of such definitions and postulates must explicitly be mentioned in the analysis; it is equally important as the derivation of defined logical/mathematical problem.

Earlier we quoted Russell on complexes and we repeat it:

> Attributes and relations, though they may be not susceptible of analysis, differ from substances by the fact that they suggest structure, and that there can be no significant symbol which symbolizes them in isolation.
>
> (Russell 2007 [1924]: 337)

A thing/substance, we may call it $\mathbb{T}$, is always a positive fact per se. If we negate this, $\neg \mathbb{T}$, this will mean $\varnothing$ per definition. With respect to a symbolic language as logics or mathematics $\varnothing \equiv \varnothing$. It is obviously nonsense to define two subspaces, $\varnothing_1 \wedge \varnothing_2 \in \varnothing$ and claim $\varnothing_1 \neq \varnothing_2$.

Furthermore a functional expression like $\mathbf{Z} = \mathsf{f}\,(\varnothing)$ is a bit difficult to analyse since $\varnothing$ can be no wars, no flowers, no spanners, mathematically $\varnothing$ can mean both an empty space or an empty dimension.

When we however come to the world around us we become more doubtful. If we look at physics for example it is indeed difficult to think of a thing or substance that is not a part of a structure and is related to other things/substances. We then remember the discussion between Keynes and Russell where Keynes maintains that a probability statement always is dependent on the actual structural relations with respect to the question the statement concerns. An interesting event illustrating this is the way the planet Neptune was found since there were unexpected as well as unexplained irregularities in the path of the planet Uranus. That caused the astronomers to study the area when and where the irregularities occurred more carefully with the result that Neptune was found.

Thus we might say that given a kind of structure where $\mathbb{T}$ is a part the non-existence, $\neg\mathbb{T}$, should affect the structure in some way relative to the existence. In natural sciences where scientists observe phenomena in form of regularities which are not possible to explain with existent models which almost always imply undetected substances or unexplained relations between existing known substances. Consequently an observed *correlation* is not a result *per se* but might be linked to a precise causal structure so far unknown, at least in form of a parametric structure.

Consequently if we have a complex, C* and specify some relation with respect to a structure which can be mirrored in a logical structure, this structure will most probably also mirror the non-existence of C*. Since being a complex C* may be related to other structures which affect our chosen relation, oil/petrol is a simple and very clear example, where its appearance in GDP-calculations may be caused by contradictory effects, due to the fact that all actions are valued in money and money values, we may add it independently of any real effects. Thus the efforts to reduce the negative effects of oil added to the GDP, the question is then if some of the effects are positive to the society and some negative is then a salary payment of 1\$ positive effect = 1\$ negative effect. Well up to now at least economic statistics claim the equality.

Final Comments

Rejecting the axiomatic structure of the neoclassical theory implies that although our analysis may consist of neoclassical functions and postulates these are not of any normative value *per se*. Using mathematical technique for economic analysis requires an analysis of the implicit time concept and inertia. The dynamic structures are normally temporal and local and thus historical studies on parameter structures render no certainty but at best some rational argument for belief in the chosen mathematical (logical) structure of defining the empirical observations.

The basic reason for rejecting the neoclassical axiomatic structure is that we must reject the axiom of reflexivity since commodities are not atomistically defined but are complexes and furthermore the agents cannot be atomistically defined since they are able to reflect and react to the aggregate result of the market process.

At the same time it is necessary to discuss the concept of rationality because physical, social and cultural structures are often inert and that means that the very existence of the individual requires 'rational' responses to these structures. This kind of rationality is however due to purposes, contextual apprehensions and environmental responses which imply that the agent which not fulfil the *ex ante* purposes has to reconsider both purposes and contextual apprehension, which in itself is a source of dynamic change.

However this kind of analysis starting from the concept of epistemic cycles leads to a radical proposition, which by all means is implicated by Arrow's paradox, namely that aggregate optimization is possible provided there exist collective bodies but this optimization is logically independent of the individual optimization. An obvious consequence is that there exists no general equilibrium.

In the light of these findings we may discuss Keynes' analysis, the economic as well as the philosophical. A basic clue to his philosophical works is his interest in atomistic logic when used for complex variables.

When we look at Keynes' development as an economist and also as a philosopher we are struck by the utmost care of his conceptual analysis. Sure it could be questioned but seldom with respect to empirical sciences but with respect to different positions in pure philosophy. Thus when Keynes discusses concepts of risk and probability he has a considerable insight of the philosophical and the empirical difficulties. Comparing with the rational expectation hypothesis the latter seems to be based on rather ad hoc postulates, where links both to the basic neoclassical axioms and to the empirical world are obscure or missing. The obscurity of the links to the neoclassical axiomatic structure appears because of the many implicit assumptions which are completely outside the neoclassical axioms. We discussed above the essentials of an a priori axiomatic theory and one feature is that either it holds or it does not. In fact we arrive at Moore's paradox which Keynes and Wittgenstein were both fascinated by. When we take a stance in an a priori axiomatic structure any assumption not consistent with the structure falsify all propositions where it appears, thus allowing false trading with respect to an error term actually falsifies the axioms if you start your analysis from an established equilibrium, but if you still believe in the theory and your derived propositions you have the case; *A is not, but I believe A*, which is the weak form of Moore's paradox. But given that Lucas and Prescott are able mathematicians and as such surely know of the logics with respect to an axiomatic structure it seems that we in fact have the strong form of Moore's paradox $[\neg a \wedge a]$. This is where Keynes started his philosophical investigations in 1905!

Furthermore Keynes' discussions on atomistic variables vis-à-vis variables which are more or less complex is indeed missing in many economic models of whatever characteristics and that also goes for the treatment of the agents, where Keynes was clearly aware of the fact that the single agent was both a subject, thus a final cause, as well as a social creature related to a net of implicit and explicit conventions. Such an approach also requires an awareness of ethics and it is symptomatic that Adam Smith, Karl Marx, John Stewart Mill as well as Keynes all started as moral philosophers.

Ekstedt and Fusari (2010: 108–109) discussed a possible ethics for the neoclassical general equilibrium theory based on the principles of a Nash-equilibrium:

the economy will be in a state of general equilibrium when all agents maximize their welfare function given their respective budgets and the welfare functions of all other agents. This formulation is rather close to Kant's (2007 [1795]: 398) imperative: 'Act externally in such a manner that the free exercise of thy will may be able to coexist with the freedom of all others, according to a universal law'.

An interesting philosophical task could then be to investigate whether any market form but pure competition according to the axiomatic structure could possibly fulfil Kant's imperative. If not, what does that mean for the stability of the theoretical approach?

A barter theory of an atomistic kind, like the neoclassical theory, has no intrinsic stability but that has to be imposed like the famous *invisible hand*. The more practical analysis like the one by Makarov and Rubinov working within a communist command economy tells us quite frankly that the one who controls the price vector decides irrespective if it is the *central agency* or the *capital market* (Makarov and Rubinov 1977: 202–203). Thus the axiomatic structure gives no help on the question of whom/what creates stability. In fact the axioms are more leaning towards chaos if not the Kantian imperative is explicitly imposed into the mind of the agents.

Keynes' approach in *General Theory* is that the social structure and its conventions are of utmost importance for the function of the market economy.

Notes

1 There is also an axiom of choice in mathematics which we will, at least indirectly, use which tells us that 'if we have a Set A which consists of non-empty mutually exclusive sets $a_1, \ldots, a_n$ there exists at least one set C such that it includes one element from each set of $a_1, \ldots, a_n$.'
2 The neoclassical global optimization process is described as a flea-market behaviour in Ekstedt and Fusari (2010, 2013: 46).
3 Which also are the roots of internal conflicts in organizations.
4 For a more comprehensive analysis of risk and uncertainty see Ekstedt (2012) Chapter 6: 'Uncertainty Money and Liquidity'.
5 In Ekstedt (2012: 115–118) there is an extensive discussion of Hicks' 1937 paper.
6 Skidelsky (2003:167) concludes:' Perhaps of most interest to the student of Keynes's thought is the contention that certain public functions are best performed by semi-autonomous bodies rather than directly by the state – which foreshadows the argument in his well-known essay of 1925, "Am I a Liberal?" The great advantage of an independent central bank was that it would shield the Secretary of State from political criticism.'
7 This aspect is further discussed in Ekstedt (2012: 203–205).
8 It was his dissertation on ethics in his civil servant exam 1908. See Skidelsky (2003: 108–109).
9 Umberto Eco (1999) has an interesting discussion of these things in Chapter 3 on 'Cognitive Types and Nuclear Content' and although he does not mention Moore's paradox his analysis is enlightening for the understanding of Moore.
10 We can think of a referendum on building a specific football arena in a city, which is the yes alternative, but some want to have a bigger arena and some want no arena at all but both these groups vote no.
11 Peano was an Italian mathematician and is regarded as one of the key figures in developing mathematical logics.

12 For example, investigating all persons who are 183 centimetres tall or more will meet the case, while alluding to our earlier example of baldheadedness will not do, except in case of utmost precision.

13 Thus those who criticize deductive reasoning as such seem to deny any logical thinking whatsoever and then there is no much left for empirical sciences.

14 Russell (1992[1903]: 512–516, §485–489)

15 P^n is Homeomorphic to P^m if and only if $n = m$.

Bibliography

Allais, M. (1953) 'Le comportement de l'homme rationel devant le risque: Critique des postulates et axiomes de l'ecole Americaine', *Econometrica*, Vol. 21, 503–546.

Arnér, M. and Ekstedt, F. (2008) Option Pricing and Volatility: A Study of Four Contiuous-Time Models. Master Thesis in Mathematics. Göteborg, Sweden: Dept. of Mathematical Sciences, Division of Mathematics. Chalmers University of Technology and Göeteborg University.

Arrow, K.J. (1950) 'A Difficulty in the Concept of Social Welfare', *The Journal of Political Economy*, Vol. 58, No. 4: 328–346

Brody, T. (1994) *The Philosophy Behind Physics*. Berlin/Heidelberg/New York: Springer Verlag.

Coplestone, F.S.J. (1966), *A History of Philosophy*. Westminster, Maryland: The Newman Press.

Davis, J.B. (1994) *Keynes's Philosophical Development*. Cambridge: Cambridge University Press.

Debreu, G. (1987[1959]) *Theory of Value*. New York: Wiley.

Eco, U., (1999) *Kant and the Platypus. Essays on Language and Cognition*. Vintage, London.

Ekstedt, H. (2012) *Money in Economic Theory*. London and New York: Routledge.

Ekstedt, H. and Fusari, A. (2010) *Economic Theory and Social Change, Problems and Revisions*. London and New York: Routledge.

Hicks, J. R. (1937) 'Mr. Keynes and the Classics – A Suggested Interpretation', *Econometrica*, v. 5 (April): 147-159.

Hicks, J.R. (1980-1981), 'IS-LM: An Explanation', *Journal of Post Keynesian Economics*, vol. 3: 139–155.

Hume, D.A. (2002 [1740]). *A Treatise of Human Nature*. Oxford: Oxford University Press.

Kant, I., (2007 [1795]) *Fundamental Principles of the Metaphysics of Morals*. Great Books of the Western World, Encyclopaedia Britannica, Chicago, London.

Keynes, J.M. (1913 [1908]) *Indian Currency and Finance*. London: Macmillan & Co. Ltd, Available at: https://archive.org/details/indiancurrencyan014875mbp

Keynes, J.M. (1920) *The Economic Consequences of the Peace*. London: Macmillan & Co. Ltd.

Keynes, J.M. (1953 [1930], *A Treatise on Money. Volume I The Pure Theory of Money*. MacMillan & Co, London

Keynes, J.M. (1962 [1921]) *A Treatise on Probability*. New York: Harper & Row Publishers.

Keynes, J. M. (1973 [1936]) *The General Theory of Employment Interest and Money*. Cambridge: MacMillan, Cambridge University Press.

Makarov, V.L. and Rubinov, A.M. (1977) *Economic Dynamics and Equilibria*. Heidelberg, Berlin: Springer Verlag.

Moore, G.E. (1993[1903]) *Principia Ethica*. Cambridge: Cambridge University Press.

Russell, B. (1992 [1903]) *The Principles of Mathematics*. London: Routledge.

Russell, B. (1948) *Human Knowledge: Its Scope and Limits*. London: George Allen and Unwin Ltd.

Russell, B. (2007 [1924]), *Logic and Knowledge*. Nottingham: Spokesman.

Skidelsky, R. (2003) *John Maynard Keynes 1883–1946: Economist, Philosopher, Statesman*. London, New York: Penguin Books.

Torretti, R. (1999) *The Philosophy of Physics*. Cambridge: Cambridge University Press.

Weisstein, E.W., (2000a) *CRC Concise Encyclopedia of Mathematics*. Chapman and Hall/ CRC, London, New York. Entries: Cantor's paradox and Cantor's Theorem

Weisstein, E.W., (2000b) *CRC Concise Encyclopedia of Mathematics*. Chapman and Hall/ CRC, London, New York Entry: Dimension Invariance Theorem

Whitehead, A.N. (1978 [1929]) *Process and Reality: An Essay in Cosmology*. New York: The Free Press.

Whitehead, W.N. and Russell, B. (1910 [1927]) *Principia Mathematica*. Cambridge: Cambridge University Press.

Wicksell, K., (1937 [1922]). London: Routledge.

Wiener, N. (1988 [1950]) *The Human Use Of Human Beings*, Houghton Miffin & Co, Boston.

Winslow, E.G. (1986) '"Human Logic" and Keynes' Economics', *Eastern Economic Journal*, Vol. 12, issue 4: 413–430.

Wittgenstein, L. (1974 [1921]) *Tractatus Logico-Philosophicus*. London: Routledge & Kegan Paul.

3 The Basics of Money

Abstract

In this chapter we will discuss the intrinsic character of money. Money as a *medium of exchange* implies that money also will be used for other reasons. In economics we mostly discuss *liquidity* and the *use for accounting and contracts*. The latter implies that contracts are written in money terms and irrespective of whether we use some correction factor for inflation or not, the very contract is written in current money terms and has a temporal meaning. Thus money represents a link between the past, the present and the future. The two latter features are not something that we add to money as extra theoretical/empirical matters but are logical consequences of the use of money as a medium of exchange.

However money has also another intrinsic feature which plays a theoretical role and that is that money at variance with real commodities belongs to so called non-proper classes referring to Russell's paradox. This implies that we get an anomaly when we transform the apprehended real value of commodities into monetary values. This is logically allowed only in a state of general equilibrium in a neoclassical meaning but not in a disequilibrium economy. Thus we formulate Proposition 2.1 which implies that when we transform real commodities to money values in a non-equilibrium monetary economy the Proposition 2.1 does not hold for optimizations in money values. This implies that the barter economy and the monetary economy are contradictive even in non-equilibrium.

Introduction

In the first chapter we concentrated our analysis on the neoclassical general equilibrium as it appears in the axiomatic structure. Furthermore we looked at the role this approach seems to play when it comes to expectation formation. What we found was that the fact that a neoclassical general equilibrium is nowhere dense, a theory of expectation built on it requires slightly peculiar assumptions, no false trading and agents are postulated to expect the same kind of equilibrium as they form the expectations.

Furthermore since the neoclassical approach has a form of a barter economy, the axioms are defined only at the positive orthant, which means that we will have no contradictive utilities. The agents are given a price vector and incomes are passive in the process of expectations, which are affected only by events in the state space, which is independent of the market actions.

In the Arrow and Debreu setting there is something which might look similar to prices as we comprehend it in daily business but that is wrong since it basically is an index of relative prices only present in the very state of a relevant equilibrium, and consequently it will change when the equilibrium price vector changes. When it comes to money in the neoclassical approach in the sense we understand it in daily affairs, it is simply not there.

In the second chapter a different approach was introduced, based on at best temporal and local equilibria, where the equilibrium has no normative value but is an ordinary mathematical model with a parametric structure based on historical development and has no general normative value. We also discussed Keynes' philosophical considerations on the subject of atomistic and complex variables and we concluded that the basic feature of our criticism of the neoclassical approach is its treatment of complexes as atomistic facts. Looking at utility theory, as Jevons treated it, the complexes were squeezed into the theory by disregarding fundamental features such as aggregation, which for example Mill touches upon. Thus with respect to microscopic theory, barter per se could be unaffected by commodities being complexes or defined in an atomistic way. The consumer knows, as we at least can postulate so, which dimensions of the complex are relevant and acts with respect to atomistic commodities. The distinction between complexes and commodities defined atomistically only matters when it comes to aggregation and thereby the macroscopic analysis.

The barter analysis was contrasted to Keynes' economic and most of all philosophical considerations on the concepts of probability and induction which are in its deepest sense always at the bottom of expectations formation.

Fundamental for Keynes' analysis is the understanding of propositions concerning complex variables which are at variance with the proposition concerning atomistic variables. In fact probability statements with respect to Kolmogorov's theorems *only* concern atomistic entities.

In this chapter we introduce the money economy and starts by discussing the intrinsic characteristics of money. Money is remarkable because introducing the concept in the theoretical barter economy makes the theory break down, but introducing it in a loosely defined non-equilibrium setting, it works quite well.

Money, Equilibrium and Non-equilibrium

The theoretical results of our analysis in Chapter 2 are so far entirely negative in the sense that when we reject the additive aggregation, there will be no logical link between optimization on the microscopic level and optimization on a macroscopic level, which is expressed in theorem 2.I. However the kind of non-equilibrium concept that we discuss in Chapter 2 is interesting since there is no logical obstacle to introduce money in the reasoning.

Money as we understand it in the daily economy consists of three basic characteristics: a medium of exchange, in normal conditions the highest form of liquidity, and a denominator of historical and future contractual values of assets and liabilities. These three characteristics are formally and logically separated from each other and affected by different markets and related to different needs of the agents, but still the two latter features are firmly linked to money as a medium of exchange. The three characteristics obviously also affect each other not as some stable interrelation but as a result of the character of market actions. General liquidity crunches may appear as a result of a booming economy but can also be a result of a general lack of confidence in the market as we were reminded of in the aftermath of the credit debacle in 2008. The contractual values of assets and liabilities are affected by inflation but might still be tolerable in case of stable and high real growth.

The central point is however that these considerations only concern money as one single concept and its intrinsic complex features, which also means that depending on the macroscopic characteristics the intrinsic characteristics may even become contradictive. Dealing with money in either of the mentioned aspects implies that we also affect the other intrinsic features directly or indirectly.

Medium of Exchange

Let us concentrate on money as a medium of market exchange but keep other features in our memory. When rejecting general equilibrium, any exchange is a business between the supplier and the demander at a precise spot in time and space, and furthermore since we are looking at the exchange in a kind of time dimension we have by necessity also changing epistemic cycles. This is in fact already observed by Aristotle when he points out:

> There will, then, be reciprocity when the terms have been equated so that as farmer is to shoemaker, the amount of the shoemaker's work is to that of the farmer's work for which it exchanges. But we must not bring them into a figure of proportion when they have already exchanged (otherwise one extreme will have both excesses), but when they still have their own goods.
> (Aristotle 1990 [original around 334-324 BC]: 381, no 1133ᵃ)

From a theoretical point of view we may ask why the price formation is not more chaotic than it seems to be. One of the Dominican Friars of Salamaca during the 16th century, Luís Saravia de la Calle, discusses the matter of what is to be regarded as a just price.

> Excluding all deceit and malice, the just price of a thing is the price which it commonly fetches at the time and place of the deal, in cash, and bearing in mind the particular circumstances and manner of sale, the abundance of goods and money, the number of buyers and sellers, the difficulty of

procuring the goods, and the benefit to be enjoyed by their use, according to the judgement of an honest man.

(Grice-Hutchinson 1952: 79)

We can see that de la Calle mentions a sort of utility factor but he links this to contextual/ethical matters.

Dropping the link to macroscopic matters for the moment, the structure of individual optimization is apparent. Thus the individual optimization is fully accepted already by the Friars of Salamanca. Certainly they have opinions on market behaviour from an ethical point of view but with respect to optimization *per se* it is accepted by the Friars of Salamanca as well as Aristotle.[1]

But to have a logical link from these optimizing individuals to the macroscopic level we need further assumptions: that the society is populated with optimizing agents but the commodities are not complexes and it is only their physical appearances that are demanded, which mathematically means that the commodity space is defined on the positive orthant.

Commodities which are complexes might be contradictive among agents and could take on negative values among some agents. But still on the individual level the agents are maximizing their welfare given their budget, which include their momentary access to the credit market. Thus agents optimize, given a set of epistemic cycles, with no logical links to the macroscopic level.

Describing the non-equilibrium economy in such a way we understand that there is no unique measure for the relative prices for the whole economy but just a measure with respect to the specific exchange which the agents are involved in, and the measure is attached to the prices of the commodities and the budgets of the involved agents in the actual time and space of trading. Thus in a non-equilibrium economic system the equilibrium index disappears, but money lasts since it is not linked to any particular price vector, and the only kinds of equilibria that are left are temporal and local. Valuations in a specific context may occur even of complexes and the agreed price in a specific context may be seen as almost analogous to a similar business but if the trade is concluded in the first case it has no general logical bearing on successive trade of similar commodities but only with respect to social inertia. Jean Baptiste Say expresses it:[2]

> Nor is the position of Montesquieu, that money-price depends upon the relative quantity of the total commodities to that of the total money of the nation at all better founded. What do sellers and buyers know of the existence of any other commodities, but those that are the objects of their dealing? And what difference could such knowledge make in the demand and supply in respect to those particular commodities? These opinions have originated in the ignorance at once of fact and of principle. ...
>
> Money or specie has with more plausibility, but in reality with no better ground of truth, been pronounced to be a *measure* of value. Value may be estimated in the way of price; but it cannot be measured, that is to say,

compared with a known and invariable measure of intensity, for no such measure has yet been discovered.

(Say 1834[1803]: 246)

But even if we agree with Say that money is not a measure of value/utility we must remember that the actual sums paid can, without any ado, be added. Thus we can have a total sum of money payments for any money economy and this lead us to a kind of mystery.

Still leaving other aspects than the medium of exchange we may ask about a stability of a non-equilibrium market system. We have already discussed the stability of the general equilibrium and we find that the general equilibrium is nowhere dense which means that it either exists or not. If it exists the axiomatic structure holds for all agents and any aggregate is a vector sum of underlying levels of aggregation. Since the commodities are defined in an atomistic way on the positive orthant in the Euclidian space there are no internal conflicts between agents.

For the non-equilibrium economy things are completely different, the stability of the market system is more an exogenous problem. There does not exist a logical link between the interior mind of the agent and the commodity space but its stability is on one hand dependent on the state space in the neoclassical meaning but it is also dependent on social factors, aggregate events and similar matters. Thus the stability of the market from an aggregate point of view is a matter of social, economic, cultural, political, etc. factors which on one hand mostly are outside the market sphere and on the other on actions by individuals and different kinds of aggregates of individuals, so the dynamics is in line which is implicit in Arrow's paradox. When adding agents who are able to consider effects of other agents' actions and aggregate matters, their consideration plays an active role for the price formation. The stability, or inertia if we prefer, is not intrinsic to the market but to its socioeconomic and political frames, thus exogenous to the market.

Thus the neoclassical approach is transforming agents and commodities to logically independent atoms while in a non-equilibrium setting, agents in particular are complexes and so also are commodities. Consequently in the latter case we are not able to claim that the utility space somehow linked to the commodity space is defined only at the positive orthant since we are not dealing with commodities in their physical appearance but in their specific use by different agents. This implies that there may exist contradictions between agents caused by their very choices.[3] If so, there does not exist a meaningful index which is linked to relative prices. We may actually make such an index based just on the existing pricing. This index contains however contradictions from a neoclassical point of view.

Thus in all kind of logical analysis we have to transform our variables to atomistic variables. For complexes this means that we pick out certain dimensions which might be of importance or that we imply appropriate inertia with respect to the analysis. This is also a necessity for an analysis of non-equilibrium states.

We consequently look at a local and temporal space where the relevance of the analysis depends on assumed inertia, but since the neoclassical theory treats agents and commodities as atomistic variables as a fundamental theoretical feature which is, as is also an implicit conclusion of Arrow's paradox, to squeeze both agents and commodities into a form which by necessity cannot be other than temporal and local. Thus in the end neoclassical theory does not imply something specific on the microscopic level but maintaining additive aggregation will have specific implications linked to the specific apparatus necessary for the additivity to hold, if the neoclassical assumptions are assumed to hold for aggregates and any kind of local and temporal equilibrium of a model is seen as a general equilibrium, but still at the very moment money becomes an anomaly relative to the momentary price vector in form of a mathematical index.

It is precisely in this case money plays the important role since it has no link to any commodity and a specific relative price vector. Thus with respect to money as a medium of exchange there is no intrinsic stabilizing factor in the market, eventual stability is fully exogenous as well as eventual instability.

We have earlier mentioned that changing dimensionality of the commodity space is a major problem to handle in neoclassical theory since the price vector has to be reconsidered *in toto*. In a money economy of the one we see in most countries this is actually no problem whatsoever with respect to money per se. The problem with dimensionality is that it might appear in price investigations as inflation and give rise to policy measures which counteract the growth. We will come back to this later.

Liquidity

The feature of liquidity is fundamentally linked to money as a medium of exchange; the very market transaction necessitates liquid resources. Liquidity apart from the need for transaction has no value per se, but the value is created by other motives than the immediate need for transactions and to grant access to liquidity in the future. According to Keynes the precautionary and the speculative motives are two kinds of sets of motives. Money hoarding often is seen as supra-optimal holding of liquidity but since the optimal holding of cash is dependent on the judgement of an individual and a social state of affairs such an optimality would be hard to calculate as some kind of general norm. Thus money hoarding might, relative to some epistemic cycles, be rational. Furthermore since we have rejected the existence of general equilibrium we can hardly calculate an individual optimality on the basis of some aggregate average.[4]

To define what is precautionary and what is speculative in holding liquidity is next to impossible since actions caused by one of the motives might lead to a behaviour which usually is classified as a behaviour vis-à-vis the other motive. In a non-equilibrium approach the concept of money seems to reveal a more complex structure than as a pure medium of exchange. It must also be regarded as a medium of valuation and liquidity. This is due to the social acceptance of money as a medium of exchange. Consequently we have one form of complexity when we have economic and social stability but when we have economic instability combined with social unease there appears different forms of complexities.[5]

When we formulate a goal implying maximization of financial surplus we are in fact covering almost all outcomes of the barter trade as a consequence of money's independence of preference structures, different local and temporal equilibria, structure of price vectors and so on. The acquisition and holding of money make the individual agent less vulnerable to contextual changes which decrease the effects of future unexpected events changing the real structure. It is however wrong to say that it decreases uncertainty of the future because of its potential effects on the diffusion of money in the economy. These two aspects are often juxtaposed. Thus the very holding of money may in fact, as is well known, affect the aggregate real uncertainty due to reducing the diffusion of money in the economy, using Hume's analytical approach, in current analysis we say of reducing the velocity of the medium of exchange.

Consequently we have several different types of problems when we have the above described anomaly of money with respect to the neoclassical formulation of the barter economy but analysing a non-equilibrium money economy does not save us from anomalies and we are urged to ask whether the transformation of the individual optimization of the financial surplus in a money economy will change the outcome of an analysis relative to a hypothetical barter optimization, given a real commodity basket?

To analyse this question we must realize the extreme character of the neoclassical optimization in the general equilibrium; the agents and commodities are atomistically defined for the positive orthant in a Euclidian space, the correlate of independence of irrelevant alternative holds, the principle of revealed preference holds, and the aggregation is additive.

We have during our journey, so far, in fact rejected all these implicit effects of the neoclassical axiomatic structure. Furthermore, by introducing the concept of epistemic cycles in conjunction with postulating the agent to be a subject equivalent to a local and temporal final cause, we also introduced a formidable source of uncertainty namely the behaviour of the fellow agents per se, which is nonexistent in the neoclassical axiomatic setting.

Thus, with respect to our question we must realize that the analysis must be entirely different in a basically neoclassical setting compared with a money economy where only local and temporal equilibria exist. So the theoretical foundation matters with respect to the methodological framework at least.

Consequently when we look at for example Kenneth Arrow's famous article from 1963 the problems he envisages can only appear if we equip the economy in question with those kind of voting agents we discussed according to Arrow's paradox, and these agents are also able to adapt to the results of the aggregate behaviour. Arrow says:

> If, on the contrary, the actual market differs significantly from the competitive model, or if the assumptions of the two optimality theorems are not

fulfilled, the separation of allocative and distributional procedures becomes, in most cases, impossible.

(Arrow 1963: 943)

Thus the philosophical problem will be: if we analyse a problem vis-à-vis a defined economic model which is contradictory to the actual real economy which the model is supposed to picture, what is the empirical/theoretical value of such an analysis with respect to the actual economy? So – back to our first question again.

With respect to the market exchange our rejection of basic postulates in neoclassical theory opens for what we may call market inefficiencies in a broad sense. The fundamental one is the instalment of uncertainty with respect to the market space itself. In the general equilibrium we have a market space where we have an efficient information system via prices, the environment of the market space, and the state space affects the market space but is independent of it and subject to known risk structures.

In the non-equilibrium economy there is no unique price vector since the demand of commodities takes place according to individual sets of epistemic cycles. Thus any kind of equilibrium is dissipative and this actually drags the time dimension into the problem and consequently waiting is an economic factor. It is here that we find one of the key factors for holding liquidity. But if waiting might be profitable liquidity implicitly also contains the opposite case of necessity of liquidity immediately. As we know and also have seen recently in the 2008 debacle liquidity is not only a concept solely concerning the individual but it concerns all aggregate levels.

We generally look at money as the most liquid form of assets but as a matter of fact the financial engineering of today mostly is working to find liquid alternatives to money.

The concept of liquidity raises the question again of the intrinsic value of money and gives rise to two principle standpoints; chartalism and metallism. Each of these can in principle be subdivided into two more groups. Thus we may have chartalism with or without inflation norms. With respect to metallism we may have the real bill regime or bullionism. The two latter were during the 19th century also called the banking school and the currency school respectively. Chartalism with inflation norms is reminiscent of bullionism because it is built on quantity theory.

Chartalism and also bullionism do not regard the intrinsic value of a particular currency as fixed but governed by supply and demand conditions. The reason why bullionism still advocates money based on precious metals is foreign trade since the precious metal is supposed to render confidence to the currency. Furthermore since precious metals are accepted internationally inflation becomes known and also more difficult to manipulate by states.

The real bill approach implies that each bill in circulation has a direct value measured in gold or silver which means that the quantity restriction is unnecessary given that the precious metal has a substantially more inert supply. Henry

Thornton (1939[1802]) however showed that this was only viable if no bills of exchange and no promissory notes, were issued.

The debate on the basic character of money as we shall see to a great extent dismisses the developments of the so called financial technology, the management of debts and assets which are used as almost money. True that these are built on confidence but that goes in fact for the management of the entire monetary system. Also interesting is that money as a medium of accounting is fundamental here since debts and assets are defined nominally.

Already Thornton and Say in 1802 and 1803 respectively pointed out that the problem of liquidity enforced the existence of bank money; even in international trade the mere utilization of a bank note with no intrinsic value renders it a positive value. Say expresses it:

> Even when the absolute necessity of finding some medium of circulation of value obliges a government to invest with value an agent, destitute either of intrinsic value or substantial guarantee, the value attached to the sign by this demand for a medium, is actual value, originating in utility, and makes it a substantive object of traffic. A Bank of England note, during the suspension of cash payments, was of no value whatever as a representative; for it then really represented nothing, and was a mere promise without any security, given by the bank, which had advance it to the government without any security; yet this note, by its mere utility, was possessed of positive value in England, as a piece of gold or silver.
>
> (Say 1834[1803]: 245)

Henry Thornton also introduced the concepts of circulation and capability of circulation. He also noted that different groups use different kinds of money. Concerning bills of exchange he says:

> Bills, since they circulate chiefly among the trading world, come little under the observation of the public. The amount of bills in existence may yet, perhaps, be at all times greater than the amount of all the bank notes of every kind, and of all the circulating guineas.
>
> (Thornton 1939 [1802]: 95)

Furthermore Thornton continues in a critique of Adam Smith's position based on Thornton's distinction of capability of circulation and enforced circulation, the latter stands for 'law money'.

> ... He [Smith] represents the whole paper, which can easily circulate when there are no guineas, to be the same in quantity with the guineas which would circulate if there were no paper ...
>
> The quantity of circulating paper, that is, of paper capable of circulation, may be great, and yet the quantity of actual circulation may be small, or *vice versa*. [Original emphasis]
>
> (Ibid.: 96)

Thus whatever kind of money we consider, it represents a kind of value which is possible to utilize as basis for exchange bill or promissory bill in Thornton's meaning. This is important to keep in mind when discussing the velocity of the circulation of money. As already in Thornton's days the velocity of circulation was a problem to measure, and it is far worse nowadays. The quotes from Thornton emphasizes that neither the volume nor the velocity of circulating exchange bills are known and even foreseeable and this is written during far more simple predicaments than it is today with electronic facilities.

At the same time Thornton's analysis implies two further things; namely that access to derivatives is asymmetrically distributed and derivatives exist independently of the construction of law money.

When it comes to the intrinsic value of the very law money it is a bit intricate. Von Mises' point (von Mises 2007: 471–475) is that money directly linked to gold makes the management of the monetary system more transparent and makes it difficult for deceitful politicians to use it for dubious manipulations. Von Mises means that the money manipulation is hard for ordinary people to detect. He then speaks of the experiences from Germany in the beginning of 1920s and Hitler's supply of so called MEFO-bills; both these events were orchestrated by Hjalmar Sacht. Surely we have seen more of such things after World War II so von Mises is not bringing in an irrelevant aspect. The debacle of 2008 was due to the ruthless behaviour of banks with respect to securitizing and this was just under the very nose of the controlling authorities so one could think that von Mises would have had one or two words to say. Unfortunately there exist many ways of attaining the same effects as the MEFO-bills actually is an example of, if the political power is ruthless.

We have so far dealt with the demand for liquidity but in the very concept it is also an imperative aspect: to make a market transaction we need to be liquid. The form of liquidity per se is not important; it might be promissory notes, liability swaps or ready money, but it has to be there in agreed numbers.

Say touches on this in an example of bringing jewels to a grocery shop which would require an intermediary transaction which would obscure the price of groceries. Liquidity is a necessity for carrying out market transactions. Whether liquidity is in hard money or different forms of credit grants or liability swaps makes little or no difference with respect to the liquidity and its price. To illustrate the problem we may use the concept of lexicographic preference, Figure 3.1.

The 'normal' use of lexicographic preferences is in relation to *hedonic pricing* and deals with the question of why some people are not affected by prices whatsoever when choosing between a recording of Bach's mass in g-minor, and a recording of the latest Eurovision song contest. But the concept is actually more useful.

In Figure 3.1, A* represents the absolute necessary quantity of commodity A. This means that the preference system $I_1 - I_3$ only exists to the right of A* and that in the very point A* the price relation A/B might approach infinity.

Lack of a medium of exchange in any form may lead to severe revaluation of less liquid assets, as Say also mentions in the example of bringing jewels as a means of payment to a grocery shop. Thus there are causes affecting the market

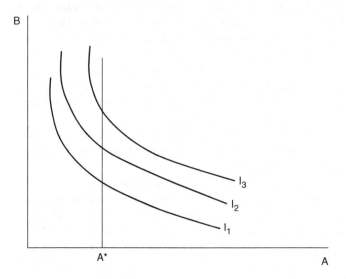

Figure 3.1 Lexicographic Preferences

Source: Ekstedt 2012: 163

sphere in such a way that liquidity needs may vary. It is with regard to these problems that we must separate the concepts of risk and uncertainty. Observe here that the price of liquidity is set by a market but that the specific character of the 'commodity' implies that prices might approach infinity.[6]

From Wicksell (1936) we have the implicit pricing of money as a relation between an average growth factor of production capital and the money market price of credits. But what we are talking about here is the question of momentary distribution of liquidity needs on a microscopic level. Since liquidity might be a separate dimension from wealth, temporal and local changes in money supply which affect the credit volume might force temporal and local changes of the price vector, particularly with respect to assets and liabilities. If so a short run credit crunch may have long run consequences for certain agents and consequently we are out of equilibrium.

Money as an Accounting Measure

Money contracts are made in a time dimension. This means that current money has to be valued in relation to historic values or future obligations. In economics we have one principle formula for valuing a future asset or liability, the present

value $v_0 = \dfrac{v_t}{\left(1+r+\left(a_1+...+a_n\right)\right)^t}$ where the a_i factors in the denominator represent other factors than the real interest rate r, such as inflation, growth and eventual other time dependent aspects such as endogenous risk growth.

If we assume that the present value above relates to a money contract we know v_0, v_t and r, the rest builds on expectations. The a_i expectations can be good or bad but they refer generally to common dynamic aspects in the economy which are to be discussed in a more general framework than in relation to the principles of a present value. That leaves us with r. What does it reflect? The funny thing is that we can, at least in principle, expand the a_i vector to cover all common aspects of the relation between now and the future; alternative returns, risks related to a common state space, technological growth/risks, changes in market structure/ market power due to innovations and so on. So what is left in r? Since all common factors somehow can be dealt with in general terms we have to turn to individual aspects. In principle there are three such aspects: life expectancy, degree of impatience and degree of systemic uncertainty.

Life expectancy includes health, living conditions of the individual and the relevant family and similar questions, affect the need of ready money. The degree of impatiens, could be business opportunities, poker debts or whatever also affects how quickly the agent wants the liquidity. The two extremes 0 and ∞ are expressed by God and the new born baby respectively, according to the Bible 1000 years are as one day and one day is as 1000 years for God, which is a pretty good explanation for a zero real interest rate.

Systemic uncertainty has to do with different forms of instabilities in the society such as doubts about the functioning of the credit/financial markets or worries of social unease.

Thus even if we concentrate on one factor with respect to the individual agent we achieve a rather complex structure which affects the individual not factor by factor but a joint effect of which we know nothing with respect to the relative dependence of the intrinsic parts. To this we add the a_i-vector which might be indefinitely complex. Obviously the market might exhibit some common principles but whether these are stabilizing or destabilizing is hard to say.

However if we take the two latter aspects, accounting and liquidity, and observe the almost bizarre scariness of becoming less liquid we realize that in the financial market there are hardly any stabilizing factors with respect to the price vector. Thus the valuation of even such things as short run money contracts might be affected during high degrees of systemic uncertainties.

Summing up the liquidity and the accounting features of money we find that each one is pretty complex with respect to the implicit value of money. But combining this with that money also has the feature of being a medium of exchange which in fact is the fundamental cause of the existence of the other features we find that it would be remarkable if money would be neutral with respect to the real economy.

The Neutrality of Money

The neutrality of money implies that an increase in money supply does not affect the real factors in the economy. This proposition is based on the money supply being completely symmetric. When it is not the proposition of neutrality of money becomes more doubtful. Obviously we can increase the number of other assumptions to avoid the effects of asymmetry but that is a bit of a boring way to analyse the problem.

The Salamanca Friars had a rather simple view of money. During the second half of the 16th century and the beginning of 17th century the inflow of gold to Spain from South America started a huge inflation in Europe in general and Spain in particular. The problem which the Friars discussed was: why was Spain with its enormous inflow of gold and an ability to buy foreign commodities still de facto poor? Their conclusion was that the basic stable form of trade was when it was based on trade between producing countries where the export of real commodities in principle corresponded to the import of real commodities. The abundant inflow of gold, which was the basic medium of exchange, implied an imbalance of shorter or longer duration. This caused also real shifts in the relative production abilities. In the case of Spanish gold inflow, the beneficiaries were the competing big powers of England, Holland and France as well as minor city-republics in Italy. The great loser was Spain. It is however important that the gold inflow to Spain was externally created and the actual development was probably not necessary. If it were the case that Spain had developed her productive abilities, which is actually suggested by Martin Gonzáles de Cellorgio (Grice-Hutchinson 1952: 108–109), it could have led to a different outcome. Anyway an external inflow of the medium of exchange will have real effects depending on how it is used and it is exactly here that the question of asymmetry of the money supply comes in.

In Spain the inflow of precious metals were directed to a rather small group of very rich which is why the great part of the population did not directly benefit from the inflow other than indirectly, namely when the inflow was 'diffused' within Spain, thus affecting demand. But since those groups benefitting directly from the inflow were rather small and very rich their demand of the possible supply in Spain became rather small and most of the inflow was the base for an increase in the import demand.

So what about an internal change in the supply of money, will that have any real effects if changed? Looking at the quantity identity:

$$M \cdot V \equiv P \cdot V$$

we can obviously say nothing since we then need to define the contained variables precisely. If they are defined in an atomistic way for example it is clear that the money supply M may affect Y as well as P. That M only should affect inflation rate requires extra assumptions. As the quantity identity appears above, it concerns only macroscopic variables and says nothing about for example effects of the money supply on the relative prices in case of asymmetries in supply or market consequences, so for the identity to hold even with respect to the structure of the price vector it is required that we dwell within a general equilibrium in a neoclassical meaning. Thus money supply, if changed, must be assumed to have symmetric effects on prices and we must assume the agents to be free from any money illusion.

So we may say that i) given that commodity demand is only affected by prices and incomes, totally and with respect to distribution, and ii) given that distribution of incomes and the price vector is not affected by the money supply, and iii) given that we start from a general equilibrium: we can conclude that money supply does not affect the real Y and that goes not only for M but for $M \cdot V$. Thus the quantity theory, which implies a specification of the quantity identity, can never derive the neutrality of money without extra assumptions about microscopic conditions.

Lucas (1995) takes David Hume as a supporter of quantity theory and partly also the neutrality of money as well. The most interesting observation is that Lucas applies a general equilibrium theory in judging Hume's discussion.

Lucas pays much attention to Hume in advocating the quantity theory as well as neutrality of money. It can therefore be of interest to se what Hume says. In Ekstedt (2012: 31–35) Hume's contributions to economics is thoroughly discussed and it is found that Hume certainly was supporting a kind of quantity approach in the line with the Friars of Salamanca. He is also keen on claiming that money as a medium of exchange was independent of the definition per se; Livre, Dinero or Pound does not really matter. Furthermore, dismissing foreign currencies, if a pound was 20 shillings or 15 did not really matter for the working of the market exchange. However money as an economic phenomenon has an enormous importance for society. To understand Hume's analysis we have to look at money in relation to barter.

> Money is not, properly speaking, one of the subjects of commerce; but only the instrument which men have agreed upon to facilitate the exchange of one commodity for another. It is none the wheels of trade: It is the oil which renders the motion of the wheels more smooth and easy.
>
> (Hume 1770 [1752]: 43)

Hume discusses 'the universal diffusion and circulation of money', thus the monetary penetration of society is important for social and cultural development.

> It appears, that the want of money can never injure any state within itself: For men and commodities are the real strength of any community. It is the simple manner of living which hurts the public, by confining the gold and silver to few hands, and preventing its universal diffusion and circulation.
>
> (Ibid.: 59)

It is rather obvious that he complies with the Salamanca Friars' position on a quantity relation of money. 'If we consider any one kingdom by itself, it is evident, that the greater or less plenty of money is of no consequence; since the prices of commodities are always proportioned to the plenty of money' (ibid.: 43). Thus basically the quantity of money affects prices but has no influence on relative prices and the pricing of productive factors, hence money is neutral to the real economy, at least in its everyday use.

However when it comes to changes in the money supply Hume dismisses the kind of static neutrality which is logically derived and he refers to the diffusion of money. A reduction of money supply in particular would hurt production and the sentiments of entrepreneurs and businessmen. Thus money supply is not symmetric in expansion and contraction. Given no money illusion expansion will have no or small real effects while contractions will.

Hume discusses a form of rudimentary expansive monetary policy, changing the supply of money (coins) irrespectively of the foreign inflow (ibid.: 51). Since decreasing the money stock would set back the enthusiasm and industriousness of the agents Hume suggests a continuous growth of money (coins of less precious metals) of some 2% per annum, which given a real annual growth of 2% would leave the relation of money quantity and commodities unchanged. Thus saying that Hume advocated a mildly inflationist policy is not correct since when he describes the diffusion of money out to the market agents he sees it as a slow process and mainly an effect of a growing market circulation of commodities, which should be the very purpose of the money increase. When Lucas (1995) discusses Hume he tries to squeeze his analysis into some form of equilibrium modelling which is completely wrong since Hume discusses a society which is changing from barter to a monetary economy.

The role of money implies that they have real effects but not in the sense that they are linked to a particular price vector but to the fact that the use of money gives access to larger markets and promotes the growth of production. A contraction of the money supply simply halts this process.[7]

An even more obvious point is the question that if there is no money illusion and money is neutral why do we fight inflation? We will come back to this question.

An interesting feature in Hume is his analysis of interest rates. In fact Hume has a rather sophisticated analysis involving a joint effect of increase in competition and growth. The interest rate on credits is a function of demand and supply;

> High interest arises from *three* circumstances: A great demand for borrowing; little riches to supply that demand; and great profits arising from commerce. And these circumstances are a clear proof of the small advance of commerce and industry, not of the scarcity of gold and silver.
>
> (Hume 1770: 65)

The quote indicates somewhat of a similarity with a Wicksellian attitude with a difference between growth rate and money rate of interest. This feeling is strengthened by his following discussion. Hume emphasizes the importance of competition with respect to the interest on credits. He claims that extensive commerce implies high competition and high growth which both decreases the interest rate and implies a lowering of profit rates, and a subsequent lowering of prices. That leads to growth of consumption and subsequently growth of industry and in spite of the lower profit rates in the individual case there is a totally higher profit stemming from the high growth, which thus alters both demand and supply for borrowed capital thus lowering the market interest rate.

However when commerce is low and concentrated to few actors it implies *per se* a high supply of credits but since the demand of credits is restrained by the low activity in commerce it leads subsequently to low growth.

Thus Hume's analysis implies that he generally looks upon the actual money stock as unimportant per se. When it comes to changes of the money stock Hume claims that a rise in stock of outstanding money has minor real effects while a reduction in the stock of outstanding money has negative effects on entrepreneurs and commerce. While the rise in money stock above the real growth faded out with respect to some minor initial real effects and ended in a general rise in prices, the reduction of the money stock implied more or less irreversible negative real effects. Thus manipulating money supply has asymmetric effects.

When it comes to the credit market, Hume regards this as more important vis-à-vis the real business than manipulating the outstanding money stock. The level of interest on credits played an important role for the advancement of entrepreneurship and commerce. He explicitly separates the interest rate of credit market from the growth rate on production and commerce. Moreover he indicates that in low growth times profits are concentrated to few actors but others suffer from the bad time. The supply of credits are high but due to lower growth rate the demand for credits are low and subsequently the interest rate is nominally reduced but the real growth is still lower.[8]

Lucas in his Nobel Prize lecture of 1995 wrestles a great deal with the question of whether Hume is a monetarist or not. First of all, such a question is wrong to ask. Hume describes an economy where money was intimately linked to the social and political evolution. Transforming the economy to a monetary economy was of central importance for the state in order to control society. Furthermore if we look at Hume's eventual policy recommendations he sooner tends to support a Wicksellian/Keynesian approach than a monetarist one.

Neutrality in the Short and Long Run and the Interest Rate

When we come to Keynesian and Wicksellian approaches things become much more complicated since quantity theory is dismissed as a general theory, which does not imply that quantity theory may work as describing one set of relations which explains inflation. Anyway; to postulate quantity theory is to postulate general equilibrium theory if we shall be able to manipulate the money supply without microscopic effects, but on the other hand money as we deal with it in a monetary economy is obviously not defined in general equilibrium theory.

However to see quantity theory as a macroscopic theory implies particularly with respect to investments that they are always equal to the saving, furthermore the return on real capital is always according to the standard marginal rules obtained through optimization. A decisive difference between a non-equilibrium approach like Keynes'/Wicksell's vis-à-vis the neoclassical one is that return on capital is a residual, a result which we will use later. This will however imply that we will have a possibility of a money interest rate to become different from the current return on capital. If so, there will by necessity be a difference between money assets/liabilities and real assets. Money as liquidity will have a price different from its eventual value as a medium of exchange. This difference is actually then institutionalized by the use of money for accounting and valuation of historical, current and future contracts.

We asked above why we should fight inflation if money is neutral and there is no money illusion. Assuming that the velocity of circulation is constant and just discussing the money supply, it seems that it creates a symmetric (with respect to agents and commodities) kind of inflation and consequently we could think of an corrective indexation which restored the nominal prices in each moment of time relative an initial price vector. But that would in fact be analogous to postulating general equilibrium. So if we have the Wicksellian/Keynesian problem of interest rates, which also Hume in a way alludes to, the inflation per se would be related to the underlying real growth and thus the kind of inflation index would not become commensurable over time depending on the relation between money rates and growth rates.

A further problem is with respect to Kalecki's critique (1944) of the real-balance effect, where he points out that inflation/deflation have strong effects on the valuation of liabilities, thus in order to have neutrality of money we also need to make assumptions with respect to the debt structure.

However neutrality of money is sometimes said to hold in the long run while in the short run it might have real effects. This is somewhat exciting with respect to the underlying time concept.

Long Run, Short Run

In Chapter 2 we discussed the concept of time and we looked at the difference between so called Newtonian time and the time concept of Einstein-Minkowski. The former concept of time is to be seen as a sort of objective axis which runs exogenous to world/universe affairs. Newton is also careful to point out that his time concept has nothing to do with our common clocks like the rotation of the earth around its axis or around the sun but is a pure mathematical abstract concept (Newton 2010[1687]:13).

The Einstein-Minkowski concept however implies in deepest sense that they reject the Newtonian objective time and make the relative changes as the true time. Given that energy is eternal in its basic existence the most basic time we can have is set by the changing entropy in space, at the universal level. In fact if we dismiss the entropy for the moment, their time concept is such that for a closed space completely random changes implies the disappearance of time in the sense that time has not any direction. Consequently time requires some form of direction which for example Hume's causality concept implies. But that is only directed locally and temporally.[9] Ageing is an absolute and ongoing process but is it continuous or even directed? Here is an example where the measure of a certain aspect/dimension influences the definition of a multidimensional concept.

That means that with respect to long run this is a sort of joint result of momentary changes of different changes in the space. As we said earlier a logical time model $S_t = S_0 \cdot e^{\lambda t}$ à la is void of any time in the meaning of Einstein-Minkowski. This is in fact also the very message in chapter twelve of Keynes' General Theory, where he claims that although we may take decisions which have long term consequences, these are not based on some specific knowledge of a long run trajectory but are based on historical knowledge and interpretations of that in conjunction with the (individual) apprehension of the current state.

I happened to see a survey from a bank dated the 22 January 2015, regarding analysts' expectations concerning H&M. H&M was to publish their report concerning Q4 (Sept.–Nov. in the financial year of H&M) on 28 January so the survey I read concerned what was expected to be in the H&M report, published one week later. Seventeen analysts were asked, they were selected by SIX News/ Industry Financials.

H&M had beaten the expected sales figures in all three months of Q4 and the result before tax was expected to be 7,898 million SEK compared to 7,337 during the same period in 2013. However the gross margin is expected to be 60.1% compared to 60.8% in same period last year.

The 17 analysts had different opinions about the report: six analysts recommended *Buy*; two analysts set *Over-weight*; three analysts set *Under-weight*; three analysts recommended *Sell*; and finally four analysts recommended *Keep*.

Probably these 17 analysts were rather prominent as market analysts. But why did they arrive at such different results? Can we make some average of the analysts' recommendations? What is the value of their average recommendations when the recommended actions are contradictive and is it possible to take notice of the recommendation without knowing how the experts perceive the market environment and relevant influences? A comparison requires a standardized form for apprehending the market and its environment.

So if we have a sum of money to invest and are eager to learn about the stock market, where is the long run aspect in the related survey and where is the consistency and rationality? It is interesting of course that all 17 experts are probably perfectly rational and consistent with respect to their understanding of the position of H&M with respect to its market environment. The question is only which market environment to look upon as relevant and how to rank relatively speaking the perceived essential aspects. Thus all 17 experts are probably exhibiting rational expectations with respect to their respective epistemic cycles.

In the described case we could of course wait until next week to make any decision but then the factual position of H&M is already anticipated so we have to reconsider our horizon of expectations as well as start from partly new knowledge.

Well – it is one week later and H&M has delivered their report for Q4 and gross earnings were 7,731 million SEK to be compared with Q4 the preceding year during which the gross earnings were 7,182 million SEK. Thus the reported gross earnings were around 2% lower than average expectations but 7.7% higher than same period the preceding year. The question is whether we invest with respect to the difference between the factual figures and the average expectations or the last year figure.

So what can we say about the H&M example? First of all is that this kind of problem would hardly appear in a barter economy. Surely expectations are important also in a barter economy but to make a revaluation of an asset you actually have to use it and become pleased or disappointed and furthermore expectations must be built on physical characteristics like storing wine (Wicksell (1936)/Böhm-Bawerk (1930 [1888]) or waiting for the crop in relation to upcoming needs changing the time-preference. In the story of H&M any price movements before the Q4 report are mostly built on the same psychology as in Keynes' beauty contest.

The second reflection we may do concerns short and long run. If we have taken pains to get information about the investment plans for the company and believe in them we could utilize the drop in the share price and if the market more and more comes to believe in them the current price will be judged as a short term drop. If we however do not believe in them the current price might be treated as reflecting the long run price. So the long run decision seems to be an action built on an expectation which *ex post* is deemed correct. But since *ex post* unfortunately does not exist *ex ante* there is no possibility to say that an action is appropriate in the long run perspective or not since it always has to be judged *ex post*.

We have a way of judging long and short run behaviour on whether we think about consequences with respect to various time horizons. But the consequences of an action depend on the development of the environment and only partly, sometimes not at all, depend on our own behaviour. Thus we may be in stable environment and have high confidence that our plans will hold, but as we will see in the next chapter even deterministic systems have points of breakdown which are mostly impossible to forecast.

Thus based on *ex post* figures/knowledge the long run character of a historical decision is seldom possible to judge and *ex ante* we know little and historical experiences are useful but unfortunately deceitful. Thus a current decision is based on a particular epistemic cycle and whether that leads to desired long run effects is to a lower or higher degree depending on luck. This was the knowledge of the Vikings who counted 'luck' as fundamental in any venture as did Napoleon.[10]

Consequently any action which has consequences on the economic environment is judged with respect to the agents' individual epistemic cycles which obviously also affects each other somehow and for that matter all such actions are part of the context in which a decision concerning short run questions or long run questions shall be taken. Decisions whose effect will be of importance for the future may give the result that the epistemic cycle for these decisions are different from a short run decision but the apprehended context is in principle the same.

Thus if there was a long run neutrality of money but not a short run would that have no long run real effects? We are then obviously affected by the short run non-neutrality but at the same time we sort out those types of decisions which are of long run character and say that these will not be affected by the current short run non-neutrality which we only will let affect the short run decisions. Such reasoning is a bit hard to understand, what is then the content of long run?

The question of long and short run is a juxtaposition between *ex ante* and *ex post*. The only way we can have long run neutrality of money is when we are in a neoclassical general equilibrium but in a non-equilibrium economy the problem is nonsensical. The neutrality of money is a general equilibrium concept and concerns only the pure exchange economy, and this is a logical result because as we have said real money as we think of it in daily affairs is a non-equilibrium concept. Money as we know it has more features than just a medium of market exchange.

Quantity Identity and Quantity Theory

We have earlier discussed quantity identity as at variance with quantity theory.

$$M \cdot V \equiv P \cdot V \qquad\qquad\qquad \text{E.3.1}$$

The identity is so because all the variables need sharp definitions. There is obviously an outstanding amount of money used for transactions which we call M. That it is circulated at a certain speed V is almost certain. There are indeed prices P and real commodities Y. Thus with respect to such considerations we may call it an identity.

Let us now look at Swedish data, there is no reason to assume that Sweden with respect to this kind of considerations collects other types of data or takes on definitions at difference with other market economies so our discussion could equally well have concerned another OECD country, save for the material content.

We look at the period 1995 to 2013 and we use data from the Central Bureaux of Statistics and the Central Bank.

We use M3, which includes all public bank holdings and holdings of short run treasury bills, as the norm for M, and thus we have the basic data as in Table 3.1. Prices P are defined as CPI and Y is GDP at market prices deflated to fixed prices. The deflator is a weighed index based on CPI and internal supply (SCB Central Bureaux of Statistics, 2015).

We transform all the series to index 1995 = 100 and we have the Figure 3.2 built on Table 3.1.

There is a rise in the M3 series, at least if we assume constant V, does not seem to follow from the development of CPI and GDPM so we may ask what happens if we assume V is constant and let the real GDP at market prices be as it is. We would then have the full effect on CPI of the increase in M3.

Thus in Figure 3.3 we can see that obviously the definitions used for CPI and M3 are not commensurable under assumptions of constant V and GDPm volume is calculated in the standard way.

So why not drop the assumption of constant V? We will then have $V = \dfrac{CPI \cdot GDPm}{M3}$ and we will get the series of V.

Table 3.1 Basic data set for M, P and Y

	M3	CPI	GDPM volume index
1995	698362366	254,94	68,1
1996	785876907	256,3	69,1
1997	817420197	257,99	71,2
1998	847455312	257,3	74,2
1999	1066486321	258,49	77,5
2000	1162535313	260,81	81,2
2001	1182074807	267,09	82,5
2002	1207609517	272,85	84,2
2003	1259276715	278,11	86,2
2004	1290986591	279,14	89,9
2005	1407955550	280,41	92,4
2006	1630603083	284,22	96,8
2007	1896177000	290,51	100,1
2008	2066300155	300,5	99,5
2009	2108280171	299,01	94,3
2010	2145925027	302,47	100
2011	2217542039	311,43	102,7
2012	2362300072	314,2	102,4
2013	2418223852	314,06	103,7

We have now created a number series of all four variables in the quantity identity of money based on working principles and definitions in Sweden during the period of 1995 to 2013.

In Figure 3.4 the full identity is defined by a number series and transformed to a diagram.

In the case of Figure 3.4 we have *de facto* definitions of the variables M, P and Y, while V is a sort of residual with respect to numbers but not subject to an actual definition of the specific variable *Velocity of circulation of money*. That however casts deep shadows over the *de facto* definitions of M, P and Y that are not in any sense proved by our investigations of the available data set.[11]

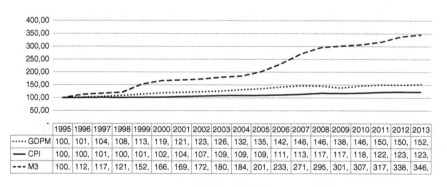

Figure 3.2 Development between 1995 and 2013

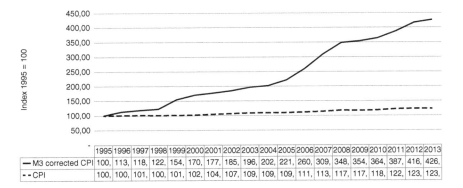

	1995	1996	1997	1998	1999	2000	2001	2002	2003	2004	2005	2006	2007	2008	2009	2010	2011	2012	2013
— M3 corrected CPI	100,	113,	118,	122,	154,	170,	177,	185,	196,	202,	221,	260,	309,	348,	354,	364,	387,	416,	426,
- - CPI	100,	100,	101,	100,	101,	102,	104,	107,	109,	109,	109,	111,	113,	117,	117,	118,	122,	123,	123,

Figure 3.3 CPI corrected for the rise in M3 given GDPm

A normal assumption of V is a relatively high degree of constancy either in level or in change, since the velocity as we look at payments for commodities, follows usually established routines in a society which are rather inert. At the same time we know that the velocity of money is affected by two aspects, at least: first, we have changes of the average individual agents' patterns, which include changes in income distribution. Second, there are changes in the number of agents which are active in the market as well as quantities and dimensions of commodities. Both aspects might be affected by

Table 3.2 Achieved Velocity given quantity identity and CPI, GDPm and M3

	(CPI*GDP)/M3
1995	100,00
1996	90,65
1997	90,39
1998	90,62
1999	75,56
2000	73,28
2001	74,98
2002	76,53
2003	76,58
2004	78,19
2005	74,02
2006	67,87
2007	61,69
2008	58,21
2009	53,80
2010	56,70
2011	58,02
2012	54,79
2013	54,17

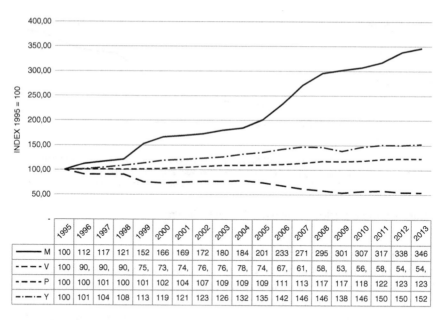

	1995	1996	1997	1998	1999	2000	2001	2002	2003	2004	2005	2006	2007	2008	2009	2010	2011	2012	2013
M	100	112	117	121	152	166	169	172	180	184	201	233	271	295	301	307	317	338	346
V	100	90,	90,	90,	75,	73,	74,	76,	76,	78,	74,	67,	61,	58,	53,	56,	58,	54,	54,
P	100	100	101	100	101	102	104	107	109	109	109	111	113	117	117	118	122	123	123
Y	100	101	104	108	113	119	121	123	126	132	135	142	146	146	138	146	150	150	152

Figure 3.4 Development of M, V, P and Y

the economic environment in the form of contractions and expansions. On the other hand innovations with respect to payment and credit forms affect the velocity. The traditional Keynesian motives to hold money is a rather good classification but those motives are most probably not constant in space and time.

Why the tradition to assume a constant V is a bit obscure to derive, thinking in neoclassical terms such a variable as velocity of money circulation is an anomaly, and we end up in static analysis but that might explain the tendency to let V be, if not constant, very inert.

It is also obvious that the derived V in Figure 3.4 depends on the definitions of M3, P and Y, but it is hard to see that changes in those definitions within reasonable frames could lead to a systematic development as exhibited in V in Figure 3.4.

Consequently we might suspect that the deterioration of the velocity of circulation of money, *whatever it is*, in the Swedish economy has to do with structural changes in the market structure or the agents' behaviour vis-à-vis market transactions.

As it is seen in Figure 3.5 there has been an ongoing process since 1975 of an increased inequality of pre-tax incomes. This has probably to do with the increased concentration of the Swedish economy and the increased export dependency. It is probably also affected by increased permanent unemployment; which on one hand is measured by the average length of unemployment but on

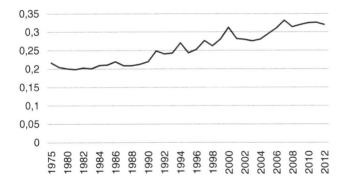

Figure 3.5 Development of the Gini-coefficient

the other quit the labour force and fade into other categories as sick leave, early retirement, redefining themselves as not belonging to the potential workforce and similar categories.

It is too early to say but the last years since 2009 there has been a growth of the household service sector due to some ease in labour taxes which households do not need to pay. It looks like it has had some effects on the Gini-coefficient but on the other hand the export industry has suffered from the high value of SEK which now has depreciated and then according to earlier experiences the profit share will increase, so the dip in the Gini-coefficient might also be explained solely by decreased profit share.

In the labour market, save for the increase in the household service sector, there is a long run evolution of increased heterogeneity and labour hoarding. The character of the industry is such that labour has been transformed from being a flexible production to becoming more and more fixed with respect to the organizational features of the company. We will come back to this evolution in later chapters.

Consequently treating quantity identity as a closed system ends up in one of the variables as a residual. Given confidence in the other three in the closed system, this residual implies that variations in the environment enter the identity and open the seemingly closed system. Thus claiming that the neoclassical approach completed with the *quantity theory of money* will be a relevant base for modelling the real world economy is indeed doubtful.

However we have focused our interest on the residual V as we assumed the other three variables bona fide, which there might be some doubts about.

What are Prices, P, and Real GDP, Y

The right hand side in quantity identity consists of two variables P and Y and are defined in economic theory in different ways. However looking at elementary textbooks, which are indeed important since they lay down the common interpretations of simple concepts, we find distinctions between real and nominal variables, for example in Mankiw (2003: 107), we are taught:

> All variables measured in physical units, such as quantities and relative prices, are called **real variables**.
>
> In this chapter we examined **nominal variables** – variables expressed in terms of money.

What does it really mean when it is said that 'All variables are measured in physical units such as quantities and relative prices', within the realm of the macroscopic level? Do we actually know the quantities or the relative prices of Consumption or Investments in their physical forms which are key variables in the analysis?

When we collect macroscopic data *all* variables are measured in nominal price terms, and then the only occasion when the price value of a commodity is equivalent to its real 'utility 'value" is when we have a *prevailing general equilibrium*. In non-equilibrium information concerning average prices of groups of commodities or prices of representative commodities is what is available, but unfortunately we have no unique price vector. Thus interpreting fixed priced items as real values is just another way of using additive aggregation.

This is an example of the juxtaposition of theoretical structures. In the textbook in question there is no sign of a discussion about equilibrium states but still the methodological features of equilibrium analysis are used although this is not relevant other than in a prevailing equilibrium.

However we may also by real entities just mean entities which are valued in fixed prices and in such a case the best option is to say that Y is giving us some hint of a quantitative turnover in the economy. Unfortunately this does not allow us to overcome the problem of non-uniqueness of the price vector.

If we look at CPI the Swedish calculations consist of 70 subgroups, which have a relative weight and the price development is measured by either the average price of the subgroup given the weight or via representative commodities for the group in question.[12] Such a method is vulnerable in relation to two factors: structural change within the subgroups and/or changes in the commodity dimensions within a subgroup.[13]

The particular case of changes in the dimensionality of the commodity basket is nasty. First of all this upsets general equilibrium theory which Keynes noted in the preface to the French edition of GT.

> I believe that economics everywhere up to recent times has been dominated, much more than has been understood, by the doctrines associated with the name of J-B Say. It is true that his 'law of markets' has been long abandoned by most economists; but they have not extricated themselves from his basic assumptions and particularly from his fallacy that demand is created by supply. Say was implicitly assuming that the economic system was always operating up to its full capacity, *so that a new activity was*

always in substitution for, and never in addition to, some other activity [emphasis added]. Nearly all subsequent economic theory has depended on, in the sense that it has required, this same assumption.

(Keynes 1973 [1936]: xxxv)[14]

Technically speaking the *dimensionality problem* stems from a central theorem in mathematics by the Dutch mathematician Brouwer. It is called the dimension invariance theorem and has the form:

P^n *is Homeomorphic to* P^m *if and only if* $n = m$

Thus to make any kind of comparisons of a set in time and space we need constant dimensionality of the set.

Let us look at a small example: a more elaborate example is found in the appendix. Let us assume for simplicity's sake a *real bill* approach, thus the price is in fact equal to some weight in a precious metal, let us say gold. Let us assume that the total gold supply is 250 grams and that all prices are expressed in grams of gold (1 ounce is 0.035274 gram). We have two commodities in period 1 A and B while in period 2 we have three, A, B and C, the supply of gold is the same during the both periods, P, Q and Y in Table 3.3 represents Prices, Quantity and Expenditures respectively.

Given that *relative prices* of A and B are constant we see that the price of C will be 10 but Com A and Com B will have a lowered price to 8 and 4 respectively. So calculations give us that given the gold supply and the initial prices keeping the relative price A/B constant we will have:

$P_A = 2i$, $P_B = i$, and $P_C = 2.5i$ which in our case leads to
$i \cdot (20 + 30 + 12.5 = 250)$
Subsequently $i = 3.2$ and we get Table 3.3.

Assume now that all the commodities are within one established commodity group which we measure through representative commodities. The appearance of C will not be seen until a more thorough investigation of the groups and their weighs is undertaken, so we will report decreasing prices of the group in question but we will at the same time report a higher portion of unexplained outlays which

Table 3.3 Effect of an increase of the dimensionality of the commodity basket

	Period 1				Period 2		
	P	Q	Y		P	Q	Y
A	10	10	100	A	8	10	80
B	5	30	150	B	4	30	120
				C	10	5	50
Total Y			250	Total Y			250

will be generally corrected as inflation. We saw that Hume wanted to allow for a 2% increase in the money supply to keep up the enthusiasm of entrepreneurs and from the above example we have nothing to say against it but of course that is under the assumption of constant velocity.

Thus we see from the above considerations that changing the dimensionality of the commodity space will have substantial effects on both nominal prices as well as relative prices which require further assumptions to solve given the money supply. If all these assumptions are not taken nobody can tell the nominal effects nor the real effects with respect to relative prices. What is long run or short run in all this is impossible to say.

First, if we accept only local and temporal equilibria we obviously have to work with some kind of average, which may have some meaning given certain inertia of the market process. But how do we then explain the link to quantities? Second, we must have an idea of the aggregation process. If we use additive aggregation how does that relate to quantities when we actually have rejected it for the barter economy?

Third, how do we compose commodity groups or representative commodities and what does that mean for the relevance of relative prices? If we speak about the *real GDP* what does that mean in quantitative terms? We know that if we are in a prevailing general equilibrium and introduce money as a medium of exchange the equilibrium will cease to exist if we take the logics of the axiomatic structure seriously. Finally commodities in general equilibrium analysis are only defined for the positive utility orthant, while our apprehension of commodities allows for commodities, as complexes, defined also for the negative utility space.[15]

The Left Hand Side M3

Figures 3.2 and 3.3 and our considerations on the velocity of money V all tell us that during the investigated period the development of the nominal GDP depends on two contrary processes of considerable strength: a substantial increase in M3 and a considerable decrease in V. As we already have mentioned V is a residual variable and the values obtained are only defined by the degree of certainty of the definitions of P, Y and M3. We have found that the essential figures on the right hand side are those of the nominal GDP. But the further definitions of P and Y are subject to a similar problem as V, namely that the important tool of construct-ing P is the treatment of inflation and given that the real Y is a residual. So look-ing at the quantity identity again:

$$M \cdot V \equiv P \cdot V$$

we receive the remarkable result that of the four variables two are residuals, P and M, M3 in our case. We have already expressed some doubts concerning the infla-tion calculations and now we have only M3 left. Are we sure that its definition is adequate? That means if the definition is adequate with respect to the right hand side of the identity, P and Y, M3, which is the bank holdings of the public plus short money promissory notes, should then define the fundamental mean of the medium of exchange. On Wikipedia there is a compilation of different money measures for the US, Table 3.4, which for M3 corresponds to the Swedish M3. So we may ask whether any of the different definitions of money corresponds to the nominal GDP.

The immediate reaction is of course with respect to notes and coins which to a large degree is replaced by internet operations. Furthermore we have easier connections of the public with financial and stock markets which affects M3.

Banks give today almost no interest rate on holdings thus the public uses other forms of savings than time and saving deposits. This development is probably strengthened in Sweden by the development of higher inequality of incomes which is illustrated in Figure 3.5.

Furthermore we have a structural change in the credit market where suppliers of commodities give credits which are outside the regular banks.

In a historical perspective Edvinsson (2007) shows that M3 as a percentage of GDP at market prices reached an all time high at the beginning of the 1930s of circa 93% and decreased systematically to around 55% in 2006. He also shows that M0 as a percentage of M3 decreased from a level of circa 37% in 1871 to around 8% during the 1930s, rising to around 15% during World War II but decreased then to around 7% in 2006. The decrease in M3 relative to GDP could be explained by a higher velocity but as illustrated in Figure 3.4 above V has actually decreased, which makes the explanations of M3 relative to GDP outside the quantity identity *per se* and concern M3 as a relevant definition of money.

Thus, although the measure M3, or any other definition of money, is rigorous from a formal point of view its relevance in quantity identity is less clear. Other means of payments next to money are successively created and the official money will change in relation to the nominal GDP.

Table 3.4 Modern Typology of Money

Type of money	M0	MB	M1	M2	M3	MZM
Notes and coins in circulation	X	X	X	X	X	X
Notes and coins in bank vaults		X				
Federal Reserve Bank Credit		X				
Traveler cheques of non-bank issuers			X	X	X	X
Demand deposits			X	X	X	X
Other checkable deposits			X	X	X	X
Saving deposits				X	X	X
Time deposits less than $100 000 and money-market deposit accounts for individuals				X	X	
Large time deposits, institutional money market funds, short-term repurchase and other larger liquid assets					X	
All money market funds						X

Source: http://en.wikipedia.org/wiki/Money_supply

Some Elementary Conclusions

Our considerations of quantity identity have led us to a rather remarkable result: out of the four variables M, V, P, Y, two are to be seen as residuals, V and Y, and get their trustworthiness from the definitions of P and M. However the inflation calculations are built on assumptions of inertia which with respect to some periods might be doubtful, these assumptions are not necessarily inappropriate but more an adaption to keeping down costs of the exercises. Furthermore M3, although properly defined per se is doubtful with respect to the relevance within the realm of quantity identity.

Thus with respect to some kind of quantity theory it is certainly possible to believe in the potential existence of such a theory but then we need to be more convinced of the appropriateness of the variable definitions.

Money and its Intrinsic Contradiction

Money as we think of it in daily affairs is a non-equilibrium concept in relation to the neoclassical equilibrium. It can be used in business where the relevant price vector is only defined locally and temporally. This conclusion is based on the fact that money in its daily conception is not only non-existent in a general equilibrium setting but also actually contradicts the general equilibrium so it is a kind of negative proof based on the observation that it actually works in daily business (Samuelson 1969).

Furthermore we have shown that the barter economy defined as in the neoclassical axiomatic structure only holds for atomistic defined agents and commodities. This stems from the axiom of reflexivity, which partly gives rise to Arrow's paradox. Thus the agents, as we know them from daily experience do not behave as postulated in the axioms. Consequently we have rejected the existence of general equilibrium and thereby *also* additive aggregation.

But this rejection of additive aggregation is only valid for the barter economy. Thus it says nothing with respect to the money economy since transferring real purchases into money values has no bearing on our analysis of the barter economy.

Earlier we had it that neoclassical theory a priori transforms agents and commodities to atomistic variables and our rejection of the axiomatic structure actually targets this very feature as well as the feature of additive aggregation. Doing so we could derive a relatively strong theorem for the barter economy with respect to relations between different aggregate levels in Proposition 2.1, but this has *per se* little to do with the money economy.

So now we have to set out for analysing money in a disequilibrium economy with only local and temporal price vectors. Fundamentally however we have still the same problem as before and which is expressed in Russell's paradox and concerning complexes in relation to atomistic variables.

The difference, as we already have pointed out, between an atomistic variable and a complex variable is that the former belongs to non-proper classes, that is the universal class belong to itself, but the latter belongs to proper classes, that is the universal class does not belong to itself. So we bring in a medium of exchange which is money and which is defined in a physical sense, by coins, bills, figures on a paper or in a computer file, called monetary assets/liabilities/promises. Thus it has some kind of inter-spatial and inter-temporal *physical* representation. Remember that the neoclassical price index does only exist in a mathematical structure of unclear spatial and temporal existence.

Arrow and Hahn (1971: 356–357) express it nicely:

> Keynes wrote that 'the importance of money essentially flows from it being a link between the present and the future', to which we may add that it is important also because it is a link between the past and the present. If a serious monetary theory comes to be written, the fact that contracts are indeed made in terms of money will be of considerable importance.

As we have already seen and will see further on, this aspect of a physical representation of a value in time and space is of huge importance when discussing the concept of inflation, growth and monetary policy.

So – how about the market process and values? Let us imagine an economy in general equilibrium at a ruling price vector. If we in such an economy lend some money, whatever that may mean, our liability is defined in real terms and thus has a real value and since the general equilibrium must be of almost eternal duration our liability will have a physically defined money of constant real value.[16]

However the sloppy non-equilibrium we discuss here has no generally persisting price vector, only one that is locally and temporally defined, and therefore there is no logical link between the value of money and the ongoing market process in the economy in question. There are obviously links of social, socioeconomic nature but these links are due to what Samuelson calls a historical dynamic trajectory which is constantly affected by current events. Think of a visit to a castle, like that in Compiègne, outside Paris, for instant. When you walk through it you pass through different chambers, rooms, banqueting rooms, closets, back stairs, magnificent marble stairs and so on. When you pass the different rooms and stairs you must adapt to the shape of the rooms, passages, and eventual pieces of furniture and art, but still you have a kind of direction, but the general direction cannot be seen as a norm for local conditions (and of course vice versa) irrespective of the shapes of the rooms you so far have passed through and eventual average patterns you may imagine. This has bearing on the discussion of GDP when some people in the media particularly, mostly non-professional economists, claim, at least implicitly, that GDP is some kind of welfare measure, which is completely wrong. It is an index of the money turnover in the economy. But assuming rather inert social and economic structures an increase in the turnover can be linked to increases in consumer demand and higher employment but such conclusions depend on structural matters of the economy in question.

Say describes the money as non-equilibrium measure in relation to physical measures in an elegant way which we quoted in Chapter 1 (Say 1834 [1803]: 247).

Jean Baptiste Say as well as Henry Thornton firmly rejected money as some kind of global measure and that was in line with their rejection of general equilibrium which Say rejected explicitly in pointing out that all price vectors were only local and temporal. Thornton implicitly rejected it in his criticism of Smith's real bill approach and both stuck to the analysis by the Friars of Salamanca represented by the earlier quote from de la Calle (see page 110) and that means that any kind of average norm for judging prices will have distributive consequences if somehow implemented in the economy and unfortunately any standard assumption on the stochastic measures a priori is bound to be of the same character as other ad hoc assumptions.

Consequently any kind of money value has a general meaning in the current context from a social point of view which means that for particular groups of commodities you could find a set of price intervals which are more or less temporally and locally inert. However if we look at a market result in real terms for a certain period of time, it means that with respect to a certain aggregate commodity basket this has little to do with the supplied assets and liabilities during the same period. A very simple example is the exchange rate in a small open economy like Sweden where the cross-border flows due to financial operations are approximately ten to fifteen times larger than those due to export/import operations and these different streams have in the short run little to do with each other. Thus art valuation, jewellery valuation, car valuation, food valuation occur in more or less closed compartments and when we speak of money value which of those compartments mentioned would we rank as most important for keeping the money value stable? However we may also think about a stable money value in relation to outstanding assets and liabilities and we certainly find a more vivid interest in the latter problem but how will that affect the mentioned commodities of the first question?

How the current valuation of money relates, if at all, to current and future production/consumption is perhaps the most intriguing question. As we have discussed earlier with respect to non-proper classes: what happens when we transform a set of complex variables into money values is that we also drain them of any real content. Thus there is no intrinsic link in the market exchange which hints to us what dimensions in the complex are valued. Nowadays we see that commodities are linked to dimensions as appropriate from environmental points of view, we have so called 'fair trade' commodities and similar. Thus we have to specifically point out certain dimensions and of course find control systems to fight frauds.

So the barter deals with complexes and thus we can derive proposition 2.1 that additive aggregation does not hold and furthermore that optimization at individual levels and aggregate levels are not logically connected.

But bringing in money in its daily sense, which does not fit into the barter equilibrium, implies inducing an atomistic variable. Money, which has indeed several intrinsic features which are, at least partly, at variance with each other, is still defined as an atomistic variable in the sense that money irrespective of assigned value or patterns of use belongs to non-proper classes, thus the universal set of money, and money values, belongs to itself.

This means that we are actually free to aggregate individual money values irrespective of any kind of *real utility* of the commodities in question: 'Pecunia non olet'.

If we go back to Russell's paradox again it is evident that money belongs to so called non-proper sets. A ten-dollar bill is equivalent in value to ten one-dollar bills, a hundred-dollar bill is equivalent to ten ten-dollar bills or a hundred one-dollar bills. Possibly there might be an aspect of convenience which we dismiss from our mind.[17] Furthermore there are no problems of adding different prices of the same type of commodity at different times and/or places and the sum will have an economic meaning, in relation to a budget restriction for example. All aggregations of money values take place in space time and are added for a geographical/administrative area and over a time frame irrespective of any local and temporal equilibria. The numbers of any kind of paper, transformed to the same currency, denoting assets/liabilities/promises can be added and have an economic meaning.

This leads us to a surprising analytical result. Proposition 2.1 holds aggregation of real entities, thus when we discuss the neoclassical axiomatic structure we are bound to reject any logical link between different aggregate levels due to the aggregation per se. We may reject any form of additive aggregation of real variables, which are to be seen as complexes.

In Chapter 1 we rejected the axiom of reflexivity on the grounds that the physical item is different from the commodity in the sense that a commodity has a higher or lower number of characteristics which fit differently into different structures. Thus we rejected additive aggregation with respect to commodities. What we have done so far is to reject additive aggregation of agents as a consequence of the correct interpretation of Arrow's paradox. *But all this concerns the barter economy.*

When passing over to the money economy at the microscopic as well as the macroscopic level we actually leave the real economy and discuss only money values, which have no normative value whatsoever in a macroscopic analysis except as a sign of short term turnover of money.

So what is our logical apparatus worth? As soon as we empirically can detect some inertia we can in principle set up a deterministic model for that kind of inert structure. Obviously the neoclassical approach is a very good model for rational economic choice/exchange given certain conditions which are set by the axioms but their link to inert empirical structures are indeed week, so exactly what kind of lessons do we learn from that approach?

Thus aggregating money values in a non-equilibrium monetary economy measures at best the money turnover in the economy and which via fixed prices achieved by some standard operations give some vague idea of the commodity turnover given appropriate assumptions of inertia.

To say that the so called fixed prices give some sort of idea of a *value* which has any extension in time and space should mean that all dimensions of a commodity should be measured. Thus the so called externalities either if they are bound to the commodity in question or to the production of the commodity are dimensions of the physical item we call a commodity, irrespective of whether it is a thing or a process.

In a non-equilibrium analysis this is a necessity since the commodities are defined over the entire positive and negative space. This of course does not prevent the individual agents to just discuss a limited dimensionality in their negotiations over a market price.

Now measuring inflation in a dynamic economy is a priori not possible but requires that we assume a certain socioeconomic inertia of consumption and production structures if the acquired index should be a measurement of the development of real transactions, and when using the Laspeyre inflation index for example we have to assume constant dimensionality of the commodity space to have a proper interpretation. In fact it is, from what we have discussed earlier on complexes, rather difficult to interpret inflation and also thereby growth in a dynamic perspective. In the short run we may claim socioeconomic inertia but in the long run the social 'role' of the commodities changes, which affects the internal relations in both individual and aggregate commodity baskets. To catch that kind of processes requires rather intricate and thorough investigation and is probably not adequately met by commodity group aggregates or representative commodities. Thus short run inflation enquiries might be relevant because of socioeconomic inertia but long run comparisons are due to effects of the socioeconomic development with respect to consumption and production structures.

Strictly logically speaking however this means that when we aggregate money values we are able to perform additive aggregation and furthermore proposition 2.1 will indeed become difficult to specify since we then obviously lack measures to perform the real analysis. How do we discriminate one money value from another when we work with money values?

We have claimed that there is a considerable difference between an index with respect to relative prices in a general equilibrium and inserting a medium of exchange/measurement which is thought of as representing this index. Economists/philosophers before the so called marginal revolution like Ricardo, Say, Smith, Hume, the Friars of Salamanca and Aristotle all claimed that the introduction of a conventional medium of exchange, which was called money, always implies that the medium of exchange gets an intrinsic value from its very role of such a medium and furthermore that this is partly independent of the adequate commodities. Furthermore as mentioned before, Jean Baptiste Say explicitly rejects money as a general measure of value: it is only a temporal and local measure.[18]

As we see this fundamental problem does not arise from economic and/or mathematical considerations but springs out of a more general philosophical problem of conceptualization. If we return to Keynes' rather deep involvement in the question of atomistic and complex variables, which indeed blur the concept of probability with respect to social sciences, the passing over to analysing real things with respect to their money value, which appears in actual transactions, implies that we quite automatically specify the real variable, *irrespective of any intrinsic complexity*, as an atomistic variable. Thus the problems which Keynes struggled with are in fact already overcome in the passing over to money values as the foundation of the analysis. Furthermore the precise analysis of the barter economy is of no relevance for aggregation.

When it comes to econometric studies these are to be performed with respect to the money value of items not the items themselves. Consequently proposition 2.1 holds in a barter economy and so also for analysis where the problem with respect to the adequate real variables is so precisely defined that passing over to use the money values for the real variable in question does not change the fundamental structure of the problem. However in a money economy where the market actions result in local and temporal price vectors proposition 2.1 is affected in a curious way.

We suggest the following tentative proposition:

> Proposition 3.1
> *With respect to a real analysis equivalent to barter, the proposition 2.1 holds.*
>
> *When we pass over to a non-equilibrium analysis where goals and restrictions are formulated in monetary terms we lose all logical relations to the real economy and consequently Proposition 2.1 has no meaning.*

The second part of the proposition 3.1 implies that if we have a goal as 'maximizing the financial surplus' or 'minimizing the financial costs' given restrictions in financial terms we may very well imagine the existence of a set of individual optima which are unique to a certain universal optimum and these are measurable in the same way as any aggregate optimum.

Thus the individual optimization problems are formulated exactly as any kind of optimization for an organization on some aggregate level. A State under has in some sense the same kind of budgetary problems as individuals, apart from that the state controls the money printing. This actually gives rise to the deceitful political argument 'Dear citizens, the minister of finance has a task of balancing a budget, which is a problem we all recognize from our household economy …'. This theme is regularly used and *it is true* in some sense, but perhaps not from all perspectives?

So what have we achieved? Logical operations in the barter economy, which logically exclude a medium of exchange as money in physical sense, give rise to proposition 2.1.

We pass over to the money economy which is a non-equilibrium economy and find to our surprise that this theorem does not hold with respect to commodities and processes expressed in money values. But then we also exclude any form of general equilibrium. Furthermore we have no logical link to any form of real values.

We have reached a magnificent contradiction.

Appendix: On Increase of Commodity Dimensions

The author has come into possession of a rich material from a country store, C.G. Bergs store. The material contains of inventory lists from 1913 to 1924 more or less complete. Furthermore many farmers and their families paid the monthly purchases around the tenth of the following month, which means that there are very specific records of purchases for around ten households which are seemingly complete for at least 5 years between 1914 and 1924.

As a comparison we have also access to a rich material from a modern grocery shop Rossin's, owned by Mr and Mrs Rossin who have most generously let me study parts of their books and accounts for 2013.

Unfortunately this fantastic material cannot be analysed here since we then dig in to a fascinating microscopic world which will be a booklet of its own.

However with respect to the number of dimensions of the commodity basket we have compared the two stores.

The inventory list of C.G. Berg's General Store the 31 December 1915 had 87 different articles. A study of the actual sale based on the purchases of five households gives us that around 30 different articles or more was sold on more or less regular basis that were mostly food stuffs, egg, bread, milk, cheese, vegetables, fish and similar, which were bought from farms, hunters, fishermen. So we can say that around 120 commodity dimensions were sold by C.G. Berg.

Rossin's Grocery store made an inventory list on 26 August 2013, which held 18,423 different articles, although Mr. Rossin told that around 16,500–17,000 different articles were sold on regular basis, since the store is situated in a small village close to the sea, so summer and winter sales are rather different.

The commodity dimensions of C.G. Berg were almost independent dimensions with small substitution possibilities, while Rossin's commodity dimensions is in many cases almost as direct substitutes, as toothpaste, shampoo and similar. Mr. Rossin's thought that it could be wise to diminish the dimensions by 10 to 15%. So we will land on some 15,000 relevant articles.

Thus we have 120 commodity dimensions in 1915 and 15,000 dimensions in 2013. Let us now proceed according to Adam Smith's version of the real bill hypothesis, thus the bills have to be covered by a certain quantity of gold.

Furthermore let us dismiss the quantity problem so we assume constant population and constant consumption so the same number of people consumed canned sardines in 1915 as in 2013, thus commodities are consumed in one unit and relative prices among existing commodities will be constant for the future. Durable commodities as their prices can be distributed over an appropriate time period.

Under these very simplified assumptions the average price will be directly proportionate to gold and we assume the growth to take place at a constant rate.

The growth function for $t_0 = 120$ and $t_{98} = 15,000$ will consequently be $D_t = 120 \cdot e^{0.049 \cdot t}$

Thus in order to keep the nominal prices, we need a growth of gold possessions of 4.9% annually.

We will not proceed our speculations by releasing our assumptions, suffice to say is that the aspect of increase of the dimensions of the commodity basket is an important aspect to take into consideration when dealing with inflation measures and inflation policy. It is also a bit curious and intriguing why it is so seldom that theoretical growth studies deal with this aspect besides the quantitative one.

Notes

1 We are aware of many critics today of the abundant use of rationality and optimizing behaviour but that is probably due to the juxtaposition of *how* people should optimize and *if* they should optimize.
2 Say, J.B. (1803 [1834]), *Traité d'économie politique*. Translated from the 4th edition of the French by C. R. Prinsep. *A treatise on political economy*; available online at: **http://www.econlib.org/library/Say/sayT.html**.
3 When commodities are structurally defined some dimensions might be negative for some agents while positive for others.
4 Optimality where we use global or average optimality as norms only holds in neoclassical general equilibrium theory. Given that the agents have different apprehensions of the current reality it is however difficult to have any objective norm whatsoever.
5 Such distinctions are also of value when we discuss the ordinary workings of an economy. With respect to inflation for example ordinary variations in inflations due to real causes and political measures are not seldom discussed in relation to hyperinflation. Thus some political and economic actors warn against using money supply to (hopefully) increase the market activities in an economy. Hyperinflation normally appears in a state of social disintegration and severe unease. One historical hyperinflation was administered during the early 1920s by Germany. Simply it was a way to pay the war indemnity by increasing the money supply at a higher percentage than the current depreciation of the currency. As it went out of order it was stopped at the price of individual economic catastrophes. Hjalmar Schacht, who was one of the inventors of this policy during the Hitler era, constructed the so called MEFO (Metallische Forshungsinstitut) which had the opposite goals namely to save the German Reichmark from depreciation and inflation by forcing companies and in the end also the employees to accept the MEFO-Bills the underlying value/grants of which was less or equal to the paper containing the text.
6 There is a market for quick credits which you can get on your mobile phone, called sms-loans. The effective interest rates on this market, which authorities are now discussing banning, is sometimes up to 12,000 % per annum, although a part of the interest payment is called fees.
7 It is funny to see that economists such as Hume, Thornton and Say and even the Salamanca Friars are sometimes interpreted as general equilibrium theorists. These three were from the logics of analysis non-equilibrium theorists. Hume pays much attention to the role of money in a process of social change. Thornton discusses the problem of inconsistencies between the real and the financial sector, and Say actually explicitly rejects the principle of a general measure.
   The reason for this might be that modern analysts may not observe the difference between an ordinary dynamic (or static) equilibrium and the general equilibrium as defined by an axiomatic structure.
8 This part in Hume can be interpreted as a discussion of competitive and non-competitive market structures but Hume only discusses the fact that in good times many have good profits while during bad times few have good profits.
9 With respect to our lives we often think of a straight line from birth to death. But how shall we treat the situation where we may set a probability of death, within a year for

example, for a person with a serious heart problem, but the person is treated in an efficient way which makes the probability of dying within a year lower. We cannot treat life for that person as a straight line.

10 There is a story about Napoleon that he once promoted a colonel to general who exclaimed that it was the first time he was really lucky, which made Napoleon cancel the promotion with the words: 'I have no use for generals who are not lucky'.

11 A *de facto* definition of a variable is not only used for scientific purposes but also for practical purposes in daily business. Thus we may theoretically come up with many interesting definitions which might even give us desirable answers but if so we have to explain the relations to the everyday handling of the same variables but a different definition.

12 CPI – consumption price index. Not to be confused with corruption perception index.

13 If we for example look at subgroup *410 Flat with right of tenancy, cooperative flat, garage* is indeed problematic since price of flats with tenancy rights to a high degree are negotiated centrally while cooperative flats depends, at least in bigger cities, on free market pricing. During the 1990s and 2000s there has been a pronounced change in the structure with flats with tenancy rights being transformed into cooperative flats in attractive areas. This change has therefore affected the allocation of different flats to different income classes.

14 I am not particularly happy with Keynes' references to Say since they are built on later interpretations of Say. Reading what Say actually wrote and placing the so called Say's law within a proper context of his writing Say is on one hand a no-equilibrium economist and furthermore much less categorical than is hinted at by Keynes. Given however the specific interpretation of Say, Keynes' reflections are correct.

15 Thus for example a particular car could be seen as a set of characteristics, features, of which some are much preferred by the consumer while others are not and in some cases also considered negative. However the relative importance of the specific features of the car in question depends on the very context of the daily use.

16 Remember that if there exists a general equilibrium defined by the neoclassical axiomatic structure, the equilibrium has no complement thus it is almost eternally persisting.

17 This aspect may indeed play a role, which we experience when the cash machine tells us that only 50 euro bills can be obtained for example and you just need a few euros to pay in cash. Furthermore when inflation explodes these matters it is also worthwhile to take them into consideration.

18 In fact he rejects the entire concept of general equilibrium.

Bibliography

Aristotle (1990 [original around 334-324 BC]) Politics Bno. (1257[a]), in *The Works of Aristotle vol II*, Encyclopædia Britannica, Inc. Chicago, London, p. 452, Bno. 1258[b] (Bno refers to the Berlin enumeration)

Arrow, K.J. (1963) 'Uncertainty and the Welfare Economics of Medical Care', *The American Economic Review*, vol. LIII, no. 5.

Arrow, K.J. and Hahn, F.H. (1971) *General Competitive Analysis*. San Francisco: Holden Day Inc.

Edvinsson, R. (2007) *Historisk monetär statistik för Sverige 1668 – 2008 - Årlig statistik över M0 och M3 1871 – 2006*, Ekonomiskhistoriska institutionen, Stockholms Universitet och Sveriges Riksbank. (Historic monetary statistics for Sweden 1668 – 2008 – Yearly statistics of M0 and M3 1871-2006, Univ. of Stockholm, Dept. of Economic History and Central Bank of Sweden).

Ekstedt, H. (2012) *Money in Economic Theory*. London and New York: Routledge.

Grice-Hutchinson, M. (1952) *The School of Salamanca*. Oxford: Clarendon Press.

Hume, D. (1770 [1752]), *Essays and Treatises on Several Subjects, vol. II, containing Essays, Moral, Political, and Litterary*, Printed for T. Cadell (successor of Mr. Millar) in the Strand; and A. Kincaid and A. Donaldson, at Edinburgh.

Hume, D.A. (2002 [1740]) *A Treatise of Human Nature*. Oxford: Oxford University Press.

Kalecki, M. (1944) 'Professor Pigiou on the Classical Stationary State. A Comment', *The Economic Journal*, Vol. 54, No. 213: 131–132.

Keynes, J.M. (1973 [1936]) *The General Theory of Employment Interest and Money*. Cambridge: MacMillan, Cambridge University Press.

Lucas, R. (1995) *Monetary Neutrality*, Prize Lecture – 1995 Nobel Prize in economics, December 7, 1995 http://www.nobelprize.org/nobel_prizes/economic-sciences/laureates/1995/lucas-lecture.pdf

Mankiw, G. (2003) *Macroeconomics*, 5th edn. New York: Worth Publishers.

Newton, I. (2010 [1688]) *The Principia – Mathematical Principles of Natural Philosophy'* Snowball Publishing.

Samuelson, P.A. (1969), 'Nonoptimality of Money Holding under Laissez Faire', *Canadian Journal of Economics*, Canadian Economics Association, vol. 2, no. 2: 303–308.

Say J.B. (1834[1803]) *A Treatise on Political Economy; or the Production, Distribution, and Consumption of Wealth*. Philadelphia: Grigg & Elliot, 9, North Fourt Street.

Thornton, H. (1939 [1802]) *An Enquiry into the Nature and Effects of the Paper Credit of Great Britain*. London: George Allen & Unwin. Available free at http://oll.libertyfund.org/index.php?option=com_staticxt&staticfile=show.php%3Ftitle=2041&layout=html

von Böhm-Bawerk, E. (1930 [1888]) *The Positive Theory of Capital*. New York: G.E. Strechert & Co. Available at: https://mises.org

Wicksell, K. (1936) *Interest and Prices*. London: Macmillan and Co. Ch. 9.

4 Money, Finance and Growth

Abstract

On the basis of our findings in the first three chapters in this chapter we are going to investigate more carefully the dynamic concept of money and finance. We will concentrate of the concepts of stability and growth with respect to the organization of the banking and financial sector and discuss return of the real bill principle as a consequence of globalization. We will then compare the early 19th century debate between real bill proponents and monetarist proponents, which led to a conscious choice of the monetarist view and compare this with the more or less endogenous changes in the financial system due to the globalization.

We will furthermore study the effects on real flows by revaluations of assets and liabilities, where we use the Minsky hypothesis and try to link it to enlarge the discussion by Keynes in *General Theory* chapters 17 and 18 on why the economy is unstable to a certain degree but not completely unstable.

Introduction

We have in the first three chapters run into a rather unpleasant set of contradictions. Pro primo, the neoclassical model has to be rejected on axiomatic grounds, which means that there exist no a priori links between the microscopic and the macroscopic levels of the economy. Furthermore we have to rule out additive aggregation. With respect to money in its usual daily form, there is no consistent role for it in neoclassical theory, given its axiomatic structure, apart something in the form of a mathematical index which is linked to the precise equilibrium in question.

Pro secundo, rejecting the existence of general equilibrium made money as we know it in daily business intelligible but on the other hand it allows us, contrary to the barter economy, to perform additive aggregation and when we pass over to money values it is possible to find some sort of consistency between microscopic and macroscopic levels, although this has no bearing on the real analysis. If it should have, that would imply that we must once again find an axiomatic structure transforming commodities and agents to atomistic variables, belonging to non-proper classes as money does. Thus there is a breach between the real economy and its financial picture due to a conceptual difference between money and real variables.

Pro tertio, we have shown that the neoclassical axiomatic structure has no environment; the general equilibrium is nowhere dense. If so we ask what does the concept of stability mean because if we are thrown out of a ruling general equilibrium the economy is not defined. We are then out of equilibrium and many local and temporal price vectors may exist. Thus we cannot expect an equilibrium with a unique price vector; so, what is meant by a partial local and/or temporal equilibrium at variance with a general equilibrium?

Obviously money/finance/liquidity has to be much more integrated in macro-economic thinking. As it seems now the real economy lives its own life beside the financial sector. Business is affected by the financial economy that is true, but there is no real interaction between them and the financial sector is partly seen as a mirror of the real sphere and partly independent. To some extent we have to agree with such a description, but as we have seen in the preceding Chapter 3 even the elementary concept of money implies great difficulties and our considerations of the quantity *identity* of money seems to lack the necessary definitions to make it a viable quantity *theory* of money.

The role of banks and the financial markets in relation to the real side of the economy is in principle threefold: first, there is the task of transforming financial savings into real investments; second, the task of redistributing liquidity, which combines the storage of liquid resources with a redistribution, given proper security, of liquidity not used by some agents to agents in need of liquidity. The third task is almost the same as the second but at variance with respect to the size of liquidity, and deals with transforming real inert assets into liquid assets, given proper security, which smooths the inertia and gives a higher degree of continuity.

As we see in principle we have three kinds of liquidity flows

One liquidity flow is direct between firms and households in relation to shares ownership. One is from household to banks/financial sector and one from

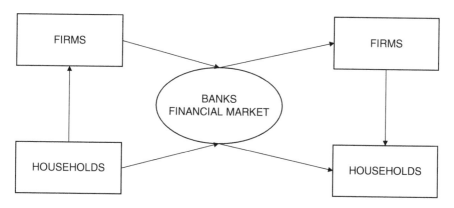

Figure 4.1 Principle Liquidity Flows

banks/financial sector to households. These flows are all based on contractual relationships and concern current as well as future affairs with respect to the flow in question. For all the flows it holds that contracts are made in current nominal money. Interest rates are negotiated with respect to current security and expectations.

Thus banks and other financial operators are a sort of transformation mechanism which, alluding to Hume, does not deal with the real economy but is a lubricant and makes the diffusion system of money more efficient. This means that basically the banks' role is arbitration at a given security level. This is actually the basic rationale for a sort of real bill system which the bullionist debate in Britain during end of 19th century and beginning of 20th century was about. The illustrious banker Henry Thornton, who was not basically a bullionist, attacked the banks within the current real bill system for jeopardizing security in order to make profits, which had certain parallels to the financial debacle of 2008. Furthermore the borders between proper credit costs and usury is always a viable problem, not so much perhaps with respect to interest rates but with respect to the focus of the credit system avoiding natural risk-taking which always is linked to entrepreneurial activities which promotes real growth.

Thus when the financial system leaves this role of a lubricant for business and production activities in order to maximize its profit it may affect the real transactions and decrease the efficiency of the market system.

Growth

The market economy builds basically on the diffusion of money in order to penetrate new entrepreneurs to develop new products and services. It is hard to see a market economy as a static organism. In this growth process the financial market is a prime actor in the diffusion process of money/liquidity. On the other hand we have seen that if we could only see money as a medium of exchange the diffusion process would be simple and straightforward, but as money is indeed complex the different intrinsic dimensions are at certain moments contradictory. One of the first to realise this was Aristotle.

Outside the neoclassical analysis, liquidity is seen as a most interesting concept and already Aristotle notes the basic features of it. It is instructive to follow Aristotle's steps in the analysis. First of all he is a chartalist, money is a social convention, although he discusses coins in precious metals:

> But money has become a convention a sort of representative of demand; and this why it has the name 'money' (ὅμισμα) because it exists not by nature but by law (νόμος) and it is our power to change it and make it worthless.
>
> (1990 [334 BC]: 381, no 1133ᵃ)

The second step concerns the future value of money:

> And for the future exchange – that if we do not need a thing now we shall have it if ever we do need it – money is as it were our surety; for it must be

possible for us to get what we want by bringing the money. Now the same thing happens to money itself as to goods – it is not always worth the same; yet it tends to be steadier.

(Ibid.: 381: no 1133^b)

The third step Aristotle takes is of great theoretical importance since he recognizes the possibilities of organizing future markets in form of retail trade and furthermore the possibility to earn money on money itself. With respect to the latter Aristotle held a strict moral code which later was pursued by St. Thomas.

When the use of coin had once been discovered, out of the barter of necessary articles arose the other art of wealth-getting, namely, retail trade; which was at first probably a simple matter, but became more complicated as soon as men learned by experience whence and by what exchanges the greatest profit might be made.

(Ibid.: 451, no. 1257^b)

This led to the possibility of earning money out of money itself:

There are two sorts of wealth-getting, as I have said; one is a part of the household management, the other is retail trade: the former necessary and honourable, while that which consists in exchange is justly censured; for it is unnatural, and a mode by which men gain from one another. The most hated sort, and with the greatest reason, is usury, which makes a gain out of money itself, and not from the natural object of it. For money was intended to be used in exchange, but not to increase at interest.

(Ibid.: 452, 1258^a–1258^b)

Consequently if we follow Aristotle's analysis, both retail trade and the different features of the financial market follow from the very concept of liquidity.

When we look at the 20th century discussions it almost seems that Keynes was the one who invented/developed the analysis around the concept of liquidity. Furthermore in the light of Aristotle it is remarkable that the non-existent analysis of money in the classical and neoclassical theory could be so central in the economic thinking.

In our analysis of liquidity, in Chapter 3, in terms of lexicographic preferences it is obvious that prices of liquidity under certain conditions even approach infinity.[1] Under such circumstances the market process is perturbed with respect to economic and/or social and ethical aspects.

Going back to the simple illustration in Figure 4.1 we realize on one hand that the 'transformation' system needs resources to work properly. This was in fact one of the conclusions of the Friars of Salamanca who more or less lifted the ban St. Thomas had placed on making money from money exchange. It is true that the Friars of Salamanca put forward ethical restrictions on just prices but nevertheless the financial operations were accepted as a normal part of a market economy.

On the other hand we must also realize that the under some conditions banking/financial system works under asymmetric conditions. Let us for simplicity's sake discuss only banks. A bank must manage two types of contract: one concerning borrowing from the public and one concerning lending to the public. Both these types of contracts are based on trust with respect to proper security; we may illustrate it traditionally as in Figure 4.2.

In such a case as Figure 4.2 shows we see that there is a kind of symmetry through which banks sell incoming liquidity back to the market agents who return it to the banking system and, given that, we do not have any systematic choice among banks and/or agents. In principle we can have a liquidity balance where the general gross liquidity change of banks' lending is zero. The moral obligations in the different directions are supported by the law in the case of banks and by real securities offered as security by the market agents. These real assets however have little or no liquidity value per se but increasing the 'enthusiasm' of the agents to stick to contractual payments.

However as we have seen the M3 have successively lost its importance in relation to GDP, at the same time the turnover of M3 has decreased. This is due mostly to financial market engineering giving particularly households better and wider access to the financial market and the stock market. But it has also changed the principles of the financial and banking system as illustrated in Figure 4.2. Although some part of the system as illustrated in Figure 4.2 still works we can illustrate an alternative structure which has grown from the middle of the 1970s to mid 2000s and illustrate it as in Figure 4.3.

The banks' direct borrowing from the public is at minimum and the banks have to finance their outstanding debt by securities sold at the market. In principle we can then categorize the outstanding debt in risk classes with different interest rates. Given a perfectly functioning financial market Figure 4.3 does not imply any principle difference in a macroscopic sense from Figure 4.2; in principle it is the households and firms who lend to banks in Figure 4.2 which buy the market

Figure 4.2 Borrowing and Lending in Banks

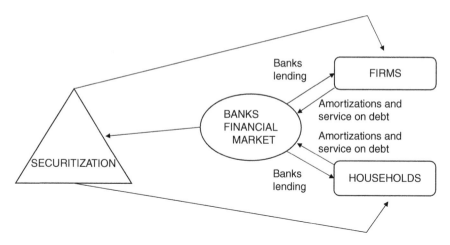

Figure 4.3 Real Bill Structure

instruments in Figure 4.3. Thus we will not have the asymmetry we mentioned above.

The difference however is that while the agents in Figure 4.2 deal with the direct flows of saving and liquidity, the securities in Figure 4.3 are part of a market choice of instruments where saving and liquid resources may change directions.

Most of all it changes the relation to inflation. Looking at Figure 4.2 we see that a given inflation rate certainly depreciates the outstanding debt as well as the amortizations but on the other hand it also affects to much the same extent the banks borrowing from households and firms. Thus what happens is that household lending will increase with inflation and so will the household borrowing. Thus as long as the real interest rate is not negative, that is the growth is above zero, the dynamic consequences for the bank system will be positive.

When we come to Figure 4.3 things are different. In our extreme case the debt has in fact disappeared from the banks' balance sheet. The banks earn money on the actual stream of loans, in Figure 4.2 banks are the guardians of the borrowed and the lent stocks of debt. What has happened in Figure 4.3 is that the market agents do not use banks as a source of income of money savings but acquire securities parallel to banks' removal of the agents' debts from their balance sheet.

This of course changes the incitement structures for the banks. Since they earn their money on the loan *transactions* they have an incitement to increase the very speed of turnover of these transactions and the former attention to the net interest rate has in our extreme Figure 4.3 disappeared. The interest rates are now set by the financial market relations.

What is even more interesting is that with respect to Figure 4.2 is that the banks' role as a guardian of debts earlier inspired them to pay attention to the underlying assets, but their role has been reduced to a transformation mechanism of loans to securities and of debt payments from the agents to the issuer of the securities.

Obviously this means that banks are protected from bankruptcies of the original borrower and their income comes from fees of transaction movements. Here the volume of transactions as well as the speed affects the incomes of the banks. This is underlying the very psychology behind the sub-prime crises.

A less observed effect of Figure 4.3 in relation to Figure 4.2 is that original real assets underlying the securities become less the asset per se but the payment abilities of the owner of the asset. Furthermore wealth as money bills/bonds upgrades the relative ability of liquid payments. Thus in fact from banks' perspectives low interest rates with tiny net interest rates are switched to increasing the volume and speed of loan transactions as long as the agents can pay their service. Furthermore there is the question of amortizations on debt – who has interest in that? True that securities mature but the horizon of maturity may well in principle be extended to eternity since in fact no market agent or bank in Figure 4.3 has any interest in that question. Thus amortizations might be a measure of controlling agents and of course they have their place when we have a mixed system of Figures 4.2 and 4.3 but in the extreme case of Figure 4.3 it is hard to see the need for amortizations as long as the market grows and then we mean the *financial market*.

A natural problem to pose is that of inflation. If we for the moment dismiss agents who have fixed incomes in nominal terms, pensioners and students on grants, these should not be neglected although they to a large extent in fact are[2] and concentrate on agents who are active at the market inflation kept within reasonable borders, has very small current effects. As we saw from our considerations and the statistics of Chapter 3 when we regard the real market we must ask who will react on a difference in inflation of 0.5%, particularly when we have a real growth in the economy, which we may define as increased turnover of commodities and production factors? None at all comes to mind. Thus with respect to Figure 4.2 the financial flows are relatively little affected by inflation. But when we are in the reign of Figure 4.3 the world is changed. All securities are defined in nominal values and banks and the issuing authorities are more or less independent of inflation since they get their incomes from the turnover of the financial resources in current price increases with inflation but the market agents who buy securities as an asset will be immediately hurt since the total wealth of nominal assets will be degraded by the increase. Thus while it is hard to see that inflation has any short term effects the financial effects on nominal wealth will be immediate and in principle of the same size as the change in inflation.

Consequently the social attitudes to inflation are completely changed when we move from Figure 4.2 to Figure 4.3. If the change is gradual, as it has been, the attitudes will change gradually, possibly reinforced by financial crises.

If we look at such a development in a historical perspective the two figures have similarities with the *bullionist* regime and the *real bill* regimes respectively. The bullionist approach was also called the *currency school* and the real bill regime was called the *banking school*.

The Bullionist-Real Bill Debate 1800–1826 in a Modern Perspective

The development of the financial market system leads us to take historical discussions between bullionist/currency school and real bill/banking school into consideration and it is fascinating to see that we today have a drift from the currency school as in Figure 4.2, which has dominated in practice more or less since World War II to the banking school represented by Figure 4.3 which is partly an answer to the globalization that has developed since the 1970s.

A Bank panic broke out in London in 1793, followed by a severe crisis in 1797 and the subsequent financial distress in England due to the wars provoked a discussion, the bullionist debate, of the monetary/financial system, which might be seen as a foundation for the monetary discussion today. The theoretical debate which was then underlying the political one, started with Henry Thornton's path-breaking analysis in 1802: *An Inquiry into the Nature and Effects of the Paper Credit of the Great Britain*. In some sense this debate came to a halt in 1826 when Ricardo's Ingot plan was posthumously published and which led to a full central bank system outlined in the Bank Charter Act 1844 when Bank of England got the sole right to issue bank notes which were tied to the gold reserves.

The early participants of the both sides respectively were David Ricardo as a bullionist and Charles Bosanquet as a supporter of the real bill approach. Concerning one of the key issues of the debate, inflation, the bullionists claimed almost a monetarist view that inflation was created by the money supply. The real bill supporters claimed on the other hand that inflation mainly was caused by real factors such as cost inflation. Henry Thornton took from the beginning a sort of middle position by claiming that both real cost factors and money supply affected inflation but in the current situation of England's financial distress he mainly blamed the careless policy of the government and most of all the fact that the money supply was not controlled. Thornton was to some extent regarded as an anti-bullionist mainly because bullionists tended not to be particularly liberal with respect to international trade in using paper credits and promissory notes which Thornton saw as an obstacle to trade and a hindrance to England's economic progress. Thornton chaired in 1807 a parliamentary committee on *public expenditures* and in 1810 he chaired the parliamentary *bullion committee*.

Thornton attacked the real bill approach and particularly Adam Smith's misconceptions of the financial system and the practice which had evolved (Ekstedt 2012: 41–53).

The debate between the currency school and the banking school has continued since the early 1800s but with variation in intensities. The currency school has dominated backed by quantity theory but economists like Fullarton and Tooke in the mid 19th century and Thomas Sargent and Neil Wallace at the end of the 20th century were/are supporters of the banking school/real bill approach.

An interesting start for our considerations might be Wicksell (1936 [1893]: xxiii) who had doubts regarding both the approaches in their absolute claims:

> I already had my suspicions – which were strengthened by a more thorough study, particularly of the writings of Tooke and his followers – that,

as an alternative to the Quantity Theory, there is no complete and coherent theory of money. If the Quantity Theory is false – or to the extent it is false – there is so far available only one false theory of money and no true theory.

We will actually follow Wicksell in our further considerations on money and the financial markets.

To follow this extensive and comprehensive debate covering a time period from the Friars of Salamanca to our time is almost equal to say that we want to cover the discussions over economic theory through time: it is impossible. We will however consider the different sides in a debate initiated by Sargent and Wallace (1982) to a sort of end comment by Sproul (2000). This debate is very interesting since the different authors actually start with references to the debate between Bosanquet, Thornton and Ricardo and with reference also to Fullarton and Tooke from the mid 19th century.

The real bill/banking school was described by John Fullarton (Sproul 2000) who wrote in 1845

> ... so long as a bank issues its notes only in the discount of *good* bills, at not more than sixty days' date, it cannot go wrong in issuing as many the public will receive from it [original emphasis].

According to Sproul (ibid.: 3–4) a good security will not cause inflation and is understood to mean: 1. sufficient – meaning that banks take a sufficient collateral value in exchange; 2. productive – that loans should go to 'carpenters and farmers' not to 'gamblers and spendthrifts'; 3. short term – generally less than 60 days. The real bill approach was supported by Adam Smith and Charles Bosanquet in the late 18th and early 19th centuries. The two most vigorous critics of the real bill hypothesis in the beginning of the 19th century blaming the reign of that approach for the bad financial position of England, were David Ricardo and Henry Thornton.

The debate between these two approaches has with varying intensity gone on since then. In the beginning it was mainly the question of the relation between money matters and inflation which was the big issue. Later on the efficiency and cost of the credit market/institutions has become more in the centre. The bullionist/currency school links inflation, partly at least, to the money supply, where the real bill/banking school approach deny such a link in the case that the real bill approach is properly managed as Fullarton/Sproul points out.

Sargent and Wallace (1981) compared the real bill hypothesis with quantity theory.[3] There are three main aspects which Sargent and Wallace consider: 1) government regulations of financial intermediaries; 2) conduct of open market operations by the central bank and the discount-window policy, 3) the definition of money.

The authors present two models, one real bill model and one quantity theory model and on the basis of the analysis of these models they conclude that:

Although our models are consistent with quantity-theory predictions about money supply and price-level behaviour under these two policy prescriptions, the models imply that the quantity-theory prescription is not Pareto optimal and the real-bills prescription is.

(Sargent and Wallace 1982: 1212)

Thus the paper by Sargent and Wallace does not deal with the empirical economy per se but is an analysis how the two approaches fit into a particular theoretical approach, the neoclassical general equilibrium theory. With respect to the early 19th century debate such an approach was not even possible since the particular conceptualization did not exist. This is also pointed out by David Laidler (1984) which we will come to later.

Anyway Sargent and Wallace claim that the real bill doctrine which suggests unrestricted financial intermediation, also proposes that there should be an unrestricted discounting of real bills since these are void of any default risk: 'The doctrine relies on market forces to prevent excessive "credit creation" by private banks' (ibid.: 1212–1213).

It is important to note an underlying assumption that real bills as credits are fully backed by real assets, gold, and other productive real assets. Under such conditions a laissez faire regime would reproduce real bills which were monetary replicas of the real economy. A credit is fully backed by real assets and the difference in time preferences between rich and poor agents would cancel out in time since the payments on debts exactly correspond to the difference in time preferences.

With respect to the quantity theory, where authorities try to separate *money* from *credits*,

The economy is such that, in absence of government restrictions upon intermediation, private credit instruments and government-issued currency are perfect substitutes from the point of view of the asset holders. Thus from quantity-theory point of view, the economy is one in which credit creation is simultaneously money creation when there are no government restrictions on intermediation.

(ibid.: 1214)

The models which the authors use for their derivations of propositions contain a specific feature which is interesting and that is a distinction between rich and poor households. Thus there are two groups of households with identical preferences but different endowment vectors. This difference between rich and poor households plays a decisive role in the analysis.

With respect to the real bill regime the private issuers of securities for loans are non-restricted with respect to the size of the securities which means that private banks can issue securities of a small size which poor households can buy, while under a quantity theory regime the credit market is restricted by the central authorities and so also the security market where authorities restrict the minimum size of securities which make the securities available only for rich households.

Thus given these latter additional assumptions to the standard perfect market assumption we end up in a situation where both the real bill and the quantity theory approach reach a monetary equilibrium, proposition 3 (ibid.: 1219) and proposition 4 (ibid.: 1222) respectively. However when it comes to full Pareto optimality only the real bill approach can produce that, proposition 5 (ibid.: 1223).

The reason why the quantity theory regime cannot produce Pareto optimum is the imputed assumption of central authorities limiting the minimum size of securities implying that the distribution of securities will change the distribution of endowments.

The Sargent and Wallace paper thus produces some kind of financial replica to the real distribution as it seems. The distribution of securities will mirror the relative endowments imputed into the Arrow-Debreu economy which given all axioms will hold.

We referred in Chapter 1 to Makarov and Rubinov (1977) and their linking of Newman-Gale dynamics to an Arrow-Debreu economy. In principle that is the kind of thinking we tend to meet in this paper, save for the lack of a production sector, so we will try to make an interpretation of the model by Makarov and Rubinov. We can think of an ordinary expected utility approach with perfect knowledge of the outcome vector and the probability structures. The endowment vectors consist of liquid resources and productive resources and a productions system which transforms the liquid resources by paying productive resources to make tools of future production, which when used pay eventual services and amortizations. We may assume that if we have two income classes, one rich and one poor, with identical utility functions, that the time preference between the two income classes are distributed with respect to the expected utility functions and that the production structure produces investment commodities as well as consumption commodities. Then the production of the investment goods will be paid ahead of the return on the investment, but since that is accounted for by the rich classes' lower time preference it will correspond to the poor classes' higher time preference.

This variant of the Sargent and Wallace models raises two questions however: why do the poor households need to borrow and why do they need to buy securities? From a Makarov and Rubinov point of view, eventual securities are identical to the remuneration of those who create capital items for future production, so the labour force, which we may suppose being the poor guys are actually paid and the rich are paid by the future returns which are properly sized by the market.

The other question is more fundamental: where are the production sectors in the respective models by Sargent and Wallace?

David Laidler (1984) criticized Sargent and Wallace on three main aspects:

> (1) The conclusions on whose basis they seek to rehabilitate the real-bills doctrine would have been anathema to its proponents; (2) what they refer to as the real-bills doctrine is not the real-bills doctrine; (3) their interpretation of Adam Smith's analysis of the social productivity of banking is quite misconceived.
>
> (Laidler 1984: 149)

Laidler's critique is worth reading in its entirety, but it is sufficient to say here that i) real bill supporters as Adam Smith and Thomas Tooke were clearly aware of the risk of 'excessive credit creation'. If we go back to the early bullionist debate, little else was discussed. Ricardo in his critique of the state of affairs expressed in an answer to Charles Bosanquet in the *Morning Chronicle* that the issue of paper money from the Bank of England in a real bill regime would transfer the Bank of England to a gold mine and we would revive the days of the inflow of gold from America.[4]

Furthermore Laidler says: 'Note that Smith does not advocate "unrestricted discounting of ... evidences of indebtedness, which ... are ... free of default risk"' (ibid.: 152). Laidler also notes 'that Smith suggests that bank lending to be confined to a certain class of customers, namely merchants, who should be thought of as borrowing to finance goods in the process of production and distribution' (ibid.: 152), and he proceeds:

> In any event, a model in which banks are permitted to make unlimited consumption loans, the only kind that exist in the world analyzed by Sargent and Wallace, surely cannot be used to rehabilitate a doctrine whose central feature, as we have now seen, was that bank lending be restricted to short-term loans to finance current *production and distribution*, only one of the many kinds of loan available in the world analyzed by Smith and subsequent real-bills advocates.
>
> (Ibid.: 153)

Then the question is still there: where are the restrictions Adam Smith makes and where is the production sector? With respect to that it is hard to see how rich households can lend to poor households.

The Sargent and Wallace paper is remarkable since they try to squeeze a discussion based on non-equilibrium thinking into a general equilibrium setting, and refer to the participants in a similar debate in the early 19th century who did not have even the slightest idea of concepts such as general equilibrium and Pareto optimality. To do so however the authors take assumptions which are contradictive and to some extent even contrary to the originators of the approach they want to defend.

However let us go back to the days of the early bullionist debate which in other terms was a debate between supporters of the currency school/quantity theory and banking school/real bill. Let us however start with Figures 4.2 and 4.3 above to understand the naming of the two sides. In Figure 4.2 the banks are borrowers/lenders in a defined currency supplied by the central authorities. The crucial problem is then the effective quantity of money which is the money supply in relation to the transaction velocity. Though if we had means to at least define and observe the velocity and it was not defined as a residual we would be able to relate the money supply to the velocity and thus control the effective money supply exactly. One problem is of course that the velocity may be different for different sectors like the real estate market in relation to the consumer market.

In that case we may have an asymmetric price development and since the real estate market also affects the wealth of the households we may have an unbalanced growth of wealth. Thus if real estates are financed by long term bonds we may affect the wealth of the household as well as the assets in the banking side and this way we may have an increase of credits. However this could be controlled by the authorities by using cash ratios and liquidity ratios where the bonds are included in the liquidity ratio. We must agree with Sargent and Wallace that such asymmetric processes highly affect the distribution of wealth and the banking system illustrated in Figure 4.2 indeed does not impose any neutrality with respect to wealth distribution.

In Figure 4.3 the credit creation is undetermined in the sense that if we can sell the securities we are free to go on lending to households and, as already mentioned, the incitement structure of the banks shifts from the net interest rate of assets and liabilities to the financial transactions speed. In principle we can think of a development illustrated by the two balance sheets in Figure 4.4.

We have illustrated the two extreme cases from Figures 4.2 and 4.3. In time period two in Figure 4.4 the liability side of the banks has been reduced to short run liabilities as check accounts and similar and owner's capital. The development has transformed the banks from guardians of stocks to a transformation vehicle in the dynamics of the financial system. The guardian aspect is now taken over by security issuers and eventual authorities and the banks are left to make a first check that the original borrower is bona fide with the proper support of the appropriate legal system. But the banks themselves have the interest of increasing the turnover of financial assets and liabilities which pass the banking system.

At the time of writing, winter 2015, the Central Bank of Sweden has decided to lower the overnight rate to -0.1, it is the first time in history that the overnight

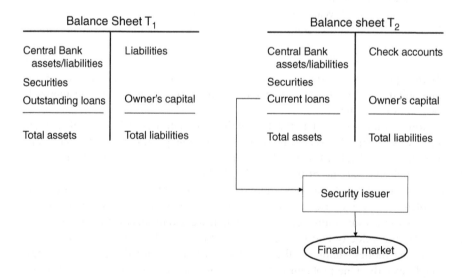

Figure 4.4 Bank balance sheet related to real-bill regime

rate is negative so it has caused some fuss in the media. However if we look at the balance sheet of time period two one may ask why should the banks have any lending/borrowing operations whatsoever in relation to the central bank?

The answer to this question is actually hidden in the very names of the two regimes. According to the currency school the central bank controls the supply of the very currency which is also necessary for the international position of the currency. Henry Thornton writes:

> The export trade to foreign countries is, generally speaking, one trade; the trade of importing from foreign countries is a second; the trade of sending out and bringing home bullion, in order to pay or receive the difference between the exports and imports, may be considered as a third. This third trade is carried on upon the same principles with any other branch of commerce, that is, it is entered into just so far as it is lucrative to the speculator in bullion, and no farther. The point, therefore, to be enquired into is clearly this, whether the pressure arising from a scarcity of bank notes tends to render the importation of bullion a more profitable speculation.
>
> (Thornton, 1939[1802]: 117)

In the case of Figure 4.3 and period two in Figure 4.4 the main importance is the underlying original value of the securities. But in a globalized system of convertible currencies it is insignificant which are the actual original currencies the original loans were given. Consequently we more or less cut the intrinsic links between foreign trade and the internal financial system since this is not existent but is a part of the international system.

However with respect to big transnational companies this structural change of the financial market is not a big deal, they are already using the financial markets of many countries.

For small companies and emerging companies however it probably makes a difference and Sargent and Wallace could indeed have a point here if they had noticed the production sector but that would probably lead to re-examination of the intrinsic features of the currency school and the banking school. As we see in the extreme case of Figure 4.4 time period two the possibility of long term finance of investments is no problem for big companies with big assets of different kinds. For small companies and relatively new entrepreneurs the situation is more difficult. As seen from Figure 4.4 the banks in period two have fewer resources to lend to such companies and further on these companies seldom have any assets of substantial value to back a security. Thus the only hope they can have is if the banks/issuing agent can pool a portfolio of small companies and issue securities on that basis, this is by the way what so called risk capitalists may do but judging new private market ventures is difficult so the normal way for entrepreneurs is to to sell their innovations and thus lose control of their innovations.

Here we do have a troublesome asymmetry but that works in relation to currency school and banking school exactly in the opposite way with respect to Sargent and Wallace conclusions.

The theoretical debate after Sargent and Wallace (1982) and Laidler's (1984) respective papers was continued by a paper by Thomas Cunningham (1992) and Michael Sproul (2000). Cunningham tries to give some empirical evidence on real bills doctrine and quantity theory while Sproul mainly discuss the bullionist's critique of the real bill approach in the early 19th century, particularly Henry Thornton.

It is interesting to start with the latter which we also can relate to Sargent and Wallace (1982). Sproul's paper is a criticism of Ricardo's and Thornton's opinions, mainly Thornton's in fact. The quintessence of Sproul's critique is summed up in his conclusion:

> Henry Thornton's 'false wealth' fallacy led him to believe that privately-created money would seldom be backed by any actual property. His mistake was in failing to realize that the self interest of the parties involved in money-creation automatically assures that all derivative money is backed by the entity that issues it. Once this is understood, the remaining question is whether base money itself is backed. If it is, then Thornton's argument cannot be used against real-bills proposition that money issued on good security will not cause inflation. Every new issue of money would be backed by assets of commensurate value, and so the value of money would be independent of its quantity.
>
> (Sproul 2000: 15)

One elementary critique of this paper is obvious, Henry Thornton's critique of the real bill hypothesis and particularly in Adam Smith's version is that he actually saw the very process in his daily work and contrasted Adam Smith's examples with routines and practices used in the current financial market. This is not a guarantee that Thornton's critique of Adam Smith and the current banking system was correct, but at least if Thornton made a mistake 'in failing to realize that the self-interest of the parties involved in money-creation automatically assures that all derivative money is backed by the entity that issues it' it is Thornton's analysis of what he actually saw which is wrong. His analysis is not based only on a theoretical model but also on assumptions.

This is also important to understand from two reasons: first we claim above that the more or less endogenous change of the financial system today due mainly to the globalization process will change the incitement structures for the banks and second Sproul's critique of Thornton implicitly claims that self-interest of the parties would create the appropriate control of the system. Thornton indeed failed to realize this, as did supporters of the real bill hypothesis. Laidler writes:

> Smith therefore understood the potential of price-level fluctuations for redistributing wealth in an arbitrary fashion, and he feared that potential: words such as 'injustice,' 'fraudulent,' and 'cheat' enter his vocabulary when he discusses these matters (see, e.g., p. 350). Such sentiments are not confined to Smith. All subsequent important adherents of the real-bills doctrine held

similar views. Thus, when Thomas Tooke, a leading figure in the banking school and a real-bills advocate, argued that the maintenance of the convertibility of currency into specie at a fixed price was 'the sine qua non of any sound system of currency' (1840, p. 177), he was expressing a view that had been a commonplace on both sides of the real-bills-quantity theory debate for four decades and was to remain so well into the twentieth century.

(Laidler 1984: 151)

Thus we realize from Figures 4.3 and 4.4 the necessity of backing the securities. What we may say is that it is not only a question of ethics here, which obviously is crucial as we learnt from the debacle in 2008 and the so called NINJA-bonds, but it is also a matter of revaluations of assets and liabilities due to the growth process of the economy.[5] Sad to say, economists often see growth of an economy in abstract aggregate terms; with respect to this there is indeed a need for a microeconomic foundation of the concept to realize the enormous power of structural changes both of the consumption side as well as of the production side which are not neutral to distribution of incomes and wealth, neither to allocation of productive resources.

In the above considerations Henry Thornton is a kind of central figure. He is in many ways a predecessor of Wicksell and Keynes and like Wicksell in the earlier quote he does not take any extreme position; he on one hand criticises Adam Smith's position with respect to real-bills, on the other hand he criticises the state central banks in their mixing of public and private affairs, thus defending the independence of Bank of England:

> ... the banks of Petersburg, Chopenhagen, Stockholm, Vienna, Madrid and Lisbon, each of which issues circulating notes, which pass as current payment, all in the most direct and strict sense government banks. It is also well known that the government residing in these several places have not those easy means of raising money, by a loan from the people, which the minister of Great Britain so remarkably possesses. Those governments, therefore, have in times even of moderate difficulty, no other resources than that of extending the issue of the paper of their own banks; which extension of issue naturally produces a nearly correspondent depreciation of the value of the notes, and a fall in the exchange with other countries, if computed at the paper price.

(Thornton 1939 [1802]: 108)

The essence of Sproul's critique of Thornton which we quoted above concerned the backing of the securities and the quality of that backing with respect to private interests. This is certainly a part of Thornton's discussions. But as seen from the quote on state interests with respect to money supply it is a bit difficult to see that Thornton's concern about the backing of the securities should be interpreted only in the state–private dichotomy; it has sooner to do with the difference in incitement structures of different agents with different purposes. Thus with respect to ethics we can say that imposing an ethical standard on an organization which in some sense contradicts its accepted purposes is a problem. You may limit the purposes within certain restricted areas but to impose rules which contradict the purposes in a general manner is unwise and lead to confusion and inefficiencies. For example private agents should not be expected to take part in control systems of private agents at variance with their own basic purposes. It is true that markets are generally a balance between conflicting interests but the control of the market function itself is quite a different thing as also Arrow's paradox to some extent shows.

Anyway Sproul focuses just on a part of, and perhaps not even the most essential part of Thornton's analysis. His critiques of Adam Smith's version of the real bill principle basically concern the circulation of money/papers/securities:

> The error of Dr. Smith, then, is this:—he represents the whole paper, which can easily circulate when there are no guineas, to be the same in quantity with the guineas which would circulate if there were no paper; whereas, it is the quantity not of 'the thing which circulates,' that is, of the thing which is *capable* of circulation, but of the actual circulation which should rather be spoken of as the same in both cases. The quantity of circulating paper, that is, of paper capable of circulation, may be great, and yet the quantity of actual circulation may be small, or *vice versa*. The same note may either effect ten payments in one day, or one payment in ten days; and one note, therefore, will effect the same payments in the one case, which it would require a hundred notes to effect in the other.
>
> I have spoken of the different degrees of rapidity in the circulation of *different kinds* of paper, and of the consequent difference of the quantity of each which is wanted in order to effect the same payments. I shall speak next of the different degrees of rapidity in the circulation of the *same* mediums at *different times*: and, first, of bank notes.
>
> (Thornton 1939 [1802]: 96)

Theoretically speaking we could say that Thornton analyses the eventual intrinsic contradictions of the 'moneyness' of different bills/securities/money. It is interesting to note that Sargent and Wallace (1982:1213–1214) partly at least note this aspect when they claim that while the currency school tried to separate the contractual aspect of money from the aspect of money as a medium of exchange, the banking school actually wanted these two aspects to be present in the money used. Sargent and Wallace actually advocate the latter, however their observation is correct. This is actually the essence of the bullionist debate.

Thus Thornton's problem is that a medium of exchange directly linked to gold, which was used for foreign affairs and for hoarding in times of unease would lead to uncomfortable variations in circulations of the medium of exchange which could have effects on the variations of prices. We have mentioned David Hume on this matter that he saw variations in the accessibility of the medium of exchange as asymmetric in the sense that a lack of medium of exchange led to more severe consequences than an excess of medium of exchange. Thornton takes the same attitude. With respect to the bank crises of 1793 he writes:

> The alarm, the first material one of the kind which had for a long time happened, was extremely great. It does not appear that the Bank of England notes, at that time in circulation, were fewer than usual. It is certain, however, that the existing number became, at the period of apprehension, insufficient for giving punctuality to the payments of the metropolis; and it is not to be doubted, that the insufficiency must have arisen, in some measure, from that slowness in the circulation of notes, naturally attending an alarm, which has been just described. Every one fearing lest he should not have his notes ready when the day of payment should come, would endeavor to provide himself with them somewhat beforehand. A few merchants, from a natural though hurtful timidity, would keep in their own hands some of those notes, which, in other times, they would have lodged with their bankers; and the effect would be, to cause the same quantity of bank paper to transact fewer payments, or, in other words, to lessen the rapidity of the circulation of notes on the whole, and thus to encrease the number of notes wanted.
>
> (Ibid.: 97–98)

The point is that the circulation of guineas and the papers directly linked to those were actually hoarded by country banks while in London it led to shrinking liquidity which threatened the punctuality of commercial payments.

The crisis was partly solved when 'a loan of exchequer bills was directed to as many mercantile persons, giving proper security, as should apply' (ibid.: 98). These exchequer bills were not backed by gold but provided a sufficient security. We have quoted Say in Chapter 3 when he claimed that even if an English paper not backed by gold and thus virtually worthless in France has a proper value if the paper is accepted in England/London and consequently it can be used among French merchants dealing with trade in England.

A diminution of notes of England based on guineas would lead to serious consequences and lead to further hoarding of gold guineas/real bills;

> Gold, in such case, would unquestionably be hoarded through the great consternation which would be excited; and it would, probably, not again appear until confidence should be restored by the *previous* introduction of some additional or some new paper circulation.
>
> (Thornton, 1939 [1802]: 114)

As also Laidler (1984) points out the dismissal of the production system from the analysis is devastating if we try to understand the bullionist debate. Thornton is quite aware of the difference between promissory notes used as medium of payments in commerce and production but this is on different terms with respect to the consumer market exchange. Thornton is not only aware of this but he actually treats commerce/production matters differently from the consumer market.

In commerce the different agents on one hand trade with large sums and on the other have profit as a main purpose. Then securities, properly backed, may be used as intra business payments. The securities are then interest bearing which is an advantage since they are held as profitable but they also are appropriate for business exchanges of large sums even if they are slower than both gold and bank notes in circulation. Even business however needs ready cash in terms of daily affairs. Thus neither gold nor bank notes pay any interest but gold/real bills are the very basis of valuation and thus a bank note, not linked to gold directly, which is in practice some sort of promissory note without interest has no hoarding value but as a medium of exchange and thus good for cash.

To conclude we can say that Thornton's analysis concerns mainly the speed of circulation of different more or less liquid assets and he stresses the point that the aspect of liquid assets as medium of exchange should not be 'corrupted' by other intrinsic features of money. He mentions the ethical aspect which Sproul claims is the key aspect of Thornton's analysis but this is in fact a minor aspect in his considerations. Furthermore Thornton's analysis strictly concerns the very financial system he was working with in his daily business as a banker. To squeeze Thornton's analysis into a general equilibrium setting or to the financial system of today is rather meaningless since those two matters were not actually discussed 1803.

Lessons from the Bullionist Debate and Wicksell's Doubts

What can we learn from the bullionist debate in early 19th century? When looking not only at Thornton but also at Ricardo, Smith, Say and Hume, their awareness of the difference in conditions between production/entrepreneurship, commerce and consumption respectively is a vital part of their analysis of even macroscopic questions. They indeed have a microscopic foundation of their macroscopic analysis. However this foundation is not based on abstract theoretical modelling but awareness of the particulars of different types of agents as well as of distribution and allocation problems. Thornton and Smith for example were well aware of the difference between London and the rest of Britain both with respect to commerce production and banking and these differences were a vital part of their analysis.

Thornton and Ricardo were the two leading figures on the currency side so to speak. In modern terms we could perhaps be tempted to call them early monetarists, but that is wrong. Thornton never mentions something even remotely similar to the quantity theory but still his analysis deals with the variables contained in quantity theory. He discusses, that's true, effects on the real production due to a diminishing quantity of money and also a price effect by excess supply of money. But he also discusses differences in the circulation speed depending on different mediums of exchange. Furthermore he differentiates the economic agents into different groups/classes, both with respect to commercial companies and production companies as well as poor and rich consumers. He also discusses the regional effects of using different kinds of medium of exchange between London as the commercial centre, the areas where other production took place and the countryside where agricultural production was dominant. Thus it could be seen as an outline of a sort of input-output model completed with financial streams, underpinned with regional and sectorial models. Extremely complex, that is true but still an impressive effort of systematic analysis, it would certainly be hard to find a straightforward way to express it in mathematical terms.

Thornton criticizes the real bill approach the approach which was working in the late 18th century in England and which was analysed by Adam Smith not some general equilibrium variant. Still however Thornton is not to be seen as a quantity theorist. He accepts in principle quantity identity but having said that he does not regard the circulation speed as constant but dependent of variations in the real economy as well as of institutional matters and the other features intrinsic to money. He was well aware of the possibility of using different forms of money but these were not symmetric with respect to different kinds of agents and different kinds of economic sectors. Thus quantity identity could not be uniquely specified as a coherent theory.

In a way Thornton underpins Wicksell's doubts about the existence of any kind of true theory of money, and it is indeed doubtful whether any coherent theory of money ever can be formulated in the sense of logical consistency since the inherent features of money, although stemming from the very fact that money is the medium of exchange, are partly or on the whole contradictive, but these contradictions vary in strength due to the understanding of the state of the economy and its socio-political environment.

Thus creating a system of behavioral rules is certainly possible but unfortunately due to institutional, social and political inertia in relation to human innovativeness and creativity, such a system will be obsolete and even internally contradictive as time goes by. The idea of formulating a set of universal and inter-temporal axioms which generates logical conclusions, is to no avail.

Where are We Now?

Following the bullionist debate into the present is indeed interesting. In the early 19th century England had mainly lived with the real bill system which in the 1790s was upset by the shockwaves of the French revolution and the warfare between France and England which started around 1792/93 and led to the Napoleonic wars. These events led to a conflict between private and collective interests in England which also contained the monetary system. We have to look at the bullionist debate from this perspective; both Ricardo and Thornton realized this conflict and proposed a system where the central bodies, i.e. Bank of England became solely responsible for the control of the money supply mainly outlined in Ricardo's Ingot Plan 1826. Thus the bullionist debate basically was about a *political decision* between two systems where the bullionists claimed the necessity of controlling the monetary system and also to avoid financial crises which, if not regularly, not seldom occurred by excess credits. England in the early 19th century was in the process of *political recreation* of the financial system.

The bullionist debate although of great interest and dealing with much of the same questions as we today have to consider had a completely different political, socioeconomic and institutional environment than we meet today.

If we look at the world in the aftermath of World War II, we started with a rather coherent international system built mainly on the ideas of the currency school, the Bretton Woods system. This broke down mainly due to an internal weakness that one of the member countries, USA, also issued a basic currency which created a dual system of financial markets; one outside the US and one inside which were connected in kind but not with respect to the real conditions. The Bretton Woods system worked surprisingly well for a long time but when the general growth created by World War II ended at the end of the 1960s competition increased and growth diminished which uncovered the intrinsic weaknesses of the Bretton Woods system. After its breakdown we had a period when the states upheld internal monetary regimes with more or less floating currencies. The creation of the EMU was an effort to create a system more built on Keynes' principles in the Bretton Woods system of which the natural consequence was a single currency. However the working of the EMU is partly transnational and partly national. This leads to inconsistencies in the sense that the formal rules for the different governments in the system does not de facto recognize the single currency, furthermore the institutional underpinnings on national levels are different between the member countries.

However since the breakdown of Bretton Woods, globalization has continued and necessitated practical solutions for business and production companies. Thus we have had a growth of 'promissory papers' as Thornton names them for business purposes and the growth has been little observed by the general political world and media, as Thornton says:

> Bills, since they circulate chiefly among the trading world, come little under the observation of the public. The amount of bills in existence may yet, perhaps, be at all times greater than the amount of all the bank notes of every kind, and of all the circulating guineas.
>
> (1939 [1802]: 94)

As we saw, in Chapter 3, from the statistics and the reports from the Central Bank of Sweden M3 has diminished with respect to PY in the quantity identity. The development from the extreme case of Figure 4.2 to that of Figure 4.3 has in fact proceeded for many decades but it is important to realize that we have never have been in the full regime of any of the illustrated cases but both regimes exists simultaneously to higher and lower degrees. Anyway with respect to the quantity identity there is no clear cut definition of money and consequently M3 loosely in relevance.[6]

In the case of Figure 4.3 the logics of quantity theory loses completely its relevance since, which in fact is in line with the Sargent and Wallace analysis, we can increase the outstanding securities *provided they are properly backed* towards infinity. Limiting money supply is an inefficient mean and manipulating the interest rate from the central bank will at best have price effects on some sectors, particularly housing, but in an internationally integrated market efficiency will be diminished. Open market operations will have effects but even these effects will be more limited to those sectors who mainly deal with the national markets, particularly the housing market.

Thus the central banks in the extreme case of Figure 4.3 will be left as a controller of banks, a lender of last resort and to some extent manipulating the interest rate with open market operations. But in a globalized world which still contains countries which set, at least partly, their own rules and pursue national economic policy the efficiency of monetary policy will be undermined particularly with respect to inflation.

Inflation can of course be explained by excess credits but then also we must reconsider the wording 'properly backed' securities.

Thus our current problem is not to choose between institutional systems but to cope with a more or less endogenous change of the financial market in response particularly to globalization.

Sargent and Wallace and Sproul draw very optimistic pictures of the real bill hypothesis in a theoretical world. We have gone through some criticisms mainly Thornton's which was built on his experience of the working of the system. Much of that critique is of course specific for those times but some aspects are still valid. One difference between the modern analysts and Thornton is that the latter discussed banking papers backed by gold while the modern analysts discuss securities based on unspecified assets. With respect to gold Thornton pointed out the risk of mixing the medium of exchange with the ultimate security and thus having the problem of variations in hoarding. With respect to securities based on credits Thornton discusses this in relation to commerce and production and observe a lower rate of circulation due to the interest bearing of the papers and also to the tendency to save that type of security exchange for transactions of larger amounts. These comments induce us to suspect that such a system will favour larger customers both with respect to business and private credits in order to have an appropriate backing of the securities, which is contrary to Sargent and Wallace's theoretical deductions when assuming a banking system of small local banks dealing with their neighbourhood in issuing securities at variance with the huge centralized private banks today issuing securities for an unspecified international market.[7]

We have seen that even proponents for the real bill approach have considered the necessary ethical standard in issuing securities and it is interesting that Sargent and Wallace and Sproul take this aspect lightly since their thought is that the market is self-regulating. This stems most probably from their basic general equilibrium methodology of analysis. Furthermore assuming both with respect to microscopic as well as macroscopic levels the postulate that saving is identical with physical investment and subsequently a separation is not required between money as a medium of exchange and money as credits and a denominator of assets and liabilities. When analysing a non-equilibrium economy such an assumption is indeed doubtful. Our analysis in preceding chapters to show the impropriety of the general equilibrium model as expressed in the axiomatic structure of the Arrow-Debreu approach puts in reality focus on the inertia of the economy. In such a non-equilibrium economic world particularly profits are problematic since they are to be seen as residuals and that give the result that the identity between physical investments and saving does not hold. Furthermore we showed in Table 3.5 that in Sweden there has been an ongoing process of increasing inequality of incomes which makes the saving/investment identity even more spurious.

In Chapter 3 we quoted Hume on interest rates where he also mentions the difference between the high competition market and the monopolized market and the effect that would have on interest rate. Both Hume and Thornton stress the importance of the competitive economy; not in a static manner of the 'perfect completion model' but in the sense that competition provoked new solutions in business and new dimensions of commodities and to obtain such a situation it was necessary to separate the diffusion of money in the society from the market for credits and securities.

They are also clearly aware of the importance of the circulation of money. David Hume uses the expression *diffusion of money* and that is actually a good expression and probably illustrates the thought behind the neoclassical general equilibrium theory as an efficiency norm.

The ethical side of security issues is evidently important but it is probably intertwined with aspects outside the control of the issuing agents, such as rules and habits in the technique of valuation and revaluation of assets and liabilities.

The Enlarged Input–Output Matrix

A great help in analysing the joint problems of the real and financial markets is to use the technique of the input-output matrix.

In Figure 4.5 we have enlarged the standard input-output table with a transaction scheme for financial flows. However it is important to see this completed tableau in a dynamic perspective so we also enter opening and closing assets and liabilities for a period, as well as the created resources for respective sector during the period. However to have a complete picture of the dynamics we also need to add revaluation vectors for assets and liabilities respectively.

From a static perspective all the entries within the matrices are given and constant and then the whole system is just a mechanic accounting system. We can add dynamics but then it has to be of the Neumann-Gale type which put restrictions on the agents which makes the whole dynamics meaningless. Real dynamics must therefore include revaluation of assets and liabilities but such revaluations are always exogenous to the matrices and this implies, (after some consideration), that the parameters of the matrices will develop differently with respect to the nature of the revaluations.

However in Figure 4.5 we illustrate a sort of non-equilibrium tableau where the revaluation vectors are partly due to structural changes both on the real side as well on the financial side, but they are also due to expectation formation.

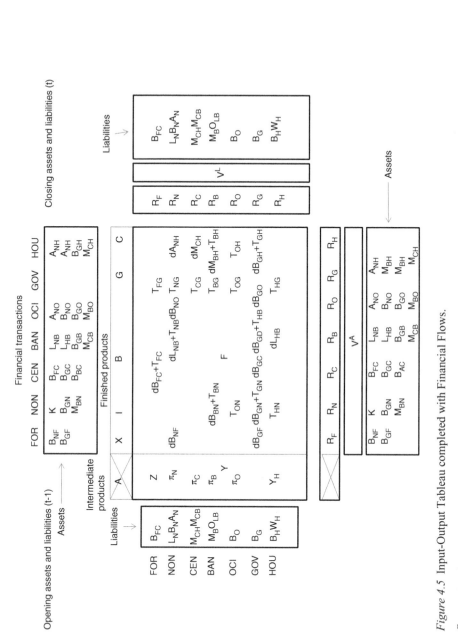

Figure 4.5 Input-Output Tableau completed with Financial Flows.

Source: Westberg 1983

It is important to realize that we are only using the tableau for illustrative purposes, so although it feels tempting to attach a mathematical structure to the tableau that would require assumptions which either were meaningless from a mathematical point of view or destroyed the illustrative value of the tableau.

The flows of the F-matrix consist both of reallocations of opening assets and liabilities as well as the produced resources during the period. The R-vectors are the total of real and financial resources created. But if we now look upon the Y-vector (incomes) which in a non-equilibrium economy is a sort of residual; partly with respect to profits, partly with respect to changes in salaries and partly with respect to changes in unemployment we will have changes in the financial flows due to the Y-vector but then this will most probably cause changes in expectations which further cause revaluations. Thus the closing assets and liabilities will not be a simple addition of the opening position and the real and financial flows of the period.

If we look at a three-period sequence in Figure 4.6 we have the principle inter-temporal connections indicated by the arrows.

Consequently the only time that we can make a consistent mathematical model of the dynamics of Figures 4.5 and 4.6 is when we assume a persistent equilibrium. If that is not possible we are unfortunately in a situation of non-additivity where we of course can make assumptions of the character of the revaluation vectors but the relevance of these are due to the inertia of the socio-economic system.

If we look at the changes of the financial system which we indicated in Figures 4.2 and 4.3 the F-matrix is built on the traditional system of Figure 4.2 completed with intra-business flows working in principle as Figure 4.3. However as Figure 4.5 indicates, the actions of the central bank concern mainly the dealing with government bonds, households and the foreign sector in affecting the money supply and the interest rate. Thus the direct links in the financial matrix of the tableau in Figure 4.5 illustrate a considerable division of the credit system and the governing of the management of the medium of exchange.

With these assumptions, transactions are driven by actual events and/or expectations. We disregard transactions which are a consequence of supply/demand transactions and regard only transactions dealing with real and financial assets and liabilities which do not involve (in principle) an exchange of real items but only the grants of ownership.

We thus have the financial flows of the period linked to production/demand between different agents which results in a summation of financial resources, assets and liabilities respectively in the R-vectors but in order to get the closing assets and liabilities for the period in question we must add a revaluation vector V^A and V^L respectively.

Apart from these revaluation matrices the financial matrix is as mechanical as the rest of the input-output table. So from where come the revaluations? It cannot come from the intra-table transactions since these just describe a financial mirror. So the only explanation mainly has to do with three things: exogenous shocks, inflation and revisions of expectations.

In the first instance we have the discrepancies between the expectations for the current period and the actual results, an ex ante/ex post analysis. Thus why was

Time

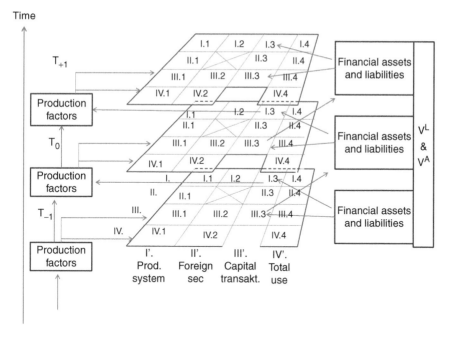

Explanation

We have four sectors in the rows and transposed to columns: I: Internal Production System, II: Foreign Sector, III: Capital Transactions, IV: Income Use We have also added a box of the revaluation vectors V^A and V^L to the right. Entries:

I.1 I/O-system	**I.2** Export	**I.3** Gross Investm.	**I.4** Consumption
II.1 Import	X (Empty)	**II.3** Net Foreign Assets	**II.4** Current net foreign transfers
III.1 Consumption of Capital	**III.2** Capital transf. from abroad	**III.3** Internal fin. Transactions	**III.4** Saving
IV.1 NDP	**IV.2** Net Cap. Inc. from abroad	X (Empty)	**IV.4** Disposable NDP

Figure 4.6 Dynamics of the enlarged input-output tableau.

Source: Westberg 1983

not the epistemic cycle closed in some cases? As we discussed before, such a question has the potential to lead to reconsiderations of the contextual apprehensions and reconsiderations of goals. Such reconsiderations lead in many cases to revaluations of assets and liabilities. All these factors may lead to revisions of the market behaviour of individuals which beside the revaluations also insert new causal structures with respect to Figures 4.2 and 4.3.

A powerful factor here is the rate of discount irrespective if it is based on official interest rates completed with inflation expectations or if it is based on conditions internal to the organisation/individual.

It is here that the inflation factor becomes devastating for stability and where modern inflation policy has its roots. A discount factor as Minsky discusses it has the form

$$d = \frac{1}{r + dp + g}$$

E.4.1

Where r is the running market interest rate, dp is expected inflation and g is expected growth factor. This formulation gives a tremendous leverage effect and even small changes in expectations may lead to large effects on valuations. The two assumptions we have taken have in principle no effects on expectations per se but the almost frictionless revaluations with respect to the physical process affects obviously the volatility and with respect to that there is an abundance of models in following and developing the Black and Scholes model. But more important, room for second thoughts is diminished.

The expression E.4.1 should be compared with the proposition by Modigliani and Miller somewhat moderated, to give rise to a reaction rule:

$$r_e^d = r_e^e + \frac{D}{E} \cdot \left(r_e^e - r_d \right) \quad given \quad r_e^e \geq r_e^d$$

E.4.2

Equality in E.4.2 means in principle non-action. The two expressions represent more or less the same thinking although E.4.1 looks as suitable at the macroscopic level and E.4.2 is more on the microscopic level. The latter expression is clearly linked to the matrices in Figures 4.5 and 4.6 but still the interest rates and the expectations have to be exogenously added.

Real Growth and Growth in Money Terms

Our discussion in this chapter has so far concerned the diffusion of money and financial assets and liabilities. The introduction of the enlarged input-output tableaus illustrated that dynamic changes are brought about in principle by three aspects; changes in demand, changes in production capacity or production technology and financial revaluations built on expected returns. However now we approach the problem which we discussed in Chapter 3: the anomaly between the real and the financial sides. We come to the question of what is growth. Expectations of an individual agent are built on a set of epistemic cycles. That means that contextual apprehension plays an overwhelming role. Thus expectation theories can never be internal to a specific economic theory or model.

When we define a dynamic model of any character we will be able to speak about equilibrium but that is then defined by the parameter structure within the very model we are working with. But if we for example think of two different economies which have the same growth rate in money value sense while one of the economies seems to have a high degree of social stability, the other has considerable social discontent this will affect the valuation of the growth as a numerical figure, both with respect to economic as well as political valuations. We will impose different risk/uncertainty apprehensions. In expected utility terms we might say that dynamics of the state space require a specific analysis to complete the economic. The contextual conditions also affect the individual as well as social apprehension of utility/welfare.

The choice optimality will thus be dependent on contextual developments; in times of social stability both the market results and individual choices may be contradictive as well as inconsistent making the creation of a consistent social welfare function most difficult, while in crises individual preferences tend to be narrowed and social welfare functions are demanded by individuals. Amartya Sen writes the following and we may fill in other scenarios which could be added to the quote:

> When distributional issues dominate and when people seek to maximize their own 'shares' without concern for others (as for example in a 'cake division problem', with each preferring any division that increases her own share, no matter what happens to the others), then majority rule will tend to be thoroughly inconsistent. But when there is a matter of national outrage (for example, in response to the inability of a democratic government to prevent famine), the electorate may be reasonably univocal and thoroughly consistent.
>
> (Sen 2002: 76)

A well-known aspect which we have to contemplate with respect to the enlarged input-output matrices in Figures 4.5 and 4.6 is that the revaluations of assets and liabilities are 'quick' variables, they are instantly affected with respect to asset/liability pricing, which set the financial conditions for the coming period.[8] This means that given that expectations could be based on a rather diffused contextual apprehension rationality would also become blurred and furthermore alluding to passion's priority over reason, an obscure context affects probably the agents more and for a longer time than a clear state which is of a negative character. The latter can be dealt with but not the former.

The quote from Sen above sets from the beginning however the fundamental problem: stability and dynamics in an inert physical system is something different from stability and dynamics in social systems where the agents are subjects. This does not exclude the use of logics/mathematics but conclusions and interpretations of a mathematical analysis in the two cases must be based on different foundations.

We have several times alluded to Keynes' criticism of Tinbergen in his letter to Harrod on the vain purpose to find empirically justified parametric structures for models. The quote from Sen expresses in fact the same sentiment. Mathematics/logics are strictly deterministic methods of thought. In principle we can, given sufficient inertia, set up a mathematical model whatever the problems are, and the treatment of this model must follow the same principles irrespective of if the model is said to describe a psychological or a physical structure. There is one little caterpillar in the salad: the variables must be defined atomistically and this is probably the only problem but it is also the key to understanding Keynes' critique as we discussed in Chapter 2.

We mentioned in Chapter 1 Lucas' (1976) critique which introduced a learning/saturation element in the individual's reactions to collective measures. Although somehow within the same realm Lucas' critique is outside what we discuss here, which deals with the difficulty of defining human purposes as well as conceived context. Nevertheless our problem will affect the relevance of Lucas' critique in the sense that learning/saturation is also dependent on the degree of complexity of variables as well as the system per se.

That means that we, in line with Keynes' view, can regard human society as a set of started and ongoing causal processes, some inert, some dissipative, some bound to fail, some successful by chance, and try to make a dynamic analysis on the basis of some historical period which seems virtually impossible if we try to find relevant parametric structures. One of the more basic factors is that the agents interact with the macroscopic structure in a way which is mostly hidden to research efforts. Since humans also are social creatures, ethics and other behavioural patterns create inert structures, but these vary both locally and temporally.

As has already been pointed out, our basic view is that of Keynes' in his letter to Roy Harrod where he claims that in economic modelling studying forms is relevant but to find exact parametric structures is not only in vain but also leads the researcher into a false path of analysis. Variables and parameters are not linked to physical inert structures but to subjects and their idiosyncrasies.

Notes

1 Examples of absurd consequences are poor countries whose people are forced to sell their children for different uses, body organs and even themselves into slavery in order to survive or to give their children better lives.
2 Ekstedt and Larsson (2008) discuss the intricate question of what will happen if a majority of the electorate get their incomes from public transfers. This is currently (2015) a pretty hot political question in Sweden and it has probably caused the pensioner collective to become more politically volatile. Sweden is rather close to the point that Ekstedt and Larsson discussed.
3 Please observe that we now pass over to quantity theory in standard terms and we are consequently not discussing its role in relation to quantity identity.
4 Correspondence of David Ricardo, Vol. 3 Pamphlets and Papers 1809–1811 [1809]. http://oll.libertyfund.org/titles/204
5 NINJA means No Income No Job Assets and leads in practice to no backing of the security.
6 In a discussion with a representative at my local bank I asked about the bank's preferences with respect to giving people loans for buying cars or boats for instance. She said if the client owns a house, which often is the case, the bank prefers giving a loan with the house as security. The loan would then be securitized. An ordinary bank loan would be of certain inconvenience for the bank. Thus the development we describe in the movement from Figure 4.2 towards Figure 4.3 has now reached the consumption level, which it has in fact done many years ago.

7 In discussions with banking officers one often meets a concern about small innovative business which they have to reject because of banking rules with respect to securitization. I have met such sentiments not only in Sweden but also in France and Spain.
8 A period is not necessarily referring to the clock and the almanac but might be more attached to the Einstein-Minkowski approach where we look at the very changes as setting the pace.

Bibliography

Aristole (1990 [original around 334-324 BC]) 'Politics', in *The Works of Aristotle vol II*, Encyclopædia Britannica, Inc. Chicago, London, (Bno refers to the Berlin enumeration).
Ekstedt, H. (2012) Money in Economic Theory, London and New York: Routledge.
Ekstedt, H. and Larsson, T. (2008) *Growth, Productivity and Democracy in an Ageing Society.* The Swedish Case. Paper presented at the EAEPE International Conference in Porto.
Laidler, D. (1984) 'Misconceptions about the Real-Bills Doctrine: A Comment [The Real-Bills Doctrine versus the Quantity Theory: A Reconsideration]', *Journal of Political Economy*, University of Chicago Press, vol. 92, no. 1: 149–155, February.
Makarov, V.L and Rubinov, A.M. (1977) *Economic Dynamics and Equilibria.* Heidelberg, Berlin: Springer Verlag.
Sargent, T.J. and Wallace, N. (1982) 'The Real-Bills Doctrine versus the Quantity Theory: A Reconsideration', *The Journal of Political Economy*, Vol. 90, No. 6: 1212–1236.
Sen, A. (2002) *Rationality and Freedom.* Cambridge, MA and London: The Belknap Press.
Sproul, M.F. (2000) *Three False Critiques of the Real Bills Doctrine*, Department of Economics, California State University, Northridge. Accessed at http://www.csun.edu/~hceco008/critique.htm
Thornton, H. (1939 [1802]) *An Enquiry into the Nature and Effects of the Paper Credit of Great Britain*, George Allen and Unwin, London, available free at http://oll.libertyfund.org/index.php?option=com_staticxtandstaticfile=show.php%3Ftitle=2041andlayout=html
Westberg, L. (1983) *Finansiering i ekonomisk teori* (Finance in Economic Theory) Memorandum Dept. of Economics, University of Göteborg.
Wicksell, K. (1936 [1893]) *Interest and Prices.* London: Macmillan and Co. Ltd. The original appeared in German 1893 as *Geldzins und Güterpreise*.

5 Structural Stability in Models and Reality

Abstract

In dynamic models there are mainly two concepts which are central: bifurcations and perturbations. Briefly we may say that *bifurcations* are intrinsic to a multi-dimensional model, where the dynamics of the different trajectories create non-stable forms.

Bifurcations are therefore dependent on the complexity of the problem and the higher the dimensionality of the problem the more difficult it is to calculate the stability.

The other factor creating instability perturbations is linked to bifurcations when the parametric structure is upset for one reason or another. Thus the reason for a perturbation is exogenous to the dynamic structure, causing some parameter(s) to change. It is linked to bifurcations in the sense that the parametric change may cause the dynamics of the trajectories to come into a neighbourhood of an instability point. Other parametric structures may be very stable even when faced with substantial changes in some parameter(s).

In a technical sense both bifurcations and the sensitivity of perturbations are examples of what we can call structural (in)stability. A bifurcation maybe called a catastrophic or a chaos point of the dynamic structure, but we need to remember that we are then talking about a different chaos than the grand universal chaos of a system, and it is a *deterministic chaos* intrinsic to the system.

Mathematically a bifurcation in almost all cases has to do with the sacred number of zero which is involved, generally in the denominator. We may use the two concepts outside mathematics to describe developments of the real world but it is difficult to do so in a consistent way.

Introduction

In dynamic models there are mainly two concepts, which are central; bifurcations and perturbations. Briefly we may say that *bifurcations* are intrinsic to a multidimensional model, where the dynamics of the different trajectories create non-stable forms. Breaking waves is a 'simple' illustration where the depth of the water and the initial wave height are interrelated. As long as it is relatively deep the waves are not affected by the bottom, when it grounds up however we will have friction with the bottom causing the water molecules in the lower part of the wave to move slower in the wave direction at the same time as the mass of water is compressed to heighten and finally the asymmetric speed of the different parts of the waves cause the base of the wave to vanish in relation to the top and the wave breaks.

As we see several forces are important: the wind, the depth, the topology of the bottom. Thus in principle changes in any of these three factors make the shifts in the break of the waves.

Bifurcations are therefore dependent on the complexity of the problem and the higher the dimensionality of the problem the more difficult to calculate the stability.

In mathematics a bifurcation somehow involves zero, often in a denominator for simple functions and for matrices when the determinant is zero, which is important in dynamic analysis. In the nature however we have no such rules. If we take water we have a very exciting triple bifurcation point: the fluid can be transformed to a solid (ice) or gas (steam). This occurs when the temperature is around 0.01 C° and the pressure is around 612 Pascal (to be compared with around 101 300 Pascal at the sea level). However if we look at the simple function

$$y(t) = \frac{1}{x(t)}$$ E.5.1

it gives us the nasty trajectory in Figure 5.1. This is in fact the basic mathematical explanation of sudden bifurcations in a system.

We may use the two concepts outside mathematics to describe developments of the real world but it is difficult to do so in a consistent way. In economics we can of course create mathematical models with variables which represent/are called consumption, investment and so on, but how to describe the real

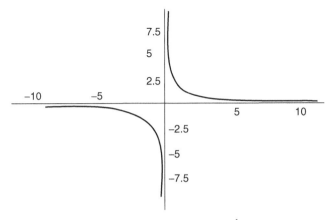

Figure 5.1 Trajectory of the function $y(t) = \dfrac{1}{x(t)}$

phenomenon is more difficult with respect to the complex environment in relation to the assumed variables. It is with respect to the question of constructing a model and how to choose representative variables the so called Occam's razor is as most deceitful.[1] Per se this is almost tautologically true but only as the limitations of the system is known and the variables are defined in an atomistic manner, and this is unfortunately a problem as we have seen, particularly in social sciences. Equally true is that you need more cards to build a house of cards than to keep it standing, and that goes also for other houses. Thus Occam's razor is a good scientific principle which does not necessarily work in building a model of the reality or to detect the central structure of a part of the reality. The reality created by the supreme demon of Laplace or God may always work according to Occam's razor but a sub-model of universal creation does not necessarily do so because if it did you would have also found the true universal model. This is actually the working of the neoclassical approach built on the axiomatic structure. So if we have not found the true universal system Occam's razor is a good principle to have in mind but knowing its exact meaning in a particular empirical study is indeed difficult.

In November 1985 there was a public discussion arranged by Salvador Dali at his house in Figueras, north of Barcelona, between the Nobel laureate in chemistry Ilya Prigogine and the great French mathematician René Thom. The latter was one of the portal figures in the development of the mathematical theory of structural stability (Thom 1972 [1975]). In the discussion the following exchange of opinions took place:[2]

THOM: You should very carefully distinguish between what belongs to mathematical theory and what belongs to real systems. Mathematics has nothing to say to reality.

PRIGOGINE: That's your point of view, it is not mine.

We must here realize the two entirely different perspectives. Thom is coming from mathematics and bases much of his thinking on examples of real forms and structures, while Prigogine is coming from an empirical/experimental science and looks at mathematics as a source of getting ideas of forms and particularly the moulding of forms. Mathematics is providing us with an abundance of experimental possibilities with forms which costless (in money effort terms) can be used to produce ideas. So both attitudes are acceptable but, since we work in an empirical science, we must always remember that costless findings of mathematical structures do not hold in real structures which are due to differences in inertia, contradictive forces and so on. It is well worth having Hume's scepticism in some nook of our brain.

> ... that there is nothing in any object, consider'd in itself, which can afford us a reason for drawing a conclusion beyond it; and that even after the observation of the frequent or constant conjunction of objects, we have no reason to draw any inference concerning any object beyond those of which we have experience.
>
> (Hume 2002[1740]: 95)

Accepting Hume's scepticism as a basis for empirical work, we may still utilize the relative simplicity of analysing forms and thus get patterns for ideas for approaching empirical/historical processes, but it can never be so that we bluntly apply a set of mathematical models and squeeze a real development into them.

A good example is chaos theory. Such an approach may be exciting when looking at price movements, when looking at seemingly unexplainable breakdowns of certain evolutions and so on, but all explanations must be afforded by the very empirics themselves and not to be searched for in a priori modelling. That is what we have criticised in the neoclassical theory, which as such is extremely well analysed and well founded in a clear axiomatic structure.

Nevertheless we shall look at some examples of mathematical structures which are attached to often-used forms. Let me first go back to Thom and his predecessors for a while. Thom, as the title of his book from 1972 tells us, studies structural stability and morphogenesis. The latter word can be interpreted as the study of natural forms and is used in biology where the classical work is D'Arcy Thompson (1992[1942]), *On Growth and Form*, a work which influenced René Thom very much and he says:

> That we can construct an abstract, purely geometrical theory of morphogenesis, *independent of the substrate of forms and the nature of the forces that create them*, might seem difficult to believe, especially to the seasoned experimentalist used to working with living matter and always struggling with the elusive reality. This idea is not new and can be found almost explicitly in the classical book by D'Arcy Thompson, *On Growth and Form*, but the theories of this innovator were too far in advance of their time to be recognized: ...
>
> This general point of view raises the following obvious question: if according to our basic hypothesis, the only stable singularities of all morphogenesis are solely by the dimension of the ambient space, why do not all phenomena of our three dimensional world have the same morphology? [Original emphasis]
>
> (Thom 1975[1972]: 8)

In economics we are not particularly used to speaking about morphology or forms in a geometrical/topological sense. Above we discussed the mathematical character of commodities and money in terms of medium of exchange, and arrived at the conclusion that these two items took different mathematical forms with respect to class logic which through the axiomatic structure were transformed in to one class. It is obvious that this will affect the analytical patterns and imply a violation of the reality, to put it strongly. An argument that it will simplify logical/mathematical analysis is both with respect to Hume and Thom a false argument. To be a bit unkind we could call it street-lamp research after the story of the policeman asking the drunkard, who he was helping to find the door key, if he was sure he lost it under the street lamp and got the answer 'no it was over there but it is so ... dark there.'

At the same time we are well aware of the fact that reality offers a rich supply of more or less catastrophic shifts in development of societies but the causal structure behind such events is normally rather difficult. To take a mathematical technique and apply it more or less ad hoc to real developments and claim any form of explanatory power seems rather frivolous.

Causality

Central to the stability concept is the concept of causality. That is that events/ actions will have consequences of some sort for the context/environment of the event/action in question. We have already mentioned as a result of Arrow's paradox that the consequence of agents' ability to consider actions/decisions by other fellow agents as well as the macroscopic structures, given their comprehension of the relevant structures imply that agents themselves constitute the most fundamental uncertainty.

This of course could lead to complete chaos if there were no limiting forces for the actions of the individual.

As Luigi Amoroso (1938:10) says in his analysis of Pareto's contributions to economic theory:

> In general the meaning of obstacles is that economic goods are limited; until violence and fraud, theft and donation are excluded, a thing cannot be had except by giving in exchange for it one of equal value pro tempore; that every product is the result of a certain combination of the factors of production in harmony with the laws of techniques, as they are known pro tempore; that legal order and the economic organization fetter individual actions; and so on. ---- It is at this point that the crux of Pareto's system becomes apparent. The internal forces of the economic system are not susceptible of a theoretical representation as simple, elegant, and universal as is the case for the applied forces. They are not only, as for the material macrocosmic systems, forces of conservation, by which – to express it elegantly – the dead city dominates through inertia the living city; they are also directed forces or forces of impulsion, through which the living city forms or attempts to form the city of the future. The internal forces, therefore, are History, they are even Ethics and Politics, something powerful, but vague and indistinct, which is not susceptible of mathematical representation; an expression of the freedom of the will, which does not allow itself to be enclosed in the meshes of a mechanical representation, and, because it is mechanical, determinist.

A stable society is some sort of balance between the 'directed or impulse forces of the living city to form the city of the future' and the conservative forces of historical structures, ethics and politics. In fact democracy can in certain periods be a revolutionary force but in other periods a conservative force. Amartya Sen (2002:76) note such a duality with respect to the possibility of formulating a collective welfare function, which we quoted in the preceding chapter.

This means that we live in a world with considerably high physical inertia, although disasters such as hurricanes, earthquakes, excessive heat and rain remind us of the increasing entropy, which of course can be affected by the collective actions of societies. We have also biological inertia in the sense that evolutionary forces are difficult to detect and observation of these are mostly *ex post*, although humans try to affect them with the help of microscopic techniques without understanding its macroscopic effects. We, as Amoroso points out, have social inertia, although individuals mostly look upon this as too narrow a jacket.

The role of inertia, if we may express it like that, since inertia is hardly something we control, is to actually create physical/social/economic structures where we might have causal structures which as a matter of fact also make it possible to create a future. As we said, humans strive towards a change but are also reluctant to change. In the 1963 film by Visconti, *Il Gattopardo*; Don Fabrizio (played by Burt Lancaster) says something like 'For things to remain the same, everything must change' which is also the sentiment in Lampedusa's book (1959) with the same name.

But what are we going to change in order to remain the same? To express it in technical words, some structures have changed while some others are as they were which creates tensions and social unease. This calls for obsolete structures to be changed in order to keep ethical and social values which lay the foundation for rational behaviour.

So basically causality is about rational behaviour and when it comes to social structure, the ability of foreseeing actions and reactions. Tensions created in society created by evolution make it necessary to change obsolete social, political and economic structures but on the other hand if these changes are too frequent we approach chaos. This is also the deepest meaning of the quote from Amoroso, by whom Giuseppe Tomasi di Lampedusa most probably was well known.

The relation between mathematics and causality is indeed delicate. A causality relation can, ideally, be expressed as an 'if … then' proposition, thus a deterministic setting. This goes for objects as well as subjects. In the latter case we must have a purpose, an action space (the market) and an event/action (the actual exchange). But as we earlier mentioned in relation to Wittgenstein this mathematical setting has to be exactly interpreted in its proper environment. A complicating factor with respect to mathematics is the irreversibility which gives rise to a time direction, since $A \Rightarrow B$ implies that A appears before B in a time dimension. Thus equivalence always presumes full determinism which excludes causality. As we showed in Chapter 1, equivalence between A and B with respect to market exchange in neoclassical equilibrium is a desired feature since that gives rise to the principle of revealed preferences.

Thus we may ignite a paper with a match but also with a magnifying glass but the time components are generally different. This implies that by only watching a fire we are not able to say something about the cause other than in probability terms. When we make enquiries of subjects such differences are important to notice when we for example think of a continuous stream of information and differences in epistemic cycles.

Determinism and Probability

Mathematical models of parts of the reality are deterministic if we think that we should find a parametric structure which describes the relations between the variables. Based, hopefully, on observation and inductive reasoning, we create a model of the causal relationship between variables and then by statistical methods we deduct the parametric structure, given or not a stochastic analysis of these parameters. Whatever the issue of research our observations are mostly turned into a causal model and this model predetermines the causal relations for further research so they may form a deductive system. What are the weaknesses and the appropriate use of such a model? What is the expected 'life-time' of the model? Such questions are solved at the pleasure of the individual researcher or team of researchers. When it comes to established models we understand the attitude 'you cannot go on testing standard models all the time'.

Judea Pearl raises a word of warning in employing statistics too frivolously as well as deterministic models to model causal structures:

> An autonomous intelligent system attempting to build a workable model of its environment cannot rely exclusively on pre-programmed causal knowledge; rather, it must be able to translate direct observations to cause-and-effect relationships. However, given that statistical analysis is driven by covariation, not causation, and assuming that the bulk of human knowledge derives from uncontrolled observations, we must still identify the clues that prompt people to perceive causal relationships in the data. We must also find a computational model that emulates this perception.
>
> (Pearl, 2000: 42)

It seems that we come to a kind of junction which means that we either work in purely deterministic spirit where we fully control the transformation of our observations into intellectually satisfactory sets of mathematical/logical models of a deterministic character, *or*, that we specify the deterministic model in a probabilistic environment which actually feels like letting in the 'devil's advocate' into our creative work.

In a sense the latter happened to Hume, which as we said before let the doubts get a grip on his soul and he became almost completely sceptical with respect to induction and empirical work and this was mostly due to this watershed between determinism and attaching a probability setting to the causal analysis.

As Hume points out the multitude of causes linked to a certain effect, both necessary and contributory necessitates a probabilistic attitude in describing causation in terms of a joint probability distribution with respect to some observed causal structure. But Hume takes one further step: the experience and the analytical patterns of the observer/researcher affect the judgement of the environment/context and this affects the judgement of the space of outcome as well as the probability structure.

How do we look at such kinds of probability structure? Does it appear because we so to speak truncate the problem too soon, which means that a more detailed scrutiny should have revealed the true deterministic model? It seems then that we replace specific environmental knowledge with a probabilistic model based on general historical observations. As Judea Pearl says 'we must still identify the clues that prompt people to perceive causal relationships in the data'. (2002: 42)

We now realize that the step to determinism is a rather short one. Determinism in the classical form à la Laplace is seldom outspoken within scientific circles although it may appear. Evolutionary theories sometimes appear similar but the logical basis is different. The famous words by Laplace:

> We may regard the present state of the universe as the effect of its past and the cause of its future. An intellect which at a certain moment would know all forces that set nature in motion, and all positions of all items of which nature is composed, if this intellect were also vast enough to submit these data to analysis, it would embrace in a single formula the movements of the greatest bodies of the universe and those of the tiniest atom; for such an intellect nothing would be uncertain and the future just like the past would be present before its eyes.
>
> Pierre Simon Laplace, A Philosophical Essay on Probabilities

Although Laplace was not a Christian, at least not very faithful, it seems that he was a kind of deist; his works on Newton's system that in many cases brought it into theoretical perfection, made it easy for him to look at the world/universe as a kind of machine. As we see his determinism concerns all possible microscopic and macroscopic levels.

However on the Christian side the above quote has a rather precise counterpart in pre-Thomistic theology. St. Bonaventura makes a distinction between the human probabilistic world and Divine determinism in the 13th century. Etienne Gilson (1965:174) describes it:

> The root of the matter is that St. Bonaventure's Christian universe differs from the pagan universe of Aristotle in that it has a history: every celestial revolution, instead of following indifferently an infinity of identical revolutions, coincides with the appearance of unique events, each of which has its place fixed in the grand drama which unfolds itself between the Creation of the world and the last Judgement. Every day, every hour even, forms part of a series which is ruled by a certain order and of which Divine Providence knows the whole reason; *si dicas quod statum ordinis non necesse est ponere nisi in his quae ordinatur secundum ordinem causalitatis, quia in causi necessario est status, quaero quare non in aliis?*[3]

St. Bonaventure refuses to admit not only causes but also events acciden-
tally ordered. [Original emphasis]

The two quotes are interesting since both Laplace and Bonaventura separate the
possible knowledge of the highest intelligence from that of the partial and sometimes erroneous knowledge of humans. It is important however that there exists
an abstract form of knowledge which links precisely the Now and the Past and
the Future. Our feeble thinking is not able to see it, but as knowledge increases,
secular in Laplace's case and about God in Bonaventura's case, we may be able
sometimes to detect it.

Thus basically the role of probability in empirical sciences is a sort of systematic treatment of lack of (divine) knowledge. This attitude is a bit difficult to
understand since human actions built on ignorance and erroneous analysis seem
not to affect the divine determinism so it must be a rather adaptive system.
With respect to causality, apart from the mentioned problem, no true causality
can appear in a complete determinism, in fact causality and any form of determinism are contradictions in terms. The main reason is that while causality is a relation which can be very complex between some factors, say A and B, but it can be
completely independent of other parts of the environment. When it comes to
determinism between A and B this cannot exist independently of its environment.
Thus If we can relate two variables A and B exactly and which are linked in
Laplace's way, then we on this basis can determine the whole system. This is
actually equal to our reasoning with respect to the neoclassical general equilibrium theory. A deterministic system cannot not have an environment; it is
nowhere dense.

Furthermore a deterministic relation requires only one final cause and at the
universal level there is one possible eternal final cause and that is present in the
creation. The quote from Laplace is interesting since it combines the macroscopic and microscopic determinism in every possible level. A conclusion of this
is that whether we are working with complexities or atomic facts with respect to
probability does not really matter. Anyway in such a world there is no causality
whatsoever. Thus causality and determinism are contradictions in terms at a
universal level.

Aristotle made the first more systematic classification of causality: material
cause, formal cause, efficient cause and final cause. Particularly the latter one, the
final cause, is of interest to us in which the word (causality) is used for the end;
as a matter of fact this is the simple basis for claiming humans as a subject.
We may also see the role of the neoclassical axiomatic structure, which deprives
the commodities of their substance and transforms them to atomistic variables,
and makes the concept of optimal choice meaningless in an Aristotelian sense.

Somebody/something has a purpose and acts according to that purpose.
Aristotle takes walking as an example:

This is what something is for, as health, for example, may be what walking is
for. If asked, 'Why is he walking?', we reply, 'To get healthy', and in saying

this we mean to explain the cause of his walking. And then there is everything which happens during the process of change (initiated by something else) that leads up to the end: for example, the end of health may involve slimming or purging or drugs or surgical implements; they are all for the same end, but they are different in that some are actions and some are implements.

Aristotle (2007: 271, Bno 194-5).

This gives rise to a standard syllogism: 1. Walking is good for health; 2. A is walking; 3. A will improve his health. Much modelling of humans takes its stance in Aristotle's analysis on final cause.

The modern attitude to causality is based on David Hume's analysis. Although his analysis led him to a deep scepticism towards the principle of induction, he does not deny a priori the possibility for humans to scrutinize causal structures and detect causal relationships. His doubts concern the posterior probability structures.

Hume summarizes the logic of causation in eight conditions:

1   The cause and effect must be contiguous in space and time.
2   The cause must be prior to the effect.
3   There must be a constant union betwixt the cause and effect.
4   The same cause always produces the same effect and the same effect never arises but from the same cause.
5   Where several different objects produce the same effect, it must be by means of some quality, which we discover to be common among them.
6   The difference in the effects of two resembling objects must proceed from that particular in which they differ.
7   When any object increases or diminishes with the increase or diminution of its cause, 'tis to be regarded as a compound effect, deriv'd from the union of the several different effects which arise from the several different parts of the cause.
8   That an object, which exists for any time in its full perfection without any effect, is not the sole cause of that effect, but requires to be assisted by some other principle, which may forward its influence and operation.

(2002[1740]: 116–117)

We can divide causality into three groups: experimental, observational and structural causality. We leave the latter, structural causality, for a while since that involves some difficult philosophical aspects. The first two however are the everyday experience of natural and social sciences. That is the natural sciences have with respect to the microscopic level the possibility of making precise experiments implying a limitation of the environment and the repetition of such experiment makes (hopefully) the parametric structure converge to a statistically satisfactory model structure of the involved causality. However the weaker the limits to the environment and the higher the complexity of the model means the more random noise and/or unobservable structures will enter the research design.

We have to admit however that the natural sciences have been successful to some degree to overcome Hume's scepticism both methodologically and technically.

However Hume does not discuss an important aspect which in a way alludes to Popper's rejection ability of a proposition, so called *counterfactual propositions*. Let us assume that low inflation causes increased growth, which means we may show that there is a strong correlation between inflation and growth. The question is then if this correlation shows a *necessary* and/or *sufficient* cause or may be just a *contributory* cause. Can I say without causing an uproar among colleagues that 'if this inflation had not been so high we would have a higher growth'? Using counterfactual propositions has a wider consequence than just rejecting a proposition on causation; it also stresses the boundaries of the proposed causation. The importance of counterfactual propositions is that causality, apart from elementary cases where the cause and effect are technically determined, can be detected by using a probability setting in which, as Pearl claims, co-variation is also a possible interpretation. That means that the cause/effect relationship if it should fulfil Hume's criteria must have a precise analysis of the environmental limits and thus be stable within these limits.

The natural sciences have, due to improvements in statistical methodology, better technology of observation and the possibility of controlled experiments has reached a high degree of sophistication in isolating causation. However the price for this is the possibility of efficiently controlling the role of the environment which, as we for example have seen in pharmacological studies, has led to too optimistic introductions of pharmacological substances into a wider clinical environment.

This is not true for the social sciences. A science like economics has to a large extent entertained the methodology of natural science with a substantial portion of a priori deterministic theoretical foundation. An elementary first step is therefore to eliminate a priori structures and accept humans as subjects and thereby a local and temporal last cause.

Doing so will throw economics into a jungle of new conceptualizations of standard concepts and accepting only local and temporal models which might be inconsistent with each other.

Unfortunately we also have to accept that economics is no experimental science but our only hope is that our observations should be systematic and consistent enough to allow us at least to discuss the form of eventual causal relations. To find a satisfactory parameter structure seems a rather remote dream, if possible at all. With respect to Keynes' letter to Harrod he also claimed this dream of finding the 'true' parameter structure that misled the research in a wider perspective in leaving the study of what a topologist would call *the study of forms*.

The conceptual definition by Hume leaves very few degrees of freedom. It is then important to remember that the conceptualization concerns the case where with full certainty we can establish a causal link. Counteraction causes, such as the match was wet so we could not light the paper, occur. We have a multitude of causes and counteracting causes, thus we can at best discuss causes in terms of probabilities where the 'chance in itself' contributes nothing to the explanation but reveals the degree of uncertainty of causes. Thus as long as we have not established a precise link between different causes and effects we cannot use the probability per se as viable information of the causal structure since on one hand probabilities measure the relative structure of causes but on the other hand it can also be seen as a measure of the uncertainty of the environmental effects and un-observables as we will discuss according to *structural causality* later on.

Thomas Brody (1994: 100) discusses this matter in relation to quantum physics and concludes:

> Causality and chance, therefore, are not counterposed; they are complementary. The only opposition is between chance and those determinisms which, like the Laplacian determinism, can have no place in physics.
>
> This thesis evinces the lack of solidity that affects traditional arguments regarding causal implications of quantum mechanics. From the fact that quantum mechanics utilizes the concept of probability in a form which is not susceptible to reduction we can neither conclude that it does not admit causality, nor that we can go further in physics; rather it indicates that our understanding of the links between a quantum system and the rest of the universe is incomplete: which is precisely what Einstein was telling us half a century ago.

Applying this quote from Thomas Brody to social sciences clearly displays our problem. Historical observations can never be a foundation of causal structures thus precise links between some causes and their effects simply cannot be established with respect to parametric precision, but still worse is that not only individual purposes may be affected by social interaction but also the contextual conception. Under such circumstances stochastic approaches may make a mixture of logically separated probability structures. From that point of view it is easy to understand that many economists stick to the neoclassical theory since its conceptualizations and logical structure are consistent and it is easy to derive precise empirical hypotheses from it. So the price we have to pay for looking at economics from a more realistic logical foundation is that traditionally used concepts are being muddled and there is no clear link between the microscopic and macroscopic levels.

It is important to realize that causal analysis although from the beginning was an inductive hypothesis, it can be transformed to a deductive system where due to claimed inertia (*ceteris paribus*) we translate the objects of analysis and the parameters into mathematical/logical symbols and then the similarity between Aristotle's example of the utility of walking and a standard syllogism can be tempting to enlarge irrespective of the strict limitations of the analysis.

We have stated above that determinism in Laplace's sense omits causality but we actually transform the causality into determinism in deductive theories and under some circumstances we admit that this is allowed given assumptions of inertia. If we look at neoclassical theory we obviously make such a transformation and as long as that is limited to a particular point in space-time, according to Debreu, it is no problem but if we enlarge the analysis to allow for inter-temporal analysis, economic growth for example, we are very much on a doubtful analytical path.

Consequently when we look at economics it is obvious that the social and individual inertia in many cases are sufficient to investigate and to give a mathematical form but to find a parametric structure similar to experimental physical sciences is fruitless enterprise. It is not a mathematical/technical question, it is a matter of the research object being subjects.

But then we have already passed the border to logics and left the empirical world. With respect to theoretical reasoning we can of course find out almost an infinity of complex structures but these are not decisive since causality in the physical world must be observed or, at least as Hume hints, be in the memory of the agent. When it comes to the agents themselves we may have theories about the cause of their behaviour but to the author's knowledge there is no physio-/psychometric device such that exact measurements can be done. Thus the agents must be regarded as subjects and bearing in mind our earlier discussions about Arrow's paradox nothing sure can be said about an aggregate of subjects because of a lack of further information from the members of the collective in question. Furthermore the individual actions do not need to give any particular information of the individual's action within a collective. It is true that humans are social creatures and we can assume that many behavioural patterns are inert, but for societies which are open to external influences such inertia seems to be less important.

In natural sciences where on one hand it is possible to make controlled experiments and on the other hand the research objects are indeed objects, we may not build on experimental data but relays on historical observations, under a less controlled environment experimental/technical causality may well develop into observational causality. Social sciences, however, are only built on observation since eventual experiments are generally of a statistical character or they might also be linked to the very individual subject. Furthermore all observations and experiments in social sciences imply that subjects interact while we in natural sciences have at least one side which although it can be affected by observation/experiments does not *interact*.[4]

The result is that it is hard to detect any structural causality in social sciences where subjects are involved. With respect to our concept of epistemic cycles we may even assume that purposes are constant but since the contextual apprehensions vary the stability of a given epistemic cycle is doubtful. Thus in this respect the social sciences are closer to Hume and his doubts concerning the principle of empirical induction than natural sciences are. The time dimension becomes therefore particularly sensitive.[5]

The standard syllogism may therefore hold in one direction given certain limits and locally but is not reversible since we might have contradicting causes combined with a multitude of causes with respect to a certain effect.

Structural Causality

Althusser (1970 [1968]) in his study of Marx observed that Marx discussed the dynamics of behaviour on one hand with respect to the kind of causality as we so far have discussed but he also introduced something which could be called *structural causality*.

A tentative explanation just to start with is that based on the logical analysis of individual behaviour we can never understand society as a whole nor the behaviour of the socialized individual. Thus saying that humans are a final cause still lacks an explanation as to why the behaviour of individuals are not completely chaotic particularly when we consider the complexity of deterministic systems and the complexity of their estimation which we have discussed. Each society is also affected by un-observables affecting the individual choice of action. A set of such un-observables is intrinsic to a particular society and contains power structures, explicit or implicit ethical norms, technological structures and restrictions and so on. This set creates restrictions and patterns of behaviour of dos and don'ts which affect the action/reaction patterns and thus the social causal structure.

To some extent social research can expose such structures but the obstacles are different from, at least the normal, obstacles of natural sciences. The scientist is a part of the society in question and remuneration, status and even survival matters affect the questions and design of the research.

Our introduced concept of epistemic cycles contains in principle these un-observables which imply the existence of power hierarchies. A society does not have a simple hierarchy of dependencies but simultaneously existing structures which are kept in the whole by the same kind of un-observables which create the differences between substructures. Althusser (ibid.: 26) explains:

> ... the Marxist whole .... is a whole whose unity, far from being the expressive or 'spiritual' unity of Leibnitz's or Hegel's whole, is constituted by a certain type of *complexity*, the unity of a *structured whole* containing what can be called levels and instances which are distinct and 'relatively autonomous', and co-exist within this complex structural unity, articulated with one another according to specific determinations, fixed in the last instance by the level or instance of the economy. [Original emphasis]
>
> (Ibid.: 26)

Althusser's explanations are supported by a quote from Marx:

> The different limbs of the society are converted into so many separate societies, following one upon the other. How, indeed, could the single *logical formula of movement, of sequence, explain the body of society, in which all relations co-exist simultaneously and support each other?* [Althusser's emphasis]
>
> (ibid.: 27)

This aspect of what we may call structural causality is indeed important to bear in mind when we create and/or interpret deterministic modelling into the real world of causality. Above we showed a very simple structural instability of a very elementary mathematical model but such a model is an arm-chair construction: what about describing real structural instability and its (non-) deterministic structure?

Causality and Correlation

Thus causation is not deterministic a priori but a posteriori a given cause determines a certain effect and as usual if we have sufficient inertia in this relationship we can describe it with deterministic models which give rise to statistical hypothesis. The problem however is that a causal structure might be quite complex. One of the first to discuss these matters in statistical terms, *Correlation and Causation*, was Sewall Wright (1921). Wright was a geneticist and did some pioneering work in the detection of genetic paths. He worked at the interface of clinical and statistical analysis and he had therefore rather precise genetic models to analyse which meant that the aspects of environmental uncertainty which Brody discusses where minimized.

It is obvious that principally a causal relation between two events must appear in the form of a correlation. A simple deterministic relationship XTY must have the correlation 1, following Hume. But when it comes to more complex structures like the ones illustrated in Figure 5.2.

In model 1 the role of x3 is intricate and the interdependence between x1 and x3 is almost impossible to cope with in a linear analysis without extra assumptions with respect to eventual exogenous knowledge.

Basically the analysis starts from the matrix of correlations where the correlation for x_i and x_j is

$$cor\left(x_i, x_j\right) \equiv \frac{cov\left(x_i, x_j\right)}{\sigma_{x_i} \cdot \sigma_{x_j}}. \qquad \text{E.5.2}$$

Thus given linear relations in the form of linear regressions, we may develop coefficients of multiple correlations, but observe that these are based on the

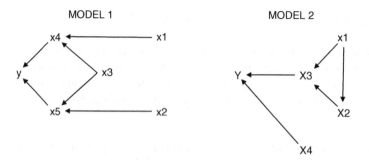

Figure 5.2 Examples of Structural Models

assumptions of linear relations. From this matrix we can calculate the different path-coefficients for the variables particularly if they are independent and linear. For dependent variables as between x1 and x3 above the calculations must be completed with judgements of the relative importance of the internal dependences, which Wright does.

As we see the technique is straightforward as long as we know the exact model. If not so, we are trapped in Hume's complications and particularly the time aspect is embarrassing.

Wright's work was developed and brought more systematically into economics by Trygve Haavelmo (1943) where he systematized Wright with respect both to statistical measure as well as a macroeconomic path of analysis which is at least partly an answer to Keynes' critique of Tinbergen. Haavelmo's contribution was directed towards the error terms in a model of structural relations.

In Figure 5.2 as well as for principally all displayed causal structures we can build a structural equation system, that is the mathematical part, but proceeding to the statistical determination of parameters requires that we somehow handle the error terms. The first question is of course 'Why do we have an error term?' In principal, according to Haavelmo (1943) and Pearls (2000) and many others there are four main factors behind the error term: i) unobservable factors ii) observable but omitted factors, iii) unknown factors and relations, iv) specification errors.

Obviously stereotype assumptions of randomly distributed residuals with a mean value equal to zero are doubtful not to say naïve.

The Copula

Haavelmo also adds another aspect which quite recently was intensively discussed: the joint distribution of errors. In 1959 Haavelmo's discussion was taken a bit further by Sklar who proved the so called copula.[6] The formal definition of the copula is:

Definition Copula [Weisstein (2000)]:

Let H be a two-dimensional distribution function with marginal distributions functions F and G. Then there exists a Copula C, such that

$$H(x,y) = C\big[F(x), G(y)\big]$$

The copula is then a continuous function picturing the joint distribution of F and G.

The financial industry was, quite naturally, the first to use Sklar's theorem in practice. Unfortunately however the H-function is dependent on the rigour of defining F and G functions which means that Haavelmo's discussion indeed is relevant for the copula as it is for the F and G functions.

The crucial question of the joint distribution is basically the interdependence of the univariate distribution functions. Rüschendorf (2013: 7) summarizes the basic questions:

- What is the 'range of dependence' covered by these models and measured by some dependence index?
- What models exhibit tail dependence and thus are able to model situations with strong dependence in tails?
- Is some parameter available describing the degree of dependence?
- Is there a natural probabilistic representation of these models describing situations when to apply them?
- Is there a closed form of the copula or a simple simulation algorithm so that goodness of fit can be applied to evaluate whether they fit the data?

It is also very important to note the two last points. We can construct complex models of causation and on basis of these derive the parameters due to analysing the theoretical correlation structures, but when it comes to applying them to real-world problems we must go back to Hume's basic discussions and to Haavelmo's and Rüschendorf's questions and even the two-dimensional case becomes complex.

Error Term and Bifurcations

Haavelmo discusses the joint error distribution with respect to a multiplier-accelerator model à la Hicks-Harrod-Samuelson which we later will scrutinize with respect to the intrinsic stability of the deterministic part, so we may introduce it here already and we also use Haavelmo's annotations.

The deterministic model is

$$u_t = \alpha \cdot r_t + \beta \qquad \text{Consumption}$$
$$v_t = \kappa \cdot (u_t - u_{t-1}) \qquad \text{Investment} \qquad \text{E.5.3}$$
$$r_t = u_t + v_t \qquad \text{Equilibrium condition}$$

r – purchasing power; u – consumption; v – investment

We get the deterministic equilibrium solution:

$$r_t = \frac{\beta + \kappa (u_t - u_{t-1})}{1 - \alpha} \qquad \text{E.5.4}$$

We will analyse this kind of solution later but now we turn our attention to the stochastic problems, which are crucial in conjunction with the intrinsic deterministic stability of the model.

Let us add residuals x_1 and y_1 respectively for the consumption and investment functions, which are assumed to be purely random with a mean value equal to zero. We thus have

$$u_t = \alpha \cdot r_t + \beta + x_t$$
$$v_t = \kappa \cdot (u_t - u_{t-1}) + y_t$$
$$r_t = u_t + v_t \qquad \text{E.5.5}$$

Haavelmo has three fundamental points: First, the residuals x_t and y_t cannot be judged according to general statements that 'errors are on the whole small' without a stochastic analysis. Second, the 'smallness' has two dimensions, on one hand they are large only at rare occasions and on the other hand that errors of a certain size occur at a particular frequency. The only analytical instrument covering these dimensions is a full stochastic specification.

Third, the point is that for a system like E.5.5 it is not sufficient to evaluate each equation using the least-square method assuming that sufficiently covers the error brought about by x_1 and y_1. In order to achieve that we must state the complete joint probability distribution of x_t and y_t.

If we look at the two first functions of E.5.5' they are linear so that given u_t, r_t, and u_{t-1} these must be jointly distributed, such that for example $E(u_t/r_t)$ is a linear function of r_t, Haavelmo sets it to $Ar_t + B$. Let ρ denote the correlation coefficient of u_t and σ_u^2 and σ_r^2 the variances. We then have that the constant A is given by

$$A = \frac{\sigma_u}{\sigma_r} \cdot \rho \qquad\qquad E.5.6$$

Given this Haavelmo evaluates A for the joint probabilities, based on the two first functions in E.5.5' he thus calculates the variances σ_u^2 and σ_r^2 and the correlation ρ. Based on this he can calculate the value of A for the first function in E.5.5', given the joint distributions, which is

$$A = \frac{(1+\kappa) \cdot \sigma_x^2 + \alpha \cdot \sigma_y^2}{(1+\kappa)^2 \cdot \sigma_x^2 + \sigma_y^2} \qquad\qquad E.5.7$$

So the first function in E.5.5' should hold under the assumptions of random values with a mean of zero for the variables x_t and y_t, it is required that the parameter α is identical to A in E.5.7, $\alpha \equiv A$, which in general is not true.

Haavelmo's exercise is important since it implies a discrepancy between the least square estimation, with its statistics based on singular functions compared with the estimation of a dynamic system. Haavelmo's contribution is also an important step toward the development of *the copula*.

However to see the full importance of these statistical manipulations we must relate them to a completely different aspect: the intrinsic instability of dynamic systems. We will develop this aspect more systematically below, but since Haavelmo is considering a dynamic system, the multiplier-accelerator model, it is illuminating to look at the intrinsic deterministic stability of the system and relate it to Haavelmo's contribution.

Let us look more closely at the deterministic setting in system E.5.5 to have a simpler case and traditional model to start from. These changes will not in any important way change conclusions on the statistical analysis.

$$u_t = \alpha \cdot r_t + \beta \qquad \text{Consumption}$$

$$v_t = \kappa \cdot \left(u_{t-1} - u_{t-2}\right) \quad \text{Investment}$$

$$r_t = u_t + v_t \qquad \text{Equilibrium condition} \qquad\qquad \text{E.5.8}$$

r – purchasing power; u – consumption; v – investment

We get the deterministic equilibrium solution:

$$r_t = \frac{\beta + \kappa\left(u_{t-1} - u_{t-2}\right)}{1 - \alpha} \quad \text{given} \quad u_{t-1} = u_{t-2} \qquad\qquad \text{E.5.9}$$

As before we look particularly at the first function since α appears in the denominator it will have a high leverage effect, so it is the most sensible parameter.

Let us start from parameter values $\alpha = 0.9$; $\kappa = 1.8$ and $\beta = 10$. The initial values are $u_1 = 100$ and $u_2 = 105.6$.

The choice of values is according to standard elementary textbooks. We can assume that the medium of exchange is white flat stones alluding to Keynes in the first chapter of *Treatise on Money* (1929).

For these values we will have a development of the purchasing power, r_t, during nine years. We do not bother with the negative values, which will be discussed later. We just look at the dynamic path of the deterministic system.

Let us now apply a deviation of u_2 with 0.095% upward.

The instability around 105.6 has nothing to do with the statistical error terms but is created by the dynamic interdependence intrinsic to system E.5.8

The change of the initial value was less than 0.1% which indeed should, by most scientists, be classified as small if it measured the error term. This gives a perspective on one hand of the precision of the calculations of the error terms but on the other hand also of the almost impossible task of estimating complex systems. The one we have used as illustration is an extremely simple system and in more complex systems we make as we will discuss later, more such critical points.

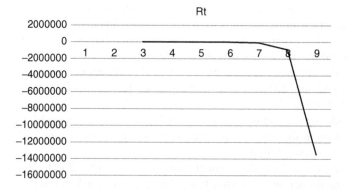

Figure 5.3 Development of r_t given $u_{t-2} = 105.6$

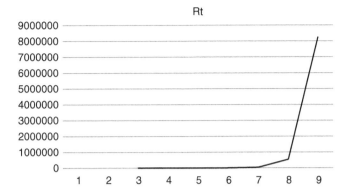

Figure 5.4 Development of r_t given $u_{t-2} = 105.7$

It is also important to note that the deterministic stability structure is completely independent of the stochastic structure although the stochastic behaviour may trigger critical points.

Thus the error term in relation to intrinsic deterministic instability is indeed interesting and important even of a rather simple dynamic model, but to see such a thing in reality, even if it appears, requires an exact specification of the parameter structure and if not our exercise can only be at best a pedagogical example. Thus following Keynes and using mathematical modelling as an intellectual tool to detect possible logical forms of instability still requires that we take pains to try to imagine a real-world picture which is parallel to the mathematical form.

Some Comments on Instability

When we use the word *bifurcation* we use a word seldom used scientifically outside mathematics.[7] Where it is used in geography and sociology it stands for a specific diverge from a principle. In mathematics it stands for a sudden change in a trajectory. The points of bifurcation are always *nowhere dense*.

It is evident that we can call an outbreak of a war or a revolution a bifurcation but looking a bit more carefully at such events we often find that there is a dynamic development of the pre-event structures such that when the event happens it is not particularly surprising.

I ask the reader to imagine a historic or social process, not necessarily economic, where we may use the word bifurcation. Let us look at three such instances where I think that the word might be used rightly or wrongly but I am prepared to meet opposition to my opinions.

If we look at the financial debacle of 2008 it was hardly any surprise since many economists actually understood the problem of subprime lending and the subsequent securitization. The problem was that it could proceed until acute liquidity problems hit the worldwide financial organizations. We also know pretty well some of the more narrow causes of the breakdown; the almost perverted increase of oil-futures in Spring 2008 curbed by the outbreak of the relatively unexpected rapid increase in the Chinese inflation in late spring/early Summer 2008 and soaring liquidity of the financial actors (investment banks). To what degree politics and expectations fuelled the process is hard to say but the presidential election campaign in the US and the uncertainty of future policy certainly had an effect. Thus the breakdown is pretty well explainable and not a bifurcation in the pure sense. But the consequences of the first events in the breakdown process revealed to the financial industry the fragility of the global financial system, which in its turn led to an almost catastrophic reduction in the systemic confidence. This on one hand affected relations between banks and on the other hand led to legislation changes. But this had a secondary effect in the revelation of the state deficits and the doubtful ability to pay mortgages. This secondary effect started something like a game of chicken with killing the growth possibilities in Europe for decades. The secondary effect would probably not have taken place if the general systemic confidence had not broken down.

So while we perhaps cannot call the event a bifurcation per se, the specific global reaction to the event seems more like a bifurcation.

A similar kind of reasoning could be applied to the events of 9/11. The event was completely unexpected with respect to time and place but similar events had occurred earlier only now the scale was dramatically increased. There existed a known threat of events of such a character so we cannot rank 9/11 as a bifurcation per se. However the scale and the character of the target led to draconian effects which changed the dynamics of the world with respect to policy and international relations, so when we look at the compounded event, action/reaction it probably can be characterized as a bifurcation.

An example of an event which might qualify in itself as a bifurcation is to my understanding the developments on the European stage the decade before the outbreak of World War 1. Reading Barbara Tuchman (1962) one gets the impression that the structure of the coalitions was indeed not evident until rather late, while the evolution towards a European war was clear to many contemporary observers. A war between France and Germany was not particularly evident, in spite of sentiments of revanchism for 1870, and Germany did not appear as a loyal supporter of Austria; they had been at war 48 years earlier. France and Russia had strong connections but Britain was not a frightfully enthusiastic supporter of either France or Russia. The events in Sarajevo brought the crisis in the Balkans to the top of the agenda and as many historians say diplomatic relations went completely out of control. I am not sure but it seems that the development was such that the tensions in Europe meant that the immediate character of a critical event could settle the future with respect to direction and structure. If so the word bifurcation as a result of a perturbation is probably correct.[8]

The point of this detour into interpretation of historical processes serves to make clear that when we use the word bifurcation in a mathematical model describing the reality this should have some form of correspondence in reality. The two examples from the outbreak of World War I as I have read from historical analysis and the 9/11 event with its subsequent consequences shows that a bifurcation process is indeed complex and the very existence of mathematical models used to demonstrate a local behaviour which is in some sense chaotic does not mean that such *models* can be used in a meaningful way. One thing which we forget in mathematical modelling is the precise composition of inert and dissipative processes. Tensions may have been built up over a long time, but the actual events may decide the direction and scale after an almost random scheme. The very outspoken distinction between long run and short run is a bit obscure, apart from sorting them according to an almanac and a clock. Our analysis of the time concept in Chapter 2 shows that *long run* analysis can possibly be defined in a deterministic model but apart from dreams and plans it has little to do with the flow of time. Keynes is said to have expressed 'in the long term we are all dead' and that is more than a joke. As a matter of fact this sentence expresses the fundamental difference between the neoclassical general equilibrium theory and the non-equilibrium/temporary equilibrium/Keynesian equilibrium theoretical standpoint. In Chapter 2 we derived Proposition 2.1 where we separated different aggregate levels from each other with respect to rationality and optimization. The sometimes confused discussion of long run versus short run on one hand is meaningless when attached to the neoclassical axiomatic structure since there is actually no time whatsoever and if we define a sort of logical time model as a Hicks/Kaldor production function the parameter structure is defined at the start and so also the dynamic rule. It is a determinism à la St. Bonaventura which we quoted from Gilson above. On the other hand: in the eagerness to find a synthesis between neoclassical and Keynesian economics the opinion that the Keynesian approach is a short term description of the dynamics of an economy, while the neoclassical approach, accepting the axiomatic structure, describes the long run dynamics of the same economy. As we have shown this is a logical contradiction, a misunderstanding of the role of axiomatic structures.

Thus different aggregate levels are independent in a logical sense but not in the sense expressed in Arrow's paradox, which means that the current individual microscopic behaviour may affect macroscopic solutions which when they are imposed often are more inert than the more flexible individual agents.

When we discuss stability in an economy it is indeed important to separate the stability problems of model structures and of real structures which cause instability/stability in the reality. Our discussion of causality aimed to show the fundamental trickiness of the very concept of causality. The analysis of dynamic processes cannot per se harbour the concept of *ceteris paribus*; it is a contradiction in terms if we stick to an Einstein-Minkowski setting of the time concept. Thus a dynamic analysis of macroscopic development must contain that economics is a social science and not something apart and isolated from the social structures in general.

Microscopic and Macroscopic Stability

To my knowledge Knut Wicksell is the first economist who explicitly mentions the possibility of different stability conditions for the microscopic and the macroscopic levels.

Wicksell looks at the microscopic level as fairly stable illustrated by figure 5.5B while on macroscopic level it is as the illustration in 5.5A. This means that a perturbation of the macroscopic state will irreversibly move the economy to a different state Wicksell (1937[1922]: 222). This is actually the same conclusion at which Hans Reichenbach (1991[1956]:207ff) arrives when he discusses more general physical systems, based on commutativity of particles and non-commutativity of structures.

The reason for this is basically that given some inertia for the agents in their respective modes of life they tend to restore these if possible, provided that the socioeconomic structures are stable. This is like Newton's stability concept; the framework of the society implies that if their life patterns are upset, agents tend to restore the mode of life within the same frames as before.

If however the macroscopic stability is upset this generally forces agents into actions because of new frames and that prevents the restoration of the old macroscopic stability state.[9]

Reichenbach bases his discussion on the concept of commutativity which is a form of reversibility. In simple algebra we have that $[a + b = b + a]$ and similar for multiplication $[a \cdot b = b \cdot a]$ where a and b are two real numbers. But if we let A and B be two matrices of real numbers we have that $[A + B = B + A]$ but $[A \cdot B \neq B \cdot A]$.

Indeed when we pass over from atomistic variable the algebra we use is normally Boolean algebra which is commutative and associative. The latter imply that for any three real numbers a, b, c holds that $[a \cdot (b \cdot c) = (a \cdot b) \cdot c)]$. While when we move over to matrices, for example describing dynamic structures, we have for three matrices A, B and C that $[A \cdot (B \cdot C) \neq (A \cdot B) \cdot C]$ this is indeed important when we pass over to a dynamic analysis of sub-systems and with respect to aggregation of structures. We will not go into these questions since they are outside our purpose, but when we pass over from elaborations of a Euclidian space to the study of abstract forms in line with Keynes' sentiment we surely have to study these kinds of matters.

Our earlier discussion leads us to a conclusion concerning the market space that aggregation could not be independent on its local and temporal environment. This must not however be interpreted as exogenous effects but more as interactions between the market space and the non-market space. As we mentioned concerning neoclassical theory it divides the social space into a market space,

A: Macroscopic stability   B: Microscopic stability

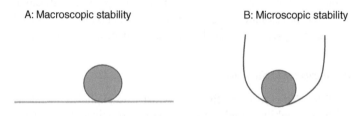

Figure 5.5 Macroscopic and microscopic stability according to Wicksell

where all information is contained in the prices, and thus the agents affect each other only through the prices, and a state space, containing the environment to the market space. Events in the state space affect the market space through the resulting price vectors but these changes do not change the state space so the communication between the two spaces are single directed. This allows us to speak about exogenous and endogenous structures. In our setting however the agents occupy seats in both spaces but in different capacities. In the market space the agents perform normally simple optimizations given earlier considerations concerning the nature of commodities, save for the influence of moral affections. In the non-market space the agents may be influenced by the revaluations of assets liabilities by the market process. The agents may also act for different kind of restructurings of the market space, such as environmental information or concerning ethical aspects, which may directly or indirectly affect the market behaviour and the market outcome.

This leads to more or less continuous restructuring of the market in conjunction with the effects of inventions/innovations and such restructurings appear and sometimes causes bifurcations or perturbations such that we locally and temporally have chaotic structures.

The individual however has the ability to adapt to new conditions when an action fails relative to its purpose, while macroscopic structures have such abilities in a very limited form, thus we will also have successive adaptions for, what is thought of as, new long run structures and such adaptions will have further effects on macroscopic structures although not of a chaotic character. Thus with respect to institutional structures in a society these might be a rational response to a problem created by the development of the increased market penetration but as time goes by the institutions in question are forced to adapt to new problems and we have a process which makes institutional structures obsolete; 'the dead city dominates through inertia the living city' and thus imposes an anomaly in the working of the public/non-market structure.

In short, the *ceteris paribus* assumption may be relevant at microscopic levels but relatively susceptible at the macroscopic level since microscopic states locally and temporally can be thought of as reversible if perturbed while the macroscopic changes are to be seen as irreversible if perturbed.

In Ekstedt (2012: 77) we used an example from the development of Volvo during the 1960s to 1980s illustrating a creeping process of structural change in the focus of the companies, which was rather typical for the Swedish economic development during the post-World War II period and completely changed the conditions for welfare policy in general and economic stabilization policy in particular. The figures are those of Volvo for years 1963 and 1987 and show the complexity of economic growth even for a single company.[10]

What we see first of all is the radically increased market risk. In 1987 one quarter of the production goes to the American market where the market share is round 1.8 %. Losing half of the market share in Sweden, which is rather satisfying and probably stable must be compared to losing half the market share in the

Table 5.1 The development of Volvo

	Sweden, %		USA, %	
	1963	1987	1963	1987
Share of Production	85	17	< 5	25
Market-Share	35	25	≈ 0	1,8

US which is not improbable given currency problems, misjudgement about supply of models and so on.

From a macroscopic perspective however it is even worse, particularly taking into consideration that Volvo's development was not on the extreme side in Sweden; in other export companies like ABB, LME, Sandvik and Atlas Copco were similar if not worse in these aspects. In all – the export share as a percentage of GDP increased from approximately 22% to 55% during these years. With this, increased attention had to be paid to the financial flows, currency matters, inflation and state budget discipline but increased attention is not enough because the government and the central bank had successively a new structure of causal relations to understand and try to diagnose.

People bought their yogurt, salad and petrol as usual and demanded their granted public welfare structure but changes at the macroscopic level were rumbling in the background and turned into a catastrophe in the beginning of 1990s when the Swedish Krona had to depreciate on the average by 43% not to speak of personal bankruptcies and unemployment. This was indeed a catastrophe and at least a widespread chaos. When did it start and what triggered the start? We may ask the same questions with respect to Black Monday in 1987 concerning the stock exchange. We may ask the same questions with respect to Autumn 2008. When do chaotic changes start and what triggers their start? No one interested in economic affairs believes in a singular act but sees them as the end of a process of development. The question is whether we can foresee such bifurcations and eventual perturbations and alter the path of the economy ahead of the bifurcation?

But forms are more than the sense in which we have used above. When we speak about dynamic structures we normally, if we limit to ordinary differential equations and anticipate in form of matrices like:

$$\dot{x}_i = f_i\left(x_1,\cdots,x_j\right), \quad i=1,\cdots,n; \quad j=1,\cdots,m; \qquad \text{E.5.10}$$

and f supposed to be linear, an assumption limiting the analysed space.

The solution of such a system will appear in form of an eigenvalue problem like:

$$\lambda^n + \alpha_1\lambda^{n-1} + \cdots + \alpha_{mn}\lambda + \beta = 0 \qquad \text{E.5.11}$$

Where the first problem we meet is whether **i** is equal to **j** or not. If *not* we land in difficulties because we then will have to analyse $\dfrac{i}{j}$! dynamic systems and their eventual interactions.

Looking at E.5.11 however we realize that this equation depends on the matrix structure

$$\begin{pmatrix} a_{11} & \cdots & a_{1n} \\ \vdots & \ddots & \vdots \\ a_{n1} & \cdots & a_{nn} \end{pmatrix}$$

E.5.12

and this structure decides the parameters a_{11} ... a_{nn}. We have then three basic problems: the first is the above mentioned problem, i.e. if the matrix is quadratic or not. If it is not, we must expect 'catastrophic points' where we enter a different dynamic pattern. It is also important to realize that a seemingly quadratic matrix may have singularities and thus reduce to a rectangular. The second is about the roots, given a quadratic matrix real roots, it will give us, within limits, a continuous development explosive or contractive, while imaginary roots will imply periodic behaviour either exploding or contracting. The third problem, which is the structural stability problem, is when we have perturbations of the matrix and what will then happen to the form of the phase-diagram in a certain neighbourhood. In certain structures of a quadratic matrix it will be extremely sensitive to perturbations while in others even rather substantial perturbations will change the numerical values but not the principle form of the phase-diagram. We will give some simple numerical examples of this.

Our discussion so far has dealt with ordinary differential systems. Non-linear systems and higher order systems imply complications but if they are possible to solve at all they can be reduced to rather simple set of structures which display the same sort of principle problems as we have discussed. Furthermore except for very well stated problems, normally appearing in financial analysis, the real economy is such that it is hard to motivate a more complicated system then a second order system if we let capital and investments have separate impacts for example. I do not think that we are analytically ready for mixing full-fledged financial dynamics with a model dealing with causalities in the real sector, but that opinion may be due to insufficient following of dynamic research.

Initial Value Problems

We have already dealt with the initial value problem in relation to Haavelmo's model above. In a higher order dynamic system a numerical solution requires some initial values. It is then rather obvious that these initial values will have a substantial effect on the dynamic pattern. Let us take a well-known example which is close to Haavelmo's model: Hicks', Harrod's and Samuelson's accelerator/multiplier model which we simplify a bit to get the points clear.

$$C_t = 0.9 \cdot Y_{t-1} \qquad \text{Consumption}$$
$$I_t = 1.B \cdot (Y_{t-1} - Y_{t-2}) \quad \text{Investment}$$
$$Y_t = C_t + I_t \qquad\qquad \text{National Income} \qquad\qquad \text{E.5.13}$$

It is dangerous to make any economic interpretations on a model like E.5.13; it is purely aimed at studying the mathematical characteristics of this kind of modelling. Nevertheless using economic terminology we may say the sensitive points are the incremental investment in relation to the incremental saving. When this relation passes zero things will happen, however the incremental saving does not occur explicitly in the model nor in the solution since incremental saving is: $S_t = Y_t - C_t$. In all dynamic systems irrespective of which, zero is to be looked out for. But the essential variable structure where zero becomes sensitive does not need to be explicitly seen but requires some additional analysis.

We solve the homogenous equation of E.5.13;

$$Y_t = 2.7 \cdot Y_{t-1} - 1.8 \cdot Y_{t-2} \qquad\qquad \text{E.5.14}$$

by transforming it to

$$s^2 - 2.7s + 1.8 = 0 \qquad\qquad \text{E.5.15}$$

And we will have the principle solution

$$Y_t = a \cdot 1.2^t + b \cdot 1.5^t \qquad\qquad \text{E.5.16}$$

The parameters a and b are technically solved as an eigenvalue problem. Thus we are looking for the point where $Y_t = 0$ which gives us the relation between a and b:

$$\frac{a}{b} = -\frac{1.5^t}{1.2^t} \qquad\qquad \text{E.5.17}$$

We may then utilise the initial value conditions Y1 = 100 and Y2 = 120. Since $100 = 1.2 \cdot a$ we get that $a = 83 \frac{1}{3}$.

Consequently we have $120 = 83 \frac{1}{3} \cdot 1.2^2 + b \cdot 1.5^2$, which implies b = 0.

We are however also interested in whether we have any bifurcation point and obviously that depends on the relation between a and b. Thus we have to solve

$$0 = 83 \frac{1}{3} \cdot 1.2^t + b \cdot 1.5^t \qquad\qquad \text{E.5.18}$$

which gives us

$$b = -83 \frac{1}{3} \cdot \left[\frac{1.2^t}{1.5^t} \right] \qquad\qquad \text{E.5.19}$$

which is true only for b = 0. So we happen to have chosen very interesting initial values. To not overload the pages with calculations we realise that for Y_2 less than 120, given a = 83 $\frac{1}{3}$, b will be negative and consequently we will always have bifurcations at some t, while if Y_t is equal or greater than 120 we have an explosive system since b will take on positive values. Obviously it holds for any n that $n \cdot \frac{120}{100}$ will imply b = 0.

If we however change the initial values to Y0 = 100 and Y1 = 119.9 we will have the solution

$$Y_n = 83.3333 \cdot 1.2^n - 1.85695 \cdot 1.5^n \qquad \text{E.5.20}$$

As we see E.5.16 will be ever increasing while in E.5.17 for a relation approximately $Y_1/Y_0 < 1.2$ there exists an $n < + \infty$ such that we will have a bifurcation and Y_t will turn and decrease.

The relation between the initial values is of course specific for the set of parameters in E.5.14 and thus the parameters of the system E.5.13, which means that the parameter in the investment function may be different, but given the initial values there will exist a critical value of that parameter where we have a bifurcation; thus we will have the case we discussed with respect to Haavelmo's model for any parameter and initial values given the value of the others. Consequently the error terms for the estimation of the parameters will interact with the deterministic structure and critical points may appear anywhere.

Consequently initial value problems are not something particular but a part of the complexity of the parameter structures.

However in a system as E.5.13 it is natural to think of 'floors' and 'ceilings in form of reinvestments in fixed capital, maintenance of stocks, renewing of consumers durables and so on. Such floors and ceilings are of course exogenous to the model and appear along the trajectory.

Paul Samuelson (1947: 315–317) has a classification of dynamic systems which is productive to use. In particular he separates so called initial value systems, which he calls *dynamical and causal*, from systems where the trajectory is exposed to external factors changing its path; these are called *dynamical historical systems*.

Hicks'/Harrod's/Samuelson's multiplier-accelerator analysis as it appears in E.5.13 illustrates a dynamical causal system, using Samuelson's notation, as

$$x = f\left[\left(t - t^0\right); \overline{x}\left(t^0\right)\right]; \qquad \text{E.5.21}$$

While E.5.13 when we insert floors and ceilings, represents a dynamical historical system and has the corresponding representation

$$x = g\left[t; x\left(t^0\right)\right]; \qquad \text{E.5.22}$$

Thus both the systems are sensitive to the initial state space but the historical system is also sensitive to successive changes in the state space over time.

Let us use the same system for illustrating what Samuelson calls a dynamical historical system. That means that exogenous event takes place during time and shifts the trajectory. Let us add exogenous control variables in the form of floor and ceiling. We do so in the simplest way as constants since the example will be complicated enough to follow. We might of course add an economic explanation for the floors as necessary reinvestments and consumption out of wealth as well as from social beneficiary systems and for the ceilings as capacity restrictions. We do not need to be particularly keen on stressing economic explanations since these often require further explanations which is unnecessary with respect to our purpose.

Anyway let us impute floors and ceilings:

Floors: The consumption cannot fall under 70 in a period
             The investments cannot fall under − 27 for two successive periods.
Ceilings: The consumption cannot exceed 140 in a period.
             The investments cannot exceed 30 in a period.

Let us start with the initial values $Y_0 = 100$ and $Y_1 = 110$. We will than have a development for 32 periods as in Figure 5.6

As we see the figure displays a certain cyclical behaviour although not particularly regular, but we can suspect that it will become more regular as time goes by. Changes in initial values, even small, will have pronounced effects. Observe that this system is, compared to the unrestricted model we analysed above, extremely complex. The floors and the ceilings although constant and well defined will affect the system in a chaotic way depending on the complex relations between the variables and the existence of 'catastrophic points'.

Let us change the initial values to $Y_0 = 100$ and $Y_1 = 105$ and we will have the following figure:

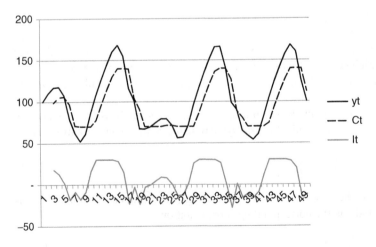

Figure 5.6 Dynamics with 'floors' and 'ceilings'

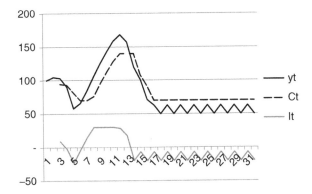

Figure 5.7 Change in initial values of a floor/ceiling model

The system will get stuck at a constant level at the floors for eternal time.

Consumption Characteristics Models à la Gorman/Lancaster

An often-used technique in consumption theory when dealing within the realms of Becker's household production approach is the so called characteristics approach, first presented by Gorman (1980 [1957]) and then developed by Lancaster (1967). The households are using commodities as means to get non-marketable qualities, characteristics, which are functions of marketable commodities. Let z_i represent characteristics and x_j commodities and we get the functions

$$z_1 = f_1\left(x_1,...,x_m\right)$$
$$\vdots$$
$$Z_n = f_n\left(x_1,...,x_m\right) \qquad \text{E.5.23}$$

Let us look at the simplest possible case of optimization, with a 2x2 characteristics matrix

$$Max\,U = z_1^\alpha \cdot z_2^\beta$$
$$z_1 = a_{11}x_1 + a_{12}x_2 \qquad \text{subject to}$$
$$z_2 = a_{21}x_1 + a_{22}x_2$$
$$\sum_i p_i x_i = B \qquad \text{E.5.24}$$

The usual assumptions in literature is that $z_i > 0$, $x_j > 0$ and $a_{ij} \geq 0$. Furthermore we must also add that the determinant of the characteristics matrix $|A| \neq 0$.

In order to get the implicit prices of the characteristics we invert the matrix and express the budget restriction in characteristics and their implicit prices.

This gives us the transformed optimization problem;

$$Max\,U = z_1^{\alpha} \cdot z_2^{\beta} \qquad\qquad\qquad \text{E.5.25}$$

$$\left[z_1 \left(p_1 \cdot a_{22} - p_2 \cdot a_{21} \right) - z_2 \left(p_2 \cdot a_{11} - p_1 \cdot a_{12} \right) \right] = B \cdot |A| \qquad \text{s.t.}$$

We develop the corresponding Lagrange expression and receive the implicit demand function for the characteristics z_1 and z_2

$$z_1 = \frac{B \cdot |A|}{\left(1 + \dfrac{\beta}{\alpha} \right) \cdot \left(p_1 \cdot a_{22} - p_2 \cdot a_{21} \right)}$$

$$z_2 = \frac{B \cdot |A|}{\left(1 + \dfrac{\alpha}{\beta} \right) \cdot \left(p_2 \cdot a_{11} - p_1 \cdot a_{12} \right)} \qquad\qquad \text{E.5.26}$$

Thus we can see from the expressions E.5.25 and E.5.26 that the demand functions for the characteristics are more complex than in the usual demand functions and we see that we are going to get discontinuous shifts due to relative changes of p_1 and p_2, which will also imply discontinuous shift in demand for the commodities.

Observe that the characteristics matrix does not need, probably in the normal case it is not, to be a square matrix. But for illustrative purposes it is simple and shows the necessary features. Thus when we have j characteristics and i commodities we end up in $\dfrac{i!}{j!}$ solutions and furthermore, when i > j satisfying the consumer needs to an outlay means that some commodities will not be consumed and when i < j consuming any commodity combination means that some characteristics will not be satisfied. As we saw even the simplest case when i = j gives us also problems of bifurcations depending on variations in relative prices.

With respect to the case of a square characteristics matrix we now have two types of bifurcations. One is the type intrinsic to the square matrix we have discussed above and the other type occurs when we have a rectangular matrix and price changes create different effective square matrices.

Perturbations and Structural Stability

Our description of the changes in the Swedish industry structure above is an example of a systematic change in the structure. The change which might be seen in *ex post* statistics will probably be hidden by evolution in other dimensions which means that the government bodies responsible for economic policy may not notice the changes in the structural composition of the industry and pursue a policy which may well be not only suboptimal but also have destabilizing effects. If we look back on the subprime problem which was known and discussed at least 4/5 years before the crisis actually occurred this was still a rather simple problem to detect since it concerned changed rules and changed praxis. Movements in the real economy are generally slow and hidden in the multitude of counteracting forces. Even if we actually observe a specific evolution we are seldom in the position to analyse the relative causations among the different events occurring. Our models for example give us one view but if fundamental structures are changing it is hard to see in what ways this affect the models. David Hume (2002[1740]: 58) puts it nicely

> When we infer effects from causes, we must establish the existence of these causes; which we have only two ways of doing, either by an immediate perception of our memory or senses, or by an inference from other causes; which causes again we must ascertain in the same manner, either by a present impression, or by an inference from *their* causes, and so on, till we arrive at some object, which we see or remember. 'Tis impossible for us to carry on our inferences *in infinitum*; and the only thing, that can stop them, is an impression of the memory or senses, beyond which there is no room for doubt or inquiry.

Thus a changing structure will change the working of our models but how do we detect that when the change only affects certain parameters leaving others unchanged which implies that our focus and priorities will also become a factor which obscures the analysis. Even if we observe the essentialities of a change, the political and economic feasibility is still an obstacle to overcome. In this connection we are remind of the contradiction between Proposition 2.1 in Chapter 2, which deal with real aggregation, and Proposition 3.1 in Chapter 3 which holds when we only deal with monetary values.

To give examples of structural stability in mathematics is a simple task. It is easy since the systems are deterministic (even stochastic systems) and repercussions are possible to analyse a priori. Still analysing large systems means that we have internal communication problems to put it in general terms. Our computer programs will detect the critical points of a *given system* but how do we know about the implicit causalities between the reality and the mathematical system when we have temporal changes? I have chosen the expression 'internal communication problems' from a discussion in London in the middle of 1980s of the LINK-system which was linking macroeconomic models from different OECD-countries into one gigantic model system with more than a million equations and several thousands of people working on the model. Imagine the internal communication problems! It is wise to have the quote from Hume somewhere in our minds.

Anyway Ekstedt and Westberg (1997) made some tentative suggestions in the line of Ragnar Frisch's ideas about a close cooperation between politicians and econometricians, but it was about dynamic modelling. Given a certain problematic area we could probably systemize the dynamics into a matrix of differential equations, say for five sectors, the interesting thing then is to see zeros and +/– signs in the matrix. This outline could then be used for interviewing people experienced in particular areas to get opinions of the zeros and the signs and then to preform computer experiments on singular points, bifurcations, to get some views on structural stability. They thereby developed a small illustration of the complexity of structural stability/instability.

Let us look at a small dynamical model with respect to sensitivity of parameter changes. In Ekstedt (2012: 242–243) we discussed asset pricing and expectations. We particularly discussed extrapolative expectation in relation to a model developed by Arrow and Enthoven (1956). We use this model to show the relative complexity and subsequent sensitivity of relatively small differential equation models, although the assumptions are unrealistically simplified and designed to have a pedagogical value.

Let X denote prices; X^0 current prices and X^e expected prices and $\dot{X}$ time derivative. The respective parameters elasticities as usual and we write

Expectation formation:

$$X_1^e = a \cdot X_1^0 + b \cdot X_2^0 + \eta_1 \cdot \dot{X}_1 + \eta_{12} \cdot \dot{X}_2$$
$$X_2^e = c \cdot X_1^0 + d \cdot X_2^0 + \eta_2 \cdot \dot{X}_2 + \eta_{21} \cdot \dot{X}_1 \qquad \text{E.5.27}$$

Adjustment speeds:

$$\dot{X}_1 = \alpha_1 \cdot \left(X_1^e - X_1^0\right) + \alpha_2 \cdot \left(X_2^e - X_2^0\right) + \beta_1 \cdot \dot{X}_1 + \beta_2 \cdot \dot{X}_2$$
$$\dot{X}_2 = \alpha_3 \cdot \left(X_1^e - X_1^0\right) + \alpha_4 \cdot \left(X_2^e - X_2^0\right) + \beta_3 \cdot \dot{X}_1 + \beta_4 \cdot \dot{X}_2 \qquad \text{E.5.28}$$

In Matrix notation we can write the systems E.5.27 and E.5.28 as

$$X^e = A \cdot X^0 + N \cdot \dot{X} \quad \text{A and N are square matrices} \qquad \text{E.5.29}$$

$$\dot{X} = P \cdot X^{e0} + B \cdot \dot{X} \quad \text{P and B are square matrices} \qquad \text{E.5.30}$$

Inserting E.5.29 into E.5.30 gives us

$$\dot{X} = P \cdot \left(A - I\right) \cdot \left(I - P \cdot N - B\right)^{-1} \cdot X^0; \qquad \text{E.5.31}$$

I denotes the identity matrix

The expression E.5.31 is indeed of a rather complex nature where the parameters are nested and where we in the calculations will most probably end up in parameters which are zero or close to zero. Thus the internal sensitivity of E.5.31 is in many cases substantial.

Let us define

$$K = P \cdot (A - I) \cdot (I - P \cdot N - B)^{-1} \qquad \text{E.5.32}$$

The solution of E.5.31 can be written

$$X_1 = k_1 \cdot X_1 \cdot e^{\lambda t} + k_2 \cdot X_2 \cdot e^{\gamma t}$$
$$X_2 = k_3 \cdot X_1 \cdot e^{\lambda t} + k_4 \cdot X_2 \cdot e^{\gamma t} \qquad \text{E.5.33}$$

where λ and γ are the eigenvalues of E.5.32 and k_1, k_3 and k_2, k_4 are the respective eigenvectors.

Let us look at a small example.

We assume the following matrices:

$$A = \begin{bmatrix} 1 & 0.2 \\ -0.1 & -0.9 \end{bmatrix} \quad N = \begin{bmatrix} 0.1 & -0.45 \\ 0.4 & -0.7 \end{bmatrix}$$

$$P = \begin{bmatrix} -1 & 0.6 \\ 1 & 0.9 \end{bmatrix} \quad B = \begin{bmatrix} 0.7 & -0.7 \\ -0.6 & 0.7 \end{bmatrix}$$

$$I = \begin{bmatrix} 1 & 0 \\ 0 & 1 \end{bmatrix}$$

The corresponding eigenvalues of E.11 are $\lambda = 0.271$ and $\gamma = -0.873$. The corrresponding eigenvector matrix is $k = \begin{bmatrix} 0.927 & 0.628 \\ 0.371 & 0.778 \end{bmatrix}$. We thus have the solution

$$X_1 = 0.927 \cdot e^{0.271t} + 0.628 \cdot e^{-0.873t}$$
$$X_2 = 0.371 \cdot e^{0.271t} + 0.778 \cdot e^{-0.873t} \qquad \text{E.5.34}$$

We thus have that the system form a saddle-point solution, where the system in the X_1-dimension explodes while in the X_2-dimension it will converge. In Figure 5.8 we show the phase diagram of the system.

Let us now change the parameter in the left upper corner of the A-matrix from 1 to 1.05, a rather small change. Solving the system we get the solution

$$X_1 = (0.582 + 0.368i) \cdot e^{-(0.705 - 0.624i)t} + 0.725 \cdot e^{-(0.705 + 0.624i)t}$$
$$X_2 = (0.582 - 0.368i) \cdot e^{-(0.705 - 0.624i)t} + 0.725 \cdot e^{-(0.705 + 0.624i)t} \qquad \text{E.5.35}$$

The dynamic properties are completely changed and we have now stability in both dimensions, although with a fluctuating pattern. In Figure 5.9 we show the phase diagram of system E.5.35.

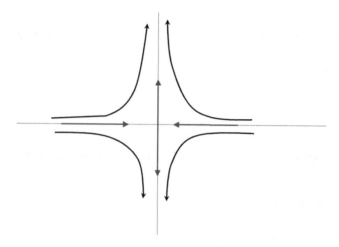

Figure 5.8 Phase-diagram of system E.5.34

The post-change dynamics is illustrated in Figure 5.9 and as we see the system is dynamically stable.

The question is of course if a *ceteris paribus* assumption for the system is ever appropriate with respect to numerical specification if we are not aware of on the mathematical side the singularities and on the empirical side the possibility of perturbations of parameters. Structural stability concerns most probably not only the specific parameter which we changed but all parameters of the entire matrix A, and also other matrices implicit in the in the K-matrix. To start with a numerical specification, which is held as true, makes us unable to find any clear sign either singular points or variations of the sensitivity of perturbations. Thus the

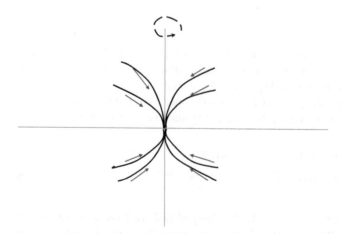

Figure 5.9 Phase-diagram of system E.5.35

complexity of the K-matrix hides the critical points but at the same time we know that these critical points are possible to detect since it is a deterministic dynamic system. These considerations are, partly at least, a rational for Keynes' views expressed in the letter to Harrod, quoted in the Introductory chapter.

We may conclude from the mathematical examples we have briefly discussed here that for any deterministic complex dynamic system we have critical points which are *nowhere dense*, where the system in question will change its dynamic structure. We call these bifurcation points and such points are part of the complex structure. We could also say that the dynamic form is changed to lean against D'Arcy Thompson's (1992 [1942]) discussion on form and growth.

Technically we define such points as *nowhere dense*.

Definition of Dense Sets:

A set is dense when for any two points a and b there exists an ε such that a < ε < b. If a set is nowhere dense there is a λ such that a] λ [b. Thus a nowhere dense point has no interior.

On the internet we find many pictures of breaking waves, a rather well-known singular point in nature, which also is of importance for certain groups of people, i.e. surfers. I ask the reader to read the definition of a *nowhere dense set* carefully and then look at a good picture of a breaking wave and try to locate the bifurcation point precisely. It is indeed difficult.

It is actually rather important to realize that we are used to locate a certain event to a point in space or time while the existence of nowhere dense sets contradicts any expression of the exact location.

Stability as a State in Reality

As a mathematical process the reality may have a certain development which leads towards a point of bifurcation although until that is reached there is obvious stability in the sense that all points in the evolution of a system are apprehended as 'dense' in the sense that most observers judge the evolution as continuous. The fact that there are turning points where the evolution reverses its direction is not in itself upsetting stability since the dynamic properties of the system seems to be intact. One funny result of this is that economics make such a clear difference between long term and short term. A definition of the difference between the two regimes usually states that if all factors are to be seen as flexible then we are in the long run regime, if not we are in the short run regime. Our discussion above of deterministic systems, particularly the Hicks/Samuelson/Harrod model shows as an example of the initial-value problem that a bifurcation is practically built into a system at its very birth. But let us imagine that we have the values from empirical observations and not from a model.

We may thus ask which variable of a system will be important with respect to the earliest warning of a bifurcation.

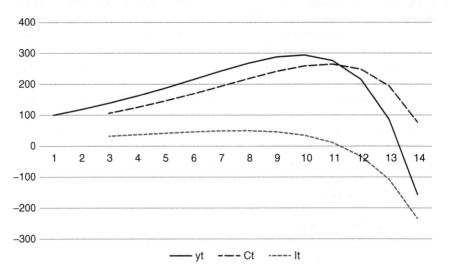

Figure 5.10 Which is the leading variable?

So when is a system begotten and when is it born and when does it break down?[11] Looking at our story above on the Volvo evolution we may ask when we find the initial conditions. Even nowhere dense points are possible to detect but how do we find them in reality? Practically we have to regard a multitude of evolutions of which we have to decide which are decisive and which are not. But those who are not; on which grounds do we disregard them? With respect to a particular theory? With respect to some empirical findings – but in that case we have to ask why we decide that these particular findings can be regarded as decisive in our question.

In economics we are used to relative quantities and sizes, which is quite OK within certain borders, such an assumption allows us to use the *ceteris paribus* presumption. But at some instant, passing some border, the scale of absolute magnitudes becomes important and this is when we pass over the pure microscopic area and get an interaction between not only the microscopic units but also interactions between microscopic levels and macroscopic levels as in Arrow's paradox which is one example; this leads to the problem which Wicksell tried to illustrate. D'Arcy Thompson (1992:16–17) describes it when the substance of an entity grows out of its form:

> We call a thing *big* or *little* with reference to what it is wont to be, as when we speak of a small elephant or a large rat; and we are apt accordingly to suppose that size makes no other or more essential difference, and that Lilliput and Brobdingnag are all alike, according as we look at them through one end of the glass or the other. ...
>
> All this is true of *number*, and of *relative magnitude*. The Universe has its endless gamut of great and small, of near and far, of many and few.

Nevertheless, in physical science the scale of absolute magnitude becomes a very real and important thing; and a new and deeper interest arises out of the changing ratio of dimensions when we come to consider the inevitable changes of physical relations with which it is bound up. The effect of *scale* depends not on a thing in itself, but in relation to its whole environment or milieu; it is in conformity with the thing's 'place in Nature', its field of action and reaction in the Universe. Everywhere Nature works true to scale, and everything has its proper size accordingly [original emphasis].

This is indeed important. In our insertion of the concept of epistemic cycles we focus on the contextual considerations of an item and we so to speak take a step further from considering the commodity as a physical item, as implicit in the axiom of reflexivity, and consider its role for the individual. The neoclassical axioms take a step back from the commodity as a physical item and transform it into single scale of relations, the Euclidian space. The neoclassical commodities are therefore robbed of every possible characteristic except for a numeric notation which is not even bound to natural or rational numbers but to real numbers. We speak in economics of indivisibilities and how to eventually overcome the problem and come back to Euclidian relations. But then when we come to environmental and health economics for example, we meet a world of absolute scales in a non-Euclidian world.

We can proceed and talk about growth. The mainstream growth concept is simply an equalization of real growth and the turnover of money. But how to measure real growth if it is not equal to the turnover of money? We will later come back to that problem but suffice to say here that if we stick to the quote from D'Arcy Thompson 'it is in conformity with the thing's "place in Nature"', growth in production of different industrial sectors and service sectors will affect future possibilities of growth both environmentally, socially, politically and economically differently. It is very possible that the human ability of adaption and innovation/ invention will solve upcoming problems but at what consequences and what efforts? The saying '*the market will solve it*' is an absurdity. There will instead be some kind of market solution but at the price of social and political adaption of which costs and prices are impossible to calculate and thus is of no interest to ideological market economists.

Get me right – I do not claim that the market process is an unimportant factor in the adaption to substantial structural changes but the market process is affected and affects the social environment in a way which is not possible to measure by prices and is therefore a part of the social and political structure. This is completely neglected in the neoclassical axioms and has therefore seduced economists for some hundred years to think of economics in terms of modelling *ceteris paribus* where only prices and quantities sold at the market counts.

This is not a problem which can be added to the mainstream theory but requires other types of questions and scientific approaches.

Conclusions

The purpose of the chapter was to discuss the concept of causality; its meaning and measurement in economics particularly in accordance with Keynes' critique of Tinbergen in his letter to Harrod.

We start from the rejection of the existence of general equilibrium. Keynes divides the use of mathematical/logical models in two areas: one purpose is to discuss possible forms of dynamic evolution and temporary equilibria using mathematics as a tool for experiments; another purpose is to find an exact form and an exact parametric structure to picture the real world economy or at least parts of it.

Furthermore causal processes are developing in a time dimension; as time goes by revelations or earlier unknown or timely unordered events fundamentally may change the causality structure.

Based on Hume's analysis of the concept of causality we have found it doubtful both with respect to mathematical modelling and probabilistic analysis to find both an exact logical form of the causality structure as well as finding a precise parameter structure.

We therefore agree with Keynes' in his critique of Tinbergen.

Notes

1 *Non est ponenda pluralitas sine necessitate* meaning that a multitude of causes should not be postulated if not necessary.
2 The discussion is available at www.dalidimension.com
3 If you say, that it is not necessary to posit a standing still of an order, except among those which are ordered according to the order of causality, because among causes there is necessarily a standing still; I ask, "For what reason (is there) not (such) among others?" Translation from www.franciscan-archive.org Commentaries on the Four Books of Sentences of Master Peter Lombard, Archbishop of Paris BOOK TWO COMMENTARY ON DISTINCTION I
4 Norbert Wiener (1950) has in his texts expressed it that the natural sciences have an honourable opponent while the social sciences have not.
5 We use the concept of time dimension as in Einstein-Minkowski which says that at low relative speeds the perceptions become more space-like while at high speeds the perceptions become more time-like. So in the space like states time-rods are meaningful.
6 Sklar (1959; 1973) contain the basic thinking and the Theorem. For a more intuitive and informal discussion see Ekstedt (2012: 203–11). For a stringent mathematical discussion see Rüschendorf (2013: Chapter 1).
7 To me there are only two sciences besides the natural sciences (physics and chemistry) which use the word bifurcation: geography and sociology/anthropology. In geography the word denotes when a river divides into two branches only to further downstream unite again, Tärendö River in the north of Sweden is such an example of a bifurcation. In sociology/anthropology it stands for a linguistic difference in denoting mother's and father's kinship. So for example mother's sister is denoted separately from the father's sister. English for example make no such difference, aunt in both cases a collateral principle, while Swedish differentiates, bifurcates, mother's sister is called moster, while father's sister is called faster.
8 I apologize for the very superficial narration which could be wrong but as I have understood it I still claim that it is a narration which could describe a sort of bifurcation.

9 I try to avoid using the word equilibrium since the economy always is changing. A state of stability which basically is a socio-political concept is more appropriate.

10 The table appeared in a seminar paper 1989 at the School of Public Administration at Univ. of Gothenburg.

11 I watched a programme on TV about the famous Swedish photographer Lennart Nilsson who took pictures of the 18-week-old foetus which appeared on the cover of the April 30, 1965, issue of *LIFE* magazine. He was asked by the reporter: 'When is a child born?'. Lennart Nilsson answered: 'At the first kiss?'.

Bibliography

Althusser, L. and Balibar, E. (1970 [1968]), *Reading Capital*. London: New Left Book.

Amoroso, L. (1938) 'Vilfredo Pareto', *Econometrica*, Vol. 6, No. 1

Aristole (2002 [original around 334-324 BC]) *Politics*, in *The Works of Aristotle vol II*, Encyclopædia Britannica, Inc. Chicago, London.

Becker, G. S. (1976) *A New Economic Approach of Human Behaviour*. Chicago: University of Chicago Press.

Brody, T. (1994) *The Philosophy Behind Physics*. Berlin/Heidelberg/New York: Springer Verlag.

Di Lampedusa, G.T. (1960 [1959]) *Leoparden* (Il Gattopardo), Bonniers, Stockholm

Ekstedt, H. (2012) *Money in Economic Theory*. London and New York: Routledge.

Ekstedt, H. and Westberg, L. (1997) *An Early Warning System*, Quarterly Commentaries, Sanders Research Associates, London

Gilson, E. (1965) *The Philosophy of St. Bonaventure*. Paterson, New York: St. Anthony Guild Press.

Gorman, W. (1980) 'The demand for related goods: A possible procedure for analyzing quality differentials in the egg market', *Review of Economic Studies*. Vol 47. First circulated as Journal Paper no. 2319, *Iowa Agricultural Experiment Station* November 1956: 843–956.

Haavelmo, T. (1943) 'The Statistical Implications of a System of Simultaneous Equations', *Econometrica*, Vol. 11, No. 1: 1–12.

Hume, D. (2002 [1740]) *A Treatise of Human Nature*. Oxford: Oxford University Press.

Lancaster, K. (1966) 'A New Approach to Consumer Theory', *Journal of Political Economy* Vol. 74: 132–157.

Pearl, J. (2000) *Causality: Models, Reasoning and Inference*, Cambridge: Cambridge University Press.

Reichenbach, H. (1991 [1956]) *The Direction of Time*. Berkeley, LA, Oxford: University of California Press.

Rüschendorf, L. (2013) *Mathematical Risk Analysis: Dependence, Risk Bounds, Optimal Allocations and Portfolios*. Berlin and Heidelberg: Springer Verlag.

Samuelson, P.A. (1947) *The Foundations of Economic Analysis*. Cambridge, MA: Harvard University Press.

Sen, A. (2002) *Rationality and Freedom*. Cambridge, MA: The Belknap Press.

Sklar, A. (1959) 'Fonctions de répartition à n dimensions et leurs marges', *Publ. Inst. Statist. Univ. Paris* 8: 229–231.

Sklar, A. (1973) 'Random Variables, Joint Distribution Functions and Copulas', *Kybernetika* 9: 449–460

Thompson, D'Arcy W. (1992 [1942]) *On Growth and Form*. Cambridge: Cambridge University Press.

Thom, R. (1975) *Structural Stability and Morphogenesis: An Outline of a General Theory of Models*. New York: Addison-Wesley.

Tuchman, B.W. (1962) *The Guns of August*. New York: Macmillan.

Wiener, N. (1950) The Human Use Of Human Beings. Boston: Houghton Miffin & Co.

Wicksell, K. (1937 [1922]) *Lectures on Political Economy*. London: Routledge.

Wright, S. (1921) 'Correlation and Causation', *Journal of Agricultural Research*, Vol. XX, No.7: 557–585.

6 Inflation and Unemployment

Abstract

In this chapter we will mainly discuss two macroeconomic hypotheses: Phillips curve and Verdoorn's law, which seem to be accepted and added to modelling in different forms irrespective of whether it is Keynesian or neoclassical theorists or other types of heterodox analysts. It seems that the two are accepted more as empirical fact than theoretical hypotheses. We will however also pay attention to the interaction between the real and financial variables with respect to stability matters. Central to our discussion is the concept of inertia in different forms particularly so called labour hoarding and its underlying causes and consequences.

The Phillips hypothesis and Verdoorn's law both deal with the cyclical behaviour of the economy and both are based on a perceived statistical correspondence which have little support in theoretical consideration either of neoclassical or Keynesian character. There have been many different explanations, some based on the behaviour of the agents and some based on structural characteristics.

Our view is that understanding of the two hypotheses cannot be based on macroscopic studies but requires sectorial and even microscopic studies at lower levels and then the two approaches are parts of more complex structures and questions of long and/or run validity becomes relatively uninteresting.

When we come to the issues of inflation, unemployment and growth we enter really a blind alley from a theoretical perspective. In mainstream economic analysis we have a mixture of theoretical fragments and methodological patterns which indeed does not lead to a general clarification of the conceptual meaning and the interrelation between the concepts.

The intrinsic complexity of the concepts implies that we run into contradictions particularly with respect to policy measures.

Introduction

From our earlier discussions we could infer that economic theory is one thing and what practical economists do is another. Thus we may take on any theory and complete it ad hoc with any kind of assumptions irrespective of the consistency with respect to the theory but fitting it in to the context of experience. We may mix different theories even if they are basically contradictory but the so-created 'hotchpotch' seems to meet the actual situation we want to analyse. As long as we know what we are doing there is not something entirely wrong about this since the reality indeed seems full of contradictions, particularly in social sciences and one could say that different theories focus on different aspects of the reality and that they all contain some important aspects to consider in relation to the reality.

The problem is however that the theory, any theory, suggests interpretation of concepts and patterns of systematic thinking and therefore applying a kind of 'hotchpotch' may hide such inbuilt structures and thus the mixture may seem rather frivolous but in reality it hides a priori structures which are not analysed with respect to the current mixture of theoretical fragments, which is particularly prevalent in mathematical modelling. Furthermore using a particular theory as a *norm* in any way seems to be rather doubtful. The neoclassical theory for example deals with barter and given enough social inertia even a monetary economy may behave as a barter economy although there is a logical contradiction in mixing the two. For microscopic levels the traditional microeconomic theory works fairly well locally and temporally and even welfare economics may work provided that it is handled with care.

In the preceding chapter when we discussed causality and structural stability we saw the fragility even of mathematical systems when they become complex, how many more problems do we meet in dealing with the reality when we analyse a non-equilibrium economy where we have contradictions already in the basic concepts as money and where epistemic cycles of individuals as basis for action often are to some extent contradictory or even contrary. All this can however be dealt with locally and temporally under the condition of enough inertia. As long as we are looking for generic structures and behaviour we do not need to be afraid of contradictory elements in our hypothesis as long as we can explain them.

The problems come when we try to generalize our results and when we make some normative statements. Generalizations of social systems normally require that we abstract to philosophical levels and making general models imply that they are almost void of any material substance.

A rather astonishing example of this is the concept of unemployment. Do we define unemployment with respect to the social structure or with respect to the economic? The neoclassical theory lacks any kind of socio-economic structure but trusts price flexibility and the subsequent *invisible hand* obviously defines unemployment with respect to those actually employed while those who regard structures of social, demographic, physical, financial character as fundamental for economic organization must have a different kind of employment/unemployment concept.[1]

So in this example two theoretical approaches give rise to two entirely different employment concepts and that will subsequently lead to different kinds of policy recommendations. However this does not mean that we must choose one approach and reject the other, because, as said, the reality is sometimes contradictory but it means that we end up in a problem of diagnosis.

We have in earlier chapters met several examples of similar contradictions: the problem of aggregation with respect to the real economy versus monetary values; money used for valuation in commodity exchange versus valuation of financial assets and liabilities; stability of equilibrium versus social stability, and so on. Neoclassical theory has basically two gigantic problems with respect to the real world: the definition of utilities which holds only for the positive quadrant and the problem of zero. These two problems imply that neoclassical theory is unable to deal with anything except a barter economy. This has nothing per se to do with contradicting commodities but with contradicting 'utilities'. Furthermore lack of certain commodities may not only be a problem for the very commodities which are lacking but destroys the entire substitutability in changing the basic socio-economic structure for the individual. In these matters the naïvety of economists supporting a true market economy also in reality is somewhat trying and in principle they are Marxists of a different colour. Turning to the Keynesian approach, it suffers from the drawback of using basically neoclassical definitions of concepts and seldom accepts the complexity of the used concepts, a sacrifice for the mathematical simplicity perhaps.

What we can say about the normative role of economic theory is that the present state of knowledge is not sufficient for any form of general normative statements.

Thus claiming that public interference in a market economy always impies losses in the efficacy of the working of the economy is certainly true if we thereby mean the very barter process but public interference seldom has the purpose of regulating the market process per se but regulates the behaviour of the agents and promotes social stability and this will normally be at variance with some agents' preferences while others are enthusiastic supporters. Unfortunately the answer to the question comes when social stability is not obtainable any more.[2]

As long as economists do not realize this distinction between stability of the economic system as a subsystem of the social system as a whole with respect to the development of economic theory they will well fit in with Keynes' expression of 'defunct economists' whose idiosyncrasies are hovering in the air. It has to do with how to regard the agent and the societies and if they really are machines void of will and passions, alluding to Hume.

This means that in the light of our discussions in Chapters 1 and 2 on complexes we have to realize that it is not the knife or the gun that decide their purposes but the agent and the purpose of buying a commodity is linked to the purpose of using the commodity. The commodities become complexes not by themselves but by the will of the agent.

All these contradictions which we can identify already at the microscopic level do not disappear at the macroscopic level. As a matter of fact it is hard to say anything about what happens in the aggregation process. As some kind of generic rule with respect to social aggregation is that it often sets limitations but whether that is good or bad depends on the perspective of the commentator. Anyway we seldom see the principle of additive aggregation discussed but we see additions to mainstream theory which are more or less independent of any theoretical links.

The issues of inflation, unemployment and growth are indeed difficult in economic theory. In the neoclassical theory base on the general equilibrium axiomatic structure the concepts of inflation and unemployment are anomalies, they cannot exist within the axioms. Economic growth is difficult partly because it is with respect to causes are an anomaly within the general equilibrium concept. We have Solow's growth model and Neumann-Gale's but both these approaches keep the causes of the growth exogenous. Furthermore most discussions on the growth problem is, at least implicitly, referring to a commodity basket of constant dimensionality which is fundamentally different from dealing with growth when the dimensionality of the commodity basket changes.

This has developed into a situation where we have no consistent theory but only a mosaic of theoretical fragments where the different concepts are loosely related to each other and mostly interpreted ad hoc.

In this chapter we will mainly discuss two macroeconomic hypothesis, Phillips curve and Verdoorn's law, which seem to be accepted and added to modelling in different forms irrespective of whether the analysis is a Keynesian or a neoclassical theorist and also other heterodox analysts seem to accept the hypothesis as more an empirical fact than a theoretical hypothesis.

The two hypothesis may in some sense contradict each other, not per se but with respect to analytical consequences. Both hypothesis deal with cyclical behaviour and for the both there are controversies whether they are purely short run cyclical phenomena or have bearing also in the long run. Both hypothesis have their roots in a statistical correspondence between variables and seems to have little connections with basic economic theory, neoclassical, Keynesian and other types of economic theories. The controversies concerning the hypothesis deals generally if they are both long and short run phenomena or if they are to be seen as just short run phenomena.

The Philips curve concerns a negative relation between unemployment rate and inflation and Verdoorn's law defines a positive relationship between productivity and output.

From a methodological point of view these hypotheses are very interesting since they are anomalies with respect to a smoothly functioning market economy and as well as being partly contradictions in terms they are also partly evident consequences of each other.

Already Ricardo and even Hume discussed the case of improving technology with subsequent increases in productivity and effects on prices. Hume merely discussed the problem with respect to foreign trade while Ricardo also discussed it with respect to employment and particularly different qualities of the workforce. He then raised the problem of partial unemployment as a result of technological change. Jean Baptiste Say is very clear with respect to this when he discusses technological change in relation to unemployment of unskilled labour. Thus in fact the two approaches have their root in the microscopic conditions of certain production structures but it is not those of a perfect neoclassical theory of homogenous production factors with perfect flexibility but those of a world of inertia and heterogeneity. Whether the approaches of Phillips and Verdoorn can actually be detected at the macroscopic level is a matter of structural composition of the economy, the data although regarded as macroscopic are the sum of microscopic behaviours that have dynamic patterns which might cancel out at the macroscopic level. Thus, and we will show an example of this, the Phillips curve may exist for sectors but since these have different dynamic behaviour the Phillips curve will disappear at the macroscopic level. If we in such a case assume perfectly flexible labour the vanishing of the Philips curve at the macroscopic level will also mean that the whole problem disappears but if we assume heterogeneous non-flexible labour the problem will still exist.

The disappearance of the Phillips curve may actually be due to non-sufficient analysis of the aggregation process, and although the Phillips relation still exists it might be hidden. That does not mean that effects cancel out; they may still have considerable effects at the sectorial level and thus affect the ongoing reorganization of the structural composition but the variations of different sectors have different time structures. In the preceding chapter we discussed the development of Volvo and its complete change in risk structure and also its changed position vis-à-vis economic policy. If we now think of such permanently ongoing processes at the microscopic level the macroscopic variables will certainly be affected.

The two approaches are, as we have said, not implied by theoretical considerations but have appeared from statistical investigations. The Phillips curve is a negative relation between inflation and unemployment and Verdoorn's law is a positive relation between growth and productivity. Both approaches seem to be macroscopic phenomena.

Without going deep into trade cycle theory it is fairly easy to regard both the approaches as purely cyclical without any long run consequences.

We may look at them in relation to an elementary production possibility locus like Figure 6.1.

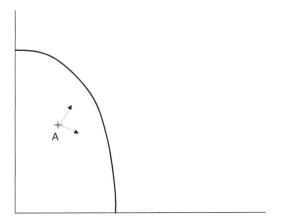

Figure 6.1 The Production Possibility Curve

Low labour demand in A as well as low commodity demand implies low pressure or even downward pressure on prices as there is unemployment. When capacity utilization approaches the production possibility frontier there is a pressure upwards on labour costs due to increased search costs, particularly if labour is heterogeneous, and high demand on commodities which imply a strong upward pressure on prices.

However the picture becomes a bit more complicated if we add Allais' equimarginal principle which is a mixture of trade cycle effects and growth effects (Allais 1987 and Ekstedt 2012:95–101). Neither trade cycles nor growth are purely macroscopic phenomena particularly not when we have heterogeneous capital and labour, but both have different effects on different sectors. The equimarginal principle is the constant search of firms for concavities which may imply at least temporal increasing return to scale due to innovations either of products or with respect to production systems. The *product cycle* process is an example of such a dynamics which leads to high initial profits but in a longer run decreasing profits due to innovations and imitation increasing competition, thus local concavities are transformed in to convexities (Ekstedt and Fusari 2010: 192–195).

This means that the production possibility curve in Figure 6.1 is on one hand static and on the other hand it presupposes perfect substitution. According to the equimarginal principle we in principle can find a production possibility curve for each sector which also includes both convex as well as concave parts.

Consequently when we look at broad aggregate approaches like the Phillips curve and Verdoorn's law we should not be surprised if we find clear signs of respective approach on sectorial levels but not on the aggregate level. We will later discuss a paper by Navarro and Soto (2006) who show this problem with respect to pro-cyclical variations in productivity and we will also discuss Swedish data which show the same tendency.

There is no reason at this stage to suspect any long term Phillips relation or long run effects other than the normal which follows from the fact that long run is built by short run decisions. If we link it to the equimarginal principle combined with the product cycle we could expect some form of Philips relation but that would not occur regularly and will hardly appear at the macroscopic level. If we assume that there is a Philips effect which is cyclical with respect to the trade cycle we could imagine that when the production sectors hire relatively homogenous labour and the trade cycles are regular we could expect to notice it at the macroscopic level. But if labour force is developing into heterogeneity and trade cycles are splitting up due to export to different regions then we might expect that even if it still exists a strong Phillips effect at the sectorial level we would not see it, neither in the short run nor in the long run. There is also a more sophisticated explanation first discussed in Ekstedt and Westberg (1991). We will come back to this later.

The point is however if we have a picture of the economy working as in neoclassical theory a microeconomic foundation of the macroeconomic theory hardly implies anything for the empirical research except for even more assumptions and mathematical obscurities.

It is necessary with a macroeconomic theory at least partly built on a microeconomic foundation but such a foundation must include structural changes, heterogeneities, and a mixture of non-competitive and competitive behaviour as is discussed in Maurice Allais' equimarginal principle. It is also important to realise that cyclical behaviour in the production/market system is dependent on structural composition of the economy and may therefore vary over time and space.

With respect to Verdoorn's law it is a bit different. Looking at cyclical matters we might expect, starting from A, that approaching the production possibility frontier may in the beginning lead to a high productivity depending on under-utilized capacity and subsequently a high growth but this will vanish when we reach the full capacity utilization where the only factor creating higher per capita growth and increase in productivity is technical change and that is a rather slow process. Thus in the early stages of the trade cycle upturn we could expect a high productivity growth as well as a high growth. Furthermore if we look at a combination of the equimarginal principle and the product cycle model we could see Verdoorn's law at the early stages of the product cycle while in the late stage we may even have a contrary development. Consequently it seems that in the long run for the macroscopic level, Verdoorn's law is more dubious.

The General Character of the Primary Concepts

We will consider Phillips' and Verdoorn's approaches along with a more microscopic discussion of productivity, profit and labour demand and also do to some 'playometrics' concerning some stability aspects.

The two hypotheses of the Phillips curve and Verdoorn's law are together a rather intricate system of relations which is also noted by 18th and 19th century economists although not with respect to the names we use. So if we try to sketch the problem we may have a picture like the one in Figure 6.2.

Figure 6.2 is organized in four nodes and pairwise relations. The two diagonal relations relate to the Phillips and Verdoorn hypotheses respectively so we have four triangular systems; two with the Phillips hypothesis as the hypotenuse and two with the Verdoorn relation as the hypotenuse.

Consequently as we see the figure catches almost the entire basic content within macroeconomic theory. Looking at textbooks in economics the macroeconomic content is normally organized around the four nodes. The reason is of course that the traditional macroscopic goals concern employment, inflation, growth and competitiveness at the international market and the intrinsic relation of the four nodes becomes of central analytical importance.

But this leads also to some kind of mystery. How does it come to be that two hypotheses of central importance as the Phillips curve and Verdoorn's law are more or less theoretically unexplained and at the same time more or less accepted as empirical 'facts', disputed – yes, but also at the centre of macroeconomic

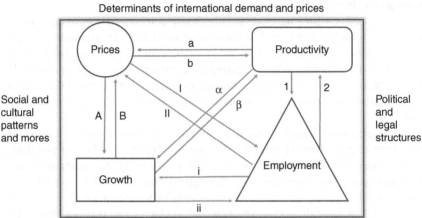

Figure 6.2 Employment, growth, prices and productivity

theory although it remains to a large extent unexplained by the central theoretical approaches, irrespective of whether it is Keynesian or neoclassical.

There is also an environment to the system which we have indicated. The interaction between the system and its environment is known 'piecewise' but to a large extent unknown which unfortunately makes the explanations of the 'system' rather diffuse.

When we look at the nodes per se: prices, productivity, employment and growth, the basic difficulty is to establish the aggregate level of the variables. As we earlier mentioned it is quite possible that a variable/relation may be possible to define at a macroscopic level but along the structural development it requires more and more microscopic underpinning. Furthermore both productivity and growth can be defined vis-à-vis physical as well as monetary aspects which call for a specification of the analytical purpose.

Prices and Productivity

When we look at the pairwise relation between prices and productivity it is indeed a bit obscure what we are looking for. Prices can obviously be seen as relative prices at a lower aggregate level, sectorial for example; we mentioned above that the Phillips relation may exist on sectorial levels but these cancel out when looking at the highest level. Thus looking directly at overall inflation may tell us little. But if we change attitude and go from overall inflation to sectorial price changes we also open for a structural effect which we do not have at the highest aggregate level or at least the structural effects will have delayed effects on the highest level.

When it comes to productivity we are in even more serious difficulties. If we first look at how to measure it we may choose between: $\dfrac{d\left\{\dfrac{p\cdot q}{w\cdot l}\right\}}{dt}$; $\dfrac{d\left[\dfrac{p\cdot q}{w\cdot l+v\cdot k}\right]}{dt}$;

and $\dfrac{d\left\{\dfrac{p\cdot q}{l}\right\}}{dt}$. The first two alternatives are both related to profit share; gross profit share and net profit share respectively and furthermore the second alternative, net profit share involves depreciation of capital which is a systematic unpleasant variable to measure and which becomes even worse when we regard profits as a residual. The gross profit share is, as we will see later, an important variable partly at variance with labour productivity measured as in the third alternative.

However productivity can also be measured in physical terms, which partly triggers the 'Baumol's disease'.

Let us define the physical productivity as $\rho = \dfrac{d\left\{\Delta q / q\right\}}{dt}$.

Any kind of productivity measure is in principle meaningless if it lacks a link to an efficiency concept. Why should we promote increased speed in different aspects? When we look at the productivity measures involving prices above they are all connected to an efficiency criterion connected to an end: in business 'maximizing profit'. Here we can see perfectly clearly the conflict between the equilibrium thinking and the non-equilibrium thinking, the conflict between Proposition 2.1 in Chapter 2 and Proposition 3.1 in Chapter 3, and finally between atomistic definitions of commodities and the acceptance of complex commodities.

Let us start with a small example. Playing a piano-concerto by Mozart today takes a considerably longer time compared to playing it on a pianoforte from Mozart's times because of the richer sound of a modern grand piano. This implies that the physical productivity of playing a piano concerto has decreased but increased quality of sound may well compensate for that.[3]

We may also suspect that most listeners feel that it is not appropriate to transform a certain tempo chosen for a piano concerto by Mozart to also be the norm with respect to the tempo of a piano concerto by Bartók. We may even have some doubts of the appropriateness of having an a priori norm for tempi with respect to different piano concertos by the same composer.

Thus commodities are complex and the reason why people buy them is not their existence as a thing but the suitability with respect to a certain perceived context of the consumer in question. With respect to this the aspects of the so called Baumol's disease is nonsense since the market, from a theoretical point of view, ought to be able to handle commodities with different price developments, at least the ordinary non-equilibrium market. This was actually discussed by both Hume and Ricardo, but of course they were also aware of the ethical aspects. However Baumol's disease is usually used in relation to public sector production as non-profit production of services which is at variance with market production.

How do we increase labour productivity in money terms n education? Let us

choose $\dfrac{d\left\{\dfrac{p \cdot q}{l}\right\}}{dt}$ as our measure, obviously, given the length of the time period,

there are three possibilities: increasing p or q or decreasing l. Many, as it seems, enquiries indicate that education has not only individual benefits but also has beneficial effects on the socio-economic structure, it would perhaps be wise that at least up to a certain level to have free education. In that case the price would be paid by the taxpayers. Thus we obviously have to increase q or reduce l, and we might have a similar conflict as with respect to the speed of piano concerts between physical productivity and economic productivity, but that only can happen if education/teaching have qualities which are affected by increased q or reduced l. However if this is the case the taxpayers have to pay relatively more for education in terms of produced things where we have no such conflict between physical and economic productivity, thus we have an example of Baumol's disease. There are three ways out of it: i) privatize the education system and do not bother with the positive socioeconomic aspects; ii) go on letting the taxpayers pay the bill; iii) have a separate system for rich and poor families where education for poor families is reduced to a few necessary dimensions good for the socio-economic structure. The same reasoning could be applied to health care, certain sectors of the infra-structure, and most types of social services.

Consequently Baumol's disease is not a unique exogenous economic phenomena but a natural part of the economic system and it deals with the valuation of different dimensions in a specific commodity and obviously it appears in a non-equilibrium monetary economy.

On the more philosophical level the considerations are based on whether we look at agents and commodities in an atomistic way or not. If we have the picture of the society consisting of agents and commodities as atoms with no interaction then the whole discussion above, all the chapters are void of any meaning. If however we think that it might be that consumers buy a certain commodity in order to obtain a certain purpose with respect to a particular context, thus both agents and commodities are complexes, then our discussions have at least some meaning.

Consequently if we look at the relation between the two nodes prices and productivity, we have a rather complex problem which involves both sectorial and regional problems since production sectors have a physical allocation. If we go back to our example from the development of Volvo earlier we can see that as long as it is mainly produced for the internal Swedish market the effect of inflation and wage lifts was rather low but when the focus of Volvo came to be towards the international market this sensitivity increased considerably, particularly when between the 1976 and 1992 Sweden aimed at a stable currency in relation to a foreign currency basket. This problem was actually discussed already at the end of 1960s and early 1970s in Sweden since the relative increase of export sectors became more and more significant. In 1970 the three economic advisors to the white and blue collar trade unions, Edgren and Odhner respectively and Faxen from the employer's organization, published a book where they presented the so called EFO-model (Edgren, Fáxen and Odhner 1973). The aim of the book was to show how a combination of differences in productivity between the export sector and the service sector in conjunction with wage negotiations where the basic principle was equal wage for equal jobs irrespective of sector, could lead to or/and aggravate inflation.

A simple example: assume an economy with two sectors; A which is exposed to foreign completion and B which is protected from foreign competition. The A-sector has an intrinsic drive to find ways to increase productivity while that is lacking in the B-sector, not only by the lack of competition but also by the character of the production, service sector, public sector and similar. It is also important to realize that production in the B-sector is in many cases a precondition for the productivity in the A-sector.

The wage spread goes partly through ordinary labour market competition and partly through central agreements to limit the wage spread, a feature of the Swedish labour market going back to the 1930s.

We can illustrate the reasoning in Table 6.1 which is based on the original report, Edgren et al. (1973).

Thus the A-sector may increase salaries by 6% without affecting factor income distribution but that increase will spread onto the B-sector which needs to increase prices or claims on public finance. The resulting inflation creation is then the difference in productivity increase multiplied by the B-sector's share of the labour market, consequently 2.7% in our example. To this comes eventual imported inflation.

For Sweden and for any small open economy, the result of these enquiries led to a principle for wage negotiations which said that wage increases of the export sector should be the restriction for other sectors. If we however remind ourselves of the discussions in the preceding chapter on the structural change of the financial sector we may also add that even the internal inflation created by productivity changes nowadays affect the magnitudes of the cross-border financial flows to a substantial degree which was not so in the early1970s.

Interesting is that David Hume actually discussed differences in productivity between different countries and the role of international competition which in some cases induced low productivity countries to utilize low wages to compete with high productivity countries, which also put pressure on the necessary productivity increase. Since until rather recently exports in all essentials have

Table 6.1 The EFO-model

	Share of market	Productivity increase	Wage increase	Resulting inflation
A-sector	1/3	6 %	6 %	
B-sector	2/3	2 %	6 %	2.7%

been commodities of physical production, the conflict between physical productivity and economic productivity with respect to services has been substantial. In the latest decade we have had a substantial increase of services in many countries. What effects those changes will have on the internal conflicts between internal and export production it is a bit early to say but some signs in media reports and from the political debate both in Sweden and also in EU give some hints about the necessity of an accelerated increase in human capital, particularly education and health care due to the increased dependence of labour with particular characteristics. In Sweden, where the educational system has been neglected for many years the representatives of industry are actively proposing increased resources to the education system on virtually all levels.

Thus as we see the interrelations between the price node and the productivity node are rather complex and naïve models based on atomistic definitions of commodities implying an oversimplification of productivity dismissing the complexity of physical and economic productivity may be relevant for specific limitations of sectors but not as a general picture of the theoretical problem.

Prices and Growth

Let us go on to look at the two nodes of prices and growth and start to ask one of the most frequently asked question in economics: Why should inflation within reasonable limits, that means that it is not regarded as a sign of social/economic/political instability, have anything at all to do with growth in the absence of money illusion?

It is clear that price increases due to real factors should have effects on economic growth if the substitution is not perfect. But why should inflation as a proportional change in all commodity and factor prices have any effects? The fact that some people live on nominally defined incomes implies a distribution and/or and indexing problem. But apart from that, given that foreign trade strictly adjusts to PPP, why should growth have anything to do with inflation in a closed economy? One answer could be that we are not dealing with a perfect world and that is a proper answer since we then have to deal with a non-equilibrium world. With respect to the latter problem of foreign trade it is obvious that if we have a conflict between cross-border financial flows and real trade flows due to structural changes in the financial sector we have a problem with inflation in its proper form of symmetric changes of all prices. But then we already left the equilibrium world.

Thus inflation, in its proper form, could have effects on growth not so much per se but due to conflicting interests. One side want to preserve the nominal prices of financial assets and liabilities and one group wants to promote growth even at the expense of increasing inflation, however then we mean inflation in the estimated form which cannot separate between increases of commodity dimensions and inflation.

It is hard to see any growth in an economy without inflation. That is mostly a theoretical construction from the neoclassical equilibrium analysis which assumes no variation in inertia and no uncertainty plus the other aspects we discussed in Chapter 1. An introduction of a new commodity dimension has rather substantial side effects on infrastructure, the judicial system, information/ marketing system and so on; some are contained in the price of the commodity in question, others are not. Thus we may expect a higher velocity of money turnover which may be interpreted as an inflation if we do not constantly revise the commodity baskets and their intrinsic relations.

However the most important part of the relations between the macroscopic growth process and prices goes through the relative prices and the subsequent structural changes of demand and production. These changes are partly dependent on technology and partly on changes in preference structures; these two aspects are also interrelated. But one price change, which we go through currently and which is an underlying problem to meet for all societies is the steadily increased real costs of energy. Energy is present in *all* production processes and has different forms and characteristics. Energy prices are in the short run completely demand dependent but demand differs between different forms of energy. The current problem is that the cheapest form of energy seems to have become substantially more expensive in real terms.

Globally access to energy is an absolute condition for all societies for the foreseeable future. This applies to not only energy per se, but also the form of the energy used. When it comes to petroleum this source of energy is remarkable. It is relatively easy to distribute even on the lowest possible aggregate level. If you have a car and a tank of some size you may fetch your petrol at some place and use it according to your needs. It is relatively free from external effects, it sounds maybe a bit surprising, but comparing with bio-energy, nuclear energy, generally the distribution systems of electricity has rather substantial effects on environment and the measures to reduce these external effects must be taken on a rather aggregate level while in the case of petroleum measures against external effects can be more decentralized. This latter argument is also valid when it comes to distribution systems. Petroleum will indeed affect the structure of the society but that is mostly through the possibilities which open up, which are desired. When it comes to all kinds of systems based on electricity, on the societal level the system-changing effects are due also to the very creation of access to the electrical utility and on top of that we have the desired effects. Thus when it comes to energy the substitutions between forms of energy is a substantial problem. This also counts for energy saving policy. The mere technical problem of energy saving is to a large extent solved but the problem to apply it to the society and to the global levels is a completely different question since it requires rather draconian changes of the societal structure in order to be efficient.

From our point of view however the most interesting thing is that: pro primo – energy is an input in all human activities, pro secundo – there most probably exists a lowest limit of energy use necessary to uphold the current structure in a society, pro tertio – energy, irrespective of form, is measurable in well-defined physical entities.

Let us first settle the conditions with regard to petroleum. The easiest accessible oil which exists today is in the Middle East; most other new oil fields consist of shale oil which after a while needs recovery. Thus the geologists can forecast the maximum oil production, save for new findings which are relatively sparse, with rather high precision. Their technique goes back to the American oil geologist Ron Hubbard, the so called Hubbard curve.[4]

In Ekstedt (2003) a Hubbard curve, based on actual consumption between 1960 and 2000, was derived as in Figure 6.3.

We can see that the maximum possible production would peak between 2005 and 2010 and the maximum production in 2030 would be on the same level as at the end of 1960s. Consequently we are, globally speaking, in for rather severe changes in energy forms which most probably imply systemic changes in the world economy as well as in the different countries. The nature of such changes is of course due to natural, social, economic and political characteristics and the outcome is pretty difficult to forecast. A glance at the geo-political map sometimes creates an impression that the warfare in the Middle East is not a pure coincidence in relation to the important oil reserves.

At the bottom of all this however there is a price of utmost importance. We have claimed the insufficiency of money to be a general measure and store of value but EROI – Energy Return on Energy Invested, is a solid price in physical terms.[5]

$$EROI = \frac{Energy\ gained}{Energy\ required\ to\ get\ that\ energy}$$

It tells us how much energy we have to use in order to get energy. So if we need to put in more energy to get an extra quantity of energy we have a purely negative income effect for all societies. True, it can be distributed differently in different societies but at the macroscopic level the economies will experience a deterioration in the total production at a given state of technology; we are thus in for a Malthusian problem. Human innovativeness is certainly at stake when it comes

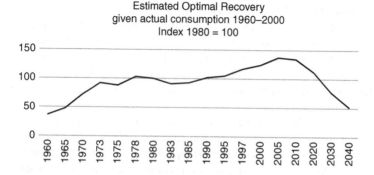

Figure 6.3 Estimated Maximal Available Oil Production

to finding efficient forms of energy saving but the grand challenge is the social, economic and institutional flexibility and adaptive ability. Killing people in wars, and we may also invent other forms for that, is of course the traditional form of solving problems of this kind so we will have a sort of test of the maturity of mankind both as a collective and as individuals. Joseph Conrad's remarkable character Lord Jim went through this process:

> He paused again. 'It seemed to come to me,' he murmured. 'All at once I saw what I had to do ...'
>
> There was no doubt that it had come to him; and it had come through war, too, as is natural, since this power that came to him was the power to make peace. It is in this sense alone that might so often is right. You must not think he had seen his way at once.
>
> (Chapter 26)

When we look at figures of EROI for different forms of energy we meet a rather ugly message.

From Murphy and Hall (2010: 109) we have for USA that EROI for domestic oil in 1930 was around one hundred while for both domestic and imported oil in 1970 it had decreased to between twenty-five and thirty and for 2010 the imported oil was down to around twenty and domestic oil below that. A sort of average EROI according to Murphy and Hall for other sources less than twenty except for coal and hydroelectricity which are between sixty and seventy for coal and thirty and forty for hydroelectricity, but then for coal the environmental consequences are large and still not controlled. Figures of EROI are varied with respect to distributional and environmental costs which vary considerably between countries, therefore the figures from USA will be sufficient as an example.

An example of this is that ethanol from sugarcane has an EROI between 0.8 and 10 depending on modes of distribution and production. Ethanol from corn has an EROI of 0.8 to 1.6 and biodiesel 1.3. Thus ethanol from sugarcane under some circumstances may locally where the production takes place, have a substantial energy potential but distribution costs are considerable and the environmental effects which from the start were very positive based on the result of the Brazilian sugarcane biofuel project have been revaluated when put into a more general setting which includes the distribution system (Larson, E.D. 2006; Davis, S.C. et al. 2009).

Thus the general problem is the distribution and transport of energy. Biofuels for example are, as in the case of sugarcane ethanol, a possible source of energy but the demand for transportation facilities are huge and as the biofuels are less efficient used in transportation at current technology the total value of biofuels is reduced. Then the same can be said about hydropower. It is clean, it is very efficient in some uses but not in others and unfortunately the transportation is a weak spot on the societal level. Hydroelectric power requires huge centralized systems of distribution, and with respect to transportation using air cables is cheap but insecure and under-surface cables are secure but expensive. Most of all however the ability to diversify the distribution with respect to sectorial differences in applicability is much more limited than for petroleum and this goes also for its use in the transportation sector. These aspects reduce the efficiency of hydropower from the perspective of society. There are a lot of studies about these matters which are a bit outside our scope but let us conclude that the peaking oil and the relatively quickly declining Hubbard curve at current consumption indicate a need of severe systemic changes in virtually all economies.

The EROI is a price, it is a real price underlying all other relative prices. Obviously it could be used in ordering the relative prices of all other commodities but that would require that the ultimate accepted purpose of the market behaviour would be to save energy which is a bit unrealistic, so EROI will somehow appear in the cost functions depending on productivity. The pricing of remaining commodities will work as usual as an interplay between supply and demand, save for regulatory taxes and similar public interventions. But EROI represents a source of genuine cost inflation, which is inescapable.

Growth and its Meaning

Growth is a tricky word. The very word imputes a norm into the discussion since it requires that we talk about what is growing and growth also has a direction. In neoclassical theory in its axiomatic form it is crystal clear that it is the utility/welfare of both the agents *and* the society which is *increasing*. This is however granted since the commodity space is defined in R^{++} in a two dimensional setting, which is the positive orthant more generally speaking. This means that even if we talk about a more neutral concept of preferences every increase of the commodity basket is by definition an increase which is desired to the pre-increase state via the axiom of local non-satiation. Due to the axiomatic structure, which implies additive aggregation, we then can conclude that growth both on the macroscopic as well as the microscopic level is unambiguously positive.

So what do we get when we reject the neoclassical axiomatic structure and have to accept Proposition 2.1 in Chapter 2? It is hard to say that we by growth only mean economic change since that has no direction from an ethical/normative point of view, even if we today hear many speak about a desirability of a society without growth or even with negative growth, which I think is a juxtaposition of growth in general terms and growth with respect to a certain commodity basket. It is desirable to keep the directed form of the concept growth of something entirely positive but how can we motivate that in a non-equilibrium monetary economy?

First of all we must accept that growth is positive at the individual level. A consumer is supposed to be rational and optimizing which means that all commodities in the relevant basket given the particular epistemic cycle are defined in the positive orthant. But here the Proposition 2.1 enters: epistemic cycles of different agents may be contradictive which imply that the collective growth on the macroscopic level is ambiguous.

We also, as we have mentioned before, have a Gorman/Lancaster setting of the consumer analysis, that consumers are looking from specific 'characteristics' which might be a function of a set of commodities but some commodities appearing in certain characteristics as positive arguments are negative in others.

It is natural to normalize this growth with respect to population of an economy so we can talk about production per capita. However the latter is a measure of importance in relation to the size of the part of the population which are not participating in production. Most western countries have an increasing number of retired persons and a discrepancy between total growth and growth per capita tells us about necessary productivity of the production system. However per capita growth is of no help in discussing the distribution of growth. This means that growth is a relatively meaningless concept if it is not related to distribution of resources and that is also irrespective of how we look at the growth concept per se since it is evident that if we define growth on the entire real space $R^+ \cap R^-$ growth can imply using some agent to achieve a higher growth without remunerating the labour properly. Consequently we may run into a discussion as in theoretical welfare theory of Hicks/Kaldor (1939) and Little (Arrow 1951) but in a far more complex way. This kind of problem will not and cannot pop up within the neoclassical theory from a strictly logical sense, since the commodity space of the neoclassical theory is only defined on R^+.

If we reject the very concept of general equilibrium as we have done in this book we completely lose this normative role of the neoclassical theory and the best we can say is that growth represents an increased turnover of money in the money economy. But since we have lost the strict definition of commodities to belong to R^{++} with respect to utility/welfare we cannot tell anything a priori about whether the increase in turnover of money is positive or negative for the agents and for the collective. However we know from empirical studies that an increase in the turnover of money usually is linked to an increase in employment which is good for short run judgements so the turnover of money is probably a reasonable measure of growth.

Since we have rejected additive aggregation growth, and commodities as complexes are defined even over the negative orthant, growth simply means an increase in the turnover of money in a society and has no particular bearing on the real welfare if we look upon it from an ethical perspective. Why have traffic rules and supervision of traffic when repairing cars, health care, and funerals increase the turnover of money?

But even comparing turnover of money inter-temporally requires that that we need to manipulate the nominal figures. This is an effect of the Propositions 2.1 and 3.1 in Chapters 2 and 3 respectively.

There is another way of measuring growth which is possible and which also implies a normative judgement, as the neoclassical growth concept implies in the sense that growth is commonly accepted as a positive factor, we measure growth vis-à-vis politically defined dimensions such as some definition of living standard, health, education, environmental standard. Even such things as personal freedom could/should enter such a set of dimensions.

If we use the first kind of approach an apparent problem is that growth is only meaningful in the short run given appropriate inertia and has no normative meaning beside the fact that the increased turnover of money implies that employment increases and people have more commodities. The second approach will imply rather in-depth structural changes of the society and will also probably imply rather advanced control systems of the market. Furthermore the political process will also have to deal with rather complicated distributional matters. Not that it by necessity implies a command economy but such questions have to be at the top of the political agenda since the market is in a macroscopic sense void of ethical standards. The neoclassical theory of the market implies such a standard given one possible interpretation that we touched on earlier and that is the Kantian imperative, which in fact implies a command economy, given the axiomatic structure, which Makarov and Rubinov (1977) also implicitly show (Ekstedt and Fusari 2010: ch. 4). *Thus this second approach to growth is the ethical equivalence to the neoclassical growth concept in the non-equilibrium economy.*

As a form of conclusion we may say that at the macroscopic level the relation between prices and growth is complex and that even if we could properly measure real growth of the neoclassical kind the complexity of the commodities and distributional matters make the growth concept in relation to prices difficult. Obviously the plain material standard is very important and looking at the distribution in a global perspective material standard is certainly to be seen as almost a basic condition for other dimensions that people in the rich countries regard as fundamental. However with respect to warfare and environmental damages in a broad meaning, not all material standards are unequivocally positive.

A real price in its full sense like EROI implies that a growth with respect to the *present* macroscopic commodity basket is hardly possible and that we will sooner or later be forced to change it. However since humans are both adaptive and flexible to compelling circumstances and further have the ability of both inventions and innovations, a new commodity basket will grow and become the norm. So, in the long run, if we regard our current way of presenting real growth with respect to price manipulations, growth will accelerate from a dip from the transformation period to new heights and growth will thus continue as an 'perpetuum mobile' (Ekstedt 2007). Thus the elementary interpretation of growth used mostly for macroeconomic policy is the fact that it measures turnover of money in the economy and as such it is relevant in the short run given adequate inertia. Long run growth is mostly to be seen as a political process and unfortunately there are no inter-temporal measures in a democratic society other than political and social stability. Somehow the latter long run growth has to do with the prices but if so it is rather probable that social and political stability is already lost.

Growth and Employment

From a macroscopic point of view growth and increase in employment are almost always connected in a positive way almost irrespective of how we define it or measure it. The problems appear at the microscopic level when we have periods of considerable technological change, Hume, Ricardo and Say are all discussing this problem but from different angles. The simple production possibility curve in Figure 6.1 shows a static view of the problem and Allais (1987) in discussing the equimarginal process shows a more dynamic development where at the bottom we have an intricate relation between technological growth, innovations with respect to the commodity basket and consumer saturation. This is a social process where human desires for security and ventures in a curious way are intertwined.

Thus in the short run we may have the occurrence of structural unemployment and growth at the same time which seems more as a distributional problem. During such periods which might be prolonged by policy mistakes and particular idiosyncrasies it is necessary to protect people from destitution in order to avoid social and political distress.

Long run matters are mostly a question of increase in human capital, health and education, and avoidance of social distress and which way it takes is known only by future generations but our role is to cultivate our world in time and space.[6]

Verdoorn's Law and Phillips Curve

Our discussion on the meaning and interpretations of the nodes in Figure 6.2 has given a rather divided picture of the possibility of forming a consistent theory out of it. We see that Figure 6.2 consists of four different triangular sets of relations, two where the Verdoorn's law relation is the hypotenuse, and two where the Phillips relation is the hypotenuse.

It seems as these hypotheses are used so that the hypotenuse will in the particular triangular context be seen as the main *explicandum* while productivity and growth must be seen as *explicans*. However we may also interchange the explicans and explicandum so growth and productivity become the primary causes and the Phillips and Verdoorn relations are to be the effects. Given that both are detected in statistical relations at the microscopic level it seems as if the latter interpretation is the more plausible so both the Phillips and Verdoorn relations are some kind of function of productivity and employment which basically are derived from microscopic relations.

Generally when we discuss the figure it is almost impossible at the macroscopic level to form any kind of hypothesis for any of the binary relations in the figure depending on their complex relation to the other nodes and binary relations. The nodes and their pairwise relations are strongly dependent upon the structural composition of the particular economy at the microscopic level so when we perform practical political analysis it is indeed tricky to claim that there are any general patterns. On the other hand such structural patterns are normally rather inert which in some sense create an 'analytical stability'.

In Figure 6.2 the specific economic factors and their relations have an environment: international, historical, social/cultural and political/legal. This environment may be seen as inert but periodically there are considerable bifurcations and perturbations. The relations between the interior of the system and its environment are discussed piecewise in economic theory but there is no systematic knowledge or theoretical framework mostly due to the differences between macroscopic and microscopic analysis.

Above we mentioned that the two hypotheses Phillips and Verdoorn are not embedded in any systematic theory but are based on some kind of statistical patterns added to economic modelling and the explanation for this addition varies considerably depending on theoretical idiosyncrasies. Thus the analysis must be a sort of mixed microscopic and macroscopic perspective. When we look at the nodes of Figure 6.2 we find that these might be defined at both microscopic and macroscopic levels but then also have different analytical forms due to non-additive aggregation. Thus a rather simple concept as productivity which might be defined differently with respect to different sectors then becomes a very obscure concept at the macroscopic level. Dynamic patterns found on sectorial levels are hidden on the macroscopic level due to counteracting sectorial dynamics and thus cancel out at the macroscopic level with respect to data which is additively aggregated, and there are tangibles and non-tangibles, there are standardized units and there are heterogeneous standards for measuring quality. There is momentarily measurable productivity but also commodities, like education and health care, which must be measured over a time span. Furthermore the aggregation of productivity of firms/sectors in different phases of their specific trade cycle may imply that the firm/sector specific patterns cancel out.

For employment we have similar difficulties. In an economy of perfectly homogenous production factors and perfectly flexible production we can obviously use additive aggregation for most economic aspects but as most economists are fully aware of the heterogeneity of production factors and inertia of economic decisions are features/problems at the top of the agenda in modern societies creating permanent unemployment and excessive uncertainty. We have discussed the problems of prices and growth which neither have a clear-cut microscopic foundation nor a macroscopic foundation but are dependent on manipulations and assumptions outside the concepts themselves.

Furthermore the discussions of the two approaches, Verdoorn and Phillips, are further obscured by adding different time perspectives since both the approaches have very little theoretical support but are seen as statistical patterns which are added to eventual theories, some economists claim that they are only short run and vanish in the long run; some others even reject them as statistical misconceptions.

Particularly the discussions about the Phillips curve has been interesting in the sense that the macroeconomic level of discussion seems unaware of rather interesting microscopic findings and that the microscopic discussion seldom deals with the question of whether eventual findings have effects at the macroscopic levels with respect to certain theories. It seems like a consequence of the belief in additive aggregation, which indeed is a curse to economic analysis.

There is another analytical error which is somehow philosophically defended and that is unsuitable simplification with some reference to Occam's razor.[7] But this principle, desirable as it stands, shall never be imposed when trying to find causal structures. Our earlier discussion on Hume's scepticism with regard to finding causal structures where an inductive method could be used is indeed a warning. Hans Reichenbach (1938) separates two phases in the research: *concept of discovery* and *concept of justification*. Thus we can never start a scientific venture, concept of discovery, by referring to Occam's razor. However when we are in the phase of *concept of justification*, it is the proper principle to keep in mind. The phase of concept of discovery should sooner be characterized by Levi-Strauss' (1962) concept of 'wild thinking'.

When we in Chapters 1 and 2 rejected additive aggregation we could derive Proposition 2.1. It implied that both microscopic as well as macroscopic concepts have to be defined independently. Thus the microscopic concept of productivity is fairly easy to grasp with respect to the single firm and even often to a specific sector but the macroscopic concept of productivity, dependent on social, political and structural matters, has to be defined independently. For example a group of people who become unemployed, because of technical progress and due to heterogeneities and other factors, will create a macroscopic problem in a non-equilibrium economy.

If we think of all these obscurities which occur when dealing with concepts which have both macroscopic and microscopic use and can be statistically measured at both the levels we see the importance of the difference between the Propositions 2.1 and 3.1, in Chapters 2 and 3, concerning the barter economy and the monetary economy respectively.

The neoclassical tradition has made an equivalence between the real economy and measuring its valuation in prices which are seen as money values. It is easy to see that the orthodox results of the neoclassical analysis is not relevant for the money economy and we must provide for that in our analysis. But the basic technique of using money values as equivalents for real analysis is accepted of Keynesians and even other theoretical approaches critical to the neoclassical theory.

It is then important to spell out that, apart from very limited microscopic studies *we have to use* money values of some form in our analyses in order to get any analytical results at all but we have to be aware of and provide for the problem spelled out in propositions 1 and 2.

Verdoorn's Law

The central relation in Verdoorn's approach is productivity and growth depicted by the arrows α and β in Figure 6.2.

Obviously there could be a strong relation between productivity change and growth, particularly at the microscopic level where the concept of productivity is relatively simple to define and measure. However whether the effect of productivity increases on the microscopic level has any effects on volume of production or only on factor incomes and their distribution within the sectors concerned is hard to say without empirical investigations. Thus nothing prevents at the microscopic level that a productivity increase will have no effects on supply but only at employment and factor incomes and its distribution. In fact a very interesting early study by Joseph Bower from the 1960s supports such a behaviour with respect to the failure risk as shown in Table 6.2, (Bower 1970: 3). It also supports our earlier discussion of Volvo's development.

As we see from Table 6.2 an increase in productivity may appear within the context of particularly the first two types of investment but it is only with respect to capacity increasing investment that we have a strong link to growth of the company. Investment in a new product is irrelevant with respect to productivity. It is in the first instance a matter of getting the product sold.

For cost reducing investment the purpose is more to hopefully decrease the risk of the company and the supply is probably left more or less unchanged, so we have no growth of supply but possibly higher profits. If we look at the macroscopic effects of the cost reducing investment it depends on whether it includes reduction of employment or not. If it implies a reduction in employment either the unemployed must find other jobs or the productivity increase must be proportionally higher than the reduction in employment in order to have a growth effect, but if the latter we will have a distribution problem.

It is however doubtful that due to structural changes we can reduce unemployment to a distribution problem. We will discuss this aspect more in the epilogue but the utilitarian habit to look at work as a disutility is indeed doubtful in a social sense; being in work makes at least some people included in the society. If you are out of work you lose control of your life which no allowance can replace.

Table 6.2 indicates however that at the microscopic level there is no self-evident link between productivity and growth in the very investment purposes. This aspect is certainly important from a theoretical point view. Whether or not it plays an empirical role is difficult to say. Bower's investigation was in form of a follow up of 50 investment projects in a big American company for ten years and to our knowledge no similar investigation has been pursued since then.

However in 2011 the Swedish Agency for Economic and Regional Growth conducted an investigation of approximately 19,000 small and middle sized companies in Sweden where the Owner/CEO was asked about important factors for development and growth of the company. This investigation is completely different from Bower's but still it reveals a complexity in the investment decision which makes the relation between productivity/profitability and growth troublesome even at the microscopic level. If we look at the simple relation of growth of employment and growth of output for those companies which announce themselves ready to grow, we get the results in Table 6.2 which tells us that in a considerable portion of the growing companies with respect to output this has

Table 6.2 Actual Return in relation to Calculated Return

Type of investment	Ratio of actual return to calculated
Cost reducing	1.1
Capacity increasing	0.6
New product	0.1

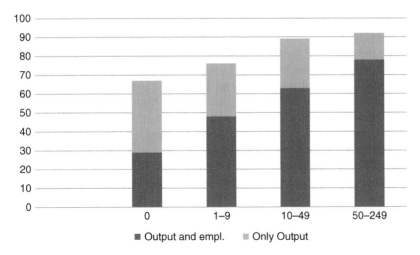

Figure 6.4 Effect of Investment on output/employment in companies of different sizes

probably little or no links to change in employment volume. The reason for this might vary from cost-reducing investment to overcapacity of invested capital.

Anyhow we see that this portion tends to decrease with the size of the company. Table 6.3 shows however a more complete picture. There is no doubt that the percentage figures will vary over time and with capacity utilization but the year 2011 was generally a rather optimistic year for Swedish industry so bearing that in mind Table 6.3 is of a great interest.

We see that for small companies there are some specific factors which are less important for the biggest companies in the investigation, but apart from that there are two factors by far the most important and they are competition and the lack of suitable labour, particularly for the group of medium-sized companies between

Table 6.3 Factors hindering growth of company according to Owners/Managers (%)

	Number of employees			
	0	1–9	10–49	50–249
Competition	18.5	22.8	32.0	41.9
Insufficient demand	8.6	8.0	9.7	13.3
Profitability of the company	13.9	14.0	13.9	13.4
Access to the credit market	9.1	11.7	14.2	12.1
Access to external share capital	8.5	9.4	10.0	5.9
Lack of suitable Labour	15.0	24.6	33.0	26.8
Access to relevant infrastructure	4.2	3.7	5.8	6.6
Insufficient capacity of current fixed capital	6.1	9.0	13.1	12.4
Owners' lack of time	29.4	31.0	26.4	-
Laws and bureaucracy	20.1	23.1	23.7	14.5

50 and 249 employees. This group of companies have been of the highest importance for creating new jobs in Sweden during the last decade.

The competition factor is quite natural since a growth of the company will
change the risk structure; the factor concerning suitable labour is of a completely
different character. We use to speak of *heterogeneous* labour but what does this
concept mean? Hume, Ricardo and Say all discussed labour of different qualities,
mainly due to education and training, and adding health we end up in Gary
Becker's 'Human Capital' (1964). We will later discuss this more in detail with
respect to consequences; suffice to say here that there is a strong link between
labour heterogeneity and labour hoarding.

With respect to the macroscopic level even the precise definition of the
concepts imply difficulties and factors both inside and outside the market sphere
are of importance. Which of the two concepts, productivity and growth is the
cause and which is the effect is even harder to say since growth, or perhaps
we should say evolution, in some sense 'releases' particular structures which
might trigger technological innovations. Koestler (1970) tells the story of the
British engineer who got a patent in early 1870s of a cow-watering machine.
A student in classical languages read in the collected works of Heron about such
a machine and he (Heron) also provided exact drawings according to Koestler.
Further investigations, by a student of Heron's works, revealed that the engineer
had actually copied the drawings from Heron and sent them to the patent authorities. Thus in this case it took about 1800 years to detect the economic usefulness
of this machine which perhaps depended on the fact that the structure of cattle-
raising had changed in such a way that this machine became economically
beneficial.

So what comes first and what comes later is difficult to say particularly when
we are mixing different levels of aggregation. As we earlier have discussed
macroscopic and microscopic levels are *interdependent*.

We may now complete the lower right triangle and add employment. As Hume
describes the money economy is open for a faster market penetration of the society which triggers socialization and development of new commodities, this also
opens up new areas for inventions and innovations. Historically the growth
process is firmly linked to development of the monetary economy and the intertwined process of marketization and diffusion of money. This is however purely
on the macroscopic level in a historical perspective.

In a more narrow time perspective, still at the macroscopic level, we may say
that as long as the general growth of commodity demand is higher than the
general growth of production efficiency we may expect/suspect a statistical positive correlation between growth, productivity and employment, as described by
Verdoorn's law. Otherwise however the relations between the three nodes are
more complicated and calls for studies of the structural composition as well as the
more precise conditions for the different relevant production sectors in an
economy.

Whether or not Verdoorn's law describes a long or short run relationship is
difficult to say. Following Hume's analysis and looking at very long historical

perspectives it seems as if the Verdoorn relation is plausible in principle but making it into a mathematical model seems rather meaningless. It seems like a kind of evolutionary model which is observable *ex post* but for *ex ante* use it is blurred by structural changes, social and political upheavals and similar exogenous processes. In the short run it is more problematic: it seems that it worked during the aftermath of World War II when the economic development could be described as a kind of greenhouse effect (Eichengreen 1995). The war had a significant effect on demand and capacity needs but this effect seems to have matured at the end of the 1960s, furthermore the breakdown of Bretton Woods took place shortly afterwards. The Verdoorn effect seems to have been measurable during 1950s and 1960s but after the maturing of capacity and the breakdown of Bretton Woods Verdoorn's effect seems to have vanished more or less, save for some signs of resurrection during the latest years probably due to the low capacity utilization. To use Verdoorn's law as a generic description at the macroscopic level seems rather doubtful, particularly if we take Tables 6.2 and 6.3 into consideration.

The Phillips Curve

The Phillips relation is even more complex. We all know the discussions about whether it is short run or long run relationship or if it exists at all. Such discussions are often built on aggregated data of price and employment figures. At the same time sectorial and microscopic studies from different countries on productivity and labour mobility grow and give us a more detailed picture of what happens at the microscopic level which we may use to explain the phenomenon of the Phillips curve. Needless to say, a general equilibrium approach consistent with its axiomatic structure is meaningless.

From Table 6.3 it is seems plausible that the heterogeneity of labour plays an important part for the firms' operations. On the microscopic level it is generally based on the development of the *factor income distribution*. This is important from two different angles: on one hand it is the base for profitability and on the other hand it is basic to the financial reserves to defend an inert production organization against risk/uncertainty. By inert organization we do not only mean the capital stock but also eventual complementarities between physical and mental capital and labour.

Generally speaking however we can look at the interaction between productivity and employment as based on the development of the demand in relation to technological change. With respect to foreign trade has already Hume discussed this and he was also aware of the possibility of a competition between high productivity/high wage countries and low productivity/low wage countries, but he also was aware of the fact that spread of technology and thereby the raising of wages could change the situation in a longer perspective.

With respect to the macroscopic level the interaction between productivity and employment is considerably more difficult to analyse. First of all this depends on the structural composition of the economy and the share of non-profit maximizing activities.[8] We have earlier mentioned the EFO model which describes how price changes are brought about by a combination between productivity changes and the wage structure which gives us a hint of the importance of structural conditions.

Things have evidently changed since the beginning of the 1970s. Wage spread and heterogeneity of labour have increased as well as international competition but the illustrated process is still to be found although in new forms and together with different explanations. The increase in heterogeneity for example sometimes has the effect of creating labour niches which are independent of sectors. An early example of this was seen in Sweden in the beginning of the 1990s when in a severe recession the steel industry fired a considerable share of the working force. However in 1994 there was a very strong upswing in the international steel sector and a subsequent demand increase also for the Swedish steel industry causing it to suffer from heavy capacity problems depending on insufficient labour forces since those fired were attractive in other sectors so the *average* wage increase in the steel industry went up between 45 and 50% in order to attract experienced labour. This manoeuvre upset the labour market stability quite considerably and became a nuisance for the whole export sector.

Wage inflation caused by sectorial differences and heterogeneity of labour is a considerable factor as a theoretical element but it varies according to cultural and institutional differences, which means that its modelling probably varies with respect to the investigated economy. The consequence of this however is that we can suspect some form of *labour hoarding*.

Labour hoarding is defined as:[9]

> Labor Hoarding
> The practice in which a company does not lay off employees when it otherwise would (as during a recession). Labour hoarding is high risk as it reduces a company's profitability during a difficult time, but it guarantees employee talent will be available to that company (and, just as importantly, not to its competitors) when growth resumes.
> (http://financial-dictionary.thefreedictionary.com/Labour+Hoarding)

This definition is in line with common knowledge and thus usable. The companies which engage in labour hoarding naturally have expectations of continuing operations after a recession, but we do not discuss such expectation formation which might be considerably different between for example a small company for which the labour hoarding is more or less necessary to the big companies which also have the ability to use consultants to solve problems at peak periods.

In an interesting paper from Institute for employment research on labour hoarding in Germany Dietz, Stops and Walwei (2010) conclude:[10]

> As a consequence of the global financial crisis Germany has experienced the deepest slowdown of its economy since World War II. However, at least up to now the German labor market has not shown a strong reaction to the

financial crises. Given the sharp decrease in GDP the levels of employment and unemployment are still quite stable. German companies continue to face stringent regulations for standard work arrangements, so atypical and more flexible work arrangements have gained importance during recent years. These work arrangements provide external flexibility at least to a certain degree and are accompanied by a set of measures aimed at internal flexibility within the core workforce. Both strategies facilitate adaptation to macroeconomic shocks and form a protective shield against job losses among the core workforce, which is responsible for the stability of the German labor market until the beginning of 2010.

(http://www.lsw.wiso.uni-erlangen.de/VfS/Vortr__ge/Walwei.pdf, p. 24)

The issue of labour hoarding is relatively old in economic literature going back to the 1960s, Brechling (1965). From the mid 1970s, the issue was discussed regularly and we particularly recommend the comprehensive analysis of labour hoarding in British industry by Bowers, Deaton, Turk (1982). Biddle (2013) is a recent survey of the concept which links the concept to the pro-cyclical character of the labour productivity.

The quote from the Dietz et al. paper tends to look at labour hoarding as a deliberate decision to save valuable labour but that is only one aspect of the problem of labour inertia. Physical and organizational technology is as important to explain labour inertia and complementarities between labour and capital. A broad view of the theoretical literature reveals that much of the labour hoarding and complementarities between labour and capital is down to the skill of labour dimension which traces its roots back to Say, Ricardo and Hume. Skill of labour is certainly an important factor in analysing this, but equally important is to employ the necessary functions to manage the working of the production capital from a volume point of view. The inertia with respect to the actual persons is certainly due to skill, training, social competence in team work and similar things and from a principle point of view we can look at the cost-productivity relation of new employed people as in Figure 6.5. This figure deals with mere on the job training and is relatively independent of formal skill achieved by education.

Obviously the form of the curve varies among individuals and among types of work but the principle form of the curve implies an inert factor of more or less importance.

But apart from the individual aspects of skill, training and similar factors are the very formal functions of the jobs in question. Since the days of Ricardo and Say societies have been incredibly more complex which means that already production organization per se is affected. Today the competitive environment requires both a sophisticated information structure and an organization to develop the product; these factors were present at the days of Ricardo and Say but not of essential importance with respect to labour costs. The legal environments are more accentuated partly through the increase in scientific knowledge and partly through improved information. This aspects becomes even more vital since most production organizations work internationally and meet a multitude of legal,

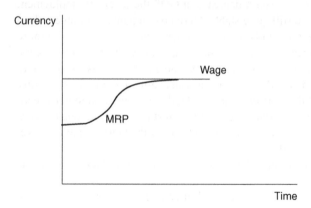

Figure 6.5 Productivity and costs of newly employed labour

cultural and social discrepancies, furthermore a single firm may meet different such environments on both the production side and the selling side. The communication and transport infrastructure is vastly more complex than in the days of Ricardo and Say, both with respect to legal issues and to varying modes.

A further aspect is what we might call the management of the organization. The competitive environment of the firms requires both the ability to adapt to environmental changes and flexibility to change important aspects of production. This means that the labour has an almost constant need of new training and education. It is true that much of this can and is bought from consultancy companies but seen from the production cost side this does not change anything essentially in the principal problem.

It is indeed fascinating to see how many economists still continue the analysis of Ricardo and Say on the dimension of skill as an overall concept forgetting the immensely increased complexity of the required skill. This complexity makes the production organization inert per se since it increases the number of inert dimensions of the production organization. The author has experience from a shipping company of which the total amount of labour, ship and shore, was some 70 persons of which only the CEO had a semi-free position; all the other functions were defined either by the capital stock mainly implying ships given regulations, legal matters which were about sea regulations, dangerous and technically complicated goods, and sale and sales promotion. Thus the working force was defined irrespective of the capacity utilization of the two ships.

The degree of inertia varies of course among different types of firms but to my experience it has increased drastically since the 1960s/70s. Partly based on Tachibonaki and Taki (2012: 20) we may categorize the reasons for labour inertia and a seemingly complementary relation to capital.

First, we have of course the factual relation between the working of the production capital and necessary labour. This consists both of the current working and technical and organizational development.

Second we have the market and market information in both directions. This aspect depends to a great deal on the dispersion of product characteristics, particularly in the service sector. There is a vast amount of relatively recent, from 2000 and forward, reports of the development of the service production. On one hand the direct production for sale to consumers has both increased in quantity but also in degree of sophistication, particularly as export commodities (Mishra et al. 2011 and Anand et al. 2012). On the other hand physical goods productions becomes to a higher degree linked to service supply which only to a degree directly is linked to current production, Growth in Services, OECD Report 2005, Chien-Yu Huang (2012). This service is sophisticated and requires indepth knowledge both with respect to the product and its environment in different dimensions. Thus the skill-factor is indeed complex.

The third fundamental aspect of inertia of labour is the organizational aspect. The modern firm operates in an intricate net of legal, social, cultural and ethical dimensions of which some concern the choice of actual individuals and some affect the volume of organization. The 'face' of the firm becomes more and more important and this is clearly visible in many production organizations to a higher and lower degree.

Thus the reasons for labour hoarding, and inertia of labour are simple to under-stand in a cyclical perspective and also with respect to a longer term perspective. The very existence is mostly a choice of the firms themselves as a response to environmental conditions both with respect to market factors and non-market factors and there is no reason to claim some kind of sub-optimality or irrationality in their decisions. However the macroeconomic consequences are a bit tricky both with respect to short and long term and comprise both the Verdoorn's law and the Phillips curve effect. Ekstedt and Westberg (1991: 42–66) suggested a kind of synthesis of the effects from a macroscopic perspective which was elabo-rated in Ekstedt and Fusari (2010: 221–229), and we will follow their path.

Basically labour hoarding/inertia of labour, independent of whether it is directly linked to the capital stock or not, is creating an implicit complementarity between labour and capital at least with respect to short/medium cyclical varia-tions in output/demand. These variations are furthermore not restricted to some precise level of capital stock but are more due to a planned level of production operations. Thus we might speak about an organizational inertia with respect to a planned level of output. This is of course changeable but due to the specific combination of the employed level this will not only have temporary effects but also change the capacity in medium term.

We may illustrate the principle for a single firm as in Figure 6.6.

The labour productivity relation which is invested in is O^*/L^* which is also the optimum level of production with respect to production costs. The two function $F_1(L)$ and $F_2(L)$ are examples of short run production functions which to the right of L^* imply decreasing returns to labour and to the left the case of labour hoarding which also implies decreasing returns to labour. With respect to profit share it decreases on both sides of the optimal level of capacity utilization. Furthermore the firm in question will be happy if at the right of L^* market prices of the produced

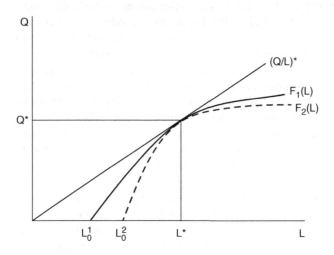

Figure 6.6 Optimal level of capacity utilization

Source: Ekstedt and Fusari (2010: 224)

commodity would rise and to the left we may guess that the firm is rather reluctant to reduce its output prices. The particularly sensitive problem is the variations in productivity and profit share with respect to the degree of capacity utilization.

The curves illustrated in Figure 6.6 vary of course with respect to the character of the firm, as said before the principle shape has not a priori something to do with labour intensity or level of skill although these matters clearly affect the shape in many cases. With respect to cyclical variations in product demand the inertia of labour creates a pro-cyclical variation in productivity and the factor income distribution. Munley (1981) discussed these phenomena and in his discussion he also mentioned the periodical under-utilization of labour. Uemura (2008) discusses growth and profit rate in the Japanese economy and observed a counter-cyclical behaviour of the wage share which means a pro-cyclical behaviour of the profit share. Navarro and Soto (2006) reported pro-cyclical variations in the Chilean manufacturing industry during the period 1979–2001 in most sectors but when they looked at the aggregated manufacturing industry this was not particularly observable, which depended, according to the authors, on the differences in pattern of demand between sectors. Basu and Kimball (1997) analysed the pro-cyclical patterns of the American manufacturing industry within a dynamic model of cost-minimizing, and discussed seven types of explanations: i) imperfect competition, ii) increasing returns to scale, iii) unobserved changes in utilization, iv) unobserved changes in technology, v) unobserved fluctuations in the factor prices, vi) unobserved fluctuations in the shadow price of output, vii) the non-existence of a value-added production function. In their broad analysis there are many interesting results although with respect to our discussion they found that the strongest correlation was with the utilization variables. They end their paper:

We doubt that variable utilization will rescue RBC models, however our work provides a direct way to study the effects of technology change on output and employment. One of the most generally-applicable results in our paper is that we derived model-based proxies for utilization that are valid under very general circumstances. Using these proxies, we find in preliminary empirical work going beyond the scope of this paper that aggregate technology change, corrected both for utilization and for aggregation biases emphasized by Basu and Fernald (1997), is actually be *negatively* correlated with contemporaneous employment changes. The result presents a challenge to standard Real Business Cycle theory. [Original emphasis]

(Basu and Kimball 1997: 2)

The phenomena which have been widely analysed by economists are also linked to Tobin's Q since there are frequent observations of pro-cyclical variations in asset prices particularly in goods producing industry. Generally it is found that labour productivity is pro-cyclical but in some cases counter-cyclical productivity is found which is also understandable. Tobin's Q tends to be pro-cyclical and also investment to capital ratio while consumption to capital tends to increase counter-cyclically. Tobin's Q and asset prices tend to follow each other, thus asset prices tend to be pro-cyclical, at least on the sectorial levels. In an interesting paper Dia and Casalin (2009) discuss the relation between investment and Tobin's Q and they found that the relation was generally weak except when firms were in need of external finance but for internally financed investment no such link to Tobin's Q was found. The result generally supports the co-variation between Tobin's Q and asset prices.

In a paper from 1995, Christiano and Fisher found 'equity prices are pro-cyclical, while investment prices are (weakly) counter – cyclical. Although the literature on Tobin's q prepares one for the possibility that these two prices are not identical, we were nevertheless surprised to find that their business cycle dynamics are so very different'.

Christiano and Fisher explained their findings:

The basic features that we use to account for the asset pricing phenomena are habit persistence preferences and limitations on the ability to quickly move factors of production both cross-sectionally and inter-temporally. These same limitations, by slowing the economy's ability to respond to shocks, have effect of introducing persistence. At the same time, limitations on intersectorial mobility, coupled with habit persistence, have the effect of making employment across sectors move up and down together over the cycle.

The result in this paper and in the BCF support the notion that the same frictions needed to account for the salient features of asset prices and returns are also useful in understanding the salient features of business cycle.

(Christiano and Fisher 1995: 38)

The conclusions are indeed interesting and in line with those of Ekstedt and Westberg (1991) for the Swedish economy.

The discussion above on the relation between productivity and employment has mainly dealt with investigations on the microscopic level and sectorial levels. The relations seem however generic for the modern economy why we should be able to enter a macroscopic discussion. We need however to add some words of warning about the importance of the sectorial composition of an economy. Navarro and Soto (2006) found for the Chilean economy clear signs of pro-cyclical productivity at the sectorial levels but almost no sign at the macroscopic level; they explained it by the sectorial composition of the Chilean economy. Ekstedt and Westberg (1991) on the other hand found clear pro-cyclical productivity at the macroscopic level since the Swedish manufacturing industry is dominated by export industries with high capital intensity and few sectors. But for both the economies the relation is there at the microscopic levels.

On the basis of our discussions we may now interpret the curve in Figure 6.6 which then illustrates the relative cost pressure of a firm during variations in the capacity utilization. Given the capital costs and the price of inputs we may illustrate the short/medium term average labour costs as in Figure 6.7 and it has a very traditional form as in a textbook.

Let us first make some methodological comments. Figures 6.6 and 6.7 are indeed trivial. Figure 6.7 at least appears in virtually all textbooks on micro-economics together with a marginal cost curve. One small detail which might be worrying is that the curve in Figure 6.7 the given salary cannot be brought about by the most popular production function, Cobb-Douglas function. We solve this by changing our reasoning a bit. But the most interesting thing is that we, after having depicted the marginal cost curve, start to tell about optimal production given market prices, the firms *choose* the profit maximizing point. We then discuss the short and long run curves and consequences for the optimal choice; in the short run some costs are flexible and some are fixed and in the long run it is possible to

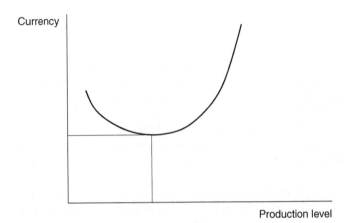

Figure 6.7 Cost pressure of the firm

change the relation between the factors of production. All these exercises are perfectly good and necessary given the limits of flexibility, or should we say frictionless production. All marginal conditions are met according to theory. This means that profits in optimal capacity utilization are results of a conscious decision.

What Keynes does when it comes to these kinds of consideration is that he says that profit is a residual, given the production organisation, and that the behaviour of the entrepreneur/manager is affected by many different dimensions as a result of genuine uncertainty. Rational decisions are necessary to meet the combination of inert production conditions and uncertainty of prices demand and technology. A behaviour like labour hoarding is therefore as much a rational decision as the decision not to hoard labour from an a priori point of view.

Thus when we look at the curves it is from the perspectives of the existence of different forms of the inertia of production and uncertainty of future demand and prices.

Consequently we have a point in Figures 6.6 and 6.7 where the capital is optimally utilized but the variations in demand of the production and the market prices are to a great extent exogenous to the company. Monopoly power may change the degree of exogenous dependence but most analysis on this show that it is of limited importance (see for example Lafourcade 2003).

We thus take the view of the CEO/firm owners who have the financial responsibility of the firm, consequently the central current operational target is that the invested capital is optimally utilized during a time horizon possible to grasp. Given this the next step is to plan possible actions for a more remote future. That implies then that investments might be relatively independent of the character of variations in productivity, profit rate and Tobin's Q, which is also reported in different investigations like in Dia and Casalin (2009).

It is of central importance however that we have emphasized the factor income distribution and consequently the profit share sooner than the profit rate because they also indicate the financial position of the firm. The variations dependent on the inertia of labour is directly affecting the financial position and that also to varying extent explains the pro-cyclical asset prices.

One problem however is that aggregating the sectors gives no evident result which is measurable in ordinary statistical investigation on macroeconomic data. The interesting and comprehensive investigation for the Chilean economy by Navarro and Soto (2006) shows this in a fairly certain way; on the other hand Ekstedt and Westberg (1991) found that the macroscopic data showed the same pattern as the sectorial level for the Swedish economy. It is no mystery, but as we said above it depends on the sectorial composition of the economy, but then the question arise whether the sectorial composition on the macroscopic level may prevent some of the cyclical and long run effects by the inertia of labour on lower aggregate levels. This question requires a rather comprehensive investigation of the economy during a substantial time period and to our knowledge no such investigation has been performed.

Consequently our analysis is limited to the logical consequences of the pattern given that it is found also on the macroscopic level.

Let us start as usual with an assumption: we assume that prices are constant but that demand varies. As such this assumption need not be particularly unrealistic for a firm selling its products on many markets and with respect to the aggregate economy the relation between external and internal demand is of central importance and prices could then vary in the same patterns or the opposite.

Figure 6.6 displays a cyclical pattern around L* where the maximum labour productivity is reached. Let us call this point 'the optimal capacity utilization'. Consequently the factor income distribution will display the same pattern. This implies that the financial position of the firm deteriorates as a function of the distance between the actual L and the optimal L* in both directions, since we have assumed fixed prices but varying quantity of production.

There are clear signs that the inertia of labour as depicted in Figure 6.6 increase with technical progress and increased organizational needs depending on complexity of demand and markets and if so we might have a process illustrated in a change from function $F_1(L)$ to $F_2(L)$, which means increased variability of productivity and the profit share. In a dynamic perspective we could then have a development as in Figure 6.8.

The increased variability in profit share implies an increased financial risk of the operations which has to be taken into account in investment decisions. This implies that if we assume that at the start our firm operates at L* as the point of optimal capacity utilization implying Q_1*, it will have the short run variations along the $F_1(L)$ function. Profit rate and future prospects seem positive so our firm decide to invest and do so but now in a more labour saving technology illustrated by the $F_2(L)$ function. The variability of the profit share however makes the firm reluctant to invest into a capacity increase which makes the optimal capacity

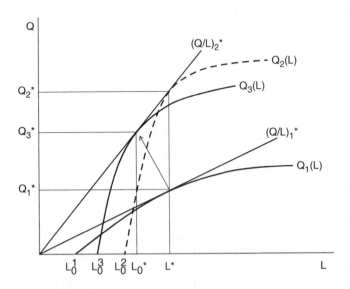

Figure 6.8 Financial Risk on Capital and Growth of Capital Stock

utilization remain at L* which implies a production of Q_2* but limit its investment to an optimal capacity utilization point L_2*/Q_3*, thus we have a lower demand for labour in the optimal capacity utilization.

Obviously the price pressure would be high at the right side of the optimal capacity point but if the firm actually can compensate for the increased cost depends on the character of competition, inflation policy and probably other aspects. This actually shows the link to the macroscopic levels.

Some Final Comments

The question is how well this dynamic development also is applicable at the macroscopic level. Looking at Bower's (1970) investigations from the late 1960s resulting in Table 6.2, the investigation of Swedish small and medium companies reported in Table 6.3 gives us an impression on one hand of the riskiness of investing in new capacity and new ventures and on the other hand of the difficulty in finding appropriate labour force. The investigations by Ekstedt and Westberg (1991), Christiano and Fisher (1995), Lafourcade (2003) Navarro and Soto (2006), and Dia and Casalin (2009) all give hints of the relevance of a dynamic process like the one described on the microscopic level, but also on difficulties to detect the very mechanisms as Basu and Kimball (1997), Basu (2006), Bentolila and Saint-Paul (2003) give examples of.

The process is clear at a disaggregated level but the sectorial composition may hide it with respect to data on the most aggregate levels, is a conclusion which one is tempted to accept.

In Ekstedt and Westberg (1991) the macroeconomic development after World War II is discussed. It is widely accepted that the production and market conditions during the 1950s and 1960s could be thought of as a kind of greenhouse effect, which Eichengreen (1995) calls it, Hobsbawm (1994: 6) calls it 'a sort of Golden Age'. In virtually all sectors there was an excess demand which however ended at the end of the 1960s at more or less the same time as the breakdown of the Bretton Woods system as Lundberg et al. (1975) and Boltho (1982) report. Nobody to my knowledge has made an analysis of the interaction of the two processes since the breakdown of Bretton Woods is mostly blamed on the Vietnam War. But it is my belief that such an investigation would be of great value.

Anyway the development during the aftermath of World War II was such that there was a more or less constant need for more capacity which vis-à-vis Figure 6.6 implied that the firms tended to choose an investment rate given by the labour supply, thus given L* as the projected maximum labour volume they choose an optimal capacity output of Q_2*. Things changed however at the end of the 1960s and beginning of the 1970s and labour saving investments were chosen at a relatively decreasing rate of output growth. So a rather useful relation to look at if there is access to data is the growth of physical productivity in relation to the estimated growth of demand in volume terms for relevant sectors. This reasoning is however partly upset by the introduction of new commodities and new sectors so we also need to handle that problem which is indeed important in our discussions on inflation.

Let us have a closer look at Figures 6.6 and 6.7. On both sides of the optimal capacity utilization at (L*, Q*) average costs will increase as a function of the distance between the optimal labour force L* and the actual labour force following the short run production function f(L) in Figure 6.6, which means that the profit-share will reach its maximum in L*. There is however a substantial difference between the two sides of L* and that is the fact that to the left the product demand is declining, while it is increasing to the right of L*. That means that if we drop the assumption of constant prices and furthermore that prices are reasonably flexible, then to the left of L* the firms will meet rising costs due to labour hoarding which in itself in the regime of constant prices will lead to decreasing profit share and a deteriorating financial position but to this comes now the eventuality of declining prices. This is indeed an ugly picture.

If we now look at the right side of L* we know that at constant prices the profit share will also decrease but in this regime the product demand will be rising. Thus if we now drop the assumption of constant prices and allow for price increases the firms may be able to meet the cost increases by higher prices and consequently the profit share/financial position can be saved.

As we see this kind of price increase is not created by money supply but has its roots in structural relationships. Furthermore this upward pressure on prices may vary between different sectors and it will not appear as a parallel increase in wages so in inflation enquiries it will appear as a 'clean' form of inflation, unexplainable by traditional macroeconomic thinking but it is still there.

With respect to our earlier discussions of the concept of complexity we see here an example where the traditional 'atomistic' and 'additive' attitude to commodities and production factors actually miss a possible explanation intrinsic to the very organization of production at a given moment and the specific form of rationality to be executed in that moment.

Now we meet the financial side and policy matters in our analysis. If we now have a situation such that the state commits itself to anti-inflation policy in order to prevent a deterioration of values of financial assets and liabilities we create a very peculiar situation which in fact is rather dreadful in the long run and can also be one part of increasing permanent unemployment. This is rather interesting when alluding to Hume. He claimed that while an increase of the medium of exchange was relatively harmless to society, the reduction of the medium of exchange was indeed harmful.

We have mostly discussed inflation caused by an unnecessary supply of money and we have claimed that its effects on financial assets are negative. But what about inflation due to real causes, how do we think about that? The answer is of course it depends. Inflation can be caused by excessive price rises out of a situation of insufficient competition in certain sectors; of excessive wage increases due to trade unions' monopoly power. Such causes of inflation are indeed of little or negative value from a macroscopic point of view, but to take measures against such causes by general means which negative affects sectors not involved also are affected which might be even more negative.

But there is also inflation due to rising of prices in fundamental commodities for production like EROI development with respect to energy, raw materials and similar where the prices rise due to current and/or expected shortage. Attacking that form of inflation leads generally to excessive real income decreases and changes in distribution of incomes as well as uncertainty of allocation of productive resources which appears in a decrease in real investment. Such a policy is harmful to society both in the short and long run.

If economists on the basis of an a priori theory describing a medieval barter economy recommend such a policy, it would hardly be more harmful than letting a fortune-teller or a shaman be an economic advisor.

However if we have a hard anti-inflation regime and most sectors work under the conditions described in Figure 6.8 we would end up in a long run development as the illustrated, and this is independent on different cyclical patterns for the different production sectors.

It is important to keep in mind that much of the theoretical development in economics took place during the end of 1960s and the 1970s when we were actually in the middle of the breakdown of this 'Golden Age' and set out for a different growth pattern both on the microscopic and the macroscopic levels. It also partly explains why Keynesian thought has grown in importance during 1990s and the 2000s.

Notes

1 It is tempting to believe that this is a problem of a closed economy and an economy open to foreign trade would escape the problem but a short consideration forces us to realize that it does not matter.
2 An interesting observation is that big investors in some kind of real production are not that keen on social and political freedom but sometimes prefer rather draconian control measures à la Machiavelli's recommendations in *the Prince*.
3 There are purists who claim that old music always should be played on contemporary instruments. I do not agree and what is more important Mozart himself engaged rather deeply with a piano manufacturer in Mannheim to improve the piano, both the sound and the control of the sound by adding a pedal.
4 Much is written about the Hubbard curve. It is based on the Gauss distribution function with respect to exhaustible resources. Two very comprehensive studies which also describe the technique are Richard C. Duncan and Walter Youngquist (1998) *THE WORLD PETROLEUM LIFE-CYCLE*. A paper presented at the PTTC Workshop "OPEC Oil Pricing and Independent Oil Producers" Petroleum Technology Transfer Council. Petroleum Engineering Program, University of Southern California, Los Angeles, California, October 22, 1998. Albert A. Bartlett (2000) *An Analysis of U.S. and World Oil Production Patterns*. Mathematical Geology, Vol 32, No. 1.
5 Murphy, D.J. and Hall, C.A.S. (2010), *Year in review – EROI or energy return on (energy) invested*. Annals of the New York Academy of Sciences. 1185(2010) 102-118.
6 When this was written in February 2015 the Swedish government had invented an 'Innovation Board', which can be seen as social engineering in all its glory. Perhaps

the author is a bit doubtful but in any case it contributes to the diffusion of money in the society.
7 *Numquam ponenda est pluralitas sine necessitate.* Plurality shall not be assumed without necessity.
8 The rather boring discussion set by the neoclassical theory that we will have a better society if the economy runs as the neoclassical theory prescribes is in our analysis dismissed in Chapter 1 and there is no reason to discuss normative general propositions concerning the macroscopic level except for specific economic policy actions to achieve limited stabilization effects or effects on growth.
9 A comprehensive discussion of the concept is found in Biddle, J.E. (2013) *The Genealogy of the Labor Hoarding Concept*, Dept. of Economics, Michigan State Univ., available at https://www.msu.edu/~haider/LaborDay/biddle.pdf
10 The article also appeared in *Applied Economics Quarterly*, (2010) Vol. 61, Issue Suppl.: 125-166.

Bibliography

Allais, M. (1987) 'The Equimarginal Principle; Meaning, Limits and Generalization', *Rivista Internazionale di Scienza Economica e Commerziale*, Vol. 34, No. 8.

Anand, A., Spatafora, N. and Mishra, R. (2012) *Structural Transformation and the Sophistication of Production*, IMF Working Papers 12/59, International Monetary Fund.

Arrow, K.J., (1951) 'Little's Critique of Welfare Economics', *The American Economic Review*, Vol. 41, No. 5 (Dec.): 923–934.

Bartlett, A. A. (2000) 'An Analysis of U.S. and World Oil Production Patterns', *Mathematical Geology*, Vol 32, No. 1.

Basu, S. and Kimball, M. S. (1997) *Cyclical Productivity with Unobserved Input Variation*, National Bureau of Economic Research, Working Paper 5915

Basu, S., Fernald, J. G., and Kimball, M. S. (2006) 'Are Technology Improvements Contractionary?' *American Economic Review*, 96(5): 1418–1448.

Becker, G. S. (1964) *Human Capital: A Theoretical and Empirical Analysis, with Special Reference to Education.* New York: Columbia University Press.

Bentolila, S. and Saint-Paul, G. (2003) *Explaining Movements in the Labor Share*, ftp://ftp.cemfi.es/pdf/papers/sb/sharebe2web.pdf

Biddle, J.E. (2013) The Genealogy of the Labor Hoarding Concept, Dept. of Economics, Michigan State University. Available at https://www.msu.edu/~haider/LaborDay/biddle.pdf

Boltho, A. (1982) 'Growth', in Boltho A. (ed.) *The European Economy: Growth and Crises* (pp. 9–37). Oxford: Oxford University Press.

Bower, J. L. (1970) *Managing the Resource Allocation Process, A Study of Corporate Planning and Investment.* Boston: Irwin

Bowers, J., Deaton, D. and Turk, J. (1982) *Labour Hoarding in British Industry.* Oxford: Basil Blackwell.

Brechling, F. P. R. (1965) 'The Relationship between Output and Employment in British Manufacturing Industries', *Rev. Econ. Studies* 32 (July 1965): 187–216.

Christiano, L.J., and Fisher, J.D.M. (1995) *Tobin's q and Asset Returns: Implications for Business Cycle Analysis.* Federal Reserve Bank of Minneapolis, Research Dept. Staff Report 200.

Davis, S.C., Anderson-Teixeira, K.J. and DeLucia, E.H, (2009) 'Life-cycle analysis and the ecology of biofuels', *Trends Plant Sci.* 14, 140–146. doi:http://dx.doi.org/10.1016/j.tplants.2008.12.006.

Dia, E. and Casalin, F. (2009), *Aggregate Investment, Tobin's q and External Finance*, Newcastle Discussion Papers in Economics: ISSN 1361 – 1837, Newcastle University, Business School.

Dietz, M., Stops, M. and Walwei, U. (2010) 'Safeguarding Jobs through Labour Hoarding in Germany', *Applied Economics Quarterly*, Vol. 61, Issue Suppl., 125–166. http://www.lsw.wiso.uni-erlangen.de/VfS/Vortr__ge/Walwei.pdf

Duncan, R. C., and Youngquist, W. (1998) *The World Petroleum Life-Cycle*. A paper presented at the PTTC Workshop "OPEC Oil Pricing and Independent Oil Producers" Petroleum Technology Transfer Council. Petroleum Engineering Program, University of Southern California, Los Angeles, California, October 22

Edgren, G., Faxen, K.O., and Odhner, C-E. (1973) *Wage Formation and the Economy*, London: Allen and Unwin.

Eichengreen, B. E. (1995) *Europe's Post-War Recovery*. Cambridge: Cambridge University Press.

Ekstedt, H. (2003) 'The End of the Dream – Some Comments on the Oil and Energy Situation'. Quarterly Commentary, Sanders Research Associates, London, August 12. www.sandersresearch.com

Ekstedt, H. (2012) *Money in Economic Theory*. London and New York: Routledge.

Ekstedt, H. and Fusari, A. (2010) *Economic Theory and Social Change, Problems and Revisions*. London and New York: Routledge.

Ekstedt, H. and Westberg, L. (1991) *Dynamic Models for the Interrelations of Real and Financial Growth*. London and New York: Chapman & Hall.

Growth in Services – Fostering Employment, 22 Productivity and Innovation – © OECD 2005.

Hobsbawm, E. (1994) *Ytterligheternas tidsålder: Det korta 1900-talet, 1914-1991*, (Age of Extremes; The short twentieth century, 1914 – 1991) Stockholm: Rabén Prisma.

Huang, C. and Ji, L. (2012) *Knowledge Intensive Business Services and Economic Growth with Endogenous Market Structure*, Presented at Conference of Dynamics, Economic Growth, and International Trade, 2012, Milan, Italy

Kaldor, N. (1939) 'Welfare Propositions in Economics and Interpersonal Comparisons of Utility', *Economic Journal*, Vol. 49, No. 195: 549–552.

Koestler, A. (1970) *The Act of Creation*. Bugay, Suffolk: Richard Clay Ltd.

Lafourcade, P. (2003) *Valuation, Investment and the Pure Profit Share*. Federal Reserve Board, Washington.

Larson, E. D. (2006) *A review of life-cycle analysis studies on liquid biofuel systems for the transport sector*. Princeton Environmental Institute, Princeton University, Guyot Hall, Washington Road, Princeton, NJ 08544, USA

Lundberg, E., Ohlin, G. and Werin, L. (1975) *Dags för tillväxt?: Konjunkturrådets Rapport 1975-76*, Studieförbundet Näringsliv och Samhälle (SNS), Stockholm.

Makarov, V.L. and Rubinov, A.M. (1977) *Economic Dynamics and Equilibria*. Heidelberg, Berlin: Springer Verlag.

Mishra, S., Lundstrom, S. and Anand, R. (2011) 'Sophistication in Service Exports and Economic Growth', World Bank - Economic Premise, The World Bank, issue 55, pages 1–4.

Munley, F. (1981) 'Wages, salaries, and the profit share: a reassessment of the evidence', *Cambridge Journal of Economics*, Vol. 5, 159–173.

Murphy, D.J. and Hall, C.A.S. (2010) 'Year in review – EROI or energy return on (energy) invested', *Annals of the New York Academy of Sciences*. 1185, 102–118.

Navarro, L. and Soto, R. (2006) 'Procyclical Productivity in Manufacturing', *Cuadernos de Economia*, Vol. 43 (Mayo): 193–220.

Reichenbach, H. (1938) *Experience and Prediction*. The University of Chicago Press.

Solow, R. (1956) 'A Contribution to the Theory of Economic Growth', *Quarterly Journal of Economics* 70 (1): 65–94.

Tachibonaki, T. and Taki, A. (2012) *Capital and Labour in Japan: The Functions of Two Factor Market*. London and New York: Routledge.

Uemura, H. (2008) *Growth, Distribution and Institutional Changes in the Japanese Economy: Faced by Increasing International Interdependence with Asian Countries*. Yokohama: Centre for Corporate Strategy and Economic Growth (CSEG) Yokohama National University.

7 Epilogue
Pictures and Axiomatic Structures

Abstract

This chapter is partly a kind of summing up vital points discussed in the book particularly from a methodological perspective.

Our fundamental criticism of neoclassical theory is that it transforms humans and commodities into atomistic variables. But this implies that economic research must be performed under the condition that the economic system is only a part of the social system and that the interactions between what we call the economic system and the surrounding socioeconomic and political reality are complex, and causal structures are to a large extent unknown. We have also shown that the acceptance of a non-equilibrium approach does not make us more equipped to formulate a consistent economic theory.

We will therefore go back to an almost pre-scientific state where we ask about the pictures we may form about the monetary economy. We have seen that David Hume as well as Adam Smith started with different pictures of the economic system. The latter started from the market exchange while the former started from the diffusion of money in society, a picture we also partly find in Aristotle's analysis.

This takes us close to the anthropological analysis in asking how pictures of social structures and relations evolve into more or less axiomatic structures. A question which evolves out of such contemplation is, often touched on in both biology and mathematics, on form and content. When we in Chapter 5 discussed structures in form of matrices there were two aspects: the principle structure of dependencies and, given that structure, the parametric specifications.

Thus basic to all kinds of axiomatic structures they are based on observations and beliefs. Subsequently we can say that any axiomatic structure is a foundation of a certain faith, which then is developed by logics into a true proposition, *given the axioms, the faith*.

The vital question in economics, and Keynes touched on it in his letter to Harrod which we quoted in the introduction, is consequently our belief in certain socioeconomic structures and how this belief are formed.

Form and Content

Unfortunately we have not been able to launch any breath-taking new theory on how the economy works but mostly only negative conclusions. The main criticism unfortunately deals with the excessive use of mathematics based on dubious foundations. It would be a pity if this is interpreted as if mathematics, and even worse also logics, is a deficient tool in social sciences, which it is not. Social sciences is however about human beings and their organizations and a naïve use of mathematics in particular, when subjects are treated like objects, complex variables are treated like atomistic variables without explanations and limitations, will by necessity make the analysis go wrong if applied to the real world. This is one kind of interpretation of Keynes' judgement of Tinbergen's analysis in the letter to Harrod, which we quoted in the Introduction.

Another interpretation of the same quote is that mathematics gives us the possibility, besides the mere calculation ability, to experiment with different possible forms. Chapter 5 is an example of this kind of use. If we try the latter use it is important not to squeeze the real problem with the help of assumption into some predetermined forms but merely to experiment to see the dynamic characteristics of different possible explanations.

But irrespective if we are faithful neoclassical economists or Keynesian ones we have to halt in front of Keynes' rather brutal words on Tinbergen's achievements. They go deep into our ideas of scientific research and spread doubts on one of our most appreciated empirical techniques, econometrics.

Keynes as an able statistician and mathematician surely does not want to deprive economic science of this important empirical technique but to understand that we must go back to his philosophical background and his work on the difference between atomistic facts and complexes which is a basic difference between science of objects and science of subjects.

But still his words will sometimes hurt and sometimes be applauded; in either case they must penetrate our minds with respect to our emotional as well as intellectual reactions. Because even agreeing with Keynes implies even more difficult conceptualizations and subsequent logics.

Our emotional reactions are perhaps the most important following Hume who says that reason is the humble servant of passion. What are our feelings on precision of thought and how do we define precision? The French mathematician Réné Thom (1975) used in his book on structural stability a picture like that of Figure 7.1 where he compared two estimations of a true curve.

Which hypothesis H1 or H2 shall we choose as a basis for an analysis of R? H1 will certainly give the better numerical fit but with respect to form H2 is probably the more interesting.

The steps towards the current picture of our solar system are interesting (Koestler (1979 [1959]). Copernicus developed a heliocentric picture but he also accepted circular orbits and constant speed which made the picture less precise than the geocentric picture which, by adding some 32 epicycles corrected the speed of the earth, and then the observations became 'numerically' rather precise.

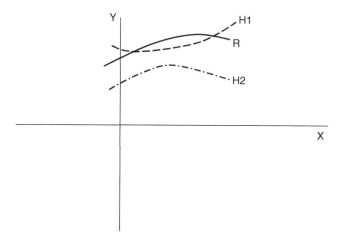

Figure 7.1 Form and Content

The Copernican picture needed some 48 epicycles and was still worse with respect to precision. When Kepler got access to Tycho Brahe's observations he developed the elliptical orbits and subsequently the non-constant speed of the planets. On the basis of Kepler, Galileo could then, with help of better instruments, develop a correct picture of the planetary orbits.

Thus we have to realize that a scientific theory not only produces figures but also form. These days the econometric technique is indeed sophisticated and it is a kind of machine producing numbers and tells us about the statistical relevance of the economic enquiry in question. What we try to do in this book is to urge the researcher to study the logical forms of the hypothesis. A commodity – why is that bought? Is it due to its physical form which is constant in all contexts or is it due to the particular set of characteristics contained in its physical form that fits a particular context? If we answer yes to the first alternative then the axiom of reflexivity in the neoclassical axiomatic structure holds since the commodity is an atomistic item; but if we answer yes to the second proposal we have to reject the axiom of reflexivity since the commodity is a complex.

Money is a typical such item, as we have seen, that includes even partially contradictive characteristics which all are due to the acceptance of money as a medium of exchange. Thus the fundamental questions in this book are about the logical forms of variables and their relative complexity in relation to eventual axiomatic structures.

The book does not give any advice with respect to economic policy although we think that dealing with economic variables which are scrutinized with respect to their logical contents should give better advice. As it now seems economic mainstream theory is rather an ad hoc theory where 'epicycles are invented to get the orbits to fit' alluding to the theories of the solar system.

A fundamental concept is equilibrium and we accept that as a solution of any kind of a dynamic system or an ordinary equation system, but we reject any form of existence of general equilibrium. The use in economics of the concept of general equilibrium theory for practical economic analysis is gravely erroneous even as a kind of analytical tool, mostly due to the difficulty in separating the mathematical conditions for any kind of conventional operation from that of general equilibrium which is from a mathematical point of view exactly the same. We tend to forget that the neoclassical axioms concern the transformation of humans and commodities to atomistic variables not mathematics per se.

In this chapter we will sum up the most important general insights but we also mention learnings of a more tentative character which are dependent on specific contexts and inert structures. The general conclusions are solely of a negative character mostly telling us that universal laws unfortunately cannot be established. The tentative conclusions relate to generic patterns found in empirical reports which can be brought to a consistent form of hypothesis provided appropriate limitations and inertia.

This makes us wonder how to proceed in a more positive way. We can of course go on with the axiomatic structure and release axioms or add some new ones in order to change the possibility to derive other and new propositions, but that is a rather boring way of theorizing, not to say meaningless, since we then forget that human thinking has many forms to be utilized.

L'esprit de géométrie and L'esprit de finesse

Blaise Pascal separates the 'l'esprit de géométrie', translated to the *mathematical mind* in English, from 'l'esprit de finesse', the *intuitive mind* in English.[1]

> The difference between the mathematical and the intuitive mind. – In the one, the principles are palpable, but removed from ordinary use; so that for want of habit it is difficult to turn one's mind in that direction: but if one turns it thither ever so little, one sees the principles fully, and one must have a quite inaccurate mind who reasons wrongly from principles so plain that it is almost impossible they should escape notice.
>
> But in the intuitive mind the principles are found in common use and are before the eyes of everybody. One has only to look, and no effort is necessary; it is only a question of good eyesight, but it must be good, for the principles are so subtle and so numerous that it is almost impossible but that some escape notice. Now the omission of one principle leads to error; thus one must have very clear sight to see all principles and, in the next place, an accurate mind not to draw false deductions from known principles.
>
> All mathematicians would then be intuitive if they had clear sight, for they do not reason incorrectly from principles known to them; and intuitive minds would be mathematical if they could turn their eyes to the principle of mathematics to which they are unused.

(Pascal 2007 [1670]: 171)

Pascal's 'Pensées' were published some 70 years before Hume claimed that reason, in the meaning of logical analysis, was the humble servant of passion; they were also published some 250 years before Wittgenstein published *Tractatus* from which we have used proposition 6.211. Pascal describes the problem between the two ways of thinking in more general terms and he also stresses the necessity of base, an analysis on both ways of thinking.

However if we read the quote of Keynes in his letter to Harrod it actually seems that Keynes will only use mathematical models as some kind of intuitive pictures since he dismisses the actual quantification of the models. It is not necessarily so. In Chapter 5 we discussed modelling and the concept of structural stability. With respect to deterministic dynamic models we showed how they both were subject to intrinsic instability points and how in some areas they were sensitive to perturbations.

When we look at economic modelling it has been mostly about formulating a static model for statistical investigations to find a parameter structure. If the statistics have been favourable the model in question has been a tool for experiments. What we suggest in Chapter 5 is on one hand to penetrate the dynamic characteristics of a model with respect to bifurcations and perturbations, but still more important is to study how these mathematical concepts of violent changes could be expressed in the real world and that implies that we have to understand the concept of complexity in its deepest sense.

It may seem that the preceding chapters have been an attack on using mathematics and logics in social sciences. It is not however. On the contrary, following Pascal, we claim that using logic/mathematics with precision is indeed important. Our exposé of different areas in economic research has brought us to the general conclusion that it is impossible to create a universal theory in the spirit of Isaac Newton which even in physics has been degraded to a special case holding for the Euclidian space and under the particular circumstances prevailing on earth, but this special case is also an approximation. These modifications brought about by the development of the physical sciences indeed do not diminish the achievements of Newton and the scientists whose shoulders he used to reach to the utmost clarification of what he could perceive with his senses and make a synthesis of by his supreme ability of not only logical analysis but of taking necessary axioms to build a consistent logical structure as a follower of the great Euclid who brought geometry of the linear tree-dimensional space into logical perfection. Then Lobačevskiĭ started and Riemann ended the enquiries of the axiom of parallels which transferred Euclid's achievements to a special case of the curved space.

This means that both Newton's and Euclid's achievements are still in use as approximations for daily earthly conditions, with a sufficient probability for practical purposes.

The greatness of Newton's as well as Euclid's achievements lies in the fact that the abstract analysis concerns daily observable matters, in principle at least. Their respective systems were synthesises of well-known observations and earlier scientific empirical analysis.

Empirical perturbations with respect to Newton's laws in their most abstract forms could be explained within the very theory with respect to the level of observational ability and precision possible during his times. It is true that for the theory such devastating discoveries as the entropy principle came relatively soon after his completion of *Principia* which changed the picture of the world entirely but as said above Newton's *Principia* is still working as a reasonable approximation and so is Euclidian geometry.

In economics however we start by reducing a picture into a logical skeleton of what economics deals with, the market exchange, which is not generally agreed to. Aristotle, the Friars of Salamanca, Hume, Thornton, Say to name some economists before the so called marginal revolution, had a much broader picture of the interactions between the social environment and the economic subsystem. Particularly in analysing Mill and Jevons we found that they had to sacrifice important features of the workings of the real economy in order to be able to squeeze the theory into a mathematical form.

Reading the quote from Pascal carefully we find that the logical/mathematical picture must be founded in an observable reality. So, we have to stop and go back, analytically, and scrutinize our pictures of the reality. Sometimes one can still hear from economists a claim that the Arrow and Debreu approach is the description of the perfectly functioning economy, not even limited to the very market exchange but enlarged to the whole empirically observable economy. This is perhaps as far as we can get from Blaise Pascal.

Anyway when dealing with pictures we do not have clear-cut logical way how to handle them and that is why Pascal singles out the two ways of thinking.

We have two sciences which particularly discuss pictures and similar. On one hand we have anthropology, in its different branches, and on the other hand we have semiology, where we study signs; pictures representing more than themselves.

Anthropology is the study of human creatures in all its varieties of activities with respect to the express generic forms; cultural forms, scientific forms, religious forms, sexual and gender forms and so on. Great emphasis is laid on how humans picture the world, themselves, the others and the nature.

On one hand it is interesting to see how pictures of natures are evolving out of classifications of species of the relevant flora. These classifications although in many cases built on magical forces and powers mostly deal with utilities/dis-utilities with respect to nutrition and medical cures and contain often a very advanced specific knowledge. Classifications of fauna is on one hand built on linking aesthetic features to ethics and on the other hand they are often classified with respect to the desirability of the assumed characters of the animals in a specific culture. Thus these pictures are often contradictory between different cultures.

When we think of the complex relation between humans as the ultimate goal of production and humans as the most important production factor on one hand on the microscopic level and on the other hand on the macroscopic, cultural, sociological level it is hard to say that the pre-scientific pictures play little role.

The same is the case when looking at gender questions, children's work, and so on. Such pictures are instead of great importance for economics and to claim that the market will arrange for a convergence in some direction is a bit doubtful.

Semiotics is in a way a study of how cultural pictures are evolving into representative signs of symbolic character. The general meaning is that in a stable culture some stylized pictures, actions, items are bearers of complex cultural signification which enlarges/limits/defines linguistic concepts and meanings.

If we look at a concept like inflation our earlier analysis has shown that on one hand it is difficult to understand its meaning from a theoretical point of view and on the other hand it is hard to measure in a correct way. So how has inflation become a key issue in the last three or four decades? When media uses the word inflation in different times and different countries what kind of connotations is brought about to the common people and how could this be changed? When the author visited a conference arranged by European Central Bank in 2002 one critic of the bank maintained that ECB had three targets: Inflation, Inflation, Inflation. Since the conversion rules still are in place such a policy must also be maintained in each member country.

In a huge market like the ECB area it would then be natural to regard local and regional variations in inflation as some sort of 'natural stabilizer'. From an anthropological as well as a semiotic point of view it would be interesting to see the pre-scientific pictures behind the specific interpretations of the concept and the policy addressed to the problem.

Outside and Inside Human Beings and Society – Looking for Signs

We have predominantly dealt with the problem of aggregation in this book. There are always two kinds of pictures, the *microscopic* and the *macroscopic*. A country which reports balanced state accountings, a stable currency and low inflation, may give a picture of stability and perhaps also of prosperity, but if youth unemployment is rising there is also growing social discontent. We may have a macroscopic picture, outside the economy, which tells us one thing while we get another impression when looking at the social and socioeconomic variables, the inside of the economy.

In a way medicine is similar to economics; it is about subjects and the doctor is dependent on their perceptions and apprehensions, furthermore it has a microscopic level combined with several macroscopic levels. Another feature is that medical research seldom is based only on observation per se but also to the purpose of act/cure detected anomalies, which separates both the subjects from physics for example. We have an outside picture of a person which may give one picture of the health status and another inside 'picture' which is at variance with the outside one. Karin Johannisson (2004), professor at Uppsala University, has followed the evolution of medicine from ancient to current times. The journey starts from the narration, the anamnesis of the patient, which was the basic information the doctor had together with the observation of corporal signs and the patient's behaviour. The meeting however was premeditated by medical science in the form of classifications of behaviour and corporal signs; a typology of humans was evolving and became objectified with respect to the individual. We know of the classical typology of temperaments and to these different types typical symptom and diseases were linked.

The objectification of the patient evolved when the meeting was transferred to the clinic, which also implied that the doctor was able to study corporal signs and behaviour apart from the normal context of the patient.

This led soon to an acceptance of physical contact, the doctor could touch the patients' bodies and by this also analyse the body fluids and excrements. Also procedures like palpation and auscultation were developed by systematization of effects of syndromes and to a certain degree also with new instruments and new techniques which often followed from the better systematization of syndromes.

Thus links to the interior of the sick body were improving. This also resulted in the anatomy of the body being completed, partial that is true, but it led to a growing knowledge of the physiology of the body. It is interesting to see the development of the interaction between the studies of sick bodies and normally functioning bodies. It was really an interaction where the medical researchers found that knowledge of the abnormal state of the body brought information of the normal state and vice versa.

Finally we reached the era of the laboratory and by that also the final objectification of the patient. The classifications became the object of experimental studies which linked the classifications to anomalies relative to the healthy body and also the dynamics of these anomalies was studied.

One of the deepest problems of medicine is the links between the macro-states and the micro-states of the individual and also the influence of the social/ psychological/economic context on the psychological and somatic state of the individual. So the enormous success of corporal medicine left the research of the mind disintegrated and almost apart from *true* medicine until the latest decades, when new observation and measurement techniques were developed.

My doctor once said that while medicine is 90% observation and 10% theory, economics seems to be 90% theory and 10% observation.

Looking at the huge amount of empirical studies in economics, particularly microscopic studies we are apt to object to such a statement, and when we look upon the development of economics from the Friars of Salamanca onwards there is a clear understanding that although the nature of economics is more difficult than medicine with respect to empirical studies, it is still a part of the daily life both on the macroscopic and microscopic levels. It is also said to be the science of allocation and distribution of scarce resources so it can hardly be separated from the individual life neither the life of the society.

By its very nature economics however must have a higher degree of philosophical considerations because the complexity of the economic reality both with respect to aspects of human/societal forms of life as well as ideologies, cultural differences and so on. Still however the search for a theory, a model is as in vain as modelling human life on earth. We can never hope more than to theorize under assumptions of reasonable inertia. This is and should be the basic understanding of all economists.

However the so called marginal revolution and the utility theory was/is seen as an important scientific step. We got a more conscious treatment of the choice situation and the individual optimization but the fault was that on the meagre foundation of the market exchange it was built an entire universe. As we have seen the final step consisted of a transformation of human beings from being living complex subjects to becoming atomistic numbers. And moreover on this meagre foundation of the act of market exchange was built a universal efficiency concept.

We accept the individual optimization and also individual rationality is only given the contextual apprehensions and the axiomatic structure only holds in the very single choice given time and space specifications.

In these respects we can say that while medical researchers and practitioners in every step forward base their studies on the observable reality the economists are forcing the economic reality in to a model of thinking which has remote similarities with Newtonian conceptualization and modelling.

We have looked at the considerations of Mill and Jevons and we have seen how they are forced to sort out almost all features which are prevalent in a society in order to make a slim picture of the individual as an atom suitable for mathematical analysis. However it is more remarkable to investigate the rational expectation theory and how it has been completely removed from the set of empirical approaches to be a pure manipulation of an a priori mathematical model where we even might suspect that the manipulations are not in accordance with correct mathematical analysis of an axiomatic structure.

Another remarkable thing is how the neoclassical theory has come to represent the theoretical expression for a free market economy when even the most basic concept, money, is an anomaly in the theory. Economic science is perhaps distancing itself from neoclassical theory, there are some signs of that, but what directions of evolution will be chosen?

Obviously we have learnt that a microeconomic foundation of macro theory is something more and other than bringing in the analysis of a barter economy.

Axiomatic Structures

An axiomatic structure, A is a set of assumptions/rules which are held as unalterable. The basic reason for A is that we want to limit the problem in order to be able to use logical reasoning. Such a system can be purely abstract as in mathematics or based on observed regularities in the real world, inductive conclusions which are held for true. The problem with the A is the intrinsic consistency; we do not necessarily need to think about the ultimate one as treated in Gödel's paradox but more about the consistency of the used concepts in A.

One of the most important achievements by the analytical philosophy during the 20th century, which is also mirrored in Gödel's paradox, was the insight that logics/mathematics is empty of any substance per se. The very content of the used concepts in the logical analysis are those which give the substance. Thus the logic is just a tool and as expressed by Hume, that reason is the humble servant of passion.

Consequently a logical apparatus can never say anything more than what is in the axioms/assumptions setting the conceptual limitations for the analysis.

A logical result per se is always true given the axioms which means that we may solve an equation system for symbols in a Euclidian space and that is true for any set of numbers which can be denoted by the symbols, but on the other hand the simple syllogism: a – all creatures walking on two legs are apes; b – Socrates walked on two legs gives the conclusion c – Socrates was an ape is also true given the premises.

All these well known facts about logics/mathematics imply that the content of the axioms becomes our metaphysical picture of the problem we are going to analyse. Any kind of logical manipulations with a set of axiom/assumptions does not say anything about the relevance or the intrinsic consistency of the axiom per se. I once heard a debate on religion among some scientists from different disciplines. One claimed that the miracles of Jesus Christ, as walking on water and making wine out of water were clearly against scientific facts. A physicist in the group answered dryly that if Jesus was the incarnated God he must obviously be above the scientific rules and was thus able to make such miracles. Faith in anything sets a sort of axiomatic system. An old expression in catholic theology about faith is *assensus intellectus veritati – the consent of the intellect to the truth.* Thus faith gives a sort of axiomatic structure and the intellect accepts this as a basis for logical analysis. This is more or less the same as Hume meant about the relation of passion and reason.

This is what we mean when claiming that an axiomatic structure basically sets the metaphysics of the logical analysis. Thus no axiomatic structure is based on reason per se. We can, as Kant did, discuss a world a priori built on pure logic/mathematics, which forms general rules for existence the world and of fundamental causes since 'it is possible to show that pure a priori principles are indispensable for the possibility of experience, and so to prove their existence a priori. For whence could experience derive its certainty, if all the rules, according to which it proceeds, were always themselves empirical and therefore contingent' (Kant 1988[1787]: 45).

Thus the principle must exist preceding the experience, must be deliberated from the accidental circumstances of the practical experience and be universal. Such a programme seems to be similar to the neoclassical approach singling out the essential structural form of the exchange economy. However Kant continues:

> It is precisely by means of the latter modes of the knowledge, in the realm beyond the world of the senses, where experience can yield neither guidance nor correction, that our reason carries on those enquiries which owing to their importance we consider to be far more excellent, and in their pupose far more lofty, than all that understanding can learn in the field of appearances.
> ...

These unavoidable problems set by pure reason itself are *God, freedom, and immortality*. The science which, with all its preparations, is in its final intention directed solely to their solution is metaphysics; and its procedure is at first dogmatic, that is, it confidently sets itself to this task without any previous examination of the capacity or incapacity of reason for so great an undertaking. [original emphasis]

(Ibid:. 45–46)

The very foundation for the empirical analysis must thus be founded in metaphysics according to Kant.

We will not discuss the discrepancies and eventual agreements between Hume and Kant. Suffice to say that Hume has a more humble earthly philosophy. However, although Hume expresses it differently from Kant reason can never produce the necessary foundation of the logical analysis:

Reason is the discovery of truth or falsehood. Truth or falsehood consists in an agreement either to the *real* relations of ideas or to *real* existence or matter of fact. Whatever, therefore, is not susceptible of this agreement or disagreement, is incapable of being true or false, and can never be an object of our reason.

(Hume, (2002[1740]: 295]

Consequently both Hume and Kant on different grounds reject the axiomatic structure underlying the logical analysis to be a part of the analysis.

The great finding of the analytical philosophy during the 20th century is that logics is empty of substance so the axiomatic structure is defining a substance in which we have faith, so while the logics tells us whether or not a proposition derived from an axiomatic structure is true the axiomatic structure is based on our faith, whatever underlies it.

Subsequently it follows that the analysis of the axioms cannot be based on the same kind of logic as is set by the axioms, which follows from Gödel. The basic analysis of axioms is about the dos and don'ts, what kind of concepts and questions fall outside the axioms and how this affects the purpose of our analysis? Looking at our earlier example in Chapter 2 of a syllogism about Socrates it seems wrong with respect to its empirical content, but if we make a study of the evolution of the species we can perhaps classify human beings as a particular form of apes and in such a particular contextual conceptualization our syllogism becomes true. But in that case we must probably give the exact limits of the conceptualization since a transformation of the meaning of apes and humans to other areas, in medicine for example, would lead to erroneous consequences.

Consequently our axiomatic structure cannot give us any hint of its truth value until its logical conclusions meet a different analysis based on different axiomatic structures and we then have to choose what to prefer and now we see the meaning of the theological expression of faith above.

We are in the end left to the decisions of passion/will/faith or whatever we call the metaphysical categories. In a way Kant's *Kritik der Reinen Vernunft* and Hume's scepticism meet each other.

Normally axiomatic structures have very precise purposes. The axioms are often radicalizations of inductive conclusions based on empirical investigations. We thus want to check on one hand the intrinsic consistency of the inductive conclusions and on the other hand look for hidden conclusions contained in the axioms as well as dynamics and reaction to perturbations. Such manipulations are as a rule a basis for refining experiments in experimental sciences and we are reminded of Keynes' discussion of econometric studies in his letter to Harrod. The propositions derived from an axiomatic structure are also defined in relation to the assumed accuracy of measurement the acceptable limits of empirical variations within the realm of the axioms.

In our discussion in Chapter 2 when we discussed Keynes' philosophical contribution we found that he focused on the scientific conditions for social sciences. His contribution did not deal with logical/mathematical analysis as such but went straight to the central point: the character of the conceptualization. Keynes had an interesting entrance into philosophy where on one side we had the moral philosophy as analysed by G.E. Moore and on the other the analytical philosophy represented by Russell, Whitehead and young Wittgenstein. Furthermore when he wrote on probability he had Whitehead as a supervisor who also made important contributions to metaphysics. That means that when Keynes worked with economic analysis he was firmly aware of the fact that science of subjects requires different conceptual categories than science of objects but also that the logical analysis as such does not change.

This side of Keynes is seldom given prominence but is of utmost importance in interpreting *what Keynes actually said*. Already in the little passage from his letter to Harrod we see his philosophical character brought to the edge; he actually more or less rules out precise quantitative methods, not as in descriptive methods, but with respect to judging logical conclusions, with respect to stochastic methods concerning investigation of subjects. We may say that this was due to the low quality of data in those days. But we may only look at the 'theory' of the Phillips curve, a relation originally built on yearly aggregate data. The data improved in the way that quarterly and even monthly observations were used and the technique of time lags made it possible to look for inter-temporal relations. We had over many years a macroeconomic debate whether the Phillips curve was short term, long term or both based on the same kind of aggregate statistics only covering shorter measurement periods. It is interesting to see that there were few efforts to analyse the form of the Phillips curve in relation to the neoclassical axiomatic structure or a set of consistent assumptions based on Keynesian approaches. As we have seen in our analysis in Chapter 6 there are several possible explanations to the appearance of the Phillips curve in aggregate empirical studies, both why it may exist and also why it cannot be seen.

Such phenomena make one ask how do we know the time structure and the relevant aggregate levels to perform empirical analysis and most of all what do we mean by different aggregate levels?

Traditionally we have two well established sets of axioms/assumptions which give rise to a consistent mathematical analysis, the neoclassical axioms and the IS-LM-model. We have rather comprehensively discussed the neoclassical axioms and their intrinsic problems.

The IS-LM system is a less strict system, which deals with aggregate variables thus accepting their insufficient definitions. A system like

$$C = a + b \cdot Y$$
$$I = I_0 + c \cdot Y$$
$$Y = C + I \qquad\qquad \text{E.7.1}$$

gives us certainly an equilibrium which is consistent, but the difficulty is the definition of the variables. As we have pointed out in Chapter 4, a system like E.7.1 presupposes that we are in a state of non-equilibrium seen from the neoclassical point of view and that means we cannot suppose that an aggregation of money values at two different time sequences are of the same real character. This means that we have a possible conflict between real and financial sectors of the economy.

Seldom have we seen discussions of the appropriateness of aggregating money values in a non-equilibrium economy. If this is a sign of ignorance or a faulty use of Occam's razor it is hard to say but it could also be so that the analytical rigour of neoclassical theory has certainly an imprint in mind with respect to additive aggregation and furthermore that so called fixed price analysis is a mirror of the real economy. This is a bit curious since an economist like Jean Baptist Say already in the very beginning of the 19th century argued in a very convincing way that prices and money values could never be a measure other than in the precise act of exchange; to use it as a general measure was erroneous. Furthermore this is an important feature of the Austrian school, von Mises and others.

From Aristotle via the Friars of Salamanca and David Hume onto Wicksell, the Austrian school and Keynes, money has been treated as measure only in the precise moment of exchange and this is also how Gerard Debreu sees it. It is then a mystery how neoclassical theory without defining the concept of money could have changed minds so that it became juxtaposed to that which is called prices in the neoclassical theory and which strictly speaking is a measure which we might describe as a measurable function (Weisstein 2000:1153):

A function $f : X \rightarrow Y$ for which the pre-image of every measurable set in Y is measurable in X. For a *Borel Measure*, all continuous functions are measurable.

Since we have transformed the market space to a Euclidian space through the axioms there always exists measurable functions on any level of aggregation. The problem is that these functions only exist in general equilibrium where money, as in daily use, is not defined.

As J.B. Say clearly pointed out: in the non-equilibrium economy there exists no general measure.

Paradoxes

At least since Zeno of Elea (490–430 BC) there has been utmost interest among philosophers on the existence and the role of paradoxes. Many interesting logical paradoxes are actually similar to each other or follow from each other. Zeno's paradoxes concerned mostly time and the so called cinematographic apprehension of time. Newton is very clear in rejecting this form of understanding time and replaces it with an exogenous continuous concept. There is thus some irony in that the Einstein-Minkowski could be seen as a sort of rehabilitation of Zeno's apprehension of space-time although we should not take it too literally.

The paradoxes we have used in this book from philosophy are Russell's paradox, Cantor's paradox and to some extent Gödel's paradox but more as extension to Russell's. In fact these three are linked together and they are also linked to the famous 'liar's paradox' dated back to Epimenides as far back as 600 BC, thus some 150 years before Zeno. It is a statement like: 'The author, who is Swedish, claims that all Swedes are liars.'

If we now look at Cantor's paradox it tells us on one hand that if we use two number lines and we make a tick for every natural number on one of the lines and a tick for every natural number plus a tick for one and two thirds of the distance between the natural numbers. We may now ask on which line there are the most ticks. The answer is of course that as long as the lines are limited there are more ticks on the latter but if the lines approach infinity, both the number series approach infinity. The other answer is however that we may use the natural numbers as a measure and then we can change the names of the line with ticks also for parts to natural numbers. Thus we use the natural numbers with respect to two different features.

So two different meanings of the same concept may be confusing.

If we look at Russell's paradox we see that Russell complexes say that atomistic items and complexes have different mathematical forms and mixtures of these two lead to confusions.

So two items of two different mathematical forms represented by the same mathematical form will be confusing.

Gödel's paradox tells us that you cannot prove the consistency of an axiomatic structure within the structure itself. Thus you have to make it plausible by other means than the intrinsic logic of the system.

Paradoxes are always interesting though they sort of exhaust an axiomatic structure. In the sense of Cantor and Russell we penetrate the concepts with respect to their precision and with respect to Gödel whose proof is regarded as a masterpiece the test concerns the question if atomic concepts can derive any substance whatsoever. If we can answer yes or no to the posed question a logical analysis will affect the substance of the analysis but since the answer is that the question is undecidable, the logic becomes empty and thus neutral to the substance of the variables.

In economics we have two well-known paradoxes: Allais' paradox and Arrow's paradox.

The first is a prompt answer to the expected utility theory dealing with future probable utilities. Allais established that the correlate of independence of irrelevant alternatives does not hold for the expected utility due to the fact that the introduction of an alternative changes the entropy/variance and will affect the binary order (Ekstedt 2012: 203–205). It is really not a paradox but a correction of an insufficient analysis. Nowadays it can be incorporated via assumptions of risk aversions, meaning that variance can be expressed as a risk measure.

Arrow's paradox is more complex. It was early seen as a problem of finding a collective unanimous choice function. It was anticipated by many political scientists as discussing efficiency problems in democratic organizations. In Wikipedia, which seems to be the new standard for interpretation of scientific concepts, we can read:

> What Arrow's theorem does state is that a deterministic preferential voting mechanism – that is, one where a preference order is the only information in a vote, and any possible set of votes gives a unique result – cannot comply with all of the conditions given above simultaneously.
>
> …
>
> So, what Arrow's theorem really shows is that any majority-wins voting system is a non-trivial game, and that game theory should be used to predict the outcome of most voting mechanisms. This could be seen as a discouraging result, because a game need not have efficient equilibria, *e.g.*, a ballot could result in an alternative nobody really wanted in the first place, yet everybody voted for.
>
> (http://en.wikipedia.org/wiki/Arrow's_impossibility_theorem)

This quote complies pretty well with textbooks on higher levels in economics.

What is interesting is that what mostly is discussed is voting procedures and eventual compliance to efficiency criteria, usually the Pareto criterion. Our view is a bit different.[2]

The axioms Arrow starts from are in fact a vector addition of the individuals obeying the neoclassical axioms. Thus the axiom of reflexivity holds and thus also the independence of irrelevant alternatives. This grants of course the additivity of the individual optima but it also makes the individuals alienated of the aggregation. The agents do not and cannot choose. Into this Arrow introduces agents who not only can vote but can also consider the macroscopic solution which is impossible if obeying the neoclassical axioms. The solution almost has to be an impossibility theorem with respect to the compliance of the two different kinds of agents.

Arrows paradox has some similarities with Russell's paradox. Russell discusses two different classes of variables, one atomistically defined and the other of complex variables to phrase it briefly. He then finds that the two are different with respect to whether the universal class of classes belongs to itself or not. Arrow actually finds that agents atomistically defined can be additively aggregated thus they belong to what Russell names non-proper classes, the universal class belongs to itself, while voting agents are complexes who are *not* atomistically defined and subsequently additive aggregation will not work, thus these agents belong to what Russell names proper classes, the universal class does not belong to itself.

Our view is that Arrow's paradox should be treated as a limit paradox for the neoclassical axiomatic structure.

In this book we have achieved quite a few paradoxical results mostly because the intrinsic features of money following from its social acceptance as a medium of exchange implies that it is used in different contexts which can be contradictory to its use as a medium of exchange. In Hume's terms we can say that the need for liquidity and its stability with respect to contracts in nominal figures may sometimes affect the dispersion in the economy and imply real effects.

Such results are however not to be regarded as paradoxes. However we have reached one paradox which is exactly in line with Russell and Arrow.

In Proposition 2.1 in Chapter 2 we showed that rejecting additively of commodities and agents as implied by the rejection of the Axiom of Reflexivity we cannot create a logical link between the microscopic and the macroscopic level within the realm of the barter economy. We then claim that the introduction of money in the market exchange is not an anomaly but works satisfactorily in the disequilibrium economy.

But then in Chapter 3 Proposition 3.1 we show that since money belongs to non-proper classes, *money values* can be additively aggregated. Thus there is a qualitative difference between the analysis of real items and the analysis of money values irrespective of if we work with current or fixed prices.

This raises the question of whether it is possible to find a sort of 'general equilibrium' when it comes to the monetary economy. What speaks against this is of course the partly conflicting features of the money concept but at least from a philosophical point of view this is an interesting question.

Back to Pictures

We have in the earlier chapters tried to comply with traditional analysis in the way that opinion at variance with established views must somehow be found in the structure of these, which is quite natural if it is an empirical science we deal with. But on the other hand changes of forms, proportions and perspectives may make different pictures of the same reality almost void of resemblance like Swift's journeys to Lilliput and Brobdingnag.

We started in the neoclassical picture with the exchange of utilities. The act of exchange is to be seen as a kind of atom in the neoclassical economic universe, this very atom was then the constant substance in the building of a general equilibrium. The atom is well defined at the most elementary microscopic level and can be used in an additive process for building a macroscopic level containing the whole economic universe. Furthermore the neoclassical atom is like the original Greek picture of the physical atom consistent and complete; in economic terms it is efficient. Since this is our fundamental building material in an additive process which does not perturb the fundamental building blocks we can prove that the macroscopic results exhibit the same characteristics as the fundamental atom: consistency and completeness. But where are the agents, the people, the persons in this picture? We may look back at Figure 1.2 and there we see that the people are built to buy commodities which are possible to use in the very exchange process, the economic atom. But they are not built by commodities in general but only by commodities which have been ennobled by the exchange; they are vectors created by the exchange process.

Thus, in the neoclassical picture the people, the persons play a completely subordinate role. All their dreams, idiosyncrasies and whatnot are expressed in the very atom, the exchange; thus, since the macroscopic creations express the same consistency and completeness as the fundamental atom there can be no additional goals or purposes which are added to the macroscopic creation. Consequently, if the individuals are free to comply with this form of market exchange we will reach the general equilibrium.

The Marxist variant is a bit different since the free exchange is in principle accepted, according to Makarov and Rubinov (1977), but the power relations of the society must be arranged properly, so the dictatorship of the proletariat takes us to the last step and we reach the communist synthesis, which seems to be much like the neoclassical equilibrium.

No much imaginative power is needed to interpret both the two pictures in religious terms where the people walk through the valley of the shadow of death but see the light and accept the salvation into the paradise/nirvana/Shangri-La or whatever we call it.

The metaphysical character of the two theories also implies that they can be used as a basis for normative statements concerning the empirical world without specifying the particular goals and purposes of individuals and the collective. Furthermore the theoretical consistency and completeness of particularly the neoclassical theory seems to imply that although many aspects/concepts of every-day economic analysis are missing the theory is seen as an ultimate description of the economy by many. It is often agreed that in the short run there are perturbations but these are dissipative and in the long run the economy converges to the ultimate general equilibrium. This is sometimes claimed without any reflections of the inherent theoretical contradictions.

The neoclassical theory is clearly normative. As we have seen from our discussions on the rational expectation hypothesis which according to Sargent (2008) is generally used, it is hardly based on empirical observations but is derived from general equilibrium theory, which means that the hypothesis only deals with a prevailing equilibrium, apart from eventual converging processes which have no theoretical meaning in the axiomatic structure. Consequently it is hard to see the neoclassical theory other than as a sort of metaphysical vision. It even has a magical dimension in the 'invisible hand' which few discuss but which de facto implicitly is a part of the axiomatic structure.

From these considerations we might say that neoclassical theory is not to be seen as an empirical science. It postulates a form of determinism which is universal and which is absolute in the sense that, as we have discussed earlier, has no environment. So it is tempting to throw it into the garbage can, but maybe we should stop and think a bit. The neoclassical and the Marxist pictures are clearly some sort of cousins and they have both an intrinsic power of imagination which for example in economics Keynes' writings do not have. It is typical that the Keynesian analysis has come to be known as Keynesianism which is firmly linked to the IS-LM model which has an easy and quickly accessible form, which has very little to do with Keynes as also Hicks (1980) admits. In many countries, Sweden perhaps most of all, it was seen as the basic tool in the social engineering.

Consequently the picture a theory alludes to is more than a set of axioms and a logical analysis. In fact we could turn it all around and say that we build a theory around a picture we want to convey. Lévi-Strauss (1962) discusses science and magic and claims that with respect to the empirical knowledge per se there does not need to be a difference but when it comes to the inherent determinism the two are different.

> Entre magie et science, la différence première serait donc, de ce point de vue, que l'une postule un déterminisme global et intégral, tandis que l'autre opère en distinguant des niveaux dont certains, seulement, admettent des formes de déterminisme tenues pour inapplicables à d'autres niveaux.
>
> ... Les rites et les croyances magiques apparaîtraient alors comme autant d'expressions d'un acte de foi en une science encore à naître.
>
> (Lévi-Strauss 1962: 19)

About magic: one could say that we use when probability calculations in areas where 'white noise' is more an expression of unknown factors than random behaviour, which Keynes somewhere, with respect to econometric studies, addresses as black magic.

In Lévi-Strauss' terminology the magical thought stands for a radicalization of a thought, a sort of utopia, and a determinism which is universal and directed. He separates magic from sciences in the sense that science differentiates between determinism on different levels and questions the single form of utopia, not to say implicitly questions the hypothesis of a single, universal goal. Thus empirical science, deconstructs pictures into parts, and furthermore works with different possible pictures on different levels; we saw this clearly when discussing the evolution of medical research and diagnostics. This also means that while magic can work with basic unity of causal dimensions, science must accept diverging causal structures, even contradictory ones.

We introduced in Chapter 2 the concept of epistemic cycles with respect to the individual apprehension of the surrounding environment and a particular context.

Originally this concept was developed by Thomas Brody (1994) in describing the interpretation of experimental data in quantum theory. Thus we use the concept for describing differences between economic scientists.

A scientist very seldom starts from collecting data, makes an inductive conclusion and creates a picture via a deductive system built on inductive conclusions.

Instead we start from a picture, a utopia, a tradition and begin to either strengthen or deny the picture in question. In principle we meet two strong pictures in economic science: the equilibrium system and the ever ongoing evolution. The equilibrium thought is per se natural. How can people who do not know each other or have the slightest contact do business in a way that keeps the prices in the system fairly stable? This was Adam Smith's question and he based the relative stability on the production price of corn, since the land rent and the workers' salary were based on the price of corn. The Friars of Salamanca however noticed the differences between different places in the Mediterranean area and based the price stability more on the local conditions of the demand and supply. Both Smith and the Friars of Salamanca were aware of the importance of the distribution of purchasing power and the social classes, particularly Smith.

The rather broad picture painted by Smith and the Salamanca Friars of the stabilizing factors was developed and formalized during the 19th century but with the so called marginal revolution the picture from Smith and the Friars went through a major revision. The picture which was based on social conditions in different respects became now a purely personal link between the intrinsic valuations of utilities of different commodities in relation to the price. We have seen how Mill tried to make the minds of the agents open to social conditions and ethics but these efforts had to be sacrificed for an efficient and logical presentation of the picture of equilibrium.

Thus Smith's and the Salamanca Friars' picture which was rather loose lost its links to the social environment but on the other hand the picture now became an eminent tool for deriving testable microscopic hypothesis and derive conclusions. The additivity concept which was impossible in Smith's and the Friars' world made it possible to enter into an exciting macroscopic world which still was partly closed for Mill but which was opened by Jevons, Menger, Walras and others and this was due to the mathematically expressed picture.

So the weakened social base of the theory was well compensated in that new ventures at the macroscopic level could be initiated.

As long as the development of the neoclassical picture was continuing, its weaknesses were hidden by derivations of new exiting theorems with respect to efficiency matters on the microscopic and the macroscopic level. Thus elaborating the a priori model and its extensions did not make the axiomatic structure more plausible since many of the derived theorems could be based on other assumptions not present among the axioms. Typically enough in the latest decades many elaborations have had the purpose to show that given certain assumptions the neoclassical model can explain certain empirical phenomena.

Thus the equilibrium thought which is quite natural in some sense cannot per se be the basis for a universal explanation. There are certainly equilibria of ordinary mathematical character which we have to examine but there are no general equilibria. The latter still belongs to the metaphysical/magical sphere.

While the equilibrium thought is quite natural in some perspectives the ever ongoing change is another picture which is natural. With respect to such a picture we have a most intriguing picture, namely the Darwinist evolution. In economics this picture is developed into evolutionary economics and at the bottom of the picture we find expressions like animal spirit, the survival of the fittest, endogenous growth and similar.

Naturally any form of change/evolution may be pressed into a variant of deterministic Darwinism and thus the status of the Darwinist hypothesis has changed, when applied to other fields into something like magic in Lévi-Strauss meaning.

Let us say immediately that Darwin's hypothesis is quite relevant but possibly there is however a small problem in applying it to other sciences and that is the problem of *ex ante/ex post* explanations and hypotheses.

When dealing with this kind of research approaches it is good to keep in mind the alleged saying by Keynes that in the long run we are all dead. Not only as a witty one-liner but also according to the Einstein-Minkowski time concept that time is created by the single changes.

Consequently it is possible to think of an evolutionary process but how do we single out that from current and historical information, and what is the direction of the evolution? Obviously we can perform a technical analysis of historical data and claim that it is all about decoding history and then we get the answer. This is opposite to the astrologers but both ways have difficulties in explaining the nearest and medium term developments.

During a discussion with the well-known sociologist Johan Asplund he said that science is about two things, the search for the holy 'grail' and the 'chaff-cutter. We try to find the ultimate atom, substance or whatever we call it from which everything originates and to find it we are prepared to deprive the concepts of our analysis of any links to the trivial and confusing reality that we belong to.

What we have claimed in this book is that the macroscopic and microscopic worlds are mutually affecting each other but the interrelations are not deterministic, not in a trivial way at least. Furthermore in social sciences we have to see the acting agents as subjects, thus final causes, which make the interrelations between the microscopic world and the macroscopic which makes interrelations between the different aggregate levels extremely difficult to postulate; detected/assumed inertia may help to create a form of inductive/deductive analysis but only partially and temporally.

Our analysis of the barter versus the money economy brought us to the utmost form of logical contradiction, with respect to the concept of money.

With respect to dynamics it is enlightening to look at Hume's discussion of money. As we have seen he was well aware of the problem of money supply as well as the different intrinsic features of money with respect to both money as a medium of exchange as well as in borrowing/lending contracts. But basically even before Hume comments on such things he tries to describe the social role of money which implies the possibility to produce in one place and sell in another. In fact he took up the Aristotelian wholesale which Aristotle regarded as suspect from an ethical point of view and regarded it from a new perspective which implied that money becomes a vital part of the socialization and civilization process. Thus money was so to say playing two roles: one with respect to the technical relations of money managing and exchange and one with respect to its social role. Naturally Hume's analysis could somehow be squeezed into an evolutionary process *ex post* but what Hume envisaged is linked to the logical working of a money system. Of course Hume is positive with regard to such a role of money but he does not tell about possible effects otherwise then in the case of tax collection which will be easier. The secondary effects of increased socialization are left to a different analysis.

Thus dynamics has somehow to be sprung out of historical and current conditions although these can be extremely complex. In Figure 6.2 in the periphery of the box with the four nodes we have hinted at the different sources of exogenous effects but we must also realize that we have reversed effects from the box onto its environment. The nodes represent factors which are tightly related but the secondary effects of these relations that cause primary effects are to a great extent 'decided' by the environment as an 'answer' to the effects of the development of the relations between the nodes in the box onto its environment.

Thus for example we have the fact that money is a social convention. It is an experience we have that the first thing which is affected by social unease is the currency, both externally and internally. This triggers the question of what is economic balance. If we use Figure 6.2 as a picture of an economy we may ask if the system illustrated by the four nodes can be in balance if the environment is in a state of imbalance, but the reversed question is also interesting, can it be unbalanced while the environment is balanced? The links between the four-node system and its environment are strong but which type of science should be claimed responsible for a research which displays these links? Has economic theory as it is apprehended in mainstream economics developed efficient tools for such research, before the marginal revolution questions about the relations between the economic system and the social system, *which the economic system was seen as a part of,* was not regarded as peripheral questions but central? Now researchers dealing with these kinds of questions are lumped together by mainstream economists as some kind of local wiseacres in so called heterodox economics. The orthodoxy in that case stems from the late 19th century and is built on an idiosyncratic axiomatic theory which is at variance per se with both the achievements in philosophy/logics and other empirical sciences during the 20th century.

Dynamics and Entropy

Dynamics, interpreted as change, has a cause. We do not need to go back to the ultimate cause as God as the first mover in St. Thomas' discussion, or Big Bang in physics, we can have a more humble purpose. For simplicity we can regard the entropy process as basic to the wearing and tearing of nature and ourselves. Let us however stop for some moments at the entropy concept, let us regard it as order. This can be used in economics in many ways as describing distributions and allocations but we will use it in a more abstract way.

Often we treat entropy as a kind of disorder and if the entropy increases the simple formula which we use is

$$E(x) \equiv -\sum_i p(x_i) \cdot \ln\left[p(x_i)\right] \text{ where p(x_i) = 0 defines ln[p(x_i)] = 0} \qquad \text{E.7.2}$$

An example is given in Table 7.1 where D1 represents the rectangular distribution which also gives the highest entropy, that is, the highest degree of disorder. The slightest perturbation of probabilities in the rectangular distribution will make the entropy decrease and ultimately the deterministic case where the probability of one alternative gives an entropy, by definition, of zero. This of course gives us rich possibilities to use the concept of entropy in economics. Henri Theil (1967) used it as an income distribution measure, Georgescu-Roegen (1971) as an environmental discussion of the distribution between utility production and scrap production and Ekstedt (2012) used it explaining Allais' paradox.

However the concept of entropy is primarily a physical concept. Seemingly we have a universal process of increasing entropy thus given the direction of change but this is only at the highest universal level; locally there might be 'islands' with sinking entropy but as seen in the table when we increase the probability of P(x_2) and P(x_3) this implies that the probability of P(x_1) decreases. We will have similar processes which might be expressed so that increasing the order of one subsystem in a closed system implies that entropy will increase, implying increased disorder in another subsystem and also the global system. In fact the general rule is that if we have a global system with a number of subsystems, the decrease of entropy in one of the subsystems will lead to a proportionally higher increase of entropy of the global system.

Table 7.1 Entropy for different distributions

	D1	D2	D3	ln(px)	ln(px)	ln(px)
P(x1)	0.2	0.18	0.99	0.321888	0.308664	0.00995
P(x2)	0.2	0.21	0.0025	0.321888	0.327736	0.014979
P(x3)	0.2	0.21	0.0025	0.321888	0.327736	0.014979
P(x4)	0.2	0.2	0.0025	0.321888	0.321888	0.014979
P(x5)	0.2	0.2	0.0025	0.321888	0.321888	0.014979
E(x)				1.609438	1.607911	0.069864
$\sum P(x_i)$	1	1	1			

In analogy with this reasoning we might discuss Figure 6.2 from a different perspective. We may look at the system of the four nodes as concerning the production system whose environment is where the people live and express their purposes of the results of the production. Thus we might see the dichotomy between humans as the ultimate goals of the production system but also as the most important production factor.

From this perspective the neoclassical is probably most interesting since it presents a set of conditions/assumptions to grant that the economy works in a completely objective and unbiased manner in relation to humans as the ultimate goal of the production. The used efficiency criteria, the Pareto optimum, is interesting since it also is a sociological dimension which might be used outside economics.

But what it is describing is utopia since the picture as it stands does not envisage any form of action to get there, neither individual nor collective, because any possible action will violate the picture itself. Not even concepts like *competition* will have room in the picture since the agents do not act but are bound to follow the price vector *irrespective* of the distribution of the initial endowments. This is actually the reason why the neoclassical general equilibrium model cannot discriminate between a market economy and a communist command economy (Makarov and Rubinov 1977).

In reality however the intrinsic relation in society between humans as goals and humans as production factors is a virtually eternal question. This question is also at the bottom of other aspects like the environmental aspect which indeed needs quick decisions and quick actions. But the monumental question then appears in block letters: QUI BONO? We know that solving many of the environmental problems is not a technical question, it is a question of implementing the techniques and the political, demographic, social and distributional effects of such an implementation. Some say that we have sacrificed growth but that is a pretty confusing statement. To remove one of the main threats to the human welfare must per se imply a positive factor of/for growth of welfare. The more constructive question of growth is to ask in which commodity basket we want the growth and which capital stock and technology to use for this. To say that the market can solve this is pretty naïve and to say that the market as described by neoclassical theory can have any form of connotations for the short run or for the long run is nonsensical.

Looking at the problem of humans as a goal and/or as production factors implies that the system of the four nodes in Figure 6.2 becomes almost totally integrated in its environment and it is hard to see where economics ends and sociology begins.

The problem of integrating these two 'cousins' in social science lies quite naturally in the conceptualizations of the two sciences. It is hard to see a complete integration since economics as we briefly mentioned in the beginning of the book has its fundamental basis in the very market exchange and the distribution and allocation of resources. This gives rise to contractual effects and changes in ownership. The Icelandic Sagas tell us about the dramatic period in the end of the10th century and the beginning of the 11th century when the old custom of *Holmgång* was forbidden and ownership in an institutional setting was introduced. Holmgång means that anybody could challenge anybody else about the possessions of the latter. This process is described in Ekstedt and Fusari (2012: 128–129). Thus the separation of possession and ownership is at the bottom of the market principle in an ordered society but that also separates the methodology of economics from the methodology of sociology. Ownership is a factor of conservation while innovations/inventions, social and demographic changes and reorganizations imply constant revaluations. The normative part of neoclassical theory which is also basic for the mainstream economics and affects current policy is to take a stance in the conservation of endowment and when discussing innovations/inventions and structural changes of production and demand these are, implicitly at least, supposed to be neutral to the relative ownership of the 'endowments'. From a sociological perspective this implies that economic change with respect to technology and demand structures will/must affect the entropy of the economic system and subsystems but also have effects on the environment to the economic system. The upholding of the fiction of the economic system as separate and independent of the social environment creates an elite in Pareto's meaning which Johan Asplund (1967:104) formulates (translated from Swedish text): 'An elite, which is closed, and does not open for persons outside the elite who has qualities which might add new dimensions to those qualities already represented in the elite, will, given other circumstances similar, be overthrown'.

Thus if economics wants to become a social science we have to combine both these principles of conservation/stability and revaluation/growth. The two sciences economics and sociology have to work side by side in close cooperation as Pareto is an example of.

Saturation and Anomie

There are however two concepts which are important to use more extensively in economics and that is *saturation* and *anomie*. Saturation, is already used to some degree and we find it in utility theory. But it is a rich concept and there is an element of the saturation phenomena in Hume's discussion of the social role of money, where money opens for access to new commodities and interactions between groups. Johan Asplund (1967: 125) treats the concept of saturation more as a macro-sociological concept than a psychological disposition of the individual. He tried to formulate a concept for saturation in the meaning of weariness of life (translation from Swedish text): 'If the set of possible experiences from the beginning is small, and/or this set is quickly consumed, the rise of saturation, weariness of life and similar states is promoted, while an initially large set of possible experiences and/or slow rate of consumption has the opposite effect'.

The expression 'possible experiences' is obviously culturally defined.

However there are some interesting additional observations from Senegal in an enquiry by Ibrahima Sy (2013). He uses a subjective methodology in analysing poverty in Senegal. People in different areas were asked about their individual perception of their economic status. As a kind of side result Sy could show that when comparing rural areas where barter to a high degree prevailed with urbanized areas where the money economy was predominant he found that peoples' subjective perception of economic status in rural areas was that their economic situation was better than was the case when so called objective methods were used. In urban monetized areas the situation was the opposite.

Here we have an example of a sort of reaction to asymmetries between people when it comes to the judgement of the set of possible sets of experiences for individuals or subgroups in relation to the set of possible experiences for the society as a whole.

We might say that there also is a limited amount of competing pictures about future possibilities in the remote areas which are at variance with urban, richer areas. Thus if we go back to our concept of saturation it generally needs counter examples of living. Thus when the general income level of an area is rather low with high homogeneity with respect to income and education the possible pictures, counter examples, are relatively few we will have less reasons for saturation.

Enquiries like that of Ibrahim Sy are highly interesting since they are directed to the very links between the economic and the social sphere. Furthermore we have a comparison of measures. Sy's enquiry shows that there is a clear discrepancy between subjective evaluation of the agents of their situation and an evaluation built on 'objective' criteria.

Going back to Hume, we may read his chapter of luxuries and find an urge for richer cultural supply and increased dimensions of living. For him the dissatisfaction with particularly the rural life in Britain was outspoken and he explicitly expresses his hope in the monetized economy to make the speed of change faster.

This problem takes us to the concept of *anomie*, which goes back to Durkheim.[3] However, Robert K. Merton has also developed the concept into a more general setting.[4] The anomie concept is mainly about the individual flexibility/adaptability with respect to rapid social changes. Durkheim has two variants: one where social norms break down leaving the individual in an ethical chaos/vacuum, in the periphery of the society, and unable to reach socially accepted and desired purposes and goals which may in the extreme cases end in *suicide*. The basic point from our point of view as economists is the inability/impossibility to link individual purposes and goals to a social structure and to limit the goals to social frames since the latter are unclear if at all visible. Durkheim also discusses the anomie concept with respect to the division of labour which might produce social subgroups at variance with more general labour force. Within these subgroups there might develop special ethical and behavioural codes at difference with the common society.

Durkheim's analysis is broad and contains concepts partly intrinsically contradictive which is to eb expected due to the extent and the number of dimensions of the analysis, but he singles out two very interesting concepts which probably have bearing on analysis à la Sy: *organic solidarity* and *mechanic solidarity*.

To phrase it briefly we may say that organic solidarity rises from a multitude of dimensions in which people are linked to each other while mechanical solidarity deals with exogenously created links as working, as Marks (1974: 354) quote from Durkheim (1933: 130):

> What justifies this term mechanical is that the link which thus unites the individual to society is wholly analogous to that which attaches a thing to a person. The individual conscience … is a simple dependent upon the collective type and follows all its movements, as the possessed object follows those of its owner.

It has to do with working conditions, common social and demographic conditions and so on.

Durkheim however places many of the anomalies in the development of the society, thus we may say that the changes and the speed of the structural decomposition on the macroscopic level causes instabilities in the position of the individual with respect to ethics and social adaptations.

Merton, according to Asplund (1967) in a way combines the two approaches by Durkheim but reverses the causality. He discusses the individual achievements in relation to common norms of success in the society. It is often called *strain theory*. Contrary to Durkheim. Merton places the failure at the microscopic level; certainly the complexity of the society contributes but the society is given and the individual has to somehow comply with it.

A failure with respect to societal norms may alienate the individual from the society and if there are groups of alienated individuals these may develop norms/ethics/generic behaviour at variance with the rest of the society. Obviously Merton's approach is more specific and depends on the homogeneity of the common attitude in defining success. Jean Michelle Bessette and Jacque Fage discuss different approaches to delinquencies and they mean that Merton in his analysis has its roots in the American society and the American way of measuring success in media (12th of June 2012, http://www.leconflit.com/article-approches-sociologiques-de-la-delinquance-2-106819543.html). Thus a wide range of accepted paths to success counteract the rise of anomie both with respect to individuals as with respect to subgroups.

Johan Asplund (1967: 130) discusses the conditions for the growth of anomie in subgroups: 'The growth of consumption in a society increases while the set of possible experiences does not increase or the set of possible experiences increases while the growth of consumption does not increases are conditions for the rise of anomie'. (Translated from Swedish text.) We can see here that the enquiry by Ibrahima Sy is indeed related to Asplund's classification.

The grown subgroups tend to turn against the very pillars of the organization of the society.

With respect to our earlier analysis both Durkheim's and Merton's are valuable. We discussed in Chapter 6 how a combination of policy, uncertainty and productivity changes could 'produce' permanent unemployment in an accelerating tempo. This is a virtual plague in Europe in these days; nobody speaks or dares to speak about 'natural unemployment' which already when the concept was introduced was an anomaly for modern scientific thinking. Today this threatens the social stability. Furthermore the anti-inflationary policy has been a fundamental theory for policy making as well as for the mainstream economic science. The debt mountains and the policy of saving the value by austere public policy have raised the question if politicians and economic advisors think that we will eat money in the future, a new variant of real bill.

Determinism/Free Will and Reversibility/Irreversibility

Through the history of philosophical thoughts there is said to be a watershed between philosophers: those apt to see man as a sort of animal machine displaying deterministic behaviour and eventual anomalies can be explained by the environment. A most radical way of expressing this is the behaviouristic approach built on John Locke's 'tabula rasa', postulating that humans are born without specific qualities but are moulded by the environmental experiences which set the frames for the animal rationality. The latter *animal rationality* is expressed by the axioms of choice of the neoclassical theory. How even this can be refined and the American economist Gary Becker builds his economic analysis of human capital and consumption theory, the so called household production theory, on Locke's philosophical principles in the sense that he assumes that all individuals are born equal and with the same desires or we might perhaps call it 'the same utility function'. Different contexts however diversify the individuals as time goes by.

Georgescu-Roegen (1971: 13) and the Swedish sociologist Johan Asplund (1967) claim that human development is conducted by the combined forces of necessity, novelty and saturation and we ultimately end up in some form of complex combinatory model.

Our attitude, although not linked to Locke, is *de facto* much like Becker's approach when we introduce the concept of epistemic cycles. This similarity does not imply that we necessarily must agree with Becker on a deeper philosophical level, alluding to Hume's discussion of causality, a particular effect might have many different combinations of causes. With respect to the human behaviour our view that humans are subjects imply that since we do not wish to develop the microscopic analysis but just want a minimal concept of human diversity in interpreting commodities and information without bringing in the philosophical problem of the free will, Becker's approach is sufficient and also more than enough complex.

The other side of the watershed, are those philosophers claiming that humans have a free will and use logics as a mean of obtaining the desires of their will. The most pronounced analysis in this direction is found in catholic philosophy built on Saint Thomas and more or less contemporary medieval philosophy, which is built on Aristotelian foundations. Aristotle, as Locke, claimed that humans were born without specific qualities but at variance with Locke he claimed that certain potentialities were provided by nature by the birth. The potentialities were however to be educated in order to be developed. This accounts also for moral virtues. Unfortunately the writings by Aristotle are rather obscure about whether or not the potentialities are differentiated between newborn humans which means that Aristotle could well be interpreted along the lines of Locke. Thus to achieve the free will the medieval philosophers refer to God who has *created* the free will. David Hume develops the Aristotelian line by stating that man is governed by passions and the will and that the logics is just a mean but also Hume is a bit obscure on the *final cause* of an eventual free will.

As we see there are no clear cut answers with respect to the question of free will versus determinism other than leaving physics and entering a metaphysical analysis, which is outside our scope. Nevertheless we can, on the basis of our earlier analysis make a distinction between a simple deterministic animal behaviour and a more complex behaviour. In the case of the neoclassical axiomatic structure we have the simplest form of animal rationality where the individual subject is determined by a preference structure provided we use the theory inter-temporally. Thus we see the subject as a decision machine, which of course solves the problem of aggregation. This means that constructing an inter-temporal model based on the axioms of general equilibrium will not be particularly successful in dealing with the reality. The prime reason of this is that the axioms allow only additive aggregation which indeed is simple to handle but hard to imagine. Arrow's paradox deals exactly with this problem although sometimes it is interpreted as dealing with politics and economics in a more general setting.

Basically we use a slightly different view of rationality in relation to the axioms of choice of the neoclassical view, actually more in the line of Locke and Becker but also strongly attached to David Hume's attitude to passion and reason which he expresses

> Nothing is more usual in philosophy, and even in common life, than to talk of the combat of passion and reason, to give the preference to reason, and assert that men are only so far virtuous as they conform themselves to its dictates. ... I shall endeavour to prove *first* that reason alone can never be a motive to any action of the will; and *secondly* that it can never oppose passion in the direction of the will.
>
> (Hume, 2002[1740]: 265)

Although we might change the actual wording a bit to make it fit into modern conceptualization, the basic content will be important to our analysis. Consequently the rationality of the individual is formally the same as the axioms of choice but they concern only the set of epistemic cycles which govern the individual apprehension of the environment and thereby also the behaviour. The same can be said about macroscopic bodies but the difference is that the decisions are based on an institutional framework regulating the responsibility as well as the relative influence of individuals.

Please observe that passion in Hume's terminology has the same status as moral virtues in Aristotle's writings, thus *passion* cannot from a logical point of view be said to impute a non-deterministic concept into the analysis, although with respect to both Hume's and Aristotle's further analysis show that it implies a definitive complication of the analysis, particularly with respect to the question of aggregation.[5]

With respect to dynamics and stability it is thus important to note that it is not the individual per se who creates the instabilities but it is the aggregation of individuals into groups/societies in which individuals are supposed to behave along certain rules or patterns, and when these rules interfere with individual desires and inter-individual relations, complexities are created. It is quite natural that if we for analytical simplicity disregard these aggregate structures and impute some human atoms which from a strict mathematical sense are *nowhere dense* it will be easier to produce theorems. The problem is, however, that we cannot pass Arrow's paradox which implicitly tells us that the humans themselves have created these aggregate structures. They thus become a necessary part of the problem we are supposed to analyse. Disregarding them is to be seen as a non-acceptable simplification of the problem.

This discussion of complexity and rationality will lead us to the questions of dynamics, stability and ultimately chaos. As we will see chaotic behaviour is not something which means lack of rationality and deterministic behaviour, on the contrary one is apt to say, but that is probably an overstatement; anyway we separate deterministic chaotic behaviour from non-deterministic behaviour.

Any discussion on stability requires a dynamic analysis and we will discuss time in relation to rationality, uncertainty and ethics. The latter is to be seen as a stabilizing factor in a society made up by subjects. Consequently before starting to build dynamic models economists should have an idea of how dynamics, stability and instability appear in the real world.

The question of determinism and free will is probably the deepest one in metaphysics and we will try to stay clear of the shadiest areas. Nevertheless the question in the subtitle triggers visions of both the individual and mankind. We have already mentioned how the two visions grown out of classical economics, neoclassical theory and Marxism chose two different paths of reasoning where the neoclassical vision starts in a microscopic world and from that derives a macroscopic one, while the Marxism starts in a holistic historic picture and from that derives the conditions in the microscopic world.

Both the visions are however deterministic. In neoclassical theory we induce limitations on the individual implicitly via the axioms. One may doubt if any of these axioms had been commonly accepted if they had been expressed in non-mathematical terms. The Marxian theory is basically dealing with a more grandiose determinism of the same kind as Bonaventura names the determinism of God and the individual is bound to the laws implicit in this macroscopic system.

However both the theories have a similar foundation in the classical economy so we may compare them in their ultimate forms. As said above they start from opposite ends in the meaning that the neoclassical individual starts from the individual and aggregate the findings up to an aggregate level, while Marxism starts from the macroscopic conditions and derives the individual behaviour.

In mathematics we have both these ways and we may compare the two as in Ekstedt (2012: 16), which is given in Table 7.2.

We see that the two ways mean that the derivation has a precise result since we so to say blow up a specific point, while the aggregation process starts from the point in question and derives possible environments where the point might be a part.

Let us see if we can see how the respective visions will be expressed.

One can say that the ultimate purpose of the neoclassical axiomatic structure is to grant reversibility (not in a temporal sense), between the microscopic and the macroscopic worlds: the *integrability theorem*. The most fundamental papers concerning this problem are Georgescu-Roegen (1936) and Samuelson (1950). Both papers concern the microscopic world and whether we can derive the utility function from income/prices data which if we add data of the income distribution make us able to derive a sort of average macroscopic utility function. The integrability theorem leans heavily on the correlate of revealed preferences at the microscopic level, and Samuelson (1948) discusses this correlate extensively. He ends his 1948 paper:

> The whole theory of consumer behaviour can thus be based upon operationally meaningful foundations in terms of revealed preferences.

On the whole we can see signs of a flare of a macroscopic utility of the same character.

It is however interesting to read the discussions, they are mostly mathematical and as such give a convincing impression. There are however one little problem, which might be illustrated by Samuelson's (1948: 246) technique by continuous approximations to approach the optimum, 'This suggests that the Chauchy-Lipschitz process will always approach the true solution curve, or "indifference curve", *from below*.' This paper was written before Arrow and Debreu published their revealing studies of the character of general equilibrium.

One could simply say that the problem with the correlate of revealed preferences takes time and the general equilibrium lacks time unless very strict limitations are imposed which rejects any kind of Chauchy-Lipschitz process.

As hinted the reversibility we discuss is just according to derivation/integration. Thus the problem of reversibility/irreversibility has nothing per se to

Table 7.2 Derivation and Integration

Derivation	Aggregation
$y = f(x) = x^3$	$Y = F(x) = 6$
$f'(x) = 3 \cdot x^2$	$F^1(x) = 6 \cdot x + a$
$f''(x) = 6 \cdot x$	$F^2(x) = 3 \cdot x^2 + a \cdot x + b$
$f'''(x) = 6$	$F^3(x) = x^3 + \frac{a}{2} \cdot x^2 + b \cdot x + c$

do with the problem of integrability since we are concerned with an equilibrium and thus eventual reversibility would be nonsensical. The reverse process is to go back to initial resources but that does not add anything to the discussion.

The Marxian vision is harder to analyse since it involves a hypothesis about the historical process of the most grandiose kind as some sort of master plan. We have earlier in the book used Makarov and Rubinov (1977) a great deal. What is interesting with this book is that it is a counterpart to Arrow and Debreu for the communist command economy. They start from von Neumann and Gale and derive an optimal production trajectory which they then link to an Arrow and Debreu economy. They do not need anything like an invisible hand, but tell us frankly (ibid.: 202): 'Finally, the last (or $(m+n+1)^{st}$) part is called the *central agency*. This organ chooses the prices of all products, i.e., it selects a vector $p \in (\mathbb{R}^S_+)^*$.'

We have earlier observed the mechanics of the neoclassical theory but as we see here Makarov and Rubinov derive the perfect form of social engineering, or at least economic engineering. We may protest against the way prices are set, but what alternative can we produce within the frames of the neoclassical axiomatic structure?

Thus the two 'cousins', neoclassical theory and Marxian economics lead in fact to the same kind of mechanics/engineering so when Friedman says that free markets are a necessary condition for democracy he cannot possibly mean that free markets have anything to do with neoclassical theory. Both the neoclassical and the Marxist variants of explaining the economy dismiss free will and are purely deterministic.

To consciously introduce free will is indeed difficult and our earlier discussed humbleness with respect to this problem in its full depth requires a metaphysical analysis sooner than a physical analysis.

We have used the word subject and regarded it as a final cause. That means that we stop the analysis so to speak when we stand in front of the interior of the human mind. Thus we define the concept of epistemic cycles but that only tells us that the individual has purposes which are subject to the apprehension of the relevant context. This actually means that St. Thomas' as well as Locke's attitudes can be covered and also behaviouristic attitude.

Notes

1 I am not quite sure that the English translation contains all the implicit connotations in the French expression, so the reader may decide according to own intuitions.

2 In Ekstedt and Fusari (2010: 59–62) and Ekstedt (2012: 70–74) there are comprehensive discussions on Arrow's paradox from the view we express here.

3 The discussion of anomie in its more specific forms is built mainly on Marks (1972) and Murphy and Robinson (2008).

4 Robert King Merton, the sociologist, is the father of Robert Cox Merton the Nobel Laureate in economics 1997.

5 It is interesting to note that Aristotle, having an explicit view of good and bad, ends up in a simpler analysis than Hume in his scepticism, actually this is one of the basic reasons why Hume in principle dismisses scientific induction.

Bibliography

Asplund, J. (1967) *Mättnadsprocesser* (Saturation processes). Uppsala: Argos Förlag AB.

Becker, G. S. (1976) *A New Economic Approach of Human Behaviour.* Chicago: University of Chicago Press.

Brody, T. (1994) *The Philosophy Behind Physics.* Berlin/Heidelberg/New York: Springer Verlag.

Ekstedt, H. (2012) *Money in Economic Theory.* London: Routledge.

Georgescu-Roegen, N. (1971) *The Entropy Law and the Economic Process.* Cambridge, MA: Harvard University Press.

Hicks, J.R. (1980-1981) 'IS-LM: An Explanation', *Journal of Post Keynesian Economics,* vol. 3: 139–155.

Hume, D. A. (2002 [1740]) *A Treatise of Human Nature.* Oxford: Oxford University Press.

Johannisson, K. (2004) *Tecknen – Läkaren och konsten att läsa kroppar.* (The Signs – The Doctor and the art of reading bodies.) Stockholm: Norstedts.

Kant, I. (1988 [1787]) *Critique of Pure Reason.* London: Macmillan.

Koestler, A. (1979[1959]) *The Sleepwalkers.* Bugay, Suffolk: Richard Clay Ltd.

Lévi-Strauss, C. (1962) *La Pensée Sauvage.* Paris: Plon.

Makarov, V.L and Rubinov, A.M. (1977) *Economic Dynamics and Equilibria.* Heidelberg, Berlin: Springer Verlag.

Marks, S. R. (1974) 'Durkheim's Theory of Anomie', *American Journal of Sociology,* Vol. 80, No. 2: 329–363.

Murphy, D.S., & Robinson, M.B. (2008) *The Maximizer*: 'Clarifying Merton's theories of anomie and strain', *Theoretical Criminology* 12: 501.

Pascal, B. (2007 [1670]) *Pensées,* Encyclopædia Britannica, Inc., Chicago, London.

Samuelson, P.A. (1948) *Economics: An Introductory Analysis.* New York: McGraw Hill.

Sargent, (2008) 'Rational Expectations', in S. Durlauf and L. Blume (eds) *The New Palgrave Dictionary of Economics.* Palgrave.

Sy, I. (2013) 'The Subjective Approach as a Tool for Understanding Poverty: The Case of Senegal', *Procedia Economics and Finance,* Vol. 5: 336–345.

Theil, H. (1967) *Economics and Information Theory.* Amsterdam: North-Holland.

Thom, R. (1975) *Structural Stability and Morphogenesis: An Outline of a General Theory of Models.* New York: Addison-Wesley.

Weisstein, E.W. (2000) *CRC Concise Encyclopedia of Mathematics.* London: Chapman & Hall/CRC.

Index